To Live on This Earth

ESTELLE FUCHS, an anthropologist, is currently Professor in the Graduate Program, City University of New York and Professor in the Department of Educational Foundations, Hunter College, City University of New York. She is the author of PICKETS AT THE GATE and TEACHERS TALK, and lectures extensively on both urban and Indian education.

ROBERT J. HAVIGHURST, Professor of Education and Human Development at the University of Chicago, is prominent in the field of educational research. Author and co-author of over twenty books on education including *Society and Education,* his long and distinguished career places him as one of the leading educators in the United States.

To Live on This Earth
AMERICAN INDIAN EDUCATION

By Estelle Fuchs
and Robert J. Havighurst

Anchor Books
Anchor Press / Doubleday
Garden City, New York
1973

TO LIVE ON THIS EARTH was originally published in a hardcover edition by Doubleday & Company, Inc. in 1972.

Anchor Books edition: 1973

Contents

LIST OF FIGURES AND TABLES   vii

PREFACE   xi

I   *The Prelude*   1

II   *Indian Peoples—the Present*   23

III   *Communities Where Indians Live and Attend Schools*   38

IV   *Mental Ability and Mental Development of Indian Children*   118

V   *School Achievement of Indian Children and Youth*   123

VI   *The Mental Health of Indian Youth*   136

VII   *Schools and Schooling as Seen by Indian Youth and Their Parents*   157

VIII   *Indian Education as Seen by Community Leaders*   182

IX   *Teachers of Indian Children and Youth*   191

X   *The School Curriculum*   205

XI   *Boarding Schools*   222

XII   *Toward New Approaches*   246

XIII   *Post-High School Education for Indians*   260

XIV *Indians in Big Cities*   273

 XV *Criticisms of Indian Education*   294

XVI *Global Evaluation of Indian Education*   302

XVII *The Indian Voice in Education*   314

     APPENDIX I   Overview of the National Study of
                   American Indian Education   327

     APPENDIX II   Summary and Critique of Research
                   Methods for Study of Indian
                   Education   345

     SELECTED BIBLIOGRAPHY   354

     NOTES   359

     INDEX   373

Figures and Tables

FIGURE 1 *Major American Indian tribes and reservations in the continental United States* 25

FIGURE 2 *Shonto community in Navajo Reservation, Arizona* 41

FIGURE 3 *Bethel, Alaska* 54

FIGURE 4 *Sells district in Papago Reservation, Arizona* 65

FIGURE 5 *Fort Apache, Arizona* 77

FIGURE 6 *Indian reservations in South Dakota* 83

FIGURE 7 *White Eagle community in Oklahoma* 92

FIGURE 8 *Robeson County, North Carolina* 99

FIGURE 9 *Residence of Indians in Chicago, Illinois* 108

FIGURE 10 *School achievement of Indian pupils* 124

FIGURE 11 *Location of Indian residence in the Los Angeles area* 278

FIGURE 12 *Location of Indian communities studied in the National Study of American Indian Education* 334

TABLE 1 *American Indian Population (1890–1970)* 24

TABLE 2   *Indian Population in States with 4000 Indians or more (1970)*   26

TABLE 3   *Selected Vital Statistics, Indians and Alaskan Natives, 24 Federal Reservation States and All Races, United States (1967)*   32

TABLE 4   *School Attendance of Indian Children and Youth (1970), Age 6–17 Inclusive*   34

TABLE 5   *Shonto Enrollment by Age and Grade (as of January 1969)*   47

TABLE 6   *Indian Oasis School-Age Survey*   72

TABLE 7   *Test Scores of Minority Group Children*   125

TABLE 8   *Mean Ratings for "White Culture" and "Indian Culture" for Indian and Non-Indian Students*   130

TABLE 9   *Relation of Self-Esteem to Attitudes Toward White and Indian Cultures*   132

TABLE 10   *Comparison of Group Mean Scores on the Semantic Differential "Myself," Age 12–17*   142

TABLE 11   *Average "Combined Self" Scores for Age Groups by Sex*   145

TABLE 12   *Mean Scores for Concepts "Myself" and "My Future" for Indian Student Groups and Non-Indian Controls*   146

TABLE 13   *Suicide Rates for Indians and All Americans by Age Group and Sex*   151

TABLE 14   *Comparison of Group Scores on the Semantic Differential, Indian Groups on "Teachers," Age 12–17*   162

TABLE 15   *Comparison of Group Scores on the Semantic Differential, Non-Indian Groups on "Teachers," Age 12–17*   164

TABLE 16   *Average Self-Esteem Score (Combined Self) of Indian Students in the Top, Middle, and Bottom Thirds of Their Class in School*   179

TABLE 17 *Comparison of Indian and Non-Indian*
          Community Leaders on Scales Indicating
          Approval-Disapproval of Schools   185

TABLE 18 *Comparison of BIA Teachers (1968) with a*
          National Sample of Public School Teachers
          (1965–66)   192

TABLE 19 *Comparison of Attitudes of Teachers with*
          Attitudes of Parents and Students   196

TABLE 20 *Cities with 1000 or More Indians in 1970*   274

TABLE 21 *Indian Students in Los Angeles and Bell*
          Gardens City Schools (1968–69)   282

          APPENDIX I

TABLE 1 *Communities and Schools in the National*
          Study   335

TABLE 2 *Number of Interviews and Instruments*
          Reported   337

TABLE 3 *Summary of Personnel*   339

TABLE 4 *Estimates of Indian School-Age Population*
          (5 to 17 Inclusive) by State (1968)   340

TABLE 5 *Number and Percentage of Indian Children*
          in Public Schools in Selected States (1967–68)   341

TABLE 6 *Number and Percentage Distribution of*
          Indian Children, Age 6–18, Reported in
          Annual School Census (1967–68)   342

TABLE 7 *Enrollment by Tribe in Schools Operated by*
          the Bureau of Indian Affairs (1968)   344

Preface

This book reports the understandings and the conclusions about Indian education which the authors have recorded over a considerable period of observation and study of Indian children and societies and of education in general. It draws heavily upon the National Study of American Indian Education, completed in 1971 under the direction of the authors.

The National Study of American Indian Education was a U. S. Office of Education funded project whose primary aim was to make a comprehensive examination of the present state of Indian education. A tremendous growth in Indian school attendance since World War II, an increase in the numbers of Indian children attending public schools rather than Bureau of Indian Affairs schools, and the growing interest in minority groups generally during the 1960s had turned attention to the need for a national review of the issues.

The importance of a national study of Indian education becomes apparent when it is remembered that there is a division of responsibility between states and the federal government in regard to the education of Indian children, that differing conditions are experienced by tribal and non-tribal Indians and that there has never been any agency consistently responsible for continuously collecting and analyzing data on a national scale for all Indians.

The National Study of American Indian Education conducted its research during 1967–71 through eight university centers: the University of Arizona, the University of Chicago, the University of Colorado, the University of Minnesota, North Carolina State

University, Oklahoma State University, Pennsylvania State College, and San Francisco State College.

In addition to compiling the current facts and figures concerning the status of the Indian population and their education, twenty-six communities with approximately forty different schools or school systems were chosen for closer study. Among the criteria used to select the schools to be studied were geographic location —schools from Bethel, Alaska, to Pembroke, North Carolina, were included; inclusion of the most numerous Indian tribes; representation of the four major types of schools for Indian youth, public, BIA (Bureau Indian Affairs) day schools, BIA (Bureau Indian Affairs) boarding schools, and mission schools. Another consideration was the degree of contact between the Indian community and the surrounding white community—distance from major urban and employment centers, educational level of parents, language spoken in the home, degree of Indian ancestry, proportion of non-Indian children in the school. Community background data, based on previous studies and on observation by the field research staff, were also compiled. The field research was planned to secure the following kinds of data on each of the communities studied: observations of the school and its relation to the community by field research staff; interviews with students, parents, teachers, and influential persons in the community; data from sociopsychological questionnaires on attitudes from students and teachers; data on mental alertness.

Throughout, the research sought to document how Indian peoples themselves perceived education and to examine the community and school contexts in which education was taking place. There were, in addition to the field work, several self-studies made in Indian communities, although fewer than anticipated.

Beyond making substantial use of the more than fifty technical papers which make up the Final Report of the National Study of American Indian Education, in the present book the authors have also drawn on the published research of anthropologists and educators who have studied Indian education during the past ten years.

This book owes a great deal to the broad experience and the skillful field conduct of the research teams from the eight universities who performed the field research of the National Study of American Indian Education. In the appendix and report in the design of the National Study at the end of this volume, the names of the principal members of these teams are given. Our appreciation for their efforts is expressed to all.

In a time when Indian people are properly suspicious of the methods and motives of non-Indians who "research" them, the National Study was fortunate in finding full cooperation in all of the communities that were studied intensively, attesting to the enormous concern for the educational issues and problems facing native Americans as well as the professional competence and respect for the communities, which characterized the researchers. The field directors obligated themselves to make responsible reports to the local communities. Community descriptions, when complete, were sent to local community leaders. Approximately half of the communities asked for and received visits from the research staff to discuss the reports and to apply any implicit criticisms to improvement in their community educational system.

Although the NSAIE was financed by the U. S. Office of Education and not by the Bureau of Indian Affairs, Department of Interior, and although there has been much recent, as well as earlier, criticism of BIA policy in Indian education, the staff of the BIA offices cooperated freely and generously with the staff of the National Study in providing data and answering inquiries.

The work of putting this book together was ably and unselfishly assisted by the following persons who are close to the authors: Mabel Frazier, manager of the University of Chicago office of the National Study, who kept a most complex operation running smoothly and with satisfaction to a variety of persons; Edythe Havighurst, wife of Robert Havighurst, who typed large sections of the manuscript; Julia Brackman and Laurie Quies, typists; and Willy Fuchs, who provided patience and moral support.

Estelle Fuchs
Hunter College, C.U.N.Y.

Robert J. Havighurst
University of Chicago

See, *Brothers:* Spring is here.
The Earth has taken the embrace of the Sun,
and soon we shall see the children of that love.
All seeds are awake, and all animals.
From this great power we too have our lives.
And therefore we concede to our fellow creatures,
even our animal fellows, the same rights as
ourselves, to live on this earth.

SITTING BULL, 1877

To Live on This Earth

I

The Prelude

The history of the white society in regard to Indian education reflects the drama of the inexorable peopling of this continent by those unable or unwilling to establish and maintain a humane, fraternal, and consistently respectful relationship with the prior residents of the land.

In these last decades of the twentieth century, official policy has turned toward both a recognition of the injustice of much of the past and an effort to design policies based on more equitable Indian-white relationships. President Nixon's message to Congress, July 8, 1970, reads:

> ... the story of the Indian in America is something more than the record of the white man's frequent aggression, broken agreements, intermittent remorse and prolonged failure. It is a record also of endurance, of survival, of adaptation and creativity in the face of overwhelming obstacles. It is a record of enormous contributions to this country—to its art and culture, to its strength and spirit, to its sense of history and its sense of purpose.
>
> It is long past time that the Indian policies of the Federal government began to recognize and build upon the capacities and insights of the Indian people. Both as a matter of justice and as a matter of enlightened social policy, we must begin to act on the basis of what the Indians themselves have long been telling us. *The time has come to break decisively with the past and to create the conditions for a new era in which the Indian future is determined by Indian acts and Indian decisions.*

Education policy for Indians parallels the troubled history of European conquest and colonization of the New World. When the Europeans first bestowed a common misnomer to the native peoples of this continent, there were several hundred societies speaking more than two hundred languages. Though they came to be known as "Indians," they differed widely in their economic, social, and religious life. However, they did share similarities in that communities tended to be kinship oriented, united by residence and constant person-to-person interaction, and by common understanding of their uniqueness as separate peoples.

During the colonial period, the various European nations exerted differing approaches to and influences upon the native Americans.

Western education and formal schooling were introduced to the Indians by Roman Catholic priests who were the earliest missionaries to America. The Jesuits, mainly French, were active in the St. Lawrence River area, Great Lakes region, and the Mississippi between 1611–1700. Their goals were to teach Christianity and French culture, following the order of Louis XIV to "educate the children of the Indians in the French manner." To accomplish this, the Jesuits removed children from their families and tribes. They taught French language and customs, and emphasized the traditional academic subjects. Singing, agriculture, carpentry, and handicrafts were also included.[1]

The Franciscans, mainly of Spanish origin, entered the south with Coronado, influencing the peoples of Arizona, New Mexico, Texas, and California. The policy of the Franciscans was to gather the native peoples into villages around missions. Families were kept intact. The schools, while teaching Spanish did not emphasize the academic subjects, placing greater stress upon agriculture, carpentry, blacksmith work, masonry, spinning, and weaving.

The Protestants also established schools, primarily in the East. King James on March 24, 1617, issued a call for the education of the Indians, and clergymen such as John Eliot took up the call. Dartmouth was founded for the education of "youth of Indian tribes . . . and also of English youth and others." Harvard was established for the education of English and Indian youth, and the campus of William and Mary included a special house for Indian students in 1723.

On the whole, education in the colonial period in all but the Spanish-dominated colonies, offered a curriculum to Indian youth that was the same as that offered non-Indian youth with major emphasis upon the area of academic study. Significantly, the school was established as an agent for spreading Christianity and the transmittal of Western culture and civilization. No consistent attempts to incorporate Indian languages, culture, or history were made in the curriculum offered. The issues raised by the white man's efforts to extend the benefits of his educational tradition to the peoples of the New World were clearly defined at an early date—and still endure. Benjamin Franklin told of the response by Indian leaders to an offer of education for Indian youth:

> But you, who are wise, must know that different Nations have different Conceptions of things; and you will therefore not take it amiss, if our Ideas of this kind of Education happen not to be the same with yours. We have had some Experience of it; Several of our young people were formerly brought up at the Colleges of the Northern Provinces; they were instructed in all your Sciences; but, when they came back to us, they were bad Runners, ignorant of every means of living in the Woods, unable to bear either Cold or Hunger, knew neither how to build a Cabin, take a Deer, or kill an Enemy, spoke our Language imperfectly, were therefore neither fit for Hunters, Warriors, not Counsellors; they were totally good for nothing. We are however not the less oblig'd by your kind Offer, tho' we decline accepting it; and, to show our grateful Sense of it, if the Gentlemen of Virginia will send us a Dozen of their Sons, we will take great Care of their Education, instruct them in all we know, and make *Men* of them.[2]

The schools of this period touched few persons and met with a conspicuous lack of success as hostilities increased between expanding settlers and Indians; as intertribal hostilities were exacerbated by warfare between the colonial powers; and as Indians resisted giving up their religions and styles of life.

The British had regarded the tribes as sovereign nations and the Continental Congress of the emerging United States of America continued this practice. The Northwest Ordinance of 1787 stated:

> The utmost good faith shall always be observed toward the Indians; their land and property shall never be taken from them without their consent; and in the property, rights, and liberty, they never shall be invaded or disturbed, unless in just and lawful wars authorized by Congress; but

laws found in justice and humanity shall from time to time be made, for preventing harm being done to them, and for preserving peace and friendship with them.

Affirming this policy, the Constitution of the new United States of America also conferred on the federal government the right to regulate commerce with the Indian tribes, make treaties, and to control the public land Indians occupied. Indian peoples continued to be dealt with as foreign nations with whom the new United States fought and concluded treaties. In addition, admission of new states to the Union could be regulated. This latter provision set the stage for requiring new states to give up any claim to jurisdiction over Indian lands—a right the original states retained. These were to remain under federal jurisdiction, creating the legal framework for the later reservation system and direct relationships between Indian tribes and the federal government.

The Continental Congress concluded a treaty with the Delaware in 1778, the first of 389 treaties made or remade with the Indian tribes between 1778 and 1871, when congressional action halted treaty making with the Indian tribes. By 1871 the Cherokee and other eastern tribes had been relocated across the Mississippi, countless battles had been fought, the Indian population severely depleted. Indians increasingly became easy targets for hostility and abuse as their territories gradually were touched by westward expansion of settlers, mining prospectors, and ranchers.

The various treaties ceded over a billion acres of land in exchange for which the federal government, with some variation from treaty to treaty, promised to allow Indians to keep certain lands as inalienable and tax exempt. In addition, the treaties usually included promises of federal services in such matters as education, health, technical, and agricultural learning.

The Indian tribes, however, remained an embarrassing impediment to manifest destiny. To those who found practices of outright extermination offensive, education to impose assimilation —to make Indians models of small farmers requiring little land —seemed necessary.

Indian education was influenced by the great religious awakening which took place in the new nation in the early 1800s. Many of the churches were evangelistic and supported widespread missionary activity. This had the effect of encouraging proselyting and education among the Indians as opposed to a policy of extermination. The Bible was the primer, and the hoe and plow the weapons of those who sought to "civilize" the Indians rather than physically eliminate them.

In conjunction with the mood in 1802, Congress approved an appropriation not to exceed $15,000 annually to "promote civilization among the savages."

In 1819, Congress, at the request of President Monroe, passed an act which apportioned funds among those societies and individuals that had been prominent in the effort to "civilize" the Indians. In this way education was turned over to missionary societies. The annual appropriation was not repealed until 1873.

The Bureau of Indian Affairs had been established first in 1836 as part of the War Department, but in 1849 it was shifted to the newly established Department of Interior. But not until 1892 were teachers and physicians placed under civil service. It was this Bureau, placed in the Department of Interior largely because of Indian lands, that became responsible for Indian education.

The decimation of Indian peoples, the enforced reservation status as wards of the government, and the frequent breaking of the treaties as westward expansion proceeded characterized relations with the Indian tribes through much of the nineteenth century.

In 1871, congressional action prohibited further treaties with Indian tribes. Indians were now confined to reservations. They were to be fed, housed, clothed, and protected until such time as Congress considered they were able to care for themselves; and a state of enforced welfare dependency ensued. The government reports in the years following called for humanizing, Christianizing, and educating the Indians.

From the beginning the federal government was uneasy about running schools itself and sought to turn over responsibility to other agencies. Continuing into the late nineteenth century, funds were distributed to various religious denominations to maintain mission schools. But public protest against federal aid to sectarian schools and the unconstitutional nature of the practice led the government to discontinue the practice. As a result, a system of federally operated schools was developed under the jurisdiction of the BIA.

Paying little attention to the multitude of linguistic and other cultural differences among Indian peoples, and ignoring the varied traditions of child rearing in preparation for adulthood in the tribal communities, the government entered the school business in the late nineteenth century with a vigor that caused consternation among the Indians. The package deal that accompanied literacy included continuing efforts to "civilize the natives." Old abandoned army forts were converted into boarding schools, children were removed—sometimes forcibly—long distances from their homes, the use of Indian languages by children was forbidden under threat of corporal punishment, students were boarded out to white families during vacation times, and native religions were suppressed. These practices were rationalized by the notion that the removal from the influence of home and tribe was the most effective means of preparing the Indian child to become an American. Paradoxically, this effort to deal with America's native population developed in part out of nineteenth-century liberal humanitarianism—an effort to substitute the primer and the plow for the policy of physical extermination which preceded it.

Although schools were institutions imposed by the whites on Indians, this did not mean that Indians previously did not appreciate the significance and values of schooling for their people. For example, as early as 1791, the Senecas had requested teachers from George Washington. Several of the tribes maintained extensive school systems operated and financed by themselves. Among these were the more than two hundred schools and academies of the Choctaw nation in Mississippi and Oklahoma which sent numerous graduates to eastern colleges, and which flourished until the 1890s.

The Cherokee Republic also developed an extensive school system, and estimates of literacy for the nineteenth-century Cherokee run as high as 90 per cent. Cherokee had a higher percentage of better educated persons than the white settler population of Texas or Arkansas. The Cherokee schools taught not only English but

Cherokee as well, using the alphabet invented by Sequoyah. The Creeks, Chickasaws, and Seminoles also maintained schools.

But by the late 1890s, these schools were closed by the federal government and the education of Indians came under the control of a paternalistic government. Cherokee education, for example, came under control of a federal superintendent in 1903, and in 1906 when Oklahoma became a state the whole system was abolished. It was not until the late 1960s that an Indian tribe once again would be in a position to direct the formal education of its children in a school.

By the 1890s, many Indian tribes had been forced into a state of welfare dependency on the reservation. But a major shift in government policy soon came with the passage of the Dawes Severalty Act (General Allotment Act of 1887, which ushered in a policy not interrupted until 1934). Both the educational and the economic policies of the allotment period led to the impoverishment of many Indians and to the shattering of their morale. The bitterness of that era remains in the memory of Indians today.

Supported by a coalition of those desirous of Indian lands, those wishing the government to "get out of the Indian business" —a euphemism for abrogating the Indian treaties, and those whose humanitarianism caused them to shudder at the reservation conditions, the act had the effect of stripping some forty-one million acres of land from Indian hands. Reservation lands were divided and distributed as individual allotments of forty, eighty, or 160 acres to people, many of whom traditionally had held land in common. Land declared surplus after distribution to individuals was purchased by the government and resold for funds for education and "civilization." As wards, individuals were unable to sell their allotments until a period of twenty-five years or longer had passed. For the plains hunting tribes this was a particularly disastrous time.

Commenting on this period the anthropologist Gordon Macgregor writes:

> The small size of allotments in areas of limited rainfall, the poor quality of the soil, the erosion that followed plowing up natural grassland ranges, the timbered allotments too small for productive operation, the rocky, infertile soil, and even in California alloted lava beds, led

to non- or inefficient use. Rental of allotments proved the only feasible solution for aged, women, and child allottees. The federal practice of granting rights to, but no ownership of, inherited lands further stalemated the allotment for assimilation policy.

The strongest barrier, however, was the cultural resistance shown among the great number of non-agricultural tribes.[3]

Education policy during this time was designed to fulfill the goals of the allotment period, a policy which ". . . if steadfastly adhered to will not only relieve the government of an enormous burden, but it is believed will practically settle the Indian question within the space generally allotted to a generation."[4]

To this end a program of compulsory school attendance with literacy training subordinated to that of industrial training was proposed. In addition, attendance of Indians in public schools rather than the federal school system operated by the BIA was encouraged. The first contracts for the coeducation of Indian and white children in state and territory schools were made in 1891. By 1901, California, Idaho, Michigan, Montana, Nebraska, Nevada, Oklahoma, Oregon, South Dakota, and Wisconsin had federal contracts to educate Indians in public schools. A total of 257 Indians was enrolled in public schools while an average of 131 actually attended, attesting to the minimal impact of state-controlled public schools among Indians at that time. Federal schools also had a limited impact despite their mandate to compel attendance.

Federal education policy did not succeed in totally destroying Indian identity, in part because so little schooling was available to Indians (there were 16,000 pupils in 113 schools, ages five to twenty-one in 1901). Also there was resistance by Indians to this kind of forced assimilation by education, a factor made evident by the Commissioner of Indian Affairs' report which reads:

> . . . gathered from the cabin, the wickiup, and the teepee. Partly by cajolery and partly by threats; partly by bribery and partly by force, they are induced to leave their kindred to enter these schools and take upon themselves the outward semblance of civilized life.[5]

Among the Navajos, for example, in 1901 there were some four thousand to five thousand school-age population, but only three schools accommodating three hundred. The White Mountain Apache had one school with a capacity of eighty pupils for 488 children of school age; among the Chippewa of Minnesota, schools had a capacity of six hundred for over 2280 children.[6]

Education for citizenship and vocations remained basic educational policy. In 1916, a uniform course of study in all federal Indian schools was introduced. It was planned with the vocational aim very clearly and positively dominant, with special emphasis on agriculture and homemaking. Expressing a concern for relevance related to assimilationist goals, the program states: "The character and amount of academic work has been determined by its relative value and importance as a means of solution of the problem of the farmer, mechanic, and housewife."[7] A complete course of study, including time allotments per subject was provided. Interestingly enough, teacher accountability was built into the program. The Commissioner wrote:

> I have directed that the teachers of the service (BIA) should hereafter be graded and judged largely by their success in passing at least 70 per cent of the pupils in their class. It will be necessary, however, for the pupil to actually accomplish the work before being so promoted, and steps will be taken to guard against any promotions which are not warranted. This will be accomplished by conducting uniform examinations for all Indian schools throughout the United States.[8]

Concurrently, those Indians attending public schools were being subsidized at a rate of almost fifteen cents per day.

World War I interfered with the strict application of the uniform policy instituted in 1916.

In 1918, Congress passed an act (Act of May 25, 1918, 40 Stat. L. 564) ". . . that hereafter no appropriation, except appropriations made pursuant to treaties, shall be used to educate children of less than one-fourth Indian blood whose parents are citizens of the United States and the State wherein they live and where there are adequate free-school facilities provided." This effectively removed large numbers of Indian children from federal jurisdiction and federal support.

By the early 1920s large numbers of Indians had attended no school. The Indian schools were very poorly financed but it was not until 1929 that Congress repealed an act passed in 1908 which imposed a limit to the per capita cost in Indian boarding schools. By this time the federal boarding schools were under severe attack and the commissioner wrote:

> ... the economies which Federal Indian schools have been compelled to practice have been harmful, and more adequate funds will have to be provided if Indian education is to advance.[9]

A majority of Indians had already become full citizens by 1924, some as early as 1817. All Indians were made full citizens by an act of Congress in 1924. Entitled to full rights including the vote in local, state, and national elections, many were nonetheless denied these rights by the states in which they resided. It was not until 1948 that Arizona and New Mexico were required by court decision to permit Indians to vote, thus extending the practice to all.[10]

The general pattern of political corruption and intolerance of cultural differences that was characteristic of American society in the 1920s pervaded the Indian service as well, and led to a Senate investigation that produced the best critical survey of federal Indian programs conducted to that date, "The Problem of Indian Administration." Popularly known as the Meriam Report, after Lewis Meriam of the University of Chicago, director of the study, the report made a severely critical review of the serious deficiencies in Indian administration.[11] Its recommendations concerning education included an attack upon the operation of the boarding schools which were seen to be overcrowded, rigid, overly demanding in their schedule of work and study, and deficient in health services and food. Teachers were considered poorly trained and salaries too low to attract better personnel.

Influenced by the prevailing progressive educational philosophies of the day, the report emphasized the value of keeping children with their families in their home communities and condemned the practice of compelling them to attend distant boarding schools. The Report stated that the boarding schools were:

> at variance with modern view of education and social work, which regard home and family as essential institutions from which it is generally undesirable to uproot children ... ultimately most of the boarding schools as they are presently organized should disappear.[12]

The Meriam Report accepted the eventual goal of educating all Indians in the public schools but warned of the government temptation "to save money and wash its hands of responsibility for the Indian child."[13] To counteract such a possibility the Report urged that "Federal authorities retain sufficient professional direction to make sure the needs of the Indians are met."[14]

The Report also spoke of the need for furnishing adequate secondary schooling, scholarship, and loan programs for Indian higher education; the need for educational specialists rather than administrators to direct educational programs; and spoke disparagingly of the use of abandoned army forts as schools.

Although sympathetic to Indian participation in the direction of schools, the Meriam Report recommendations for general Indian policy did not depart from the traditional goal of assimilation of Indians.

> The fundamental requirement is that the task of the Indian Service be recognized as primarily educational, in the broadest sense of that word, and that it be made an efficient educational agency, devoting its main energies to the social and economic advancement of the Indians, so that they may be absorbed into the prevailing civilization or be fitted to live in the presence of that civilization, at least in accordance with a minimum standard of health and decency.[15]

While it stressed humanitarian values and recommended increased federal expenditures for Indian programs, the Report saw this as the most efficient way to "write the closing chapter of the history of the relationship of the national government and the Indian."

> The belief is that it is a sound policy of national economy to make generous expenditure in the next few decades with the object of winding up the national administration of Indian affairs.[16]

This philosophy echoed the goals of the allotment period and foreshadowed the "termination policy" of the 1950s. But the immediate result of the Meriam recommendations was to slow down the allotment of Indian lands and to help usher in a whole "New Deal" in Indian affairs.

A major reversal in national Indian policy took place in the 1930s, following the revelations of the Meriam Report. John Collier became Commissioner of Indian Affairs in the Franklin

D. Roosevelt administration, holding that position until 1945. Collier and Willard Beatty, his director of Indian education, sought to reorganize and improve the federal school system. The passage of the Wheeler-Howard Act of 1934, also known as the Indian Reorganization Act of June 18, 1934, ended the allotment period and provided the legislative framework for the Collier policies which sought economic stabilization of Indians principally on the land; organization of the Indian tribes for managing their own affairs; and departing from the forced assimilation policies of the past, recognition of civil and cultural freedom, and opportunity for the Indians.

The Indian Reorganization Act made possible appropriations for new holdings, confirmed Indian self-government, made provisions for tribal business organizations. Indians were made eligible for BIA posts without regard to civil service laws, making possible the hiring of larger numbers of Indians in schools and other federal posts. The act explicitly authorized loans to Indians for tuition in recognized vocational and trade schools and colleges. The act has come to be known as the "Indian Bill of Rights" because it provided greater autonomy for tribal governments.

Given the option to reorganize under the act or not, some tribes chose not to, for example, the Navajo, but over three fourths of all tribes eventually operated under the provisions of this act. Others adopted some of the provisions.

The educational policies in BIA federal schools under the Collier administration were radically different from those which precipitated the Meriam Report. Conscious efforts were made to encourage the establishment of community day schools. Programs in bilingual, bicultural education were instituted; active efforts were made to recruit Indian teachers. Special schools for leadership training, nurses training, and health schools were set up. Inservice education for teachers was instituted. The major thrust of the Collier-Beatty philosophy was respect for the Indian heritage of the child—a marked departure from previous policies.

Public school attendance by Indian children also continued and it was in this period that the Johnson-O'Malley Act of 1934, amended in 1936, was passed. This act provided for the reimbursement to states for the education of Indians in public schools.

World War II cut into the financing of the Collier program and it never quite regained the vigor it had attained during the 1930s. And soon, John Collier and the New Deal policies in regard to Indian affairs came under strong attack.

The point of view expressed by Meriam and Collier in regard to the advisability of phasing out the boarding schools and educating Indian children in their home communities was not without political enemies. The Senate and House Indian Affairs Committee in 1944, for example, criticized what they considered a tendency in many reservation day schools to adapt the education to the Indian and to his reservation way of life rather than to adapt the Indian to the habits and requirements needed, they argued, by an independent citizen earning his own way off the reservation. Arguing for boarding school education and expressing disdain for Indian communities, the committee wrote:

> The Indian Bureau is tending to place too much emphasis on the day school located on the Indian reservation as compared with the opportunities afforded Indian children in off-the-reservation boarding schools where they can acquire an education in healthful and cultural surroundings without the handicap of having to spend their out-of-school hours in tepees, shacks with dirt floors, and no windows, in tents, in wickiups, in hogans, or in surroundings where English is never spoken, where there is a complete lack of furniture, and where there is sometimes an active antagonism or an abysmal indifference to the virtues of an education.[17]

The conflict over educational policy was related to the strong persistence of efforts to disengage the federal government from Indian affairs. Thus the Senate and House Indian Affairs Committee further argued: "The present Indian education program tends to operate too much in the direction of perpetuating the Indian as a special status individual rather than preparing him for independent citizenship."[18]

Friction over policy caused John Collier to resign in 1945.

The years following the end of World War II saw continued efforts to end federal commitments to Indian tribes, a policy known as termination. In 1946, the Indian Claims Commission Act was passed. This act, which permitted tribes to sue for settlement of claims against the federal government, was viewed by

Congress as a necessary prerequisite for Indian acceptance of separation from the tribe and reservations, for it was thought that many Indians were staying in reservations just to remain eligible for any federal payment that might be forthcoming. Rather than encouraging Indians to leave, once claims were settled, the act has served to develop legal experience among the tribes, increased sophistication concerning their historic rights, and increased experience with investing of award monies in reservation developments, educational, social, and legal programs. While monies and land were not always used wisely, experience with the claims cases has given renewed evidence of the justification of the Indians' charge of mistreatment in the past, renewed pride in their history, and increased consciousness of their legal rights.

House Concurrent Resolution 108, passed by Congress in 1953, provided the impetus to turn federal policy in the direction of ending federal aid and protection for Indians, providing the mechanism for termination. By 1960, sixty-one tribes, groups, communities, *rancherias,* or allotments were terminated including two major tribes with large timber holdings, the Klamath of Oregon and the Menominee of Wisconsin.

As one writer has described this period:

> . . . a reversal of the government's Indian policy directed at curtailing Bureau activities and eventually terminating all federal protection sent a new wave of anxiety and suspicion of the white man's intent over the Indian country. The economic and political developments and activities of Indian communities were retarded or obstructed . . . Tribal members moved into lower class white neighborhoods and re-formed Indian groups, but they lost the potential of their income from timber and their own lands on which to work out a new community life.[19]

Although termination became voluntary toward the end of the decade, resentment and fear have continued to pervade Indian government relations. During this period, BIA ended operation of all its federal schools in Idaho, Michigan, Washington, Wisconsin, substituting public school attendance. In addition, California and Oregon assumed full responsibility for educating Indian children, and Johnson-O'Malley funds, distributed by the

BIA to the states for the special needs of Indian children, were cut off there.

The federal education policy for those Indians who were not terminated or for whom responsibility was assumed by the states continued to encourage the attendance of Indians in public schools. However, the BIA boarding school system also expanded in order to meet needs arising out of the rapid increase in school attendance, especially by Navajo and Eskimo youth, as well as expanding attendance at the secondary level. Policy during the period also included a program for relocating Indians to urban areas away from reservations, began in 1951.

Because Johnson-O'Malley monies were expended primarily to support the education of Indian children living on or near reservations in public schools, Indians who were terminated or who lived in states which assumed responsibility lost eligibility for BIA educational assistance.

When Stewart Udall took office as Secretary of the Interior in 1961, morale in the Bureau of Indian Affairs was at a low ebb. The termination policy of 1953–58 was supposedly countermanded, but Indian leaders had a deep distrust of every action of the government with respect to Indian affairs.

Secretary Udall appointed a Task Force on Indian Affairs in 1961, and in 1966 a White House Task Force on Indian Affairs was appointed. These task forces held hearings and interviewed many Indian representatives. The 1966 Task Force found that the concern over termination continued as a major issue for Indians. This Task Force reported that because of the policy of termination between 1953 and 1958, no programs could be developed which in any way indicated to the Indians that the programs might be utilized to separate him from reservation land. The report emphasized the extent the termination issue poisoned every aspect of Indian affairs at the time. The issue of termination remained, in their opinion, a major psychological barrier to Indian socioeconomic development.[20]

After 1961, there was rather slow progress in the Bureau of Indian Affairs toward giving greater responsibility to Indians for the conduct of tribal affairs including the conduct of education despite support given by the new Commissioner of Indian Affairs Philleo Nash, a trained anthropologist and former lieutenant governor of Wisconsin. Critics stated that the changes in BIA procedure were altogether slow, due partly to a bureaucratic structure which slowed down decision making and partly to the unwillingness of some BIA officials to change their habits of making policy and directing practice. Here the program of another government office began to take effect.

The Office of Economic Opportunity operating under the U. S. Department of Health, Education, and Welfare managed to give local Indian tribal groups a great deal of responsibility for planning and directing aid programs. This was based on the OEO policy of "maximum feasible participation" by the recipients or beneficiaries of aid programs in the design and operation of such programs. Many Indians were employed as directors of local Community Action projects. As they and their community leaders gained experience, they gained confidence and began to claim the right to govern themselves in various areas of community activity, including education.

By the mid-1960s, it became clear that the BIA had changed its mission—to that of assisting the economic development of the Indians, rather than the more passive function of "taking care of" the Indians. An indication of this was Senator George McGovern's introduction in 1966 of a concurrent resolution in the Congress which stressed a policy of Indian self-determination and economic development.

At this time the White House Task Force on the American Indian was appointed and produced a report which stressed economic development of the Indian people together with an improved educational system. This Task Force consisted of twelve people, with Walsh McDermott of the Cornell University School of Medicine's Department of Public Health as chairman. The members were drawn from universities, industry, the law, and the BIA educational system. The report recommended that substantial government funds be put into economic development programs, with an immediate twenty-million-dollar, on-the-job training and public works program, as the first step in a ten-year, billion-dollar program to provide adequate housing for Indians on reservations and to provide sixty thousand new jobs on reservations by 1977. This was the first time that a body of men in a position to advise the Washington administration talked about a level of expenditures which could have a major impact on the economic welfare and the economic development of the Indian peoples.[21]

Just before this Task Force made its report, the Department of the Interior introduced in Congress the Indian Resources Development Act of 1967. Although this act was not passed, it also began to give economic development the top priority in Indian affairs. It provided for the creation of an Indian Development Loan Authority, to assist Indian tribes and individuals to conduct business and industrial ventures.

In March 1968, President Johnson sent a message to Congress on Indian Affairs which stressed the government's policy of supporting a stronger Indian voice in Indian affairs, directed the BIA to establish advisory school boards at all federal schools, and created a National Commission on Indian Opportunity, including Indian leaders, with the Vice-President of the United States as chairman, and assigning to it an ombudsman function.

The National Council on Indian Opportunity was retained in the Nixon administration and has paid special attention to problems of urban Indians.

The late 1960s also saw a major extensive congressional hearing on Indian education conducted by a special subcommittee on Indian education of the Senate committee on Labor and Public Welfare. Headed by Senator Robert Kennedy, and later by Senator Edward Kennedy, the committee held hearings for eighteen months and its report urged increased Indian control over education, a National Indian Board of Education, and an exemplary federal school system.[22] Although the Congress had still not approved any major economic development measure as late as 1971, this is clearly the next major step in Indian affairs.

President Nixon in his message on Indian Policy (July 8, 1970) said:

> Because termination is morally and legally unacceptable, because it produces bad practical results, and because the mere threat of termination tends to discourage greater self-sufficiency among Indian groups, I am asking the Congress to pass a new Concurrent Resolution which

would expressly renounce, repudiate and repeal the termination policy as expressed in House Concurrent Resolution 108 of the 83rd Congress. This resolution would explicitly affirm the integrity and right to continued existence of all Indian tribes and Alaska native governments, recognizing that cultural pluralism is a source of national strength. It would assure these groups that the United States Government would continue to carry out its treaty and trusteeship obligations to them as long as the groups themselves believed that such a policy was necessary or desirable. It would guarantee that whenever Indian groups decided to assume control or responsibility for government service programs, they could do so and still receive adequate Federal financial support. In short, such a resolution would reaffirm for the Legislative branch—as I hereby affirm for the Executive branch—that the historic relationship between the Federal government and the Indian communities cannot be abridged without the consent of the Indians.

President Nixon closed his message as follows:

We have turned from the question of *whether* the Federal government has a responsibility to Indians to the question of *how* that responsibility can best be fulfilled. We have concluded that the Indians will get better programs and that public monies will be more effectively expended if the people who are most affected by these programs are responsible for operating them.

The Indians of America need Federal assistance—this much has long been clear. What has not always been clear, however, is that the Federal government needs Indian energies and Indian leadership if its assistance is to be effective in improving the conditions of Indian life. It is a new and balanced relationship between the United States Government and the first Americans that is at the heart of our approach to Indian problems. And that is why we now approach these problems with new confidence that they will successfully be overcome.[23]

President Nixon's message on Indian Affairs, in 1970, carried on the evolution of at least a verbal policy of increasing Indian power in Indian affairs and of making economic development the base of Indian policy, with educational development related to it. Later in 1970, Interior Secretary Hickel announced a reorganization of the Bureau of Indian Affairs which abolished the position of agency superintendent for a reservation and replaced it with the position of field administrator with authority to assist local Indians in developing their economic and educational institutions.

It may also be noted that the commissioners of Indian Affairs, directing the BIA, under Presidents Johnson and Nixon were Indians. Robert Bennett, a member of the Oneida tribe had worked for thirty years in the Bureau of Indian Affairs before his appointment as Commissioner. Louis R. Bruce, an Indian businessman from New York, had little connection with Indian tribal affairs before his appointment. He has taken a strong stand in favor of Indian self-determination. Furthermore, there has been a substantial increase in the numbers of Indians serving in positions of authority in the Bureau of Indian Affairs. However, the rigidities of the Bureau and the positions of authority held by old-line bureaucrats and others have slowed progress and caused continued friction between Indians and the BIA. By 1971, the board of directors of the National Tribal Chairman's Association was calling for shifting the BIA out of the Department of Interior to a position directly under the White House in order to halt what they considered to be the "bureaucratic subversion" of the "historic and courageous" policy of self-determination.[24]

With minor exceptions the history of Indian education had been primarily the transmission of white American education, little altered, to the Indian child as a one-way process. The institution of the school is one that was imposed by and controlled by the non-Indian society, its pedagogy and curriculum little changed for the Indian children, its goals primarily aimed at removing the child from his aboriginal culture and assimilating him into the dominant white culture. Whether coercive or persuasive, this assimilationist goal of schooling has been minimally effective with Indian children, as indicated by their record of absenteeism, retardation, and high dropout rates.

Historically, the first defined "problem" of Indian education was predicated on the assumption that Indians must be assimilated into the white society. Assimilationist goals have currently given way, at least in government policy pronouncements, to a recognition for the unique position of American Indians in this country and their right to self-determination.

Today the goals of American Indian education are moving away from a narrow assimilationist goal and are generally agreed upon by Indians and others when they are stated broadly. Essentially, the goals are to enlarge the area of choice and self-determination of Indian people and to respect the value of cultural diversity. Adopting the optimistic view of education held in this country, the American Indian Chicago Conference, in 1961, said, "We conceive education not only in terms of classroom teaching, but a process which begins at birth and continues through a life span. Of all the studies, surveys, and research made of Indians, the inevitable conclusions and recommendations are that education is the key to salvation of whatever ills may be, wherever Indians reside."[25]

The Declaration of Indian Purpose of the American Indian Chicago Conference read:

> In order to give recognition to certain basic philosophies by which the Indian People live, we, the Indian People, must be governed by principles in a democratic manner with a right to choose our way of life. Since our Indian culture is threatened by presumption of being absorbed by the American society, we believe we have the responsibility of preserving our precious heritage. We believe that the Indians must provide the adjustment and thus freely advance with dignity to a better life.[26]

These broad statements are being applied in various ways to the actual educational systems of Indian tribes and communities. Thus, the former tribal chairman of the northern Cheyenne, John Woodenlegs, says:

> Our goals have been:
> 1. To educate our schools and the local communities to the idea of community schools, serving the needs of the local people over and above daily education of children.
> 2. To encourage parents to be more concerned and involved with the schools, including active membership on school boards.
> 3. To help teachers get more knowledge of the Cheyennes, their past history and culture and present life.
> 4. To encourage Cheyenne resource people to go into classrooms to talk on history and culture.
> We feel our children need education which gives the best of both cultures. We feel that many of the values of our past Cheyenne society can still serve us well in this modern world. We feel we need this to give us understanding and pride in our past, just as other Americans learn their history for the same reason.[27]

The goals of Indian education need to be interpreted in relation to the pervasive Indian need to live in two cultures. An Apache member of the school board of a public school district in the Apache reservation said, during a conference of Apache citizens:

> All of us have limitations when it comes to functioning effectively and efficiently in this world. I am aware of my limitations and I'm sure some of you are too. An imaginary line seems to extend across our path. The space all the way to the imaginary line represents the Indian lifeways; the space beyond the line represents that of the non-Indian society. It seems like some of us can only go as far as the line, for we have not learned the white ways of life. If we encourage our children to do their best and to be persistent in their endeavor to receive an education, I'm sure they will make the breakthrough—which is good. Because of education they should be able to function on the other side of the imaginery line.[28]

If there is a problem in Indian education today, it is perhaps best described in terms of the need to re-evaluate goals in terms defined by Indian peoples themselves; how to better the quality of the educational environment; how to make the school more responsive to the diversity of Indian peoples and their needs; to more clearly define the roles of the federal, state and tribal governments in supporting the educational enterprise; and how to insure the participation of the Indian communities in educational decision making.

At the beginning of the 1970s, there is a much clearer government policy on Indian affairs than there was a decade earlier. Money appropriated for Indian programs has increased substantially, though currency inflation has reduced the value of these increases. Several federal agencies, besides the Bureau of Indian Affairs, are involved in programs that assist Indians: the Office of Economic Opportunity, the Office of Education, the Department of Housing and Urban Development, the Department of Labor, the Public Health Service.

The Bureau of Indian Affairs has expanded its activities in the fields of education, vocational training and placement, housing, industrial and community development. Public attention has been focused on Indian affairs by such dramatic events as the restoration of ancestral land to the Taos Indians, as well as by increased Indian militancy in regard to injustice.

The principle of Indian self-determination has now been stated by two Presidents as policy of the federal government, and has been put into effect in several tribes through contracts which give them money to use in providing education and other services.

At the beginning of the 1970s the scene is set for a new era in Indian affairs and Indian education. But the long history of vacillating policies and unfulfilled promises continues to keep Indians watchful and wary.

II

Indian Peoples—the Present

Despite the myth, fantasy, and romance which surround them, the more interesting reality about Native Americans is their extraordinary vitality and diversity in the present. Today, American Indians constitute a rapidly growing population. Close to 800,000 Indians,[1] plus 35,000 Eskimos and Aleuts in Alaska were counted in the 1970 census, about 50 per cent more than in 1960. But who is an Indian? In 1970, a person was counted as Indian if he declared himself to be one or was identified as one by an enumerator (Table 1). This relatively straightforward definition according to self-identification or recognition includes a wide range of persons.

Some persons are on the rolls of organized tribes, others are not; some Indians maintain traditional life styles and are frequently referred to as "full bloods" although they may be of mixed ancestry, others represent various degrees of acculturation in relation to the white society; some live in isolated rural regions, others in major industrial centers; some speak a native language as a home language, others have limited comprehension of an Indian language or none at all; some tribal members are "progressive" in that they lean toward institutions and political structures removed from traditional kinship and religious systems of political control, others are "conservative," their allegiance remaining with traditional systems of political control; some tribes have reservation lands and close ties to the federal government through the U. S. Bureau of Indian Affairs, Department of Interior, others have no federal trust lands and have lost, through termination, claim to special federal services, or never have had such special services; some are living on reservations which are synonymous with ancestral homelands, others have had histories of forcible removal from traditional places of occupation. In addition to differences in degree of Indian ancestry, the diversity of Indians is further compounded by a wide variety of ethnic differences among the tribes, differences in historical experiences, differences in educational levels, as well as differences between generations.

TABLE 1

AMERICAN INDIAN POPULATION, 1890–1970

Source: *U. S. Department of Commerce News,* April 22, 1971

Year	Indian Population*
1890	248,253
1900	237,196
1910	265,683
1920	244,437
1930	332,397
1940	333,929
1950	343,410
1960	523,591
1970	791,839

* Excludes Aleuts and Eskimos (of whom there were an estimated 35,-252 in 1970).

In the past, Indian education policies were imposed and undertaken by administrators and educators with the assumption that one approach was suited for all Indians. But no policy that does not recognize both the right to self-determination and the heterogeneity of American native peoples is likely to be successful, for if schools are to assist in the education and socialization of Indian children and youth, they must recognize and

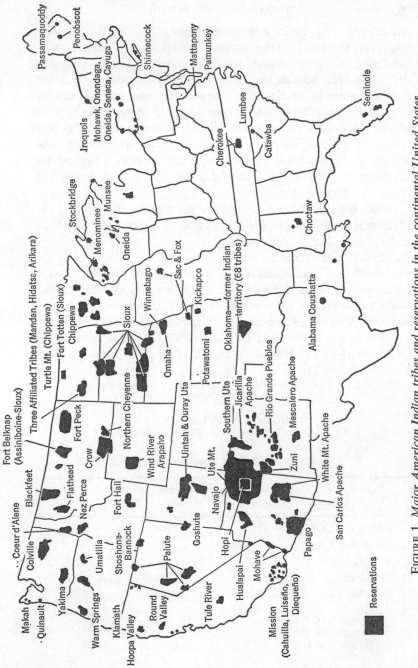

FIGURE 1. *Major American Indian tribes and reservations in the continental United States*

respect the vast basic differences among the Indian peoples. Moreover, the schools must support the efforts of Native Americans to retain those aspects of their cultural identity that they still value. The schools, to the extent possible, also must assist Indian peoples to develop those new social and political institutions Indians might view as necessary to help them in the process of adapting their community life to contemporary needs. To view American Indians simply as a single minority group in the population of the United States requiring uniform programs for development, is to be oblivious of the complexity of the issues and problems affecting them.[2]

Indian peoples today live in every state of the Union and the District of Columbia (Figure 1). In addition some 35,000 Aleuts and Eskimos live in Alaska.

Although numbers alone are not adequate for understanding the complexities of educational needs and problems, clearly, a large Indian population in a state suggests a heavy responsibility for the education of Indian children. More than 50 per cent of all Indians counted in the 1970 census live in five states, ranked as follows by their Indian population: Oklahoma, 97,731; Arizona, 95,812; California, 91,018; New Mexico, 72,788; and North Carolina, 43,487 (Table 2).

TABLE 2

INDIAN POPULATION,
IN STATES WITH 4000 INDIANS OR MORE,
1970

Source: U. S. Census of Population, 1970, 1960.

	Number, 1960	Percentage of all Indians, 1970	Number, 1970
UNITED STATES	551,669	100.0	827,091[a]
1. Oklahoma	64,689	11.8	97,731
2. Arizona	83,387	11.6	95,812
3. California	39,014	11.0	91,018
4. New Mexico	56,255	8.8	72,788
5. Alaska	42,522	6.2	51,528
Aleuts 5,755 Eskimo 22,323 Indian 14,444		Aleuts } 35,252 Eskimo } Indian 16,276	

	Number, 1960	Percentage of all Indians, 1970	Number, 1970
6. North Carolina	38,129	5.2	43,487
7. Washington	21,076	4.0	33,386
8. South Dakota	25,914	3.9	32,365
9. New York	16,491	3.4	28,330
10. Montana	21,181	3.3	27,130
11. Minnesota	15,496	2.8	23,128
12. Wisconsin	14,297	2.3	18,924
13. Texas	5,750	2.2	18,132
14. Michigan	9,701	2.0	16,854
15. North Dakota	11,736	1.7	14,369
16. Oregon	8,026	1.6	13,510
17. Illinois	4,704	1.4	11,413
18. Utah	6,961	1.4	11,273
19. Colorado	4,288	1.1	8,836
20. Kansas	5,069	1.1	8,672
21. Florida	2,504	0.8	6,719
22. Idaho	5,231	0.8	6,687
23. Ohio	1,910	0.8	6,654
24. Nebraska	5,545	0.8	6,624
25. Pennsylvania	2,122	0.7	5,533
26. Missouri	1,723	0.7	5,405
27. Louisiana	3,587	0.7	5,366
28. Wyoming	4,020	0.6	4,980
29. Virginia	2,155	0.6	4,904
30. New Jersey	1,699	0.6	4,706
31. Massachusetts	2,118	0.5	4,475
32. Maryland	1,538	0.5	4,258
33. Mississippi	3,119	0.5	4,113

a Includes 35,252 Aleuts and Eskimos, partly estimated.

Again, almost everywhere they live, Indians present a picture of broad diversity of culture, economic conditions, and legal relations to the federal government and tribes—factors which help explain the enormous complexity of American Indian education. Oklahoma, the state with the largest Indian population, includes

Indians adhering to traditional tribal customs as well as those assimilated with middle-class Oklahoma society. The original "Indian territory" Indians, resettled from the Southeast, Middle West, and southern plains, live here. Except for the Osage, Oklahoma Indian reservations have been terminated, the lands allotted to individuals and largely dissipated. Many rural eastern Oklahoma Indians live under conditions of poverty and landlessness.

Arizona includes a majority of the more than 130,000 members of the Navajo Nation, the largest tribal group in the United States, whose reservation spreads into Utah and northwestern New Mexico. The Pima, Papago, Hopi, and Apache reservations are also located in Arizona.

This area of the Southwest is rich in traditional Indian life. The reservation system is largely intact, and federal financial responsibility for the education of the children is of major importance.

Seventy-three thousand Indians including several Apache tribes live in New Mexico. Most of the existing Pueblo settlements are located along the Rio Grande River.

California is a striking illustration of trends in Indian population movements. The Indian population of that state has nearly tripled to 91,000 in the last decade. Los Angeles County, San Francisco Bay Area, San Diego, and San Bernardino-Riverside have major concentrations of Indians. The growth in the population is due primarily to the in-migration of Indians from other states to the urban areas of California. Fewer than ten thousand California Indians are native to the state. The rural California Indians, for the most part, live on or adjacent to small reservations or rancherias. They represent a wide variety of tribal backgrounds. Many of these rural Indians are employed as seasonal workers in agriculture, lumbering, and fruit-packing plants.

Marine and land wildlife resources are rapidly disappearing as industry and exploitation of the great mineral wealth of Alaska moves in upon the Eskimo. If this new economic life is not to create the social and psychological disorganization that has affected other hunting peoples, the federal and state educational systems will be called upon to provide considerably more than the usual formal elementary education and technical training for skilled jobs.

North and South Dakota are home to forty-seven thousand Indians, most of whom are descendants of the Siouan-speaking buffalo hunters of the Great Plains. These lands are suitable for raising cattle, but full use of this resource is inhibited by the individual ownership of small tracts and by an inheritance pattern which has distributed to almost countless heirs rights to use but not sell these original allotments. The present "owners" cannot legally sell, exchange, or consolidate their holdings. Unallotted and allotted lands sold to non-Indians further complicate the full and efficient utilization of the natural resources. Stock raising and commercial farming have now become big business and provide an opportunity for only a relatively few, experienced Indian operators on the limited land resources of these reservations.

Two relatively new economic opportunities have appeared in this area. One is the establishment of small industries on reservations such as small electronics parts manufacture, providing employment to Indians. The other is the great development of the Missouri River Valley through the building of dams and reservoirs to control flooding and erosion of the soil, and to provide irrigation, water transportation, hydroelectric power, and new public recreational areas. Unemployment remains a major problem.

Emigration, an obvious and seemingly easy solution, has not proved highly feasible for members of the older generations. These are the Indians who are the immediate descendants of those hunters of the plains first forced onto the reservations and who saw their means of subsistence swept away and their social and cultural institutions crumble. Under suppression and forced change and in the wake of the cultural disaster which befell the Sioux, Blackfeet, and other tribes of the Dakotas in the nineteenth century, dependency, frustration, anxiety, and bitterness have followed. Entrance into a hostile or generally indifferent world has not been easy for the young as well.

Forty-three thousand Indians reside in North Carolina, over thirty thousand of whom are descendants of the Lumbee, now living in Robeson and adjacent counties in the southeast part of the state. The Lumbee tribal origin is somewhat ambiguous but probably can be traced to several of the Atlantic Coast tribes. While they have no tribal structure, they have strong Indian identity. Most of them are engaged in agriculture as tenants or sharecroppers on tobacco, cotton, and peanut farms. A few own their own farms. A number of Lumbee are teachers and teacher aides, especially in those schools attended by Lumbee children. In Swain County, in the western part of the state, almost five thousand Cherokee Indians are living on the largest federal reservation east of the Mississippi River.

About sixty-seven thousand Indians are estimated to be living in the six mountain states of Colorado, Idaho, Montana, Nevada, Utah, and Wyoming. Several larger mountain and plains tribes reside in these states. They include the Assiniboin, Blackfeet, Cheyenne, Chippewa, Cree, Crow, Flathead, and Montana Sioux. The Nez Perce live in Idaho, the Shoshone in Idaho and Wyoming, the Ute in Utah and Colorado, the Paiute in Utah and Nevada, and some Navajo in Utah.

Forty-seven thousand Indians live in Washington and Oregon. About seventeen thousand of these reside in the metropolitan areas of Portland, Seattle, Spokane, and Tacoma. Non-metropolitan Indians who live in Washington include Quinault, Salish, and Yakima. In Oregon the Klamath and Warm Springs tribal groups live in rural areas.

Some fifty-nine thousand Indians live in Michigan, Minnesota, and Wisconsin, mostly in the northern part of these states. A third of the Indians in Minnesota are now residents of St. Paul and Minneapolis. Almost all of the non-urban Indians and most of those in the Twin Cities are Chippewa. The largest Indian groups among the nineteen thousand Indians in Wisconsin are the Chippewa, Menominee, Oneida, and the Winnebago. In Michigan among the seventeen thousand Indians, Chippewa, Ottawa, Potawatomi, and Saginaw are the largest tribal groups.

Of the eighteen thousand Indians living in Iowa, Kansas, and Nebraska, several tribal groups located in these states include the Sac and Fox, Iowa, Kickapoo, and Omaha.

In the northeastern United States the largest Indian population of about twenty-eight thousand is in New York, consisting of Mohawk, Onondaga, Oneida, Seneca, Tonawanda, and Tuscarora, former nations of the Iroquois. Some Passamaquoddy and Penobscot communities are located in Maine.

The Choctaw in Mississippi and the Seminole in the Everglades of Florida remain as viable tribal groups of some size.

Despite adjustment problems and a small attrition of families moving back to reservations, there may be as many as 250,000 Indians living in cities of 50,000 or more. Los Angeles County, the San Francisco Bay Area, Oklahoma City, Tulsa, Phoenix, Minneapolis, Chicago, Seattle, Buffalo, New York City, Tucson, and Dallas are major centers of Indian in-migration.

Though there is this broad diversity among the various Indian tribes and communities, there is an erroneous tendency for native Americans to be thought of as one group and as little different from other disadvantaged minority groups. On measures of income, educational level, and occupational prestige, large numbers of American Indians are indeed at the lower end of the spectrum, although, like Blacks, Mexican-Americans, and Puerto Ricans—America's other disadvantaged minorities—there are Indians who are well educated, economically prosperous, and hold prestigious occupations.

However, Indian Americans differ from other minorities in the country in several significant ways. They are descendants of the first Americans. They neither arrived voluntarily in search of a new nationality nor were they forcibly brought to these shores; they have a multitude of languages and cultures developed entirely in the New World—thus they do not necessarily share the values of European civilization; and, most important, many hold special treaty relationships with the United States Government.

As the original Americans, Indians have a moral as well as legal claim on the public conscience. Indians cannot easily forget the white man's attempts to exterminate their people, their forcible removal from ancestral lands, the efforts to convert them from their ancient religions, and the guarantees of rights to traditional homelands that were so often broken in practice. The record is varied, no one tribe's story is an exact duplicate of another's. But all share a history of attempts at subjugation and deliberate efforts to destroy their diverse cultures—sometimes by force, sometimes by missionary zeal.

The current census belies any notion that the American native population is disappearing. It is growing partly because more persons chose to identify as Indian. But it is also growing in actuality. Despite a relatively high infant mortality rate, the Indian birth rate in 1967 was twice as high as that of the total population, making Indians a rapidly growing and youthful population. (Table 3)

TABLE 3

SELECTED VITAL STATISTICS,
INDIANS AND ALASKAN NATIVES,
24 FEDERAL RESERVATION STATES AND ALL RACES,
UNITED STATES, 1967

Source: Unpublished data, Division of Indian Health, United States Public Health Service, 1967.

Vital Statistic	Indians and Alaskan Natives	All Races
Life expectancy	64.0 years	70.5 years
Age-adjusted mortality rate, all causes	1049.9 per 100,000 population	734.5 per 100,000 population
Infant mortality rate	32.5 per 1000 live births	22.4 per 1000 live births
Birth rate	37.4 per 1000 population	17.8 per 1000 population

There are today approximately one quarter million school-age Indian children (five to seventeen years old), an increase of sixty thousand since 1960 (Appendix I, Table 4). The largest number of these children live in seven western states—Alaska, Arizona, California, Montana, New Mexico, Oklahoma, and South Dakota —and in North Carolina. Each of these states has more than ten thousand school-age Indian children. Eight other states— Michigan, Minnesota, New York, North Dakota, Oregon, Utah, Washington, and Wisconsin—have more than three thousand children in this age group. Almost nine out of ten school-age Indian children reside in fifteen states.

Because of the unique history of Indian political relations with the federal government, Indian education developed differently from the rest of American schooling. Education for Indian children has had a unique history, in that the federal government through the Bureau of Indian Affairs was directly involved in its development. This federal commitment, which developed over the years, placed American Indians in a very special position in regard to education as compared to other peoples for whom the states and local communities assumed full educational responsibility. The federal government continues to be obligated by treaty, custom, and moral persuasion to fulfill its responsibility to provide or support educational services and facilities for a large portion of American Indians still living on or near Indian-owned and restricted trust lands.

Much of the complexity regarding Indian education involves how best to meet this responsibility and whether or not the federal government's moral commitment should extend to Indians who no longer reside on trust lands, either because of termination of their reservations or migration to cities, as well as what roles and responsibilities the states should assume in relation to their Indian citizens.

At present, two out of three Indian school-age children are considered to be the educational responsibility of the federal government. Currently, the Indian agency directly responsible for overseeing the education of those Indian youths is the Bureau of Indian Affairs, U. S. Department of Interior. This means that the BIA is the federal agency which gives direct financial support specifically for the education of over 151,000 Indian children, ages six to seventeen in sixteen states. All other Indian children are the educational responsibility of the various states, along with other children (Appendix I, Tables 5 and 6).

The Bureau meets its legal responsibility for the education of these 151,000 children in three ways. It maintains a federal school system, it makes payments to public school systems to educate Indians, and it contracts with Indian groups to run schools.

Indian children and youth aged six to seventeen inclusive can be grouped into the five categories of Table 4 with respect to the type of school they attend or their non-attendance at school.

About one third of the 151,000, for whose education the federal government is responsible, are actually attending the far-flung BIA school system. The federal government maintains a school system for over fifty thousand Indian children in 226 schools from North Carolina to Alaska operated by the Bureau of Indian Affairs. These include 77 boarding and 147 day schools, and several schools that combine boarding and day facilities.

Over twenty-one thousand of the children attending BIA schools live in the Navajo administrative area located in northeast Arizona and including some parts of southern Utah and western New Mexico (Appendix I, Table 6). Other BIA administrative areas with more than five thousand Indian children enrolled in BIA schools are Aberdeen (North and South Dakota and Nebraska), Juneau (Alaska), and Phoenix (the remainder of Arizona, Utah, Nevada, southwest Oregon, and southeast Idaho).

An issue around which there is considerable controversy and which will be examined fully in this volume concerns the fact that almost thirty-five thousand BIA-educated Indian children attend boarding schools. Almost ten thousand of these children, mostly Navajo, are under ten years of age. In addition, the BIA operated nineteen dormitories for over four thousand children who attend public school. Less than one third of the BIA-educated children attend day schools, while living at home.

TABLE 4

SCHOOL ATTENDANCE OF INDIAN CHILDREN AND YOUTH
(1970)

Age 6–17 inclusive

In BIA-operated schools	51,000
In public schools where their attendance is financed by the federal government	100,000
In public schools financed by state and local school districts	40,000
In mission or other private schools	9,000
Not in school	20,000
Total	220,000

Ninety-seven tribal groups can be found in federal schools, although seventy-six of these groups have less than one hundred children in attendance (Appendix I, Table 7). Aleuts, Eskimos, Navajos, Sioux, and Pueblos (including the Hopi) are the most numerous and make up 78 per cent of the total enrollment. Mission education, of great importance in the past, is decreasing. Only one in twenty Indian children is now educated in a mission school.

Through its program known as "Project Tribe," BIA has also contracted a few of its schools experimentally to Indian groups —among these are the Rough Rock Demonstration School and the Blackwater School in Arizona. It also finances a Navajo high school run by a local community, the Ramah School of New Mexico. The contract program is expanding.

As early as 1890, the federal government began making tuition payments to certain public school districts that enrolled Indians, and by 1900, payments were made for 246 such children. This did not become a general policy until the middle of the 1950s, when the BIA began to encourage, wherever possible, attendance in public schools. The reasons for this are complex and are related in part to assimilationist policies, to the belief in value of an integrated education, to a general reluctance of the federal government to run a school system, and to the perennial pressures to "get out of the Indian business." Today, 66 per cent of the two out of three children for whom the BIA has legal responsibility attend public schools at federal expense.

State and local school systems were reluctant to enroll Indian children living on reservations because the Indian land was tax exempt, and consequently the state or school district could not collect money from Indian parents who lived on reservations. However, three federal laws have been passed which give financial assistance to school districts with Indian pupils.

The principal source of federal funds for this purpose is the U. S. Office of Education which dispenses money under Public Law 874, providing money to school districts *in lieu of taxes* for pupils whose parents live on tax-exempt land or work for agencies which do not pay taxes. The federal payment is supposed to equal the current school expenditure per child in comparable school districts. This source of support is known as Impact Aid, since it aids school districts whose tax support is reduced by the *impact* of federal government action.

A parallel source of funds for school buildings and school facilities is provided under Public Law 815, which brought $49 million between 1951 and 1969 to public school districts, mainly in Arizona and New Mexico.

An important source of federal funds for Indian education is the Johnson-O'Malley Act of 1934 and 1936 which authorizes the Bureau of Indian Affairs to contract with state or local educational agencies for special services to meet the needs of Indian children. This act is broad enough to permit use of federal funds for educational needs of Indian students in any place where a case can be made for such needs. Thus it could be used to assist the education of Indian children anywhere, regardless of the residence of the parents. In practice, however, Johnson-O'Malley funds have been used to supplement Impact Aid funds where the latter were not adequate, for one reason or another, and have generally been applied where Indians live on or near reservations.

While the congressional appropriations are made anew each year, the amount of federal government support under Public Law 874 has been rather stable at $20 million ($21.5 million in 1968–69) and the Johnson-O'Malley funds have also been at the $20 million level. If spread equally over the approximately 100,000 Indian pupils who live on or near reservations, this would amount to about $400 per pupil, which is about the average expenditure on an elementary school child in these states.

Finally, Title I of the Elementary and Secondary Education Act, administered by the Department of Health, Education, and Welfare, provides funds specifically to improve the education of children of low-income families, wherever they live and whatever their race. Since large numbers of Indian families are "poor" as defined by this law, school districts with Indian children received approximately $22 million per year at the 1969 rate of payment. However, this money is not earmarked specifically for service to Indian children.

There is a new price on the Indian's head! Indian pupils are a source of revenue. How funds are dispersed, used, and controlled are clearly open to controversy, and later in this book we will return to an examination of these issues.

III

Communities Where Indians Live and Attend Schools

Indian children attend school in a wide variety of settings. Some live in remote isolated areas, others in major metropolitan centers of the nation. Indian communities span a broad spectrum of distance from large urban and employment centers, language spoken in the home, degree of Indian ancestry, types of schools attended, and proportion of non-Indians in the schools attended by the children (Appendix I, Table 6).

In this era of jet planes, pickup trucks, snowmobiles, migrant labor, and the ubiquitous school, total isolation is increasingly rare and conditions everywhere are in process of change. However, many Alaskan natives and many Navajos, Hopis, Apaches, and Papagos of the Southwest continue to live in the relatively more isolated and traditional Indian communities. Children in these communities come from homes where a native language is spoken and attend school with close to 100 per cent Indian enrollment. They are often the first generation to complete high school.

Although there are these similarities, the communities where Indian children live and the schools they attend vary considerably—some attending BIA day schools, some state public schools, some BIA boarding schools. The following descriptions of Navajo education in the Shonto community of Arizona, Eskimo education in the Bethel region of western Alaska, Papago education in Sells, Arizona, and the Theodore Roosevelt Boarding School in Fort Apache, New Mexico, illustrate the types of education available to children from relatively traditional communities.

The Shonto Boarding School and Community[1]

The Navajo Nation is the largest tribal group in the United States. Although parts of the Navajo Reservation, which is located in northern Arizona and parts of Utah and New Mexico, are modern and close to major highway networks, traditional life is still maintained by many and considerable physical isolation continues in this area. BIA day school and public school attendance is common, but so is attendance at the BIA reservation boarding schools.

In 1893, just a few days before he died, Manuelito, a former great war leader of the Navajo people and by then an old man, said to the young Chee Dodge, famous scout and interpreter, destined to become a tribal chairman of the Navajo:

> My grandchild, the whites have many things which we Navajos need. But we cannot get them. It is as though the whites were in a grassy canyon and there they have wagons, plows, and plenty of food. We Navajos are up on the dry mesa. We can hear them talking but we cannot get to them. My grandchild, education is the ladder. Tell our people to take it.

But, due to a combination of Navajo resistance and insufficient support for education by the federal government, in 1948 less than six thousand or only about one fourth of the twenty-two thousand Navajo children of school age were in school and only two hundred of these in high schools. About two thirds of the people had received no schooling whatsoever, and the median number of years of schooling for members of the tribe was less than one.

In sharp contrast, only twenty years later, more than 90 per cent of the forty-six thousand Navajo children of school age (six to eighteen) were in schools. The high school dropout rate compared favorably with the national average. Also, about eight hundred Navajo students were attending college under tribal and federal grants. In addition, many were participating in adult education programs.

Currently, some nine thousand Navajo children under the age of ten attend BIA elementary boarding schools. The Shonto Boarding School located in the Shonto region illustrates the complexities of this controversial type of schooling.

The Shonto area is one of the more traditional and isolated parts of the reservation.

Located in the northwest corner of the Navajo Reservation, the area is characterized by a complex system of highlands and mesas, generally referred to as the Shonto Plateau, deeply dissected by parallel canyons which drain the area. An isolated area until recently, Shonto is now connected by roads to Flagstaff, Arizona, the most important nearby urban center, 120 miles to the southwest. Tuba City, an agency town located on the reservation with BIA, school, tribal, and U. S. Public Health facilities, is located midway between Shonto and Flagstaff. Shonto is still relatively isolated since access is via a three-mile stretch of unpaved road off a dead-end paved road of nine miles. This latter road, however, is connected to the major highway known as the Navajo Trail, the visually stunning route traveled by increasing numbers of tourists yearly. (Figure 2)

The beauty of the area is tempered for the Navajo by very cold winters, with alternating freezing and thawing of the ground, as well as by the presence of fog and some snow. Summer droughts also make for serious hardship in the area. It is the mud and frequently impassable road conditions that make day travel to school from outlying districts difficult and provides one rationale for maintaining a boarding school here.

The Shonto Boarding School serves three traditional Navajo communities: Shonto, Inscription House, and Navajo Mountain, in addition to several peripheral areas such as the northern reaches of Black Mesa. Most of the region was formerly served by more distant boarding schools, and in not a few cases by no school at all. Each of the above communities has its own trader, constitutes a chapter, which is the Navajo Nation's political sub-division, and maintains a chapter house, a preschool, and usually a mission. Thus the school represents an area-based clientele, rather than a "community" in the usual sense.

The population density is low throughout the area. The Navajos of this very traditional part of the reservation live in scattered groups. These groups are extended families—related persons who live within "shouting distance" of one another. In Shonto, for example, which is about 230 square miles, there are about one hundred households representing over seven hundred persons in about thirty-eight of these residential or territorial groups. The

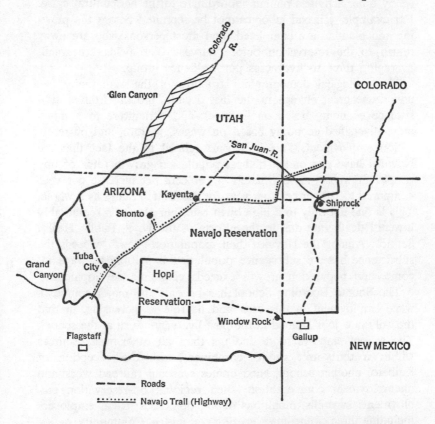

FIGURE 2. *Shonto community in Navajo Reservation, Arizona*

strength of kinship bonds makes up for the physical diffusion of the Navajo community.

Very few non-Indians live in the area. Those that do are largely associated with the Shonto Boarding School and live within the school compound, maintaining a physical and social distance from the Navajo community. Several traders, missionaries, and employees at two other schools constitute the few other non-Navajo.

Although sheepherding and livestock raising are economically more important than agriculture, traditionally most Navajos consider themselves primarily as farmers and secondarily, ranchers. Many other activities remain subordinate to the agricultural cycle. For example, railroad labor cannot be recruited before the plowing and planting are completed, and most persons who are away return to the reservation before harvest. The fields are small, averaging three to five acres per residence group.

The ecological demographic structure of the community has undergone great change in the last decade, moving from a subsistence economy based on livestock and agriculture to a much more diversified economy based on wages, welfare, and off-reservation employment. This is in part related to the fact that the Navajos have one of the highest population growth rates of any people anywhere; approximately 4 per cent net increase per year compared to 1.8 per cent per year for the United States as a whole. This is due not only to a high birth rate, but also to a remarkably lowered death rate due to the efforts of the U. S. Public Health Service. Among the Navajos then, population growth exceeds the subsistence base, a subsistence population is shifting to wage income, and population growth exceeds economic development.

The Shonto Boarding School has become the major source of wage employment in this area and its role is increasing, in that the only new jobs created in the past five years were at the school. The school employs more Indians than all other wage sources within a thirty-mile radius combined, with the exception of Kaibeto, another school. Next comes seasonal railroad work and unemployment compensation; then regional off-reservation employment: sawmills, munitions depot, domestics; tribal employees including three councilmen, grazing committee, Community Action personnel and a policeman; and a small coal mine; and the few clerks and hourly wage laborers found at the traders, missions, and National Monument. The Navajo Nation maintains dry laws on the reservation and, although illegal, bootlegging is another supplementary economic activity. Considerable controversy surrounds efforts to repeal the dry laws.

Although some Navajos hold top professional and administrative positions, most who are employed work at lower level jobs. There is considerable unemployment but unemployment must be understood as referring to wage labor only, as the same individuals might be fully engaged in subsistence agriculture and livestock raising.

The Navajo tribe sponsors economic programs in the Shonto area including a summer Youth Corps, a water system under construction at Inscription House, and ten-day relief projects. The eventual paving of a new highway may provide some new areas for economic development in the tourist services sector—gas, food, lodging. Employment opportunities for young people, however, are exceedingly limited and largely limited to replacement of school aides.

Employment assistance in urban areas away from the reservation is encouraged by the BIA, as is vocational training and higher education.

BIA employment assistance in Tuba City, about sixty miles distant, handles applications for relocation, while the state of Arizona also assists in job recruitment. A small number find tribal employment. Those leaving the reservation either generally go to vocational training programs, or to the West Coast, or another urban area.

The out-migration of Indians is to school, the army, and then relocation. Summer and fall seasonal employment on the railroads or in migrant agriculture also sees many leaving the area temporarily. Since the Shonto population grows more in number each year than the total number of jobs extant, it is clear that considerable preparation for off-reservation life should be included in the school program. However, most migrants plan to return, and many, in fact, do return, keeping up their kinship ties and grazing permits. Settling into the community is viewed by many as more

important than succeeding in an urban environment. Urban incomes which permit acquisition of pickup trucks and money for
cattle, help some Navajos to become economically established in
the traditional Shonto community. However, since few of the
younger generation have been graduated from high school, the
actual trends for the more educated are not yet apparent. The
in-migration involves those returning from urban experiences,
and, in the summer, the high school students who have been
away to off-reservation boarding schools. Sometimes the college
students also return to the reservation.

In addition to wage employment, the development of Shonto
Boarding School is associated with better graded roads, over a
hundred new houses, electricity—still not available to 90 per cent
of Shonto Navajos, one pay telephone, cable TV—at the school
compound since 1968, a water and sanitation system for compound dwellers, a graded airstrip. Also, a policeman and dentist
were added to the community.

The school, improved transportation, population growth, and
economic forces are all impinging on the lifeways of this traditional area. Much of the Navajo way remains—traditional religious practices and beliefs are both surviving and prevalent.

Although time spent on ritual activities, important in the Navajo
lifeway, has diminished over the last decade, the less frequent
major rituals, Enemy Way, a three-day ceremony, and Night Way,
a five-to-nine-day ceremony, are still performed. Minor rituals
involving singers occur about once a week year around, and more
often in winter and summer. The most frequent ceremony, reflecting the changes now occurring is Blessing Way, which is performed, before departure of students, soldiers, and migrants, and
also upon their return.

Until 1955, Shonto boasted not a single professing convert to
Christianity. The first mission established in Shonto in 1955 had
two formal converts in some fifteen months and was denied a
tribal building permit; it closed. The most active religious movement in the area involves a blending of evangelical Christianity
and certain nativistic practices, principally shaking, and seems to
be thriving. Recently, liberalized tribal practice has permitted

mission establishments at Inscription House, Navajo Mountain, Kaibeto, and Shonto.

No single change has had as great an impact upon the Shonto community as education. In 1955, less than one third of the Shonto adults had been to school. The average length of attendance was about two years and thus had very slight effect upon their subsequent lives. By 1955, school attendance was nearly universal for children from six to ten years old, with most continuing beyond that. Pupils attended the old Shonto school for the first two years, and then had to leave the reservation to attend distant BIA boarding schools. At that time, *none* of the few high school graduates had returned to live in the Shonto community. This is no longer the case, but those who return are still the exception. Today education is almost universal, with 90 per cent completing the eighth grade and most continuing into high school. The nearest high school is at Kayenta, about thirty-eight miles away, but many students attend off-reservation high schools.

Today, over 860 Indian students from the area attend classes from beginners (those with little or no English) through eighth grade.

Constructed in 1963, Shonto Boarding School is a modern complex in very good condition. Attention to landscaping, grounds, and maintenance makes the school a show place.

Over thirty-five well-appointed classrooms, utilizing modern audio-visual aids, a new library with 2500 volumes, auditorium, and gymnasium provide impressive physical facilities.

The efficient dining facilities enable the entire student body of 860 students to eat in about one hour. A smaller family-style dining room is used for familiarizing older students with Anglo table etiquette.

Four dormitories serve the 860 students. A critical understaffing problem has been reduced to a great extent by the recent hiring of over a dozen additional staff members. Each dormitory includes a large rumpus room, and outdoors there are large concrete ball courts and some playground equipment. A track and football field are nearby. The school compound also includes housing for teachers, administrators, and auxiliary staff.

The Shonto Boarding School is an on-reservation school under the jurisdiction of the BIA office at Tuba City, Arizona. The school is entirely financed and administered by the Bureau of Indian Affairs, and has an annual operating budget of over one million dollars. The Navajo tribe provides for most student clothing and eyeglasses; U. S. Public Health Service provides medical facilities in Tuba City and the resident dentist at Shonto. Johnson-O'Malley funds are used, including funds from Public Law 89-10.

Over 90 per cent of the 860 Indian students attending Shonto Boarding School come from within a twenty-five-mile radius of the school. All students live in the dormitories; no provision was made for students to live at home, even where possible. Busing would be difficult because of road conditions, but possible for almost half of the students. The Shonto preschool, however, does bus pupils. Interestingly enough, children of the compound residents are bused daily to a public day school because they live within easy access of a bus route.

In both cultural and socioeconomic terms the students represent a fairly homogeneous traditional group. Students differ most from those in other schools in that practically all use Navajo as their home language and many know little or no English when first attending. Few have been off the reservation for exposure to non-Indian ways—relocation, seasonal work, and other schools. Most students have had more formal education than their parents— parents average less than two years of formal schooling; are more conversant than their parents with non-Indian ways—from TV, teachers, older siblings, and peers; and are increasingly independent in that their elders often depend upon them for reading letters, and translating in most contacts with the non-Indian world— school, employment, Social Security, Welfare, Selective Service, Unemployment Insurance, Public Health, etc.

The distribution of Shonto pupils in the various grades is seen in Table 5. Data do not exist to estimate retention and dropout rates with any great accuracy. However, several observations are relevant. First, most students are overage for their grade. The discrepancy increases as one goes higher, despite special educational services. Considerable attrition in the number of students

Table 5
SHONTO ENROLLMENT BY AGE AND GRADE
(as of January 1969)

							Age in Years								
	5	6	7	8	9	10	11	12	13	14	15	16	17	18	19–20
Beginners	29	65	28	9	3										
Kindergarten	3	2													
First	2	22	63	5	3										
Second			11	46	64	18	1	1							
Third				4	32	41	10	1	1						
Fourth					4	29	45	26	11	2	1				
Fifth						0	19	33	16	9	3	1	0	1	
Sixth							1	19	36	24	11	7	4	1	
Seventh								6	11	16	11	8	3		
Eighth									2	8	17	16	13	2	2

enrolling by grade is observed as one moves upward in school; this is beyond that normally accounted for by population growth. Approximately 90 per cent of Shonto students would fall below Arizona age-grade norms.[2]

When this study was made, the thirty-three teachers included twenty-two white, six Blacks, four Indians and one Spanish-American. There were four white and two Indian administrators. Many local Indians were represented in the dormitory staff which consisted of two whites, one Black, twenty-four Indians; and the kitchen employed ten Indians.

The vast majority of Shonto teachers were graduated from relatively small teachers' colleges in Oklahoma and Texas. Forty per cent of the Shonto teachers were graduates of Southeastern State College, Durant, Oklahoma. It was suggested by some that this created an in-group sense of cohesion and a definite tendency to form a "transplanted" Anglo community instead of facilitating growth of an integrated community.

Shonto teachers tended to perceive their educational goal for Indian students as primarily one of assimilation, although they felt strongly there should be courses teaching local Indian history and culture. They also felt students should not be encouraged to become independent of parental control.

The teachers tended to be young, unmarried women. The limited availability of social activity for young unmarried teachers is conducive to a high turnover rate of over 50 per cent a year. Although they had favorable attitudes toward teaching Indian children, many teachers expressed a common complaint heard in many BIA schools—that they had no choice in their assignments to school nor did they have the opportunity to know with whom they would be working—a complaint shared by administrators, whose staffs were assigned to them.

Living within the BIA compound and maintaining social ties to colleagues within it, Shonto teachers have limited contact with the Navajo community.

The curriculum at Shonto is prescribed by the BIA in terms of development, selection, provision of materials, and even technique of presentation. A common teacher complaint was the inflexibility regarding course materials. Some teachers indicated that students were unable to use the textbooks provided because of oral language and reading difficulties. The curriculum is little different from standard subjects taught in non-Indian schools with the exception of drill in the use of the English language. No adult education programs were in evidence outside of in-service training for dormitory personnel, which was planned. Local Head Start programs administered by the Office of Economic Opportunity, Department of Health, Education, and Welfare, exist at Inscription House, Navajo Mountain, Shonto, and within the school a preschool familiarization program was in progress. There was a lack of communication between the boarding school and the Head Start programs, so that the two programs were not mutually understood or coordinated.

Culturally sensitive curriculum materials were not evident in classroom use, nor was any interest apparent in the direction of training Navajo teachers or of promoting education as a career among Navajo youth. No Navajo teachers existed as role models for student aspirations.

Extracurricular activities for the students included: student council, activity association—which served primarily a recreational function—movies, parties, dances, trips, homecoming and graduation events; six or eight scout troops; cheer leader pep club; an Indian club; marching club; and football, basketball, and volleyball teams. All involved staff members. The athletic and social activities were a major inducement to attend school. Many older students preferred to remain at school over the weekends to be with their peers rather than return home and share in the domestic responsibilities of hauling wood and water, herding and baby-sitting.

Although official BIA policy encourages dormitory policies which are humane, the staff-student dormitory ratio of 1:64 created a situation wherein aides spent most of their time in roll calls, escort duty, patrolling, and disciplinary actions (abusive discipline was not tolerated by the administration). Truancy or running away was considered by the staff to be a major problem. Additional instructional aides have been added so that more individualized work with the students is possible, but some children clearly wish to be with their families rather than at school.

Most student and parent complaints related to dormitory problems, theft of personal belongings, new clothes, etc. However, the institutional solutions to such problems may often contribute to problems of a higher order. This is likely the case in the removal of doors from the older girls' rooms in order to permit greater surveillance, or of locking up their cosmetics centrally in the belief this would reduce theft and health hazards. From an institutional viewpoint these may appear to be effective means of "problem prevention" while from the individual's view they become incursions into privacy and impugn everyone's integrity for an individual's misdeeds. The instructional aides generally commented that the situation was better than when they were boarding students for they had experienced harsher conditions such as corporal punishment for such things as speaking Navajo.

Shonto Boarding School has an elected school board composed of Indians from the area. This is in response to a presidential directive of several years' standing, a fifteen-page directive by the former commissioner of Indian Affairs, and action by the Navajo tribe to implement the establishment of duly elected school boards with legitimate and recognized power to make fundamental educational decisions and to direct the school on policy matters relating to their attainment.

Although official policy supports parental control through elected school boards, the school board at Shonto was essentially still in its organizational phase. Though it had progressed in defining its functions and duties, it may never become a really viable entity until it is given decision-making power commensurate with its responsibilities. It had yet to play a decision-making role.

The problem is considerably more than a local one. A manual for Navajo school boards has been compiled but is generally too vague and non-specific concerning actual implementation of the broad goals which it presents. Monthly meetings are held in Tuba City to familiarize members with the manual, but the academic nature of the manual, combined with the hundred-mile trip for Shonto members, reduces it to little more than a gesture so far as the local board is concerned.

Two aspects of community perception of the school stand out above all others. First is a very favorable general attitude concerning the school. This was locally explained in at least three ways: (1) it was closer to home than any former alternatives; (2) it provided more jobs than anything else in the area; and (3) it was a lot easier to have the government (actually the tribe) provide room, board, and clothing than to face the hassle of public schools which requires busing, book fees, meal fees, athletic fees, activity fees. Thus it was primarily the social service function of the school which drew parental approval.

The second and equally striking aspect was how little the parents knew about the academic aspects of the school in contrast to how much they knew about the dormitory life. This reflects both the parents' limited experience with formal education and their continuing limited exposure to their children's classroom experience. The average Shonto parent has less than two years of formal education, which places the average Shonto student in an educationally advantageous position relative to the parent, which the student learns to convert to his interests which are largely that of the peer group.

Politically, the most common school discussions revolve around the selection, employment, and conduct of school employees, particularly the Indians.

The non-Indians tend to view the Navajo school in terms of their own life orientations. The missionaries view education as a great inroad being made against paganism; while the trader has long lost his role as an innovator and represents more of a nineteenth-century mercantilistic orientation against the tide of the times. In the Indian community monolithic paternalism is no longer sufficient to provide a major linkage to the larger society.

Educational alternatives to the local Shonto school do exist. They include busing thirty-eight miles to the nearest public school at Kayenta which is technically a requirement for students living within one and one-half miles of the bus route. In a recent jurisdictional dispute, the public school at Kayenta claimed that some forty-eight students at Shonto should be attending public school. At issue is the fact that a significant amount of federal money, allocated on the basis of Indian pupil attendance, is involved. Another alternative for some, particularly the older students, is attendance in off-reservation schools. Where siblings or a "family tradition" or close peer attractions are operating, or when problems have been encountered in previous school experience, this option may be exercised.

Some students become involved in the placement program of the Church of Latter-day Saints (Mormon), whereby Indian students live with Mormon families throughout the school year, but attend off-reservation public schools. No figures are available for the number of Shonto families involved, but this reason was advanced to account for the slight diminution of boarding students from the previous year's enrollment. A very small number of families migrate to the cities, first because of the employment opportunities, and secondarily to place the children in public schools but have the students living at home. Finally, a diminishing but not insignificant number opt to forgo formal education and children are enculturated into the traditional roles and expectations of Navajo society. Older daughters learn how to manage the extended families, young men how to handle livestock and build a home, and, wherever elders are involved, how to provide for them.

The school is not used as a community center in the usual sense. Virtually all activities are planned by and for the school subculture; movies, programs, athletic events, etc. However, the community is always invited and a significant number of persons do participate. One basketball team from an outlying community did use the gym for its team's practice since its community was lacking in ball court facilities.

Navajo religious ceremonies are not ordinarily calendrical in nature. Most of them are more therapeutically preventive or else curative in nature and hence occur when there is a specific need to be met. It would therefore be difficult for the school to adjust its calendar to that of the traditional Navajo. The requirements for children to be with kin for ceremonials are irregular and attendance at boarding school can interfere with participation, which may influence truancy.

The tribal Education Committee has provided guidelines for school boards to augment tribal consciousness. These include a Tribal Leaders Day, a Parents Day, and an Arts and Crafts show. On occasion, local Navajo political leaders speak to the student body and they also speak at graduation exercises. It also encourages boards to select a Navajo storyteller, to recommend various speakers, and to tape additional Navajo songs.

The most obvious school efforts to further student's identity are in the way of murals depicting traditional lifeways, in the photographic displays of community leaders, and in the selection of Indian heritage books in the school library.

School communication with parents and community definitely presents a problem. Lacking mass media and with low parent literacy, the school is almost totally cut off from the community except for face-to-face dissemination of information. Channels are: the large number of Indian employees; the children, but since they board, information transmittal is sporadic; weekly events such as movies or checking out children for weekends home bring parents to the school. Official matters are transmitted via the school board, and at most chapter meetings someone is present to give a report from the school. Community contact within the trading post and Chapter House laundry provide additional means for daily communication.

In order to secure community support for its programs the school has established the school board, and has hired many local staff members. The principal has also attended many chapter meetings and discussed problems with key families in order to further understanding.

No effective systems for accountability to the community or internal evaluation of programs to measure success have been proposed; let alone designed and implemented.

Bethel, Alaska[3]

Located eighty miles from the mouth of the Kuskokwim River, Bethel is the trading, political, education, medical communication and service center of a roughly 100,000-square-mile region of southwestern Alaska. It is the farthest point up the river to which seagoing ships can travel (Figure 3). Barging activities extend approximately a hundred miles upriver beyond Bethel to supply the many scattered Eskimo and Indian villages along the river.

Transportation difficulties in this arctic area require that small planes operating out of Bethel supply small community sites up and down the Kuskokwim River, along the Bering Sea coast, up and down the Yukon River, and over the expanse of tundra. Anchorage, 419 miles by air, is the nearest large city.

Bethel is situated in an area of flat treeless tundra abounding in many small lakes. Rainfall generally does not exceed nineteen to twenty-one inches. Cold winter temperatures of −20° F. to −30° F. are made even more chilling by the characteristic winds. Winters are long and darkness falls early.

About 86 per cent of the 2000 to 2500 residents of this arctic center are Eskimo, the remainder, whites. Only a part of these people, however, forms a stable population—that is, residents who consider Bethel itself their permanent abode. To Eskimo or Indian people, a village community is more often thought of as home.

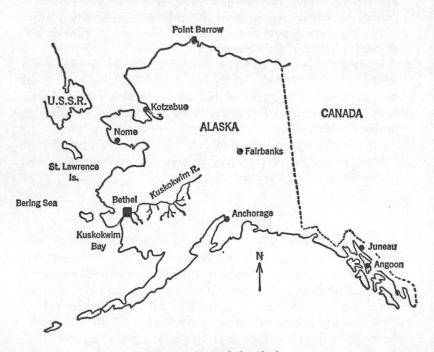

FIGURE 3. *Bethel, Alaska*

Non-Indians more often speak of Bethel in terms of a tour of duty, mission, contract or project, with some specific or approximate date of departure in mind. Nonetheless, the Eskimo population, despite its pattern of periodic transiency between Bethel and various village sites, constitutes most of the present core population. The population is youthful—the median age is seventeen years and this area has a high birth rate. Both English and Eskimo are spoken.

Founded in 1855 by a group of Moravian missionaries, Bethel is presently incorporated as a fourth-class city and is governed by the mayor and council system. There are seven council members, one of whom serves as mayor.

In addition to a K–12 public school and a hospital, the city contains a public library which is used also as an adult education classroom, polling place, and meeting place for the Bethel Women's Club. A small museum is being planned.

Several churches are in the community: the Episcopalian, Moravian, Pentecostal, Roman Catholic, Russian Orthodox, and Southern Baptist.

There are also a liquor store and three general stores.

The Eskimo name for Bethel, *Mulrekhlagamiut,* means a place to fish, and traditional economic pursuits in the area were primarily fishing, hunting, and trapping. Today Eskimo men continue to pursue these activities using high-powered outboard motors or snowmobiles. They trade their fish and mink. But many other significant changes are occurring. Although in the past they traditionally roamed the tundra for game, many Eskimos have now settled around schools, armories, stores, and jet airports, as in Bethel. Today, government agencies are the largest employers, with local private employers supplying work for less than 5 per cent of the people. The Bureau of Indian Affairs and state welfare funds augment income as traditional economies have given way to government relief, old age and National Guard pensions over the last few years.

Welfare activities and other federal and state agency services for this area of Alaska are entwined in a web of intercommunity functions and contracts, with Bethel at its center.

Prices for fresh foods imported from Seattle are high and canned foods and manufactured goods are all imported and expensive, requiring cash incomes. In an effort to improve their conditions villagers have organized a salmon cooperative, based in Bethel. There is also a politically active Alaskan Native Association group.

Housing in Bethel is very scarce and very poor for people in low-paying jobs. Some of the worst housing in Alaska is located here. A low-cost housing project is being developed for the un-employed or welfare villagers. The housing problem has led fed-eral and state agencies to provide employee housing, which re-flects the affluence and standards of the non-Eskimo world.

A fully accredited forty-two-bed hospital operated by the United States Public Health Service is located in Bethel. The medical needs of the population are very great. Infant mortality for 1965–67 was 104 per 1000 live births, and postneonatal mortality, 79.3 per 1000. Diarrhea, respiratory disease, prematurity, con-genital abnormalities, and meningitis account for the high infant death rate.

Childhood ailments create conditions that can affect children's schooling. Refractive errors, especially myopia, are prevalent. Mastoiditis is still common. Many older children have destroyed or damaged eardrums with resultant hearing loss.

Accidents, including drowning, burns, and gunshot wounds, account for 21 per cent of all deaths. One fourth of these accidents are associated with alcohol abuse. Tuberculosis remains a serious problem. Mental disease, dental caries, cancer, anemia, rheu-matic heart disease, and arthritis are also significant problems. However, diabetes mellitus and coronary artery disease are rare.

Bethel is rapidly growing and is faced with the problems of expansion: maintenance and a severe housing shortage. A native population explosion taking place over the whole Kuskokwim delta affects Bethel. The community has the determination and tenacity to survive in a harsh natural setting, despite its many problems.

Speaking of the city John Collier, Jr., has written:

> . . . in one sense Bethel is the *world* that the white man's education is selling to the Eskimo. And as a world it has most of the white man's failures. Bethel could be looked upon as a proving ground for coping with white ways and perversities.[4]

The following are views of Eskimo life in the Bethel region expressed by schoolchildren.

"The Fish Net," by Allen

During the summer after the King Salmon have migrated in the Kuskokwim River, now the Silver Salmon are migrating in the river.

So the Eskimo people are catching Silver Salmon after the King Salmon. After they are caught they are cut in two pieces and dried and smoked and stored in their food house or their cache house.

So they take the fish net out of the river before the Kuskokwim freezes and they dry the fish net and fix it for next year and put them into their cache houses or smoke houses.

So the Eskimos are having a happy time during the winter and those who don't catch fish are having a bad time.

Those who are having a bad time are asking for their food or they are going to the welfare office.

That is so they won't starve during the winter.

So their children are happy and gay after all.

"How To Prepare a Salmon For Drying and Smoking," by Mary

First you kill the salmon and then bring the salmon fish to the fish camp and then lay the salmon fish on the fish board or table and a woman comes holding an uluk and she cuts the head off. She cuts from the fish neck all the way down to the stomach and she opens the stomach and takes all the eggs if it's a female.

We make pancakes or oil egg pancakes from these eggs.

They clean inside of the salmon and from the back of the salmon we cut right straight down and stop by the little wings that are sticking out.

Cut two holes in the salmons at one end. The woman does the same things to the other salmons and after that she faces them flat.

The woman cuts lines straight across and down and after the woman cuts the salmon she hangs it on the fish rack. On a sunny day the fish will dry.

When it's going to rain, the woman puts the salmon inside the smoke hut and lets them drip-drop. When the smoke dries the fish and after days are past.

You would eat them with seal oil and salt. And sometimes agutat.

"Nicholson's Water," by Ann

Nicholson's water is very good. We get our water on Mondays and Thursday. Sometimes the water has some sand in it but it won't hurt us because it has a little Clorox in it.

In the winter the water is very cold, sometimes, but when you are thirsty you drink some water and you want to drink more and more and then you get full.

When the water is running out, the people or men driving the truck have to bring it back and fill until it is full.

Art's well is about two-hundred feet deep and it was dug about twenty years ago.

Some people buy water from Nicholson's but most of the people melt ice for water.

"The Honey Bucket Truck," by Ruth

The Honey Bucket Truck is another word for our sanitary sewer. There are two men who work for the sanitary sewer. One for the driver and one who goes into the houses and gets the honey buckets and brings them to the truck. The driver has to get out of the truck and get ready for the other man to hand him the buckets. He is the man who opens up the tank. When the tank is full, the men take it to the dump. They have a big hose that lets it run out of the tank into a big ditch. They do that every day.

"How To Train A Lead Dog," by Joe

When you want to train a smart lead dog you must pick the dog you want for a leader when he is a pup. Then you have to put him behind the lead dog whenever you go for a dogsledding.

After a month of training him try and use him as a lead dog. If he isn't doing the things you taught him, leave him behind the lead dog for about two weeks. Then after two weeks have passed, try and use him for a leader again. Then if he is doing the things you taught him right, then you've got a new lead dog.

Some things a good lead dog should know are: How to obey his master. How to lead the other dogs behind him. How to tell if the ice is safe or not. How to find his way home in a snow storm. How to lead a good path.

"Dog Team Rides," by Roy

When I was ten years old we had dogs and I liked to go dogteam riding, but when we had a new Sno-Go, Andy took the rest of our dogs and we have only one left now.

I like to go riding on a dogsled and I like to harness my dogs. I still know how to harness a dog.

"A Saturday Night in Bethel," by Wanda

A Saturday night in Bethel is a crime. Every new student or adult who comes to Bethel can't believe it. Just can't believe how the people drink, have parties, dances, and other usual things which they can't believe!

When Friday afternoon comes the men and some women go to the liquor store to buy liquor. Man! Whoever goes to the liquor store must be MILLIONAIRES or save enough SINGLE pennies for liquor. The people who buy a bottle save it for Saturday night. That is a very, very funny scene to take care of.

Saturday night seems to be a dead-end which is a kind of misery to new comers. I bet every drunk thinks Saturday night is a holiday! (I mean teenagers, too).

To the new comers they must think Saturday night is trash. That's if they don't drink as much as Bethel's people do. God help them if they don't! To me Saturday night is a crime! I can tell very easily. I go to town on Saturday night once in a great time. Every time I do go, I go by Mom's Kitchen and Joe's Pool Hall. Both are a great scene and a mess! Sometimes I feel like turning around and BURNING that liquor store.

Throw the drunks in jail and when sober have them CLEAN EVERY mess they see. If I was a governor I would do something to teach them a *lesson.*

Well, I am tired of telling about Saturday night and drunks. Anyway, I think I have said everything.

Notice: Things happen to GIRLS, too.

Bethel has had continuous schooling available in general ever since 1885, but the orientation has been in varying directions. A Moravian mission school was established in 1885; it was succeeded in 1933 by a Bureau of Education/Bureau of Indian Affairs school, and in 1947 by a school under the territory (later state) of Alaska.

Unlike the boarding school attended by the Navajo children at Shonto, the school attended by the children of Bethel is a state of Alaska public school. In 1968, there were 81 kindergarten children, 405 children in grades one through six, 240 students in grades seven through twelve, and 57 children in a special education program. Ninety per cent of the children were Eskimo.

The Bethel public school is situated in a modern L-shaped plant, one section of which houses the high school, the other, the elementary classes. The school is able to share use of the adjacent National Guard armory gymnasium. A special education program is carried on in six individual modern self-contained classrooms.

Children walk to school, the bus picking up those few who live two miles or more away. As this is a day school, no boarding facilities are available.

The school lacks an adequate library. The Bethel High School has not been accredited by the Northwest Association of Secondary Schools and Colleges.

Although there is a local school advisory committee, it is without decision-making authority and is not greatly effective. Perhaps more influential in affecting decisions is the Bethel City Council, which on selected issues has taken aggressive stands and gained hearings from state school officials and public officials in Anchorage and Juneau. The continuous operational decision making for the Bethel school is made on the state level and represented locally by the superintendent.

The teachers are hired by the state of Alaska through the Anchorage office of the Alaskan Division of State Operated Schools, Rural Schools Office. The local school is hoping to participate in the interviewing of teacher applicants in the future.

Teachers in the Alaska state system work a nine-month year. Until recently, special preparation of teachers to work with Eskimos has been generally absent. Alaska Methodist University in Anchorage, and the University of Alaska in Fairbanks are now developing programs for teachers who will be working with Alaskan natives.

The teacher turnover rate is very high. Usually few stay more than two years. A good many of the teachers are new to Alaska and conditions at Bethel are not conducive to their remaining. Housing and the high cost of living are serious problems. The average teacher earns a little over $9000 a year but the cost of living is at least 50 per cent higher than that of Seattle.

Most of the staff displays minimal cross-cultural sensitivity. People are in a low level state of culture shock and few stay long enough to become familiar with Eskimo culture. Many teachers come largely because of the appeal of hunting and fishing in the area. One high school teacher of science is an Eskimo, a native of Bethel.

A good percentage of Bethel Eskimo children do not speak Eskimo. However, children who are newly arrived from the outlying villages know very little English. On the whole, most children enter school with a limited knowledge of English. The frequency of hearing and visual defects also affects the school experience.

The curriculum in the Bethel school is state prescribed with only a few teachers utilizing local conditions. There is no bilingual program and all instruction is in English.

One first-grade class in Bethel is using an experimental program, the Alaska Reader Series developed by the Northwest Regional Educational Laboratory and the state Department of Education. Pictures of native children are incorporated into the texts.

Instruction is provided in electronics, language arts, social studies, business education, mathematics, and science. As noted earlier, the high school is not accredited.

Bethel parents represent the first generation to have attended high school at all. On the whole, the educational level is low. Most of the village adults have had only two or three years of schooling. There is a positive attitude about the school and strong approval for establishing a new, expanded regional high school serving this area of Alaska.

There is no Parent Teacher Association in Bethel.

In addition to the state public school in Bethel, other schools are available to Eskimos of the region, including BIA and mission schools. With a few exceptions, village schools within the Bethel region are federal day schools conducted by the Bureau of Indian Affairs for grades one to eight. There are no high schools in the villages. Except for those few village students who can obtain housing in Bethel by living with relatives or in foster homes, the village students who do go on to high school are sent to remote BIA boarding schools at Mount Edgecombe in southeast Alaska, Chemawa in Oregon, and Chilocco, Oklahoma. Village BIA schools have 100 per cent Eskimo enrollment.

The pattern of village life in the regions surrounding Bethel reflect the hunting, fishing, and gathering economy of the past. Many small villages are scattered some two hundred and fifty miles into the interior.

Each village has its own school containing one to five rooms. School is taught by one to three couples, with or without children of their own. The result of this is that the white teachers in village schools live in extreme isolation compared with their previous life experience.

Reporting to the NSAIE, John Collier, Jr., describes these schools and the problems for white teachers in remote villages:

> By white standards, Eskimo villages are pitifully poor, unhygienic, and shockingly overcrowded, with two families jammed into one small log cabin ten feet by twenty. As in any survival economy, per capita income would be far below even the conventional poverty line if relief and government succor were removed. Abruptly, in the midst of all this apparent squalor and staked-out sled dogs, stands the BIA school compound. Its life pulse is its diesel light plant, which makes the compound a mecca of blazing illumination in the darkness of the village. (Two villages now have their own light plants.) By day the BIA buildings shimmer in aluminum and fresh paint. Nothing has been spared to make these units ideal models of white mastery, technology, and comfort. On the one hand, the excellence of the buildings speaks for the drive of the curriculum; on the other, the technology and comforts are essential for the emotional well-being of the staff. The comfortable life style of the teachers' home culture is imported, indeed refined upon, to make life tolerable in the Arctic isolation.
>
> I am sure these comforts do make life tolerable on one level, but on another they greatly increase the isolation. Teachers exist within this comfort style and rarely go outside the walls—except to hunt, which is the only ecologically oriented outlet for male teachers in the villages.[5]

Each village school has a kitchen and a multipurpose room where hot lunches are served the children or bingo games are held for the village on special evenings. These schools employ Eskimo teacher aides, Eskimo maintenance and janitorial assistants, and an Eskimo kitchen staff.

In addition to the BIA day schools in the villages and the state public school in Bethel, the Moravians have a school, located near the village of Kwethluk, that boards and educates dependent children.

The village schools also maintained Head Start programs for preschool children.

Teachers in the village are impressed with the cheerfulness and warmth of Eskimo families and see the children as well cared for and loved.

BIA village schools are staffed by teachers recruited through federal civil service and assigned by the BIA. They face the problem of isolation as well as minimal preparation for cross-cultural education. The village schools teach a curriculum developed for non-Eskimo children. Speaking of the absence of a curriculum geared to the special needs of Eskimo children in both the BIA and state schools, Collier writes:

> Our own records . . . show very few and sometimes no items in Alaska classrooms that would suggest the schools were not in Ohio. The only consistent Eskimo item we did see was an Alaskan Airline poster that regularly presents Eskimo portraits.[6]

Schools operate on schedules which are little different from schools elsewhere, making no accommodation for such important Eskimo calendrical events as berry picking, muskrat hunting, beaver trapping, and salmon fishing.

A major problem for the Eskimo of this region is whether or not education can help in the preparation to cope with changing conditions—to make possible the survival of the Eskimo in the modern Arctic. Great potential exists in the area of trapping, the fishing and building industries. Paradoxically, however, educational success seems oriented toward exodus from the arctic, at the same time that opportunity in this region is expanding for newcomers.

> We say, the Arctic is a fine place for an Eskimo future, as much as it seems to be for eager, opportunistic white men. We believe that with balanced economic development the future of Eskimos will be largely in Alaska, and therefore they should be educated to take advantage of this future if they so desire.[7]

To this end Collier urges the teaching of modern technology combined with a respect for the integrity and dignity of Eskimo identification.

Present plans conceptualize a system of regional high schools to be operated by the state of Alaska with boarding facilities provided by the federal government. Bethel has been designated as a center for one of these schools. The extensive village school system for the early grades, run by the BIA, is likely to continue under federal supervision. Present BIA administrative offices and housing are also likely to continue to provide educational and other services in Bethel for some years. If village school graduates attend a state-operated high school at Bethel, as present plans project, rather than in remote BIA boarding high schools, as is the case at present, this will permit the education of Eskimo village youths within the Alaska ecological setting. Centers such as Bethel provide a stimulating exposure to the larger world without the distance and strangeness of boarding schools, often in isolated regions themselves.

The Sitka Conference on Alaska Native Secondary Education of December 1968 reveals the complexity of the problems involved in coordinating the operations of local district, city, borough, state, private, and federal jurisdictions. A state of Alaska bond issue for regional high schools was passed but was not expendable until such time as federal action was taken to provide dormitory space for students. The issue then arose as to whether dormitory operation should be local, state, or federal. Although all three agencies had reached accord on the matter of having the high school and the dormitories at Bethel, because the crying need for educational services in the area made it a priority, this issue remained unresolved, because of the uncertainty that the federal funds for the dormitory would be appropriated. This lack of coordination and common thrust threatened to keep the high school from being built. However, the funds were appropriated and Bethel, Alaska, will soon have a new regional high school with dormitory facilities for village youth.

The Papago—Sells, Arizona[8]

In contrast to the BIA boarding school for Navajo children at Shonto, and the small BIA day schools in Alaskan villages, Papago children in southern Arizona are attending a modern, consolidated state public school in the community of Sells, a center of administrative activity in the desert.

Stretching for over a hundred miles to the west of Tucson, Arizona, is a sparse and arid desert area. Crossed by washes or arroyos, this region of elevated valley floors is surprisingly rich in vegetation—cholla cactus, creosote, saltbush, mesquite, and the foothills and mountain ranges ever in the eye support colorful shrubs, oak, and scrub pine.

The People, known today as the Papago, have for centuries lived on this land, raising livestock, farming the small fields of beans, squash, and corn, and making rich use of the desert plants and their fruits. Now organized into the Papago tribe of Arizona, they live mainly on the Papago Reservation, established in 1917, an area roughly sixty-five miles square lying along the southern border of Arizona between the Baboquivari Mountains in the east and the Ajo Mountains in the west, with an ir-regular line south of the Gila River as its northern boundary.

In the southeastern portion of this region, surrounded by vast stretches of open range land, with the Baboquivari Mountains to

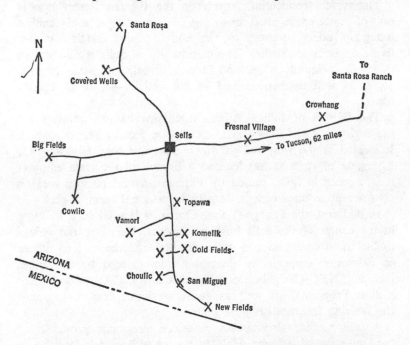

FIGURE 4. *Sells district in Papago Reservation, Arizona*

the south, is the community of Sells. Sells is the seat of Indian Oasis School District No. 40 which serves the Sells district of the reservation, and includes two of the schools in our study—the Indian Oasis Elementary and High, and the Topawa Elementary School.

The community of Sells is bordered entirely with hills to the south, and the north and west areas are flat lands. A small landing strip is located to the northwest of the community for small planes. There are no farmlands or forests of any kind in or around Sells. All of the areas around it are considered open range for livestock.

There is a large wash, or arroyo, which enters from the northwest portion of the community and a small one that joins it from the eastern end. Although dry most of the year, during the rainy seasons water flows in from the east to the west.

The typical residential pattern on the Papago Reservation is one of scattered villages consisting of groups of related families living in adobe houses, or, in some places, single families living on isolated ranches. The community of Sells is different in that it is primarily a seat of federal, tribal, and state government, as well as mission and school activity—it is an agency town.

The Bureau of Indian Affairs maintains its headquarters for the region here as does the U. S. Public Health Service, which is located at the west end of the community near Highway 86. The state of Arizona has located a branch of the state employment agency in Sells, staffed by Papagos, to aid persons seeking off-reservation employment, largely in seasonal farm work.

In addition, the Papago Tribal Center is housed in a building in the center of the Sells business district. Here are the offices of the tribal chairman and other officers, and the various offices of Economic Opportunity programs administered by the tribe, including NYC (Neighborhood Youth Corps), CAP (Community Action Program), as well as legal services. Trailers augment the housing facilities of these services.

A trailer office also houses extension programs provided by the University of Arizona. Help in regard to livestock care, home economics, and instruction in the preparation of surplus food commodities is given.

Missionary activity has taken place on the reservation since the first Jesuit missionary, Father Kino, arrived in 1698. At present in Sells there are five churches—the Nazarene located at the east end of town, the Assembly of God located south of Highway 86 to the northeast, the Roman Catholic in the southeast section, the Presbyterian in the southwest, and the Southern Baptist church at the extreme west.

Because of the numerous activities centered there, Sells has attracted service industries, among them: the Texaco service station and small cafe on Highway 86; the Chevron service station; two trading posts—the Indian Oasis Trading Post and the Papago Trading Store and Cafe; the Garcia store; and the Sells beauty shop.

There are no commercial bus lines going through Sells or any part of the reservation. A few people hitchhike to Tucson if their getting to town is urgent enough and if they don't have the finances to pay someone with vehicles to take them. Some Papagos have their own transportation, purchased from the used-car lots in Tucson or Casa Grande. Very few of the Papagos within the Sells area buy new cars but some of those with steady employment do buy new pickup trucks. Papagos without transportation usually ask those with vehicles to take them to their destinations and back home but pay or furnish gas and oil or both.

The economy of Sells is based on employment within the different departments of the Bureau of Indian Affairs, the Public Health Service, the tribal OEO programs, the Indian Oasis School, the Papago tribal office, and the stores, cafes, and service stations which have arisen to provide services.

In the Bureau of Indian Affairs, the administrative personnel and heads of the different departments are made up of non-Indians and Indians. The Public Health Service also employs Indians in senior positions since there are some Indians who have had training to do some of the administrative work. Some have seniority and have taken over positions of responsibility.

In addition, there are several men employed on Kitt Peak as

heavy equipment operators, maintenance men, and electrician helpers who commute back and forth every working day.

There are also some men who commute daily from Sells to the A. S. & R. Mining Company south of the San Xavier Reservation about seventy-five miles to the east.

The Papago tribe employs clerk-typists, maintenance men for plumbing, electrical, and other work. Also, repairmen to maintain both domestic and livestock wells on the reservation are employed.

The PHS employs thirty-eight Papagos permanently and three temporarily, as well as ten Indians from other tribes. The non-Indians consist of eighteen permanent employees, one temporary, and nine commissioned officers—all at Sells.

A Tribal Work Experience Program is administered by the Social Services and Welfare Department of the BIA. Federal government assistance, to give training to unemployed men and women, provides training slots in the Housing Department, Roads Department, PHS, and as clerk-typists for the different offices in the Papago agency and for the Papago tribe. There are 155 training slots open for the whole Papago Reservation and about 47 people are in this program within the Sells area.

Steady employment is no guarantee of adequate incomes for Papago families in this area. The Public Welfare Department of Pima County does have different types of assistance for those with inadequate income. Aid to dependent children or aid to needy and blind which supplements the meager income of some families are examples.

There is very little migration of Papagos from Sells itself, though some migration does take place among the people who live in the school district. This is mainly for seasonal work in farming areas all the way to Yuma, Arizona, and on farming areas adjacent to the reservation. Recruiting for out-of-state seasonal harvesting work is done by the Arizona State Employment Office.

The employees of the Public Health Service and the Bureau of Indian Affairs live in modern homes and apartments within two federal compounds with well-kept lawns and trees or hedges and flower beds. The Papagos employed by these two agencies have their own homes made of adobe or wood. Most of the homes are not large enough to comfortably house the large Papago families. Because of housing patterns, the non-Indians are segregated, living largely within the two compounds of the BIA and PHS.

Mobile trailer homes have recently been acquired by Papagos, but the adobe homes are still more common. Very few of the homes east of the BIA compound have running water, and water is hauled by trucks. People who do not have cars or pickups ask other people to haul water for them.

When electricity was brought into the reservation many of the villages were served, and this led to the purchase of television sets. Several of the merchants from Tucson have been on the reservation peddling electrical appliances. Many of the families budget themselves very tightly to be able to buy television and record players.

The lack of water prevents having modern bathrooms and facilities. Because of this, outhouses are seen at nearly every home outside the two federal compounds.

Children have more opportunity for racially integrated activities than do the adults. There are two integrated schools for kindergarten youngsters—one operated by the Southern Baptist church, and the other run by the Papago tribal OEO program, both encouraging children to play together during the school hours.

Since there are no other playgrounds but at the school, the smaller children play around their homes and also with neighbors. However, the school playground is open to the community at all times. Most of the parents try to keep their children near their homes where there is not much traffic to endanger the children. Nearly every home has spacious yards and open area which can be used for play.

Boys of junior age (eight to twelve) gather together in groups near their homes to play football or softball. Junior-age girls visit and play near their homes. For the teen-agers there is more to do. There is an integrated teen-age club which has been active. Some of the public schoolteachers are working with these children, and parents help as chaperones on trips or at teen-age dances. Parents also participate in fund sales for teen-age activities.

There are rodeo grounds and baseball fields in the community. The school grounds also contain volleyball and basketball courts open to all residents in Sells.

Several town events have become annual affairs. In the spring, a junior rodeo is sponsored by the students from the Indian Oasis School. Everything is planned by them with the assistance of some of the members of the Papago Rodeo Committee.

On July the Fourth, there is a tribal-sponsored pageant during which young women compete to become Miss Rodeo and Miss Papago. The winner reigns for a year. This contest is open to any unmarried, young Papago woman between the ages of eighteen to twenty-five with one half or more Papago ancestry.

The Papago Indian Rodeo and Fair takes place during the latter part of October. This event also sponsors a pageant to select a Rodeo Queen. In 1968, a high school student from the Indian Oasis School won the honors and became the Rodeo Queen. This gave her the opportunity to represent the Papago Rodeo Board on other reservations in their pageantry parades.

Cordle Hall, which is part of the public school plant, is used as a gymnasium by both the school and the community. Community meetings and events are also held in the auditorium of the large Papago tribe building. The various churches also have meeting space.

Much of the change to be observed in Sells is related to the expansion of various government services.

The Papago tribe, since its participation in OEO anti-poverty programs has acquired three large trailers to house the Community Development Program, the Legal Service, and the director of the Papago tribe OEO departments. The Extension Department of the University of Arizona has placed a trailer office near the Papago people, at their request, for help concerning livestock or assistance with home economics, such as instruction in the preparation of surplus commodity foods.

The Southern Baptists have built a home and have set up a

staff to take care of the boys and girls placed there by the Social and Welfare Department of the BIA. Additional homes have been built by the PHS for their staff, as well as additional offices for their field nurses, helpers, and interpreters. Another wing has been added to the main hospital building to serve for storage of supplies and office.

In the past three years, the BIA has had about twenty miles of road paved south of Sells, but the need for improved roads in other areas remains great.

Some of the Papago people have turned to buying mobile homes rather than to building homes out of adobe or other material. Within the past three years more trailer homes have been brought into the community. The public school has, because of the lack of space, leased about eleven mobile homes for the teachers. The BIA has, in the past year, added to the former school building; the classrooms were converted into offices; and the new addition used to house the whole BIA personnel. Three office buildings have been vacated by the BIA and presented to the Papago Tribal Council.

It is to this busy center of administrative activity in the desert that school buses converge daily, bringing children from outlying villages to the Indian Oasis School in Sells.

From the area to the south children are brought from New Fields (thirty miles), San Miguel (twenty-four miles), Choulic (twenty-one miles), Cold Fields (twenty miles), Komelik (sixteen miles), Vamori (nineteen miles), and Topawa (eight miles) (Figure 4). From the northwest come high school students from Santa Rosa (thirty-five miles) and Covered Wells (twenty-three miles). From the northeast come children from Comobabi (twenty miles), Crowhang (seventeen miles), and some from the distant village of Santa Rosa Ranch. Although some children from Topawa come to Sells, children from other villages get off the buses to attend the school in Topawa.

The Indian Oasis School District No. 40 is the public school district serving the surrounding area. In 1968–69 it maintained the Indian Oasis School, consisting of elementary school and high school grades, and the elementary school in Topawa serving grades one to eight. A total of 779 pupils about equally divided among boys and girls were in attendance (Table 6). The only other schools in Sells are under the jurisdiction of the Southern Baptist church and the tribal OEO program (Head Start) for kindergarten-age children.

TABLE 6

INDIAN OASIS SCHOOL-AGE SURVEY

(Topawa included)

Grade	Age	Boys	Girls	Total
1	6 yrs.—81	39	42	81
2	6 yrs.—2 7 yrs.—80	37	45	82
3	7 yrs.—5 8 yrs.—76	35	46	81
4	8 yrs.—3 9 yrs.—80	47	36	83
5	9 yrs.—2 10 yrs.—72	37	37	74
6	10 yrs.—7 11 yrs.—65 12 yrs.—4	47	29	76
7	12 yrs.—60 13 yrs.—32	36	56	92
8	12 yrs.—4 13 yrs.—31 14 yrs.—47 15 yrs.—1	43	40	83
9	13 yrs.—1 14 yrs.—24 15 yrs.—22 16 yrs.—10	22	32	54

Grade	Age	Boys	Girls	Total
10	14 yrs.—2			
	15 yrs.—18			
	16 yrs.—10			
	17 yrs.—6			
	18 yrs.—3			
	19 yrs.—1	24	16	40
11	16 yrs.—10			
	17 yrs.—10			
	18 yrs.—9			
	19 yrs.—2			
	20 yrs. —2	20	13	33
	TOTALS	387	392	779

The responsibility of the public schools for education of Papago children in the area is recent. In accordance with the BIA policy during the 1950s of turning Indian school plants to local public districts, the BIA school was consolidated with the public school in 1953. The BIA maintained administrative control until it withdrew completely in 1963. Federal funding, through Johnson-O'Malley funds, continues.

The Indian Oasis School is still located within the BIA compound, but new buildings have been erected including Cordle Hall, used as both a school and community meeting hall, gymnasium, and cafeteria.

The school district is supervised by a five-member elected school board. Any registered voter who submits a petition with signatures of 10 per cent of the previous year's voters may run for election. School board meetings are held twice monthly. They are open and parents are invited to attend.

The school board takes an active role in hiring personnel, including the superintendent of schools, and takes responsibility for establishing school policies.

Since becoming a public school system, independent of the BIA, Indian Oasis School District No. 40 has dealt with several important issues. It has appointed a superintendent of its own choosing. It has arranged for a system of transportation for pupils and parents. One significant action taken by the board, after conferring with various villages, was to incorporate St. Anthony's Mission School, a Catholic mission in Topawa, into the public system. When the school was incorporated, several of the teachers, who are nuns, were asked to continue to teach in the public system.

The school board is responsive to growing concern about education in the district. In 1964, only four Papago youths were in college; within three years twenty had entered junior colleges and universities, and there is hope that more will receive the education needed to assist in the new programs on the reservation.

Since the Papago Reservation is tucked away beyond the mountains and across from the Mexican border, it may seem somewhat isolated from the mainstream of Southwest urban life. Still, the roads are fairly good, and automobiles give relatively easy access to Tucson and Phoenix.

Topawa is a village almost at the southern edge of habitation. As noted above, the elementary school was a Catholic mission until just recently, and several of the teachers are nuns who simply continued to teach when the public school district took the school over.

The following excerpts from the diary of a Sister give a glimpse of teacher life:

> *Sunday, November 10.* One hour spent in a faculty meeting. The topic of home visiting was discussed. Most agreed that the present policy of visiting when and as the need arose as we have been doing is the most suitable. One problem of visiting at any time is the lack of furniture —this causes embarrassment. We noted that in some homes the only place to sit was on the bed.
>
> Several of us spent an hour visiting the local cemetery. While there we were able to console and visit with a lady of the village who had just recently lost her husband. We visited his grave with her.
>
> *Wednesday, November 13.* It was just an ordinary day—one of those when things move along pretty smoothly—not too great—not too bad —just average—until—Oh joy, Alvin finished his pre-primers. To see his little face light up when I told him that he could go to the next book was reward enough for the hours we'd spent. Alvin is in the third grade and I have been giving him special reading help.

Thursday, November 14. It was a cold rainy day—but surprisingly productive of attention and good work in school. I guess most were just glad to be in a nice warm room—and work was done in good spirits. Otherwise it was an ordinary day. The eighth grade finished a chapter on the eye and made themselves and me happy by doing well on a check test. The beginnings of a unit on fractions was another story!!

Sunday, November 17. This afternoon I got to go along to Big Fields for Mass. I have been wanting to do this for some time. We spent two hours traveling and visiting there before and after the Mass. I met several former students and the parents of some of my present ones. It is always a pleasure to share their joys and to talk to them.

Saturday, November 23. It was a glorious day so after my housework was finished and I had helped another Sister make a skirt I gave myself the luxury of an hour of reading and sun. I read part of *Modern Indian Psychology*—very good.

At five we picked up some of the students. The seventh and eighth graders were guests of the faculty at the University of Arizona-Wyoming football game in Tucson. We had a good evening—we won—and the students were appreciative. It was far into the morning by the time we had returned all the girls to their home villages.

Currently the school board is working on plans to build a new high school east of Sells. The Sells District Council has allotted fifty acres of land for the purpose; and federal funds of $780,000 have been appropriated. However, the availability of water is a problem, and drilling for well water will commence soon, although it is uncertain whether water can be found here.

Use of the school as a community center is encouraged and when open house is held, the school buses are used to furnish transportation from the outlying districts.

A Parent Teacher Council meets monthly for discussions on school affairs. This organization tries to inform the parents of their responsibilities to the school and encourages parental involvement with school problems. Many different projects have been undertaken by the members, such as volunteering to help in the different programs of the school, providing materials for curtains for the windows, and sewing uniforms. Problems that they wish brought to the attention of the school board are reported through someone delegated by the group.

Anyone can become a member of the PTC. However, a fee is set at fifty cents per person for the whole school year to help provide for refreshments and other needs. People can voice their opinions in the meetings held even if they have not paid their dues.

Current issues involve the building of the new high school and the improvement of educational achievement for Papago youth. There is discussion about the possible expansion of public education to include the entire Papago Reservation. However, parents are divided in their support of BIA, mission, and public schools.

The Theodore Roosevelt School, Fort Apache, Arizona[9]

When off-reservation boarding schools were first established by the BIA, many of them were housed in abandoned army forts, no longer serving their nineteenth-century military function. Several of these schools continue in existence, housing children sent for a variety of reasons including the isolation of their home communities and the lack of schools there. Often these schools are situated long distances from the home communities of the children attending.

The Theodore Roosevelt School, a Bureau of Indian Affairs boarding school serving grades three to eight, is an example of this type of school. It is located just south of the town of Whiteriver in the Fort Apache Indian Reservation, east central Arizona (Figure 5).

The school has a colorful history, its grounds and some of its buildings dating from the establishment of Fort Ord, later renamed Fort Apache, one hundred years ago. This military post was established by President Grant to quell Indian uprisings and insure military dominance in the Southwest, then open to settlers. Established near friendly Apache bands, the fort served as a base of operations against Navajo and other Apache groups.

Its mission accomplished, and Indians no longer a threat to U.S. expansion, Fort Apache was abandoned by the military in 1922, turned over to the Department of Interior that same year, and in 1923 was converted to a day school for Indian children.

Today the grounds of Fort Apache serve in part as a memorial to the old fort, and in part as the Theodore Roosevelt School, now a boarding school for two hundred pupils.

Theodore Roosevelt School is housed in a series of buildings of varying ages around the old parade grounds of Fort Apache (Figure 5). There is a classroom building, a boys' dormitory, a girls' dormitory, a cafeteria building, and staff housing.

The classroom building, a U-shaped structure of stucco on a wood frame, was erected in the early 1930s. It houses eighteen classrooms, one of which is used as a library; a gymnasium, also used as an auditorium; and offices. The building has a new boiler and recently the interior was freshly painted. Cheerful pastel colors are used throughout the rooms and halls.

There is a two-story boys' dormitory, built in 1932. It contains twenty sleeping rooms for groups of four, six, and in one case, twelve boys. There are a television room and recreation room

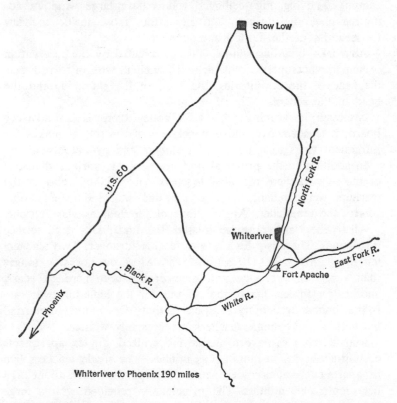

FIGURE 5. *Fort Apache, Arizona*

on each floor. The toilet facilities provide for little privacy—there are no doors on toilets and no private shower stalls.

The girls' dormitory, a stone structure built in 1931 and located on the opposite end of the parade grounds from the boys' dormitory, has similar facilities, although personal privacy is provided for in toilet facilities, and the spacious entranceway to the dormitory building is conducive to socializing.

A large cafeteria building with kitchen serves meals. Teacher housing (described below) is also available.

Although the tradition of Fort Apache as a base of operations against Indians stands as a backdrop, and the buildings do not display a chic modernity, this is, nevertheless, a spacious, pleasant campus. The big, high-ceilinged rooms have large windows admitting cheering sunshine and permitting those inside to view the beauties of the natural surroundings.

As a BIA boarding school, TRS is directed by the reservation principal, who supervises the school principal, who in turn directs the head of the dormitories, the head of the cafeteria, and the head of the school.

Although in keeping with BIA policy there is an advisory board, it is not active and the isolation of the school makes for infrequent visits to it by board members and by parents.

In addition to the principal and heads of the various divisions of the school, there are nine teachers. In 1968–69, two of the teachers were Indian; in 1969–70, one was Indian and one, Negro, the remainder, Anglo. None of the Indians was Apache.

All teachers are employed by the BIA under U.S. civil service regulations. There is a high rate of teacher turnover. Two teachers left during the 1969–70 school year. Most do not stay longer than a year or two. One staff member has been here six years, another for three. One of the reasons for the high turnover rate is the limited availability of social activity for young, unmarried teachers. All the single teachers are presently women.

Married couples have available modernized, duplex apartments costing about $57 a month plus utilities. The single teachers live in apartments in an older frame building that cost about $16 per month plus utilities. The principal is provided with a large stone house dating from the old Fort Apache compound.

Dormitory staff includes aides who are, in the main, White Mountain Apache. Efforts are being made to hire Pima aides because of the large number of Pima children resident at the school.

About two hundred pupils from thirteen tribes attend TRS. The sex ratio is about even. Almost all come from the state of Arizona, although a few have lived in California.

A wide variety of Arizona tribes is represented in the student body, with the exception that no Navajo attend. Pima, San Carlos Apache, Havasupai from the Grand Canyon, and Hualapai, and a few White Mountain Apache are among the tribal groups from which the pupils come. The degree of acculturation varies widely among the pupils. Some, like the Pima children, have lived near big cities such as Phoenix, Arizona, and indicate greater familiarity with the non-Indian world than those coming from more isolated, rural situations.

Although the school serves grades three to eight, there is a wide age range, extending from about seven to eighteen or nineteen. The youngest children are orphans who board here but attend the nearby Seven Miles School; the oldest students generally have come from isolated backgrounds, started school late, or had irregular school attendance.

Pupils are admitted to the school for various reasons. Some are from isolated regions with no day school to serve them, some have been placed by welfare authorities because of disorganized or troubled home situations, and others have been rejected by their local schools because of behavioral or academic difficulties. Some staff members see these latter children as alert, bright pupils who found their situations unacceptable and were then considered troublesome.

Local children are permitted to go home each weekend.

All pupils speak a native language.

Considerable flexibility for working within the prescribed BIA curriculum has been typical of the school recently. However, this has not always been the advantage it might appear to be. For example, textbooks selected by teachers often don't arrive for a year or two, by which time the teacher has generally left the school.

There is little Indian culture material in the curriculum. The library does have a good selection of books on American Indians but these are too advanced to be useful to the children.

Several of the teachers are markedly sensitive to the culture differences and would like to have more materials of greater interest to, and at a more appropriate level for, their pupils. One of the most popular books in the library is a Pima-English dictionary which the Pima children enjoy.

Teachers view reading instruction as a primary need. There is no special language program in the school.

Until now, the grades have been organized as follows: one combined third and fourth grades, one fifth grade, two sixth grades, two seventh grades, two eighth grades, and one combined seventh and eighth grades. The staff has developed a plan to introduce a departmental program for the 1970–71 school year. However, anticipated changes in administration of the school made long-range planning difficult.

Between 4 and 5:30 P.M. every afternoon, the pupils are allowed free time during which they play baseball, basketball, and football. There is a cheerleader group. There are no academic clubs and no socializing with the teaching staff is permitted after school hours.

Boys and girls are restricted to separate halves of the parade grounds for play. They are also separated when movies are shown in the auditorium. Every weekend, one dance is held.

There is an annual contest to select a campus queen, an Easter egg hunt, and a senior class trip. In 1970, the seniors traveled to Phoenix for two days of sightseeing and a visit to the Phoenix Indian School, where many TRS graduates attend. There is also an annual senior banquet and prom.

Much time in the dormitories is spent on clean-up activities.

Although Theodore Roosevelt School is located close to Whiteriver, which in addition to the BIA offices and Public Health Service houses the offices of the White Mountain Apache tribe, there is limited involvement of the local people in the affairs of the school. Few local Apache children attend, having available to them several day schools, and most of the pupils at TRS are from other tribes. However, Apache leaders see the school as serving a function by providing a needed place for isolated and needy Apache children. The school also provides employment. News of school events are reported in a full and friendly fashion in the *Fort Apache Scout,* official newspaper of the White Mountain Apache tribe.

In May 1970, the Fort Apache Centennial was celebrated on the school grounds by the tribe. The TRS sent its pupils home early to make the buildings available for the celebration.

As day schools become available to formerly isolated Indian families, TRS is increasingly receiving pupils who come from troubled home situations, or pupils with histories of problems at school.

At the same time, the school retains a rather traditional organization and orientation. The staff, while containing concerned, sensitive, and willing individuals, is not selected or trained for working within this developing context, and the school is without the special resources required to deal constructively with the diverse needs of its pupils. Staff turnover operates to mitigate continuity and makes uncertain the taking hold of new programs.

Despite criticism leveled against boarding schools generally, there is likely to be continued sentiment to retain TRS. The reasons for this include the functions of the school as regards child welfare, Indian employment, and the school's availability as an educational center for children who have no alternatives due to isolation and dissatisfaction with, or expulsion from, their local schools.

Bethel, Shonto, and Sells represent essentially Indian communities, non-Indian residents being there mainly because of their administrative or service roles. Their schools, together with the Theodore Roosevelt School, have all or nearly all Indian attendance. But many Indian children live in communities somewhat different from those described above, in rural areas or small cities with mixed populations. In some of these areas the Indian population is predominant. Others live in small cities were there is a larger white population and more non-Indians in the schools. The following descriptions of Cheyenne schooling in Eagle Butte, South Dakota, of schooling in Ponca City and White Eagle,

Oklahoma, and the Lumbee of North Carolina illustrate the varied nature of these communities and the different educational experiences faced by Indian children in these situations.

Cheyenne, Eagle Butte[10]

Eagle Butte, South Dakota, is the center for the BIA facilities and the tribal facilities of the Cheyenne River Reservation. Here, fifteen hundred pupils, about 80 per cent of whom are Sioux Indian, attend a large, modern, public school in grades kindergarten to twelve.

In 1959 and 1960, displaced by the rising water of the Oahe Reservoir, the Cheyenne River Reservation tribal headquarters and Bureau of Indian Affairs agency offices were moved to Eagle Butte, a town located on the Chicago and Milwaukee St. Paul and Pacific Railroad line and close to U. S. Highway 212.

This was not the first time members of the Sioux tribes had been displaced. Their right to much of the land area of the current states of South Dakota and Nebraska, established by treaty in 1868, gradually whittled away—the Black Hills and much of today's Nebraska and large sections of South Dakota were lost before the turn of the century.

The Cheyenne River Reservation is one of several small reservation areas remaining, subdivided from the Great Sioux Reservation for administrative purposes (Figure 6). About seventy-eight hundred persons, Indian and non-Indian, live on the reservation. Over six thousand are enrolled Cheyenne River Sioux tribal members of whom over four thousand or 68.5 per cent actually reside on the reservation. The others live away, some temporarily.

Before the Bureau and tribal facilities were moved in 1959 and 1960, Eagle Butte had only two stores and two cafes. There are many stores now, including some tribal enterprises, as well as four cafes. The town population has increased from some four hundred inhabitants to an estimated two thousand, counting the four hundred students who live in a BIA dormitory attached to the Cheyenne-Eagle Butte public school. Community residents perceive the ethnic composition to have changed from largely white to about 75 per cent Indian. Actually the Indian population, according to the BIA agency headquarters, is closer to 54 per cent.

Most of the Cheyenne Indian Reservation for which Eagle Butte is now the administrative center is grassland, the portions more suitable to agriculture having been lost through homesteading, railroad grants, inundation, and sale of individual land holdings. Only about twenty thousand acres are under cultivation. The principal crops are wheat, oats, corn, and some alfalfa. Due to the scarcity of water—derived from deep wells—very

FIGURE 6. *Indian reservations in South Dakota*

little land, far short of the thirty-nine thousand acres suitable, is irrigated.

Summers in this area are mild, temperatures in July average 75° F., but winters are cold, the average January temperature of 16° F. made more bitter by the prevailing winds. Only slightly more than one third of the days during the year are frost free. Welfare dependence varies with the season. In summers there are some thirty to forty cases, as contrasted with some two hundred cases involving seven hundred persons in the winter.

Currently, cattle ranching is the major economic activity extant on the reservation. In addition to some forty-six thousand cattle grazed, there are about two thousand sheep and eight thousand horses. Actually, however, cattle ranching provides a livelihood for a limited number of persons. Part of this is due to the decreasing capacity of range land—a situation typical for the entire state of South Dakota.

The Cheyenne River Reservation faced with declining agricultural employment and a growing youth population has a most serious unemployment problem.

It has been estimated that the general unemployment proportion on the Cheyenne River Indian Reservation exceeds 75 per cent. Several approaches to solving this problem include relocation outside the reservation, new private industry on the reservation, and government sponsored programs.

One of the ways of providing employment has been through the BIA Employment Assistance Service. This service provides training and placement away from the reservation. Relocation off reservation does not appeal to many tribal members, however. People do not like to leave home. This is also evidenced by the comparatively high percentage of tribal members residing on the reservation. Nor are all attempts at relocation permanent. Many persons return to the reservation bringing back with them experience of life in cities.

The tribe has also established financial operations to provide income and services for the people. A supermarket, the only Indian telephone company in the United States (service for Dewey and Ziebach counties), the tribal beef herd, a cattle auction sales pavilion, a garage and filling station, and a laundromat are all owned and operated by the tribe. An additional facility owned by the tribe is the Swift Bird Training Center, initially constructed for use as a Job Corps Center, then turned over to the tribe, which in turn has contracted with the Scale Institute of Minneapolis for the training of Indians in diesel mechanics and the use of heavy machinery.

Stone Craft Industries of Cherry Creek employs several persons in the production of tomahawks, beadwork, and the like for sale to tourists.

The stores, shops, cafes, service stations, and motels as well as the education facilities all provide jobs. There is virtually no industry in Eagle Butte, however, and few other material production enterprises exist on the reservation. The goal of the Economic Development Administration (EDA) in Eagle Butte, founded in June of 1969, is to bring industry to the reservation and to provide employment. Recently plans for a wood products prefabricating plant were approved. Two large all-purpose buildings will be constructed and turned over to the tribe. Some twenty to twenty-five persons will find employment in the plant. The buildings will be erected in the new industrial park adjacent to Eagle Butte.

Eagle Butte does not have one of the requirements for many kinds of industry—great quantities of pure water, and this impedes industrial development.

The federal programs which have provided employment include Community Action programs with funds from the Economic Opportunity Act of 1964. Included are Head Start, which enrolled some 209 children and employs many aides; Senior Opportunities and Service; Consumer Action, a credit union with over five hundred members; also, Operation Mainstream, financed by the state Labor Department, has trained men in preparation for area improvement and beautification programs.

Housing conditions, until very recently, were very poor. Mutual Help Housing has built new homes, and over 120 new homes have been built in Eagle Butte. The Public Health Service has helped provide water and sewer facilities for over 50 per cent of the homes. Electricity is now widely available on the reservation. While housing conditions are improving, there still remains a good number of dilapidated residences without adequate sanitary facilities and pure water.

The U. S. Public Health Service has identified the major diseases. Otitis media (middle ear infection) was the most prevalent. Gastroenteritis has dropped from its earlier position in first place, perhaps due to improved water supply.

There is a thirty-three-bed U. S. Public Health Service hospital in Eagle Butte and efforts to improve reservation sanitation are being made. Some of the PHS staff are concerned with establishing community relations conducive to improved understanding between the Sioux residents, and the health service staff.

The Cheyenne River Sioux Tribal Council is the legal governing body on the reservation. It is composed of a tribal chairman, fifteen councilmen, a vice-chairman, a treasurer, and a secretary. The tribe operates its own law enforcement agency and system of courts. State, county, and Eagle Butte city police also operate on the reservation, and cooperation between all agencies is good. The tribe has jurisdiction over all but one of the eleven major crimes over which state and federal government may intervene.

In addition, the tribe provides economic programs as described above, as well as legal aid services.

It is in this agency community of Eagle Butte that the Cheyenne-Eagle Butte School serving fifteen hundred pupils in grades kindergarten to twelve is located. The name reveals the dual sponsorship of the school—it is a combined BIA school with dormitory facilities for some four hundred resident students and a state public day school. This cooperative agreement states:

> The District shall expend approximately 75 per cent of all receipts in the operation of the school as agreed upon in the Annual Budget Meeting. The District shall expend its funds directly by employing teachers and other personnel and in buying supplies as agreed in the plans made at the monthly meetings. The District shall expend all general funds, anticipated receipts from taxes, and its current receipts from all other sources in fulfillment of this Agreement and in the operation of additional schools for which the District is responsible.
>
> The Board and BIA shall grant the free use of all school buildings, motor vehicles, major and minor equipment, materials and supplies now in their possession and located in Eagle Butte for the education of all children attending the Cheyenne-Eagle Butte School.[11]

Currently, the district has a school budget of some $350,000 while the BIA contributes $1,200,000 to the school's operation. These figures roughly parallel the proportion of white to Indian students attending the school. Most of the district funds are expended for teacher salaries. Of the sixty-eight persons involved in teaching and its supervision in the school, thirty-two are employed by the district while thirty-six are Bureau employees.

There are some parallels in the Bureau and the district, but most administration is handled by the Bureau. The high school recently lost its principal who was transferred to the principalship of a school in Oklahoma. The elementary school is headed by the BIA teacher supervisor and the district superintendent. Although the school leaders do not invariably agree on issues, supervision at the various levels tends to be amiable.

Facilities are divided between old, modern, and trailer classrooms. Several of the elementary grades are housed in the old Eagle Butte School which is soon to be replaced when a new high school will be built. The rest of the elementary grades as well as all of the high school grades occupy a modern building complex including dormitory facilities constructed in 1960 at the time of relocation from the Cheyenne agency. Some elementary classes are held in double-width trailers behind the high school. The high school also has a library, gymnasium, and an auditorium.

There is a teachers' room, together with a concession stand adjacent to the gymnasium. For the high school students, there is a comfortable lounge next to the library. The library is equipped with old books. There is little Sioux- or Indian-related material and very few magazines.

Housing for the staff is provided within the BIA compound. Here usually live the BIA teachers. Some BIA teachers as well as some district teachers hired by the public school system live in residential areas in Eagle Butte. Other district teachers live in the rural area surrounding Eagle Butte.

District teachers are hired on a nine-month basis and have a slightly shorter official working day. Bureau teachers are civil servants in year-round employment. Beginning salaries are fairly equal in both systems. Bureau salaries are subject to GS (federal civil service) ratings, however, and increase more rapidly than district salaries. When the greater length of the BIA teaching year and day are considered, the disparity tends to disappear.

More district teachers are employed in the elementary school than in the high school. Since the ratio of district to Bureau teachers is nearly equal, it follows that most of the high school teachers are Bureau employees. Although it is difficult to generalize, it may be said that district teachers tend to be persons from this area of South Dakota while Bureau teachers are brought into the school through recruitment elsewhere.

Teacher turnover is not a grave problem with either the Bureau or the district. Of the three new teachers hired by the Bureau for the 1969–70 school year, for example, only one was a replacement. The number of certified teachers is quite high. Because of the low teacher turnover rate few emergency certificates have to be issued. There is little informal contact between the teachers of different ethnic groups although some of the Indian and white teachers do bowl together. Teacher involvement in the community is slight.

Salary levels were never discussed in a manner indicating dissatisfaction. Bureau teachers seem to have as their reference group other Bureau employees. For most of them the Bureau is a career and there is considerable concern with promotion and GS ratings. The district teachers tend to be long-time residents of the area and thus "know all about Indians."

Most of the teachers feel that the Indian student needs discipline, since they believe he does not have suitable guidelines of behavior at home. However, in interviewing teachers a usual response was to say that they did not discriminate. This implies that the Indians are no different and that they, therefore, need not be treated differently. If it is remembered that most whites in Eagle Butte are exposed to Indian behavior which they interpret as negative, the view that the entire Indian way of life is unattractive and should therefore be supplanted by the white way tends to be reinforced.

The vast majority of the fifteen hundred students in the schools at Eagle Butte are from the reservation. The only Indian language spoken is Lakota but only by a small percentage of the students. There are no longer restrictions against the speaking of Lakota in school—a condition prevalent in the past—but most children now do not know the Indian language.

Eagle Butte Indian students, constituting about 75 per cent of the high school students, elected a full-blooded homecoming king and queen this year. Students were proud of a student lounge conducted on a student honor system. The dropout rate, however, is high.

The school is accredited by the South Dakota Department of Education. The curriculum is the same used in public schools throughout the state and is not Indian oriented. The only exception is an Indian acculturational psychology course sponsored by the BIA, although Indian language, Indian arts and crafts and an additional Indian course have been authorized and were planned. The high school government course does not include tribal government, nor does American history deal particularly with the Sioux.

The local residents of Eagle Butte are not actively involved in the administration of the school. The district does have a school board which meets monthly. Some of the members are Indians who are local businessmen. In the 1969 school board election no candidates opposed the incumbents. There is a tribal education committee but it is oriented more toward regional and national meetings than local problems. This year advisory school boards have been started in some of the outlying BIA schools and seem to function reasonably well. One of these boards aids in assuring regular attendance of students.

PTA meetings are not ordinarily well attended. In an effort to communicate with parents the district superintendent does have a ten- to fifteen-minute radio program weekdays, which reports upcoming school and community events as well as being of great informative value to the area.

Three years ago a parent-teacher conference program was initiated in the BIA elementary school. Responses were very positive. For the first set of conferences held at the end of the first nine-week period, the overall turnout rate was over 60 per cent. The lowest percentage, 50 per cent, applied to parents of bused Indian students. No comparable program is in effect in the high school.

Parents are more likely to attend teacher-parent conferences concerning their elementary children. There is little participation in the high school program although parents do come to athletic events, particularly basketball games.

Tribal law states that youth must attend school until they are eighteen years old. It is at this age that many Sioux become eligible to receive the Sioux benefit.

When the Sioux in 1889 ceded extensive tracts of the Great Sioux Reservation to the government for homesteading by settlers, it was agreed that:

> each head of a family or single person over the age of eighteen years who has an allotment of land will receive certain farming implements and oxen for agricultural purposes, plus $50 in cash for construction of a house and other buildings suitable for residence or for improvement of their allotments.[12]

The agreement was upheld by the Act of June 18, 1934, which gave the recipient a choice of selecting the items listed above or their equivalent cash value. The allocation of the cash was supervised by the Bureau. Since 1951, recipients have been given the cash directly without being required to invest it for any specific purpose such as education, livestock, farming equipment, or a business, as had been the case until then. Due to inflation, the size of the Sioux benefit has been increased repeatedly. It now amounts to almost $1300.

The pattern of spending this money seems to be based on the principle of reciprocity. In most cases the money is freely shared with relatives and friends and is gone in a short period of time. Due to the benefit recipient's generosity he becomes eligible to receive some of the money when younger friends and relatives receive their benefit. This reciprocity, based on generosity, assures anyone who shares his money freely of future financial support as long as the benefit continues to be paid. Even if it were to be discontinued others would be indebted to him.

It is clear that the tribe and school authorities encourage and enforce the school attendance law. The effect is noticeable in the relatively large numbers of those enrolling in adult education classes. Adult basic education goes to the eighth grade and concentrates on fundamental skills (reading, writing, arithmetic). It also provides the participating adults the opportunity to aid local school children through making children's clothes, etc. Programs exist currently in Eagle Butte, La Plante, Red Scaffold, and Cherry Creek. A Graduate Equivalency Degree (GED) Program is sponsored by the district and tribe. It started operation in July 1968 and has had excellent success. Ninety-eight persons have passed the examination and received their high school equivalency diplomas.

The schools include teachers and administrators, some of whom are resistant to innovation, others who are enthusiastic about new programs. On the elementary level, Project Necessities, a BIA-developed curriculum project was being tried out by two outside specialists. In the high school, an auto mechanics course was introduced several years ago. A course in Indian acculturation psychology was being introduced into the high school as an elective. Students have organized an Indian club, with membership restricted to Indians. Also, ungraded evaluation criteria were being used in some of the elementary school grades as indices of student performance.

One of the main trends in the area is toward the consolidation of outlying schools. Paved roads are currently being constructed which will allow for the busing of students from some of the smaller schools to more centrally located facilities. There is a trend toward improving and expanding the educational facilities in Eagle Butte as is evidenced by plans for a new high school which will cost close to $3,000,000.

Ponca City and White Eagle, Oklahoma[13]

In addition to those rural and small city situations in which there is a large proportion of Indian pupils in the schools, there are also many places where there is a very small number of Indians in the school population. A problem that sometimes arises in these situations concerns the relative merits of retaining small, all-Indian local schools or moving toward Indian minority attendance in large, modern consolidated schools. The communities of Ponca City and White Eagle, in Oklahma, illustrate this issue.

Ponca City, with a population of thirty thousand, is located on the Arkansas River in north central Oklahoma. It is about equidistant (one hundred miles) from the major cities in the area: Wichita, Kansas; Tulsa and Oklahoma City, Oklahoma.

The Ponca Indians who live in and around Ponca City are estimated to comprise about twenty-five hundred persons. However, probably no more than three hundred Ponca Indian families live in the city of Ponca itself. Many Ponca Indian families live five miles south of Ponca City in the area called White Eagle (Figure 7).

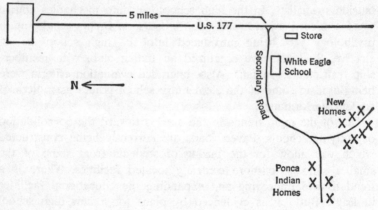

FIGURE 7. *White Eagle community in Oklahoma*

The Ponca Indians hold 935 acres of trust tribal lands, most of which are located west of U. S. Highway 177, south of Ponca City in the White Eagle area. Individually allotted lands held by the Ponca amount to 17,600 acres. Many Ponca Indian homes are located along U. S. 177 north and south of the White Eagle area. These homes, visible from the highway, in no way represent the majority of Ponca home dwellings. Most Ponca residents are scattered over a wide area of land fifteen or twenty miles from White Eagle. Some families live to the south around the community of Marland.

In sociological terms some justification could be made for designating Ponca City as a "company town," since the local economy has a heavy stake in the fortunes of the Continental Oil Company (CONOCO) which employs thirty-five hundred, and Sequoia Refining Corporation with three hundred on the payroll. Since the oil companies employ many professional people (engineers, etc.), they (CONOCO) have been strong supporters of the school system. School officials are quick to point out the good working relationship with the oil companies. Also, a number of the wives of company employees hold teaching credentials which allow them to be employed by the local school system.

By most definitions Ponca City would probably be classified as a middle to upper middle-class city. Per-household income in the city for 1968 was set at $9259. A later economic survey conducted by the combined departments of economics of the University of Oklahoma and Oklahoma State University estimated the 1970 per-person income of Kay County (Ponca City is located in Kay County) at $3457. The highest per-person income in Oklahoma was in Washington County, which contains Bartlesville and the Phillips Petroleum Company, with $5000. Kay County ranks fifth in the state in per capita income.

A drive through the community quickly impresses on the observer the general economic affluence of the white residents. Well-landscaped homes and a thriving business district create an atmosphere of general prosperity. The Negro section of the community is located in the southern leg of Ponca City. The major approach to the city from the south skirts this area. Two large road-side billboards block or screen the driver's view of the many ramshackle homes that occupy the area. Many Indian homes are located south of Grand Avenue, the major business street, and west of the north-south Santa Fe railroad tracks. Again, these homes do not seem to reflect the general economic affluence of the white community.

Another general index of the socioeconomic status of the white community can be seen in the general grooming of the senior high school students, particularly the girls. One is struck by the fashionable dress and hair styles displayed by them.

The Indian population in and around Ponca City are engaged primarily in low-level service jobs. There are no professionals, with the exception of one nurse, who is held in high regard by the junior high school girls as a model of achievement. Many of the young people leave Ponca City in their late teens, going off to larger cities for employment.

As noted above, Ponca City represents a prosperous white middle-class community with a fairly large contingent of Indian residents. Although the Indians are pitied for their poverty and generally perceived in stereotypical terms by the whites, there seems to be an emergent leadership among the Ponca Indians that is prepared to challenge the dominant group's point of view.

Promotional literature prepared for Ponca City by the Chamber of Commerce does not build on the fact that the Ponca Indians are a historical "present" for the community. One is hardly aware that Indians in significant numbers are present in the community.

An indication of the apparent invisibility of Indians in the area is that school leaders were unable to estimate the number of Indians in the school system. Probably about 5 per cent of the Ponca City high school enrollment (grades seven to twelve) is Indian. These officials were quick to point out that they did not work with youngsters on the basis of their being Indian, Negro, or white. Their apparent egalitarianism resulted in inattention to the needs and problems of the minority groups.

However, awareness of Indians and their concerns is beginning to develop. During the course of the survey many teachers and school officials spoke of the so-called "red power" movement headed by a Ponca Indian, Mrs. Clyde (Della) Warrior. School leaders were quite chagrined over the adverse publicity they felt the Ponca Indians were giving to the community—some of it via national television. Also, the publicity surrounding investigation of the nearby Bureau of Indian Affairs boarding school, the Chilocco Indian School, kept school personnel uneasy over possible investigation of their schools.

Mrs. Warrior at the time was director of the White Eagle Community Development Association (WEDA), located in an office building in downtown Ponca City. Staffing the office was done primarily with Ponca Indian women. If there is any semblance of a "red power" movement, the white community seems to associate it with the activities of Mrs. Warrior and the WEDA. Mrs. Warrior has on several occasions confronted Ponca City and White Eagle school officials with alleged acts of discrimination against Indian students as well as arbitrary policy decisions which seem to be against the best interests of Ponca Indian residents.

Funding for the WEDA has been met through a grant from the Episcopal Church. A recent grant was made to WEDA by the National Endowment for the Humanities. This ten-thousand-dollar grant is to be used to write Ponca history as seen by members of the tribe. Materials developed by the project will be available to help educate children of the Ponca community.

The WEDA probably does not speak for all members of the Ponca Indian tribe. It is, however, the most visible and vocal Indian group known by white residents in Ponca City.

In July of 1969, eight members of the Ponca Indian tribe were named to a new board of directors of the White Eagle Community Center. The community center formerly housed the White Eagle School, which was closed in 1969. Since the community center is located near the tribal grounds and a large cluster of Indian homes, usage of the facility will probably be quite good.

Tribal leaders have been concerned about securing outside funding for residential development in the White Eagle area. Home improvement, sewer lines, and site developments are high on the list of concerns of some members of the tribe. WEDA has also been concerned about attracting an industry to Ponca City that would have a pro-Indian hiring policy. Other tribal groups are interested in maintaining the social-ceremonial world of the Ponca Indians.

White Eagle School, the small public school serving the Indian community located five miles south of Ponca City, operated for many years as a grade-one-through-eight school. Before that it consisted of grades one through six. For several years before it was closed in 1969, the school was the subject of much controversy. In late 1967, Clyde Warrior, former president of the National Indian Youth Council, a militant organization of Indian youth from many tribes, became involved in community action programs in White Eagle. Initially, the action focused on the election of an Indian to the school board for the local White Eagle School.[14] In 1969, with increasing vocal dissatisfaction from Indian parents over the kind and quality of the educational offerings at White Eagle—WEDA members were involved in several school principal-Indian confrontations—a decision was made by the state and the local school board to close the school. Students were to be bused to Ponca City starting in the fall of 1969.

Although there had been dissatisfaction with the White Eagle School, many Indian parents were unhappy at seeing the school suspend operations. Several Ponca parents expressed displeasure with the prospect of sending their children to the Ponca City public schools. Some of the reasons offered by the parents included the cost of dressing their children appropriately for the Ponca City schools, difficulty the children might have competing with city students, and more demanding teachers, plus the loss of freedom in a more highly structured school setting.

When the school principal was asked why the school was closing, she replied, "No funds; it is as simple as that." One Ponca Indian leader thought that the closing of White Eagle School would be good for the Indian students in the long run. He indicated that he believed no community could be more prejudiced against Indians than Ponca City, but if the Indian students could succeed in this school setting they would be able to make their way in the larger white-dominated world.

In Ponca City now, children are attending a modern non-segregated public school system which includes nine elementary schools, two junior high schools, and one high school, plus one special school for handicapped children. Prior to the closing of the White Eagle (elementary) School, almost all secondary pupils went to the Ponca City school while the elementary children remained in the local school.

The Ponca City schools receive Johnson-O'Malley funds. There is an elected school board. In 1969–70 there was no Indian member of the board.

The Lumbee, North Carolina[15]

Although they too live in rural, small-town situations, the Lumbees of North Carolina illustrate conditions markedly different from those we have been describing. Their particular history and the absence of federal jurisdiction and responsibility in relation to them underscore the enormous diversity of Indian life in this country.

There are four tribally organized groups of Indians living in the southeastern United States. These are the Seminole and the Miccosukee of Florida, the Choctaw of Mississippi, and the Eastern Cherokee of North Carolina. Together these four groups number something under ten thousand individuals. They occupy federally supervised reservation lands in the three states, and attend local Bureau of Indian Affairs schools. In addition to these BIA-supervised Indians, there are between fifty thousand and one hundred thousand non-tribally organized, non-reservation Indians living in the southeastern coastal plains area running from Maryland to Florida.

The largest of these groups of *non-reservation* Indians are the Lumbee of North Carolina. There are approximately twenty-six thousand Lumbees living in Robeson County, North Carolina, and estimates are that an additional ten to fifteen thousand reside in the surrounding counties of North and South Carolina. In addition, there are Lumbees living in Baltimore, Maryland; Greensboro, Winston-Salem, and the High Point area of North Carolina.

The Lumbees speak no Indian language and when first recorded spoke English and lived in European-style houses. The origins and early history of the Lumbees are largely unknown, although there are reports of Indians who spoke an archaic form of English, who lived in houses, were farmers, and held slaves living along the banks of the Lumber River when the Scotch and English first started to settle the area in the 1730s.

Some credence is given in the Carolinas—and indeed by the United States Senate—to the possibility that the present-day Indian population of Robeson County represents descendants of Indian-white mixture of the Raleigh "Lost Colony," which landed on the coast of North Carolina in the area of Cape Hatteras in 1585, and the Hatteras Indians.

Although their origin and early history remain unclear, it would seem that the Lumbees do represent remnants of southeastern Atlantic Coast tribes who early in the history of our country drifted into the backwaters and swamps of the Lumber River drainage basin, and while intermarrying somewhat with whites and Negroes, kept their social identity as Indians. The Congress of the United States has given official recognition to the Lumbees' Indian status—while specifically excluding them from any benefits and claims against the federal government because of their Indian status, due in part to the absence of any treaty between the Lumbee and the United States Government.

The Lumbee Indians have held a separate legal status with respect to education in North Carolina for well over eighty years. They have had their own public school system in Robeson County since 1885 and their own college since 1887. Their present system, while no longer legally separate, still maintains a high degree of racial uniformity. The college has been integrated, and has become predominantly a white institution.

Robeson County is located in the southeastern corner of North Carolina, on the North Carolina-South Carolina border, a hundred miles or so from the Atlantic Coast (Figure 8). The county, situated in the coastal plains area of the state, is flat, with sandy soil. It is in the drainage basin of the Lumber River and much of the area of the county is, or formerly was, swampland. Many of the place names, such as "Long Swamp," "Bear Swamp," "Drowning Creek," "Juniper Branch," and "Hog Swamp" remind us of this. To be productive, much of the farmland has to be drained by ditches six feet deep. While Robeson County is one of the largest counties in the state it is one of the poorest in per capita income, and is predominantly rural.

The largest town in the county, and the county seat, is Lumberton, with approximately fifteen thousand residents. It is situated in the eastern part of the county. Fifteen miles due west of

Lumberton is Pembroke Township and the town of Pembroke, probably the largest Indian settlement east of the Mississippi, the main residential center for the Lumbee Indians and the site of Pembroke State University, formerly Pembroke State College.

Robeson County is a tri-ethnic county. Its population is almost equally divided between Negroes, whites, and Indians. The whites live predominantly in the towns of Lumberton, St. Pauls, Red Springs, and Fairmont. Negroes tend to be dispersed through-

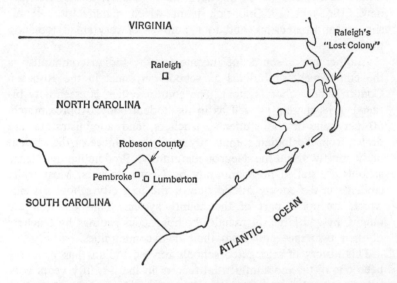

FIGURE 8. *Robeson County, North Carolina*

out the rural areas of the county and to concentrate in the towns and townships surrounding them. The Indians are most heavily concentrated in Pembroke Township and the town of Pembroke, with secondary concentrations in Lumberton.

Primary sources of income in Robeson County are from farming and from wage labor in one of the few manufacturing plants around Lumberton. It is a poor county, ranking eightieth out of one hundred North Carolina counties. Per capita income for 1960 was $1105, the median family income was $2247, and 65 per cent of Indian families had an income under $3000 per year.

The main crops in Robeson County are tobacco, corn, and cotton; minor crops include soybeans and peanuts. Farming also includes raising of hogs, cattle, and poultry. Eighty per cent of the farming in the county is done by Indians, and almost 60 per cent of the farms, which average fifty acres each, are tenant farmed. It is an area with a high rate of seasonally employed agricultural workers.

Factory employment is non-union for the most part, and is limited to a textile mill in the north of the county, to the relatively new (1968) B. F. Goodrich plant which manufactures tennis shoes near Lumberton, and to a number of very small job-shop plants.

Another major source of income for the Indian community is the employment of Indians as school personnel in the Robeson County public school system. The county system is essentially biracial in its staffing as well as in its student body. Approximately 60 per cent of the students, teachers, and administrators are drawn from the Indian community, with the balance of the student body mostly from the Negro community. Predominantly Negro schools are staffed predominantly by Negro teachers. Most white students in the county attend one of the four city school systems which are not a part of the county system. Thus children are taught, by and large, in racially homogeneous settings by teachers of their own race and from their own communities.

This history of segregated schools for the Indians has probably been one of the most influential factors in the last fifty years contributing to their acculturation in the contemporary American lifeway. Prior to 1835, Indians had attended school with whites. From 1835 to 1885, they were denied admission to the white schools and refused to attend the Negro schools. In 1885, by act of the state legislature, separate Indian schools were established, and in 1887 a normal school was set up in Pembroke for the Croatan (Lumbee) Indians.

The North Carolina pattern of minority education was a pattern of separatism as well as segregation. Negro, white, and Indian schools had Negro, white, and Indian teachers, principals and other administrators, respectively, even though the local school board and superintendent usually were white. In recent years, however, even this has been changed and Indian as well as Negro school board members have participated.

The pattern of separatism gave the Lumbees a monopoly on a group of jobs that paid regularly, were secure, and which rewarded individuals who achieved higher education. It was also a group of jobs that did not deny the holders the ability to continue in the agricultural tradition of the area, if they wished. They could be teachers and farmers.

There has developed over the last fifty years a solid middle-class community of Indians living in and around Pembroke, North Carolina. Most of them are teachers in the county system, but an increasingly large number are in other occupations—a doctor, a real estate broker and insurance man, several store owners, restaurant owners, and gasoline station owners, a few public officials, a university president, and several faculty members, a state employee or two—the range of white-collar business and professionals to be found in almost any small southern college town.

These positions have tended to run along family lines over the years. It is not unusual to find father, son, and daughter all teachers, and perhaps all teachers at the same school. The Lumbee Indian family tends to be strongly male oriented, and public school teaching even in primary grades is a high-prestige job for men. Students are taught by predominantly male teachers from as early as the fourth grade.

There is an Indian county-wide organization called the Schoolmasters' Association, which holds regular monthly dinner meetings. Its members include all Indian men in the schools. It provides an opportunity for casual social intercourse along vertical lines as well as horizontal lines within the school power structure and helps maintain a high level of morale. There is no comparable organization for the female members of the county schools.

Housing in the county, and particularly in Pembroke and Pembroke Township, is modern and in good shape.

In general, economic conditions have improved over the last decade. This is not to say that poverty does not exist, or that everyone lives in a modern home. There are still a number of dilapidated houses around, but increasingly they are being used for storage of tobacco, or simply abandoned. There are still many sharecropper houses, back off the roads, but their numbers and occupancy are decreasing, and the unmistakable impression that one gets is that things *are* getting better for the Lumbee. Prosperity, even if a bit late, is finally coming to at least some of the people.

Pembroke has a mayor and city council form of government, its own police force and fire department, a small jail, and a city clerk's office, as well as sewer and water facilities. There is no hotel or motel, but there are several rooming houses (usually filled with students), and several local residents are considering construction of a small motel in the area of the university. There are approximately thirty commercial establishments in town, almost all of them owned and run by Lumbees.

Pembroke is the site of Pembroke State University, which was established in 1887 by the General Assembly of the state of North Carolina as a normal school for the education of teachers of the Croatan (Lumbee) race of North Carolina. In the late 1950s it was integrated as a result of the U. S. Supreme Court's desegregation decision, and white students were admitted. Desegregation occurred concurrently with a rapid expansion in college attendance generally by North Carolina's white population. In the last ten years Pembroke State has grown from an institution of three hundred Indian students to one of over sixteen hundred students, the vast majority, twelve hundred, of whom are non-Indian.

In addition to the university, Pembroke is the location of a grammar school, a junior high school, and a high school. The grammar and junior high schools are located within a block of the university campus. They are both older buildings, in good repair, which have been supplemented by prefabricated temporary classrooms on the school grounds. This has restricted the play areas available to the children. Lunchrooms are available in both schools (both schools bus a number of their children), and a hot meal is served at noon. Class size averages about twenty pupils in the early primary grades (there are no kindergartens in the school system) and about thirty in the upper grades. Some teacher aides are used, mostly in the primary grades, and additional educational facilities such as school libraries, a county school system library, and audio-visual library are available, as well as specially trained teachers for art and music and remedial speech and reading.

The high school, built in 1969, is located in a semirural area approximately one mile southwest from the center of town and about half a mile from the university. It is a modern complex of buildings, built at a cost of over a million dollars. Built for an enrollment of over a thousand students, it currently houses about six hundred Indian students in grades nine through twelve.

Racially, the high school student body is composed of two Negroes, about twenty whites, and the balance Indians. The faculty is also predominantly Indian, as is the administrative staff. College preparatory, technical, and distributive education curriculums are offered. Excellent cafeteria meals are available at noon, and a brand-new physical education area adjoins the school. It is one of the newest and best schools in the county.

Not all the children in the Pembroke area attend the county school system. Several of the white faculty members at Pembroke University prefer to send their children to private or public schools outside of the area, and a few Indians send their children fifteen miles to Lumberton to a parochial school, some giving as their reason that it is a more integrated situation.

Most of the Indian school personnel who work in the county system live in Pembroke and commute to their jobs daily, often in car pools. Their children usually attend the Pembroke schools. These schools, then, draw from the best educated and highest socioeconomic levels of the Lumbees.

The Magnolia School is located north of Lumberton just off Interstate 95, part of the New York and Boston to Florida middle-class migration route. It is not really located in a community as such, but in an area. It is a consolidated school covering grades one through twelve. North Carolina does not yet provide kindergartens in its school systems.

The area around Magnolia is still rural farmland, the school drawing its students, all Indian, from the farms and crossroads settlements around it, and from the town of Lumberton, two miles to the south and east. The school was under suit by the federal government under the Civil Rights Act of 1964 for bringing Indian students out of the Lumberton city school district and concurrently busing white students from the county school district into the Lumberton city schools.

The Indian students attending Magnolia, on the average, come from homes and backgrounds less prosperous than those in Pembroke. Many of the parents are tenant farmers or day laborers. Educational level among them is below that of Pembroke parents, and few are professional or white-collar workers. One-parent homes are a more frequent occurrence among the Magnolia students, and a number of the children live with someone other than their natural parents. This is considered one of the poorer sections of the county.

Magnolia School is a complex of three sets of older buildings—one set housing the early primary grades, a second set housing the fourth through eighth, and a third set for the senior high school students, the administrative offices, the lunchroom, and the library. There are a number of temporary prefabricated classroom buildings around the complex, used for additional primary classrooms and for special education classes. Playground and outdoor sports equipment is at a minimum, but there is a gymnasium, the newest building in the complex. Housing has been provided on the school grounds for a caretaker. Teacher aides are used effectively, and the school provides a moderate amount of extracurricular activity such as a student newspaper, occasional dances, and a full sports program. One of the main drawbacks to increased use of the school after regular school hours is that almost all of the children are bused.

The overall impression that one gets when looking at Magnolia and at Pembroke is that they are dealing with two different groups of people, from a number of aspects. Pembroke is, and has been for two or more generations, a center of learning and the center of economic life for the Lumbee. Those who have come to settle there constitute a middle and upper middle class, in economic terms as well as in values and attitudes. The people around Magnolia as a group have had slightly less formal education, and at the same time are both more rural and more urban than the Pembroke residents in that more of the Lumbee migrants to the East Baltimore Street area in Baltimore, Maryland, seem to have attended Magnolia rather than Pembroke, and many of them have lived in or around Lumberton.

In recent years, Office of Economic Opportunity programs have contributed to Lumbee Indian migration from rural North Carolina to the urban, industrial area of Greensboro, Winston-Salem, and High Point, and to places in southern Virginia. In 1968, the Community Action agency, carrying out a tri-county program relocated over 450 persons, 80 per cent of whom were Lumbee Indians.

A larger number of Lumbees, however, live in Baltimore. Here, within a twelve-block area on Baltimore's East Side live approximately two thousand Lumbee Indians. Although this section of Baltimore is multiethnic and has a history of first-generation migrant settlement, it is currently the section of the city where newcomers from the Carolina countryside find kin and friends to provide hospitality and an introduction to city life.

Most of the newcomers are young, usually in their late teens and without families of their own. Temporary employment and a few months or years of exploration and excitement in the city generally suffice and most return to Robeson County to settle down and raise their families. Some move into the blue-collar or middle-class community of the city. Others get locked into the boundaries and patterns of lower-class urban life. The East Baltimore settlement is largely one of transition and acculturating process for those who pass through it.

Although most of the Indian migrants are in their late teens, some Lumbees do come to Baltimore with their families, some stay to have families, others come while still of school age and stay in Baltimore to finish school.

In Baltimore, Lumbee children mainly attend a fifty-year-old, integrated grade school of 735 students, 13 per cent of whom are

Indian. The Indian population of the school tends to be transient, registering in October and dropping out in April and May as families move back and forth between Baltimore and North Carolina. About forty-five Lumbees attend the junior high school, which has a student body of about twenty-eight hundred. The senior high school serving the area, a new plant in a thirty-two-acre setting with about two thousand students, is predominantly white. Only twelve Indians were in high school.

The Baltimore schools are markedly different from those in North Carolina for the Lumbee student because the staff and the majority of the student body are non-Lumbee. While the small urban high school enrollment may reflect only the youth of the families in Baltimore, it may also reflect a preference for secondary schooling back home in Robeson County, where the pressure of competition with the more established white and the absence of role models in the schools do not present a problem.

On the whole, the schools provide no special programs for Indian children.

For most of the people who come to Baltimore ties to Robeson County remain strong and there is frequent moving back and forth. Their ties are to the land, to the freedom and independence of the day laborer who may work for you today but is his own boss tomorrow, and to the ideal that whatever the housing in Baltimore may be like, a good home is a brick house in the North Carolina countryside.

Chicago, Illinois[16]

The diversity of Indian life and education experience is further underscored by the growing numbers of Indians living in cities, some permanently, others temporarily. If present trends continue, it is to be expected that increasing numbers of Indian youth are likely to be attending schools in large urban centers where they will be a very small part of the school population. A look at Chicago, Illinois, a city with a large Indian population, points to the complexities of Indian education in an urban, metropolitan setting.

Chicago has a long and well-documented history of waves of ethnic migration. The most recent, the spreading black ghetto, the influx of Spanish-speaking peoples, and the effects these movements have had on the older Chicago ethnic communities have captured the attention of citizens and researchers. Less visible and less well known is the small but growing number of American Indians partaking in a growing urbanization trend and confronting the myriad problems associated with life in the city (Figure 9).

Twenty years ago there does not seem to have been any one large concentration of Indians living in Chicago. There were clusters of friends and relatives scattered around the city. The Indians living here were mostly from Wisconsin—Chippewas and Winnebago—with a few from Minnesota and the Dakotas.

During the last twenty years the situation has changed with a shifting of the major concentration of residence to the north side of the city. This has been accompanied by increasing numbers of Indians moving to Chicago. While the Winnebago, Chippewa, Menominee, and Sioux are still the largest tribal groupings, there are growing numbers of Indian people in the city from Oklahoma. The 1970 census gave Illinois an Indian population of 11,413. Some seven thousand of this number live in Chicago. Actually, however, the numbers of residents vary, more living in the city in the wintertime, and fewer in the summertime when many Chicago Indians return to their rural homes.

The Indian population in Chicago falls into three major distinguishable groups. One of these is a dispersed middle-class group which is assimilating into the general middle class. They live in middle-class sections of the city. Although proud of being Indian, many do not actively participate in Indian cultural activities. There is a good deal of intermarriage with the surrounding population. This is a relatively small group and probably does not amount to more than 10 per cent of the Indian population, about one hundred families.

There is, in addition, a growing stable working-class group. They have been in the city for several years and are working at

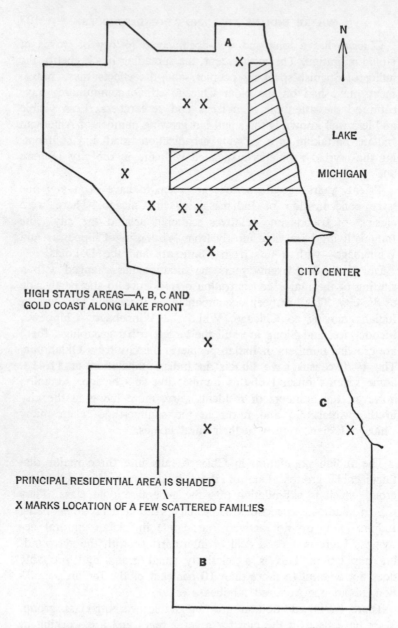

FIGURE 9. *Residence of Indians in Chicago, Illinois*

semiskilled jobs such as welding, factory assembly, stock room, office clerks, etc. This group tends to exhibit relative residential stability, to keep their children in school through high school.

They tend to be interested in their tribal culture, and to maintain contact with relatives on the reservation by going back once a year for ceremonies and sending their children back for vacations. The American Indian Center located in Chicago is a center of activity, and interest in the ideas of Indian cultural identity prevails. Although it is difficult to judge accurately the size of this group, it is probably not more than 20 per cent.

But by far the largest number of the city's Indian population falls into an unstable lower working-class group, which is marginal to the economy and the social structure of the big city. This group is practically anonymous. They have no residential stability; moving within the city very frequently is common. In addition, there is frequent movement back and forth between Chicago and a place called "home"; often a Wisconsin Indian community, and less frequently one in Minnesota or South Dakota. In terms of numbers it appears that about 70 per cent of Indians in Chicago belong to this group. They tend to be concentrated in the Uptown area (School District 24), though they are also present in considerable numbers south and west of the Uptown area.

Day wage labor, with its consequent economic insecurity; overcrowded housing; a high rate of transiency; and a low rate of use of city welfare and health agencies are typical of most Indian newcomers to the city. In a later chapter on urban Indians we shall return to a more intensive review of the Chicago Indian population and their socioeconomic position in the city.

Transiency and anonymity of the growing urban Indian population have an important relationship to schooling in the city.

Since transiency is very great both within the city and between the city and "back home" on the reservation or rural areas of former residence, it is rare for an Indian child in the Uptown area to remain in the same school for his entire elementary course. Families may average one move a year. Moving may result from employment opportunity, from family problems, or inability to pay rent regularly.

Unmarried adults move much more frequently than do families. One group of three girls interviewed had moved three times in one week. Men move more frequently than women as they move from job to job.

In examining the Indian population of Chicago, one is impressed by the ease with which an individual can fade out of sight. This phenomenon, coupled with the tremendously high mobility rate, makes it extremely difficult to locate people. An agency, for example, will set up a program for thirty or forty families, but when they get around to doing a follow-up a month or six weeks later, they will only be able to find five or six of the original number. The privacy of persons is guarded by other Indians who will tell inquirers that the family or individual has gone back home, when that family might be living close by and known to be there. School officials attempting to trace truant pupils also have this difficulty in locating families.

The use of multiple surnames also complicates identification and location of pupils. Some children have surnames different from that of their mothers. In some cases there will be three or four surnames in use by siblings and their parents. Sometimes this is due to a previous marriage or to cultural factors in the naming of children. Sometimes this is a deliberate effort to evade bill collectors, or to maintain anonymity in relation to employment agencies and government agencies. The security derived from multiple identities in the city is enormous. They are the final touches to an already bewildering array of defenses against the vicissitudes of life in the city.

Most of the adult Indians in Chicago have not been educated in that city. Those over the age of twenty have generally been educated in reservation or mission schools. Some have also attended public schools near the reservations. Only among the younger people are some who have received their education in urban schools. The majority of the adults have not completed a high school education, the largest number having left school at the eighth- or tenth-grade level.

Although some seven thousand Indians reside in Chicago, only 237 Indian pupils were found to be attending six schools located in the area of highest Indian concentration. These include five elementary schools and one high school:

Goudy	54
Stewart	41
McCutcheon	23
Brenneman	52
Stockton	48
Senn High	19

Urban Indian children are often difficult to identify. In locating Indian pupils our method was to start with children identified as Indian by teachers. There were others with non-Indian facial features, or Anglo last names who became known through their friends and classmates, or who came to us themselves and said they were Indian. Anyone with one fourth or more Indian ancestry was included in the study.

Due to the high transiency rate in the Uptown area, the enrollment numbers for these six schools are not stable. Often before we were able to meet, test, or interview pupils on the roster of a particular school it was discovered that some had transferred to other schools. Senn, the only high school in the sample, had thirty-four known Indian students when the study began in October 1969. However, when interviewing started in January, fifteen were no longer enrolled. Five of these fifteen had transferred to Indian schools outside the city, eight had transferred to other Chicago schools, and two were not attending school. Because of the high rate of absenteeism there was also trouble locating some of the other nineteen. This difficulty in locating pupils was found in other schools as well. In Stockton, an elementary school, there were twenty-one Indian pupils between the fifth and eighth grades. Of these, five rarely attended and could not be contacted and several of the other sixteen were also frequently absent.

The high rate of transfer and absence is not characteristic of the Indian population alone, however, but generally characteristic of inner city schools. In Stockton, where the enrollment is over two thousand, between September and January there were approximately one thousand transfers into or out of school. The other schools in the sample also have high turnover rates.

An interesting fact is that the five elementary schools of the sample feeding into the one high school have 218 pupils in grades one to eight, while the high school had only nineteen whom we could contact in grades nine to twelve, and of these only two were seniors. This difference may be due to in-migration of younger parents with young children and the predominance of a young adult Indian population in Chicago. There are 141 in grades one to four, seventy-seven in grades five to eight, and nineteen in grades nine to twelve. It also may be due in part to a high dropout rate among Indian teen-agers.

Of the ninety-six pupils in grades five to twelve, interviews were held with eighty-six pupils varying in age from eleven to eighteen. Data on a subgroup of twenty-one pupils show the following facts:

Five lived with both parents, eleven lived with a mother, four with a stepfather and a mother, and one with his father.

Students were asked about their feelings toward Indians and non-Indians (whom would you rather play with?). Ten indicated that they liked Indian and non-Indian friends equally well, eight preferred Indians, and two were more interested in non-Indian friends.

The great majority of Indian pupils expressed neutral feelings toward their teachers, or they said they liked most teachers. Only three said they disliked most of their teachers.

More than half of the group said their parents' feelings toward the school were neutral. "I guess they think it's all right." "I don't know; they don't say anything about it." The remainder were equally divided between parents who like the school and parents who don't like the school.

As for parent participation in school affairs, sixteen stated that their parents never visited school or came only when requested to, and five said their parents came to special school affairs.

Knowledge of their tribal language and culture was slight. Almost all of them said they did not know their tribal language, and did not hear it at home. When asked whether they would like to learn to speak their tribal language, three fourths expressed interest. On the other hand, most have no actual plans to do so. Thirteen out of twenty-one said they know nothing of their tribal culture or history. The other eight said they know just a little about tribal history, dances, and culture. Seventeen felt that the culture was worth knowing about. The other four did not care particularly to learn about their tribal background. About half of the group felt that the school should include some study of Indian culture in a history course or in other school work. The other half felt that the school should remain neutral and not include Indian culture in school classes. The younger students were more satisfied with what they were learning in school about Indians than were the older students.

When asked for their general attitude about the school, eight expressed negative feelings, eight thought "school is OK" and five had a more positive attitude. When questioned about their interest in school, two of the twenty-one said they were not interested, two more were neutral, and sixteen expressed a strong interest in certain school activities and classes.

On their perception of the relation of school to adult life, thirteen saw future employment as being the most important outcome of their schooling; four indicated other aspects of life for which the school aided them.

Teachers were asked to rank the students in school achievement in relation to the average class. The ranking for 128 pupils was:

Upper third	31	24 per cent
Middle third	40	31 "
Lower third	57	45 "

The results of the Draw-A-Man Test, a test of mental alertness administered to the Indian children of the Chicago sample indicated that the Indians were above the national average.

In most grade school classrooms, Indian students were not singled out in any way by either students or teachers. Many teachers did not even know they had Indian students. Most teachers seemed to feel that "being an Indian" was not very important to their Indian pupils; at any rate, they did not make much of it. Though not very well informed about Indians in Chicago or Indians in general, and with limited experience with Indian pupils, most of the teachers were well disposed toward Indian pupils, open-minded about them, and interested in understanding their Indian pupils better.

As far as the other pupils were concerned, most did not seem to either know or care that some of their classmates were Indians —at least in the lower grades. All of the schools which Indians attend in Chicago are very diverse ethnically. Though the majority of the pupils are southern white immigrants—"hillbilly," as the children call them—there are also Mexicans, Puerto Ricans, other Spanish Americans, Negroes, Orientals, and a smattering of other groups. Most pupils, with some exceptions, evidently come from working-class or lower-class backgrounds. Most are very transient and, according to several teachers, this leads to one of the major problems faced by a great number of children in these schools—the problem of transferring from one school to another, often in the middle of the school year. This is hard on children emotionally—they have to make new friends—and academically—as the new teacher is further "ahead" or "behind" or simply teaching something different. Moreover, the teacher does not know the child and his problems until she has had him for some time.

As far as the Indian children themselves are concerned, there are different "kinds" of Indian pupils. Some, particularly those who are not of full Indian ancestry, but including some who are, are not very conscious of being Indian. These children may be rather vague about what tribe(s) they "belong to," whether they are "full-blood" or not, etc. They do not go to the Indian Center and generally do not visit much with Indian relatives living in Indian communities or on reservations. Most of their friends are not Indian. They simply may not have gotten to know other Indian children, or they may prefer non-Indian friends.

At the other extreme are those children who are very conscious of being Indian and may feel that others in the school are prejudiced against them. Many of these children and young people have developed their closest friendships with other Indian youngsters at the American Indian Center. They go there for teen dances, athletics, pow-wows, to get help with homework, and, in a few cases, to get needed clothes or food. Most of these children spend part of vacations, especially summer, with Indian relatives in an Indian community. Many have learned Indian dances. Most, with very few exceptions, do not know their tribal language, but are interested in learning it. Many of these children express hopes of leaving Chicago when they grow up to live in an Indian community. One girl was planning to quit school soon and move with two married friends to northern Wisconsin. She is extremely bitter about her school, her mother, the city, and whites in general. On the other hand, another girl, equally bitter about whites and Chicago, replied when asked if she planned to move back to South Dakota, "Are you kidding? What could I do— bale hay?" These girls represent extremes. Even most of those in whom Indian consciousness is well developed are not so bitter toward non-Indians.

The matter of prejudice against Indians was raised by some, however, particularly the older children. Several thought that there was considerable prejudice against Indians, especially by other students. One boy reported that his brother and a friend of his had transferred to another school because they were constantly being drawn into fights. One girl reported that when she first came to her school other children called her "savage." Parents also are concerned with matters of prejudice or interracial problems. There are constant references to problems involving the number of black children in a school or to the claim that "those blond-headed kids beat up on Indians all the time." An especially traumatic occurrence seems to involve Indian children being asked if they are Negro. Sometimes a child is so mortified by this he will refuse to go back to the same school.

Although there is the belief that a high school education can be useful and is sometimes necessary, family life styles do not always support the children in school. Kinship and family obligations frequently require the child to stay home and look after the house or younger siblings while both parents are away. Poverty also contributes to a lack of money for lunch or, especially for the older children attending high school, the lack of money to purchase appropriate clothing. Frequent moves among the more transient groups, accompanied by school transfers, also contribute to difficulties in school.

There is, in addition, among many the lack of trust in higher education as the key to prosperity. Some just don't believe that Indians can get through the higher schools; some point to examples of college graduates who have hit skid row; others feel the pressure for identity with kin and peer groups and an unwillingness to be singled out as one seeking to be better or different, or "becoming a white man." There is a strong tendency for school and the resultant "improving oneself" image to be considered unimportant in Indian eyes, or even in bad form. It is putting oneself above others. Indian youth or young adults, especially after they have had some college, see the difference in values as well as limited opportunity and realize just how difficult it would be for them to go back to their home communities to help improve conditions, which they would like to do. They are torn between a developing sense of altruism and a realization that estrangement from the Indian community may be a price they must pay for an education.

The urban schools have made no special effort to diagnose these problems and provide programs especially for Indian children. This, combined with minimal support from families and peers, contributes to the difficulties faced by Indian youngsters in Chicago.

As noted above, although over two hundred Indian children were attending the five elementary schools studied, a long search turned up only nineteen at the high school level. Why this sharp drop in enrollment at the high school grades? Obviously some drop out of school. Some transfer to other schools, but then some transfer in as well. Some evidently go on to a Bureau of Indian Affairs boarding high school. Two or three transferred to the Institute of American Indian Art in Santa Fe. Two sisters went to Ganado in Arizona. Another girl moved to Wisconsin to live with relatives and go to school there. It is also probable that most Indian families are comparatively young ones, with few children above the age of twelve or fourteen.

All of these possibilities raise some interesting questions. If many drop out, how can schools be made more relevant, interesting, or bearable? If many transfer to all-Indian schools, what does this indicate about the Indians' wishes for integration into "mainstream America"? And what implication does this have for retaining BIA boarding high schools? Finally, if the Indian population is now young, should we not expect to have a substantial increase in the number of Indian pupils in Chicago high schools soon, and if so, are there any special programs or ideas which might respond particularly to their needs as Indians? As of now, there are few Indians in most Chicago schools and no special programs have been developed. If the population continues to grow, the particular needs of Indian pupils in the urban setting require careful consideration.

Although well regarded by their teachers, many Indian children are hampered in school by the absence of strong family and peer support for education, by high transiency rates, and by the absence of special programs designed to meet their needs. In the urban school setting they tend to be merged into the ranks of the "disadvantaged," attend predominantly lower class schools in the inner city, and little attention is paid to their unique characteristics as Indians.

IV

Mental Ability and Mental Development of Indian Children

The way the white man operates, whenever a job opening occurs, all the people interested are given the chance to submit their applications. Or they may express their interest personally, or else have credentials that will speak for themselves. Our ultimate goal should be to educate our children so that their qualifications for any open position will be on equal par with, if not better than, the non-Indian. This is the goal we should strive for.

WHITE MOUNTAIN APACHE speaks, April 12, 1969

We feel our children need education which gives the best of both cultures. We feel that many of the values of our past Cheyenne society can still serve as well in this modern world. We feel we need this to give us understanding and pride in our past, just as other Americans learn their history for the same reason.

JOHN WOODENLEGS, Northern Cheyenne

Two things stand out clearly in any examination of education for Indians. First is the fact that with the exception of a few innovative situations, all schools view themselves as primarily teaching the dominant non-Indian culture. Second, is that while most Indian peoples resist total assimilation, they nevertheless wish the schools to teach the skills required to participate in the dominant cash economy.

Yet despite what would superficially appear to be at least a partial coincidence of goals, the fact remains that Indian children in school do not achieve as high, on the average, when tested in academic subjects such as reading and mathematics as the national average.[1] In the past, scarcity of schooling was an important factor in keeping the educational level of Indians low. However, since World War II, schooling through the secondary level has become available to all and facilities have improved enormously.

But the relatively low academic achievement of Indian pupils remains an issue. The factors which depress school achievement are complex—they involve attention to ability, the family, the school itself, the community. They involve the complexities of culture change in the Indian communities themselves as well as the problems encountered by native Americans in relation to the larger society.

Are Indian children different from the children of other social or racial groups in their ability to perceive, to think, and to learn? There is no reason to suppose that Indian children are basically or genetically less or more intelligent than other children in America. The best evidence is that they are the same at birth, and that their experience in their early years in family and school tend to give them certain advantages and certain disadvantages, compared with children who grow up in other environments.

A number of tests are available to measure children's basic mental abilities independent of their ability to read. These form the basis of intelligence tests for young children, up to the age of seven or eight, when reading ability becomes essential for success with most intelligence tests.

One such test, which has been used widely as a test of mental alertness in a number of countries and simple and complex societies, is the Goodenough Draw-A-Man Test. This requires only a piece of paper and a pencil, and instructions to "draw a man, the best man you can draw." The test is scored by counting the number and accuracy of details in the figure drawn, without reference to esthetic values except that representation of correct body proportions and evidence of good motor coordination earn extra points. The test might be described operationally as one of accuracy of perception, or as a measure of "mental alertness," or attention given to one's environment.

Professor Florence Goodenough published a book on this test in 1926, giving a table of norms from which one can compute a child's IQ. This test works best with children aged six to ten; people do not generally improve much after eleven or twelve, unless they get special training in drawing. The test has been used hundreds of times with children all over the world, and thus permits comparison between ethnic and social groups.

The National Study tested 867 Indian and Eskimo children between the ages of 6 and 8.5 in all of the twenty-five elementary schools in the Study.[2] At the same time, one hundred Caucasian children were tested, who happened to be in the same classrooms with the Indian children—mainly in Chicago. The average IQ for the entire Indian group was found to be 103 for boys and 108 for girls. This is well above the national average for Caucasians. There is also a considerable difference between various communities of Indian children. These results are rather similar to those obtained in 1942 from the same test administered by Havighurst and his colleagues[3] to children from several of the tribes represented in the National Study.

It is also possible to compare Alaskan children of an earlier generation with children from the same communities today. In 1930, Draw-A-Man tests were given by Anderson and Eells to pupils in a number of Alaskan schools, including Bethel.[4] For 155 Eskimo children below thirteen years of age, the 1930 testing gave a DAM IQ of 94, and a Stanford-Binet IQ of 84. This is comparable to the DAM IQ of 103 for 121 Bethel pupils below age 12.5 in 1969.

There are well-standardized *performance* tests of intelligence which do not require reading or word knowledge. These correlate highly with verbal intelligence tests among middle-class urban children. The Grace Arthur Performance Test of Intelligence was given by Havighurst and his colleagues in 1942 (Havighurst and Hilkevitch)[5] to a representative sample of Indian pupils aged six to sixteen from six tribes. They made an average IQ score of 100.2, slightly above the national average for whites. As part of this study, a group of thirty Sioux pupils on the Pine Ridge Reservation made an average IQ score of 102.8, while exactly the same group, tested a year later with the Kuhlmann-

Anderson, a verbal test requiring reading ability, made an average IQ score of 82.5.

There is other evidence that Indian children develop basic mental abilities at the same rate as children from other cultures. The Swiss psychologist Jean Piaget has produced a theory of universal cognitive development in human children. Children develop fundamental concepts of space, number, and other aspects of physical reality in a logical order. Hence their minds develop through stages. Since children of various cultural groups are exposed to the same real physical world, there should be no differences between different groups in their development of concepts of physical reality.

However, environmental differences or differences in the ways various social groups tend to introduce their children to the real physical world through their language and through their handling of objects, etc., might accelerate or slow down the *rate* of development, without changing the *order* of development of concepts.

Gilbert Voyat[6] studied a group of seventy-five Oglala Sioux children aged four to ten, using exactly the same experiments and questions that Piaget had used with Swiss children. He found the same cognitive stages in Indian children that Piaget had found in Swiss children. He also found that these stages succeeded one another at approximately the same ages in the two populations.

He concluded as follows: "This study reveals a deep relationship between Indian and Swiss children. The cognitive stages as well as their succession are found in both populations, and at approximately the same time. It means that the inferiorities shown by IQ tests among Indian children are dependent upon the nature of these tests themselves, in particular their cultural content, since these inferiorities are not found when one analyzes the development of more fundamental concepts."

A number of people have noted what they consider to be unusual ability on the part of native Americans to perceive and to remember aspects of space. Examples are the ability to track animals and men, the ability to find one's way in a trackless wilderness, and the ability to draw a map of an area one has walked over. Judith Kleinfeld of the University of Alaska[7] has noted that Eskimos do very well on tasks that require one to draw figures which have been flashed on a screen for brief intervals, as well as on tests for discovering geometric figures hidden in a complex background. She compared Eskimo with Caucasian students in Alaska on their ability to copy designs from memory and found Eskimo students to be superior. When she asked teachers of village schools in Alaska, she found that 69 per cent of them believed their students showed unusual ability to recall visual details.

Whether this superiority is especially prevalent among Eskimos is not clear, since the performance of Indian students on a variety of tests requiring accurate visual perception tends to be above the average of Caucasian students. Kleinfeld noted that in the Tlingit Indian village of Angoon, children all crowd into the cinema, and they are proud of their ability to remember every detail of a movie. Teachers often comment that Indian children seem to learn especially well from films.

It follows from these considerations that the lower average school achievement of Indian children must be due to factors other than natural ability. School achievement is well known to be related to a child's experience in his family, to his school experience, and to his inherited intellectual ability. Since the Indian children do not differ from other groups of children in their inherited intellectual ability as far as we know, group differences in school achievement must be due to the family, school, or other social factors which affect the lives of Indian children.

V

School Achievement of Indian Children and Youth

Why do Indian children and youth, on the average, do less well than the national average on tests of reading and arithmetic and the other school subjects? We have seen that Indian children show about the same level of alertness as other children, and their lower achievement is not the result of any inherited inferiority.

The evidence on school achievement from several research studies is reported in summary form in Figure 10. These research studies have been made at various times since 1950, with results which confirm each other, except for one study which will be discussed later.

The data reported in Figure 10 place Indian pupils just below the national average during the first four school years, and then they drop substantially. This is shown clearly by Coleman's data in Table 7, which compare several ethnic subgroups with the white non-ethnic majority. Coleman's data are based on the same set of tests given at about the same time to national samples of the various groups.[1] Hence his data are especially useful for purposes of comparison. Coleman's sample of Indian students was not a very good one, since several of the larger Indian tribal groups were not represented. But there is no reason to suppose the Coleman data underestimated the achievement of Indian pupils.

The most extensive and most representative study of Indian school achievement was made by Coombs, *et al.*,[2] during 1951–54. His results are remarkably similar to those of Coleman (in 1965) when allowance is made for the fact that Coombs's data included test scores from about 40 per cent white children in schools in the same areas as those attended by Indian children. The Coombs study gives a table (C-2) which separates the Indian from the white children and shows in almost every area and grade that the white children exceeded the Indian children in the test. Therefore, the grade-level data reported in Figure 10 from the Coombs study would all be reduced (and made more nearly

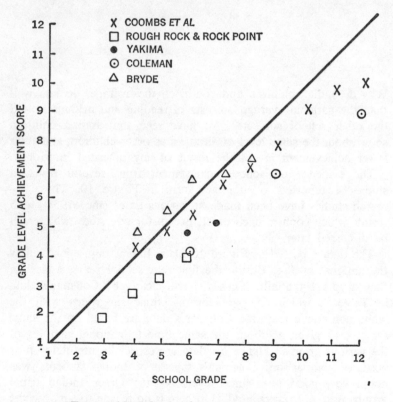

FIGURE 10. *School achievement of Indian pupils*

equivalent to those of Coleman) if scores of non-Indians had been excluded.

One of the reasons for these test results is that a relatively high proportion of Indian pupils are a year or more above the "normal" age for the school grade in which they are placed. This phenomenon is widely reported and was confirmed in nearly all of the schools in the National Study. It results from two facts. First, in BIA reservation schools and many public schools attended by children of non-English speaking families, the child, on entering school at age six, is placed in a "beginner" class for the first year

TABLE 7

TEST SCORES OF MINORITY GROUP CHILDREN

Source: Coleman. *Equality of Educational Opportunity.*
Adapted from Tables 3.121, 1, 2, 3.

Minority Group		Grade Levels Behind White Students of Non-Metropolitan Areas		
	Grade	Verbal Ability	Reading Achievement	Math Achievement
Indian	6	1.3	1.8	1.8
Mexican American	6	1.6	2.2	1.7
Negro	6	1.5	1.8	1.9
Puerto Rican	6	2.3	2.8	2.3
Oriental American	6	0.5	0.7	0.7
Indian	9	1.4	1.9	2.1
Mexican American	9	1.6	2.2	2.3
Negro	9	1.9	2.6	2.5
Puerto Rican	9	2.2	2.9	3.1
Oriental American	9	0.3	0.5	0.1
Indian	12	2.5	2.6	3.0
Mexican American	12	2.5	2.7	3.2
Negro	12	2.8	2.8	4.3
Puerto Rican	12	2.6	3.1	3.9
Oriental American	12	0.6	1.0	0.0

where he concentrates on learning enough English to begin the task of learning to read English. He is promoted to grade one after a year, and therefore is one year overage if he progresses normally after that time. The other fact is that in most school systems many Indian pupils are "held back" one or more times and thus drop further behind the normal age level for a given grade. They are not promoted generally because of much school absence combined with low school achievement.

When Indian pupils are tested on such subjects as reading and arithmetic, and are compared with other children of the same chronological age, they are likely to average below the national norms from the start of their school career. This is seen in the Rough Rock and Rock Point Navajo data in Figure 10. These pupils were one or more years below the national norms as early as the end of their second year of schooling.

There appears to be a single exception to the generalization that Indian pupils average below national norms in measured school achievement. A study reported by John Bryde[3] concerning the achievement test scores of a group of Oglala Sioux pupils on the Pine Ridge Reservation indicates that the Sioux pupils were slightly above national norms at the fourth- and fifth-grade levels, and then their performance dropped to well below national norms at the seventh- and eighth-grade levels. This has been called "the crossover phenomenon," and it has been cited quite widely. The following explanation was proposed by Bryde. The Indian children are progressing very well in school achievement up to about the sixth or seventh grade (the age of puberty), when they become more keenly aware of being "Indian" with a consequent feeling of rejection or alienation which saps their self-confidence and their desire to achieve. As a result, they cease trying to do well in school, and therefore show the dramatic "crossover" effect.

If this is so, it would be quite unusual, from the points of view of educational practice and theory, that this minority group, growing up in families which speak little or no English and generally do not read to their children or otherwise assist them in getting the basic school skills, produced children who were at or above the national norm from age nine or ten to age twelve or fourteen, after which they dropped sharply in school achievement.

Since this finding was so exceptional in research, we decided to analyze the data presented in Dr. Bryde's thesis. Bryde presents California Achievement Test data on 147 eighth-grade Indian pupils in the Pine Ridge school who came from eight elementary schools on the Pine Ridge Reservation. These pupils averaged 7.5 grade equivalent in the autumn of their eighth-grade year, when the national norm was 8.2. Many of them were a year or more overage for their school grade.

Bryde searched the school records in the eight elementary schools from which these students came, and found California Achievement Test data for 119, 73, 107, and 65 of these pupils for grades 7, 6, 5, and 4 respectively. He reported their average grade equivalents for these four grades as follows: 7.0, 6.7, 5.7, and 4.9 respectively.

There is an important unanswered question entangled in Bryde's data. He had test scores from 147 eighth graders, but only 65 of these had test data for the fourth grade. Were these 65 truly representative of the 147 eighth graders? Would it not have been wiser to sort out the 65 fourth-grade pupils and study their eighth-grade scores, so as to find out whether the 65 fourth graders exhibited the "crossover effect"? Again, the question occurs, were the original 65 fourth graders a representative sample of Pine Ridge fourth graders?

In Bryde's summary of research data on the school achievement of Sioux children, most of the studies he reports found that Sioux children were substantially below white children in the same areas on the tests. Only two references indicated that Sioux students scored at or above national norms on such tests. These both came from Aberdeen, South Dakota. One was an unpublished master's thesis and the other was a report from the Education Branch of the Aberdeen Area Office of the Bureau of Indian Affairs. These referred to scores on the California Achievement Test, given in a number of different schools. Since these studies go counter to the others in the same geographical area, it is unfortunate that the testing procedures, the ages of the pupils, the numbers of pupils in the grade but not tested, etc., are not available for careful study. No other study of measured school achievement of Indian pupils has shown a fourth- or fifth-grade group to be above national norms.

Since a variety of careful research studies have failed to confirm the existence of a "crossover phenomenon," we believe that the usual finding concerning the low school achievement of Indian children should be credited.

This is not to say that alienation and lack of self-confidence do not affect individual Indian youth in school performance and in other ways. But their school performance is probably negatively affected by environmental factors well before the age of puberty, and we shall now consider the possible influence of some of these environmental factors.

It is well known that achievement in school subjects is correlated with the pupils' family backgrounds. In studies of the various factors that determine school achievement, the socioeconomic status of the family proves to be more influential than the characteristics of the school. However, in cases where the family cannot help the pupil much, school may actually compensate to some extent.

There are several reasons for family background being a handicap in relation to school achievement of many Indian pupils in an American school. The first reason is that the great majority of Indian pupils are reared in poverty-stricken families, and poverty is generally a disadvantage for school achievement. Also, with the exception of a growing minority of Indians, most Indian families have very little formal education and therefore Indian children are far more dependent upon the school for academic instruction than children whose families are in a position to assist them in this area.

Many Indian families provide a non-English language environment which does not favor achievement in schools as they are presently oriented since almost all school curriculum is presently organized around English as a language of instruction. Conditions of poverty and illiteracy are not conducive to providing facilities which help children in school such as books, encyclopedias, and space for quiet study. In addition, the use of formal education for earning a living has not ordinarily been apparent in many Indian communities, although this is changing as employment opportunies for educated Indians increase.

These conditions strongly suggest that the average school

achievement of the children of poor families will be substantially lower than that of children of middle-class families, unless the schools perform more effectively than at present to make up for what the pupil does not get from his family and community.

Another reason family background influences school success for many Indian pupils is that the family's Indian culture can be discontinuous with the demands of schooling. We speak here of a general "Indian" culture rather than the scores of separate tribal cultures. While there is diversity among the various tribal cultures, there are certain characteristics which tend to be the same among all Indian cultures, and different from the urban-industrial culture of the larger surrounding society. These include close family solidarity and cooperation with mutual support among the kinfolk, cooperation rather than competition among members of a given age group, belief in the values of a tribal tradition, belief in tribal religion, and a tribal language.

Valuable as these qualities and characteristics are for the maintenance of the Indian cultures, they sometimes conflict with the competitive, individualistic achievement demands of the school. There is, of course, a wide variation in the extent to which these characteristics apply to any particular Indian community. Many tribal groups have all but lost their tribal language and their tribal religion. Some groups have adopted many of the economic practices and skills of the surrounding white culture. In general, however, the great majority of Indian children grow up in families where Indian cultural values predominate. (In Chapters X and XI we shall return to a more detailed view of how these conflicts express themselves in school.)

All Indian children are affected by their Indian culture and by the culture of the white society that surrounds them. They may be torn between the two cultures; they may favor one culture and reject the other; they may work out some tolerable combination of the two. Although people may participate in two cultures which are quite different and even contradictory in some respects, they have the ability to compartmentalize their behavior into separable roles which can coexist within a single life. It is this capacity that allows a person to live as a man of two cultures.

In the National Study of American Indian Education, student

attitudes toward Indian and white cultures were measured with a Semantic Differential Inventory which asked for ratings on Indian culture as a combination of the concepts *My Home, Indians,* and *Tribe's Way of Life;* and on white culture through combined ratings on *White People's Way of Life, This School,* and *Teachers.* Probably the measure for adjustment to Indian culture has greater validity than that for adjustment to white culture, since the school and the teachers may be so much a part of the local community that the child does not see them as part of white culture.

Ratings for Indian and white cultures, in Table 8, show that five of six Indian groups rated Indian culture more positively than white culture, and for two of these groups—Minnesota-Wisconsin and urban Indians—the differences in ratings are statistically reliable. However, the Southwest Indians showed no difference and the Oklahoma Indians rated white culture slightly more positively than Indian culture.

TABLE 8

MEAN RATINGS FOR
"WHITE CULTURE" AND "INDIAN CULTURE"
FOR INDIAN AND NON-INDIAN STUDENTS

(Lower score is more favorable rating)

Area	(N)	White Culture	Indian Culture	Indian-White Difference	Significance of Difference
Plains Indians	495	2.13	1.94	.19	N.S.
Southwest Indians	759	2.04	2.04	.00	N.S.
Northwest Indians and Eskimos	329	1.90	1.79	.11	N.S.
Minnesota-Wisconsin Indians	182	2.40	1.89	.51	p<.05
Oklahoma Indians	56	1.97	2.14	—.17	N.S.
Urban Indians	114	2.66	1.91	.75	p<.025
Non-Indian Controls	167	1.87	2.43	—.56	p<.05

The non-Indian control group rated white culture significantly higher than Indian culture, as would be expected.

The urban Indian group apparently had a stronger sense of differentiation between white and Indian cultures than did the other Indian groups. Perhaps they had a clearer sense of what might be called cultural boundaries and a clearer perception of cultural differences with an accompanying view of themselves as more definitely belonging to one culture and not to the other.

Another line of evidence on this matter is provided by a study of the correlation between self-esteem of Indian students and their attitudes toward white and Indian cultures, which is reported in Table 9. It was thought that the coefficient of correlation between scores on self-esteem and on attitudes toward Indian and white culture would be higher for the culture with which the Indian students identified more closely.

The correlation coefficients for the large group of Indian students who lived mainly in Indian communities indicate two things. First, there was a consistently positive relationship beween the self-esteem and the attitudes toward culture ratings, of the order of 0.4. There was no consistent sex difference. Second, there was a tendency for the correlation coefficient to rise with age for Indian culture (.34 to .45) while it decreased for white culture (.40 to .29).

For urban Indians, the correlation coefficients with Indian culture are consistently high (over .40) while those with white culture are much lower. This confirms the interpretation given to the data in Table 8, that urban Indian youth feel more alienation from the white culture than do the Indian youth who are geographically more isolated from the white culture.

It did not appear from these attitude studies that there was much sense of what some call alienation from either Indian or white cultures among the Indian students, except for urban Indians. For the majority of Indian students there is a substantial positive relationship between self-acceptance as measured by the self-esteem instruments and acceptance of both white and Indian cultures. It appeared that most Indian adolescent students viewed themselves as belonging about equally to both cultures which they tended to evaluate favorably.

TABLE 9

RELATION OF SELF-ESTEEM TO
ATTITUDES TOWARD WHITE AND INDIAN CULTURES

(Product-moment correlation coefficients, by age groups and types
of student groups)

					Age Groups										
	8–11			12–14			15–17			18–20		
Group	(N)	White	Indian	(N)	White	Indian	(N)	White	Indian	(N)	White	Indian
General Indian Group	(281)	.40	.34	(625)	.37	.36	(543)	.30	.43	(316)	.29	.45
Urban Indians	(21)	−.04	.49	(81)	.28	.46	(12)	.07	.38			
Non-Indian Controls	(63)	.51	.12	(47)	.43	.43	(57)	.34	.33			

Note: Correlation coefficients between self-esteem and attitude
toward the culture named at the top of the column.

A recent research in the Pine Ridge Sioux Reservation throws light on the family and tribal factor in the school achievement of Sioux Indian adolescents. Bernard Spilka[4] studied Indian students and their parents, and made a limited parallel study of white adolescents in the communities near the reservation. He devised a set of questionnaires to measure a complex entity which he called "alienation." This includes feelings of powerlessness, lack of hope for the future, lack of attachment to school and other institutions, and lack of standards to denote right and wrong.

Scores on his alienation instrument correlate with SES—high alienation going with low SES. Also, comparison of Indian and white students showed the Indians to have higher alienation scores. But the Indian students had lower socioeconomic status scores than the white students. Hence, the difference between the groups was apparently due to a mixture of Indianness and low SES. Spilka says:

> In the present work Indianness and socioeconomic status are often confounded. Their effects are obviously additive such that being Indian and in poorer economic circumstances go together. Combined effects are most evident in the domains of intelligence, achievement and alienation. Making certain assumptions which appear to possess some validity, an effort has been made to show the relative contribution of SES and Indianness to ability and attitudinal factors of significance in school. The results are essentially inconclusive with some suggestion that being Indian may affect measures of IQ more than low SES, while the latter may be of greater importance in the achievement realm. Even these inferences may go beyond the data. . . . If anything can be gleaned from these observations, it may be that educational innovations will have to consider equally the economic and ethnic-cultural state of the Oglala Sioux. Were the class status and job opportunities of these people to improve, the role of Indian cultural influences would also change. The likelihood of graphic change in ethnic status is probably even poorer than the probability of great economic variation, thus posing a continuing extremely serious situation for the schools, educators, Indian children and their parents.

Another way to evaluate the school achievement of Indian youth is to study their staying power in high school. Graduating from high school and going to college are marks of successful growth for young people in the dominant democratic industrial society. However, since some of the more stable Indian cultures do not provide roles for high school graduates on the reservations or in the home community, there is some question how valid the extent of high school graduation is for evaluating the educational system.

Nevertheless, nearly everybody seems to believe dropout rates are important, and therefore it is useful to have accurate data on them. Fortunately, there are fairly good data on graduation from high school among Indian youth—much better than the data for other minority groups. It has always been difficult to get valid school dropout or high school graduation data, because so many young people transfer from one school to another, or drop out for a semester or a year and then return to school, and schools rarely keep track of the students who leave without graduating. Thus there is a wild assortment of figures, and as a result one can usually find figures to suit his prejudices.

A report to the Senate Subcommittee Hearings on Indian Education said, "Most surveys have estimated the national dropout rate for Indian school children in all types of schools to be 60 per cent."[5] Yet two very careful studies of dropout rates were completed in 1968 and gave lower dropout rates. The Northwest Regional Educational Laboratory studied the Indian students in a sample of eighth grades in six northwestern states in 1962. The eighth-grade students were identified by name. Each one of these young people was followed for five years or until he graduated from high school, or dropped out of school, or died. The high school graduation rate for this group was 52 per cent.[6] A parallel study was made in six southwestern states by the Southwest Cooperative Regional Educational Laboratory. The high school graduation rate for this group of eighth-grade students was 61 per cent.[7] If we average the graduation rates from the studies, we get a rate of 57 per cent, or a dropout rate of 43 per cent.

This graduation rate of 57 per cent compares with a national rate of approximately 77 per cent at about 1967. The graduation rates for other disadvantaged minority groups are not known with any exactitude, but they are probably no higher than the Indian rate.

The conclusion seems necessary that Indian students are handicapped in their school achievement by poverty. Actions taken by the government to assist Indian groups to work out the problem of poverty are almost sure to result in improved school achievement by Indian children. But such actions are also very likely to result in greater acculturation of Indian people to the surrounding urban and industrial culture.

It is inevitable that Indian groups should feel some strain, in this situation. However, the Indian students do not appear to be in much danger of emotional stress. On the whole, the evidence indicates that given the opportunities, they possess the strength and mental health to resolve these problems.

VI

The Mental Health of Indian Youth[1]

As in so many other aspects of Indian life, tremendous misconceptions abound concerning mental health. For example the coordinator of an Indian studies program at a western state college published a paper not long ago in which he said, "Most Indians have a very low self-concept. . . . The schools are geared to educating white middle class students, so that Indians do not do well and their ideas of inferiority are reinforced. . . . Like other people, Indians do not like to fail; thus, rather than take a chance on failure in an institution where there is little chance for him to succeed, the Indian student refuses to compete and thus never obtains a college education."

This is so typical of the perception of many sympathetic white observers who come into contact with Indian youth in college that we purposely do not identify the author. This is the explanation that contemporary educators commonly give to explain why Indian students have, on the average, achieved poorly in high school and college by the usual academic standards.

Yet this is not an accurate or adequate statement of the state of mind of Indian young people, according to the facts we have learned in the National Study and according to our critical reading of the work of others who have reported on this situation. The implication of the statements quoted above is that Indian youth have poor mental health—a "low self-concept." It has been stated repeatedly that the suicide rate among Indians is very high, with the implication that this signified poor mental health. This also is an error, both of fact and interpretation.

While the attitudes of Indian youth toward education, *on the average,* are rather unfavorable for good academic achievement, the reasons for this are *not* that Indian young people feel inferior, depressed, and powerless in a general sense, which is the erroneous impression gained by some people.

Accordingly, we have investigated the mental health of about two thousand young people in the communities which we have studied. We have used the methods of the social psychologist— not those of the clinical psychologist or the psychiatrist.

These methods consist of asking young people how they feel about themselves and their future. It is expected that the answers to these questions will tell us whether Indian youth feel good or bad about themselves. Since similar methods have been used to study youth of other groups, comparisons can be made of Indians with these other groups. Admittedly, these methods are open to the objection that the young people who answer the questions may attempt to "cover up" their real feelings by answering the way they think other people would like to have them answer. This objection has been considered carefully in a number of studies where the individual's actual behavior could be compared with his written responses to such questions, and the general result is to confirm the validity of the social-psychological method, with the qualification that a minority of the respondents do respond untruthfully, and with the further qualification that the respondent must be able to read and understand the questions he is asked about himself. Since Indian youth, on the average, read below the national average level, it is important to watch carefully for this kind of difficulty. Consequently, we did not "test" anybody below the fifth-grade level, and we built in a check for consistency of response to one of our instruments by presenting several questions twice, in slightly different forms, and looking for inconsistent responses. We discarded some 20 per cent of the student protocols on this basis.

Defining Mental Health and Self-Concept

We define good mental health as a combination of the following qualities: the person perceives himself positively, he has a realistic perception of the world around him, he has the ability to be a part of society and still maintain his individuality, he has an integrated personality, including a purpose and meaning in life, tolerance for stress, and ability to recover from setbacks.

Clearly, the concept a person has of himself is relevant to his mental health. Therefore we studied the self-concept of Indian youth, or their self-esteem, with two social-psychological instruments. A Self-Esteem Inventory, and a Semantic Differential Inventory. These are both aimed at discovering and evaluating the respondent's "phenomenal self," which is a person's conscious awareness of who he is and how he stands in relation to his total environment. It is a global perception by a person of his or her relationship to the world of persons, objects, and institutions around him. It is not meant to designate a person's unconscious personality style, which is sometimes referred to as his "ego."

The Self-Esteem Inventory consisted of twenty statements which each respondent was asked to check as "like me" or "not like me." Examples are:

> I think I'm as good as anybody else.
> I usually do the wrong things.

This gave a possible range of scores from zero, indicating low self-esteem, to twenty, indicating high self-esteem.

The Semantic Differential Inventory asked the respondent to rate the concepts "myself" and "my future" on a set of seven adjective-pair scales like the following:

Good ⌞____|____|____|____|____|____⌟ Bad

The other six adjective pairs were: worthless-valuable, happy-unhappy, weak-strong, lazy-active, smart-dumb, and friendly-unfriendly.

A score of 1 was given for a respondent who rated himself at the extreme positive end of a scale, and other scores from 2 to 6 were given to ratings at the other positions of the scale. The average of ratings for "myself" on all seven scales was taken as a measure of the self-concept.

We also studied with the Semantic Differential test the attitudes of Indian youth toward their school, teachers, Indians, the Indian way of life, and the white man's way of life.

There were two measures of the self-concept—one from the Self-Esteem Inventory, and one from the Semantic Differential. These were combined by a simple statistical procedure into a third "combined self" score with a range from 3, indicating low self-esteem, to a high of 40, indicating high self-esteem.

Results of the study of self-esteem and self-concept will be reported here in two ways. The first will be a comparison of the Indian data on the Semantic Differential with data from a number of other groups which are comparable in age, who responded to these same semantic differential items during recent years. This permits a test of the hypothesis that Indian young people are similar in self-esteem to other well-defined groups of young people.[2]

The second report will present relationships of the combined-self scores to age, sex, and tribal group within the Indian groups who were studied in the National Study of American Indian Education.

Comparison of Indians with Other Groups in Self-Concept

Boys and girls from the ages of twelve through seventeen were asked to rate the concept "myself" on the following adjective scales: good-bad, happy-sad, strong-weak, and active-lazy. These four scales were used for this comparison, because the same scales had been used with similar groups as follows:

Chicago Working-Class Students. In 1961, a group of fifty boys and fifty girls in the eighth and eleventh grades of a Chicago suburb were tested. These students were all from upper working-class families.[3]

Buenos Aires Students. In 1961, fifty boys and fifty girls in Buenos Aires were given the same form of the SD that was given in Chicago, but in a Spanish version. They, too, were from upper working-class families.[4]

Puerto Rican Students. In 1967–68, a field study was made by Professor Guy Manaster at the University of Puerto Rico, which was parallel to the Chicago-Buenos Aires study. An upper working-class sample was given the SD, in the Spanish version. The students were from the cities of San Juan and Ponce, and from a rural area in central Puerto Rico.

Chicago and Colorado White Students (Controls). White students in the same schools with Indian students that were studied by the Colorado and Chicago research teams in the National Study were asked to respond to the SD so that their scores might be used for comparison purposes. There were fifty-two boys and fifty-two girls, aged twelve to seventeen.

Rees-Virginia White Students. The SD was administered by Miss Martha Rees of the Colorado research staff to a group of high school students in a Virginia middle-class suburb of Washington, D.C. There were twenty-five boys and twenty-five girls.

Kansas City Maladjusted Boys. In 1964, a group of fourteen- to fifteen-year-old boys in the Kansas City public schools were given a form of the SD which was comparable with the form used in this study. There were approximately three hundred boys, all screened out in the seventh grade as possible dropouts and delinquents. These boys were studied through the following years, and assessed at the age of about eighteen as belonging in one or the other of two categories: adaptive and maladaptive—127 in the first and 150 in the second category. These are only comparative terms, since the adaptive group was barely at the level of minimal competence in school and at work. Thus this study provides us with two comparison groups of boys who were visibly maladjusted at the ages of thirteen and fourteen, and with marginal adjustment or serious maladjustment at the age of eighteen.[5]

Table 10 shows how the Indian youth as a group compared with several non-Indian groups. The non-Indians were all from working-class homes except for the Rees-Virginia group, who were mainly middle class. As is shown in the table, the Indians do not differ much from the other groups in their average scores. All groups have a rather favorable self-concept, since the range of possible scores is 1 to 6, with low scores indicating a favorable self-concept.

The most directly comparable groups are the Chicago-Colorado "controls" and the Chicago and Plains Indians. (Chicago and Plains Indians are included in the larger group labeled "Indian.") The "controls" are the non-Indian students in the same schools and classes with the Indian youth who were studied. For boys the average self-evaluation score is 2.06 for the controls and 2.11 and 2.16 for Plains and Chicago Indians respectively. These differences are not statistically significant. For girls, the controls have an average score of 2.07, while the Plains and Chicago Indian female groups are 2.19 and 2.38 respectively. These differences are statistically reliable, but not great enough to make much practical difference.

We may summarize the comparisons of Indian boys and girls with Anglo-American youth as follows. There is no reliable difference, on the average, between Indian boys and Anglo-American boys of the same socioeconomic level. For girls there is a slight but statistically reliable difference, the Anglo-American girls rating themselves more favorably.

The Latin-American scores show a relatively large sex difference, with boys giving a more positive picture of themselves than girls do. We would interpret this hypothetically as a correlate of the often-stated Latin-American belief in male superiority. Latin-American boys rate themselves more positively than Indian boys and Anglo-Americans, but Latin-American girls rate themselves at about the same level as Indian girls do, and below Anglo-American girls.

Table 10 also indicates that the Indian boys and girls have about the same level of self-evaluation (on this instrument) as Anglo-American boys and girls. For boys we have a set of comparison scores from Kansas City, from boys who were definitely maladjusted, and were rejected by their teachers and by many of their age mates. These boys have definitely more negative self-evaluation than the other Anglo-American boys, and definitely more negative self-concepts than the Indian boys.

Thus the evidence from the Semantic Differential Inventory when used to compare the self-evaluation of Indian with non-

TABLE 10

COMPARISON OF GROUP MEAN SCORES ON THE SEMANTIC DIFFERENTIAL "MYSELF", AGE 12–17

MALES

Group:	Anglo-American					Latin-American		
	Chicago 1961	Chicago-Colorado 1969	Kansas City 1964 Controls	Adap. Mal.	Virginia-D.C. 1970	Buenos Aires 1961	Puerto Rico 1968	Indian 1969
Number:	*50*	*52*	*127*	*150*	*25*	*50*	*150*	*743*
Good-Bad	2.18	1.94	2.41	2.64	1.43	1.69	1.54	2.12
Happy-Sad	1.52	1.97	2.18	2.52	1.68	1.66	1.61	1.84
Strong-Weak	2.16	2.23	2.30	2.36	1.81	2.05	2.25	2.08
Active-Lazy	1.73	2.11	2.26	2.52	2.17	2.00	1.94	2.21
Average	1.90	2.06	2.29	2.51	1.77	1.85	1.84	2.06

FEMALES

Group:	Chicago 1961	Anglo-American Chicago-Colorado 1969	Kansas City 1964 Controls Adap. Mal.	Virginia-D.C. 1970	Latin-American Buenos Aires 1961	Puerto Rico 1968	Indian 1969
Number:	50	52		25	50	150	750
Good-Bad	1.81	2.02		1.65	1.87	1.72	2.11
Happy-Sad	1.79	1.63		1.72	1.86	2.12	1.95
Strong-Weak	2.58	2.30		2.35	2.92	3.17	2.45
Active-Lazy	1.72	2.15		2.30	1.95	2.25	2.33
Average	1.98	2.07		2.01	2.15	2.32	2.21

Note: The low score is the more favorable response.

Indian teen-agers of comparable socioeconomic status, indicates that the Indians have about the same level of rather favorable self-evaluation as non-Indians. When the self-evaluations of Indian boys are compared with those of distinctly maladjusted groups of Anglo-American boys, the Indian boys appear to be in a relatively favorable situation.

Further light may be cast on the problem of mental health of Indian youth by comparisons between and among Indian groups. For this, we have the "combined self" scores, a combination of scores from the Semantic Differential and the Self-Esteem Inventory (Table 11).

While most self-concept studies show stability from one age to another for white subjects, some Indian studies claim to have found a kind of "adolescent crisis" phenomenon among American Indians; i.e., a drop in level of personal-social adjustment, school achievement, and self-esteem that occurs about the beginning of adolescence. The Indian adolescent, according to this view, is caught in a cultural conflict between his native Indian culture and the dominant white culture; he has few adult role models, suffers from what the psychoanalyst Erik Erikson calls "identity diffusion," and exhibits clinical symptoms of alienation and depression.

To examine this hypothesis, the National Study divided the "combined self" data into four age groups—preadolescent group, ages eight to eleven; and three adolescent groups, ages twelve to fourteen, fifteen to seventeen, and eighteen to twenty. The comparison of these groups is shown in Table 11.

The data in Table 11 indicate a tendency for the Indian groups to drop slightly in self-esteem score between the ages of eight to eleven and twelve to fourteen, but the non-Indian controls also dropped. Between ages twelve to fourteen and fifteen to seventeen, there is a slight tendency for the self-esteem scores to rise. Thus the hypothesis of a decrease in self-esteem at adolescence is not confirmed for the Indian youth in this study.[6]

Looking at age changes in the two sexes, it is apparent that Indian girls were more likely than boys to show a significant decrease in self-esteem from preadolescence to adolescence. Thus, if the adolescent crisis hypothesis holds at all, it would appear to be a more accurate description of girls than boys. It may also be

TABLE 11
AVERAGE "COMBINED SELF" SCORES FOR AGE GROUPS BY SEX

Group	Age:	MALE				FEMALE			
		8–11	12–14	15–17	18–20	8–11	12–14	15–17	18–20
Plains Indians		26.8	27.2	26.1	26.5	27.9	24.5	24.9	26.5
Southwest Indians		26.9	24.9	26.2	25.9	26.6	23.8	24.4	23.8
Northwest Indians and Eskimos		28.6*	26.5	27.3	29.3	24.7*	23.9	24.5	27.3
Minnesota-Wisconsin Indians		25.1*	27.1	26.0	–	27.5*	23.7	26.5*	–
Urban Indians		26.5*	25.9	23.8*	–	24.4*	25.3	23.3*	–
Non-Indian Controls		29.7	28.0	28.8	–	31.2	30.0	28.0	–

* Number of subjects is less than 20; score is unreliable.

noted that Indian boys tend to rate themselves higher than Indian girls do, at ages twelve to seventeen. To some extent, this is due to the presence in the Semantic Differential of the adjective pair "strong-weak," on which boys rate themselves much more positively than girls do. However, there seems also to be a tendency for the Indian girls to be more self-critical and self-doubting than the Indian boys, on the self-concept instruments.

The attitude which a person has toward his future is often noted as one indication of his state of mental health. For Indian youths, who are members of one of America's most neglected and impoverished minority groups, there is reason to expect that the future might be seen as a time of uncertainty and doubt. To test this hypothesis, the Indian youths were asked to rate "my future" across the same adjective pairs in the Semantic Differential as were used in rating "myself." The results are shown in Table 12.

It is clear that all groups of Indian students rated their future more positively than their present self. This trend was consistent across all age groups for both sexes. These results would seem to indicate that Indian students looked toward the future with feelings of optimism and hope, as a time when they expected that life would be better than it was in the present and as a time

TABLE 12

MEAN SCORES FOR
CONCEPTS "MYSELF" AND "MY FUTURE" FOR INDIAN
STUDENT GROUPS AND NON-INDIAN CONTROLS

(Lower score is more positive rating)

	N	"Myself"	"My Future"
Plains Indians	495	2.12	1.86
Southwest Indians	759	2.30	1.98
Northwest Indians and Eskimos	329	2.12	1.63
Minnesota-Wisconsin Indians	185	2.37	1.80
North Carolina Indians	57	1.70	1.37
Oklahoma Indians	65	2.26	1.78
Urban Indians	114	2.29	1.76
Non-Indian Controls	167	1.92	1.56

when their personal aspirations would be fulfilled. In no sense do these data indicate a feeling of what some researchers have termed alienation or a view of the future as a time of hopelessness and frustration. There appeared to be no difference between the comparative views of the Indian students and the non-Indian controls in this regard. Both groups saw the future significantly more positively than the present, and neither appeared to be alienated in the sense of looking upon the future pessimistically.

It is now appropriate to consider the mental health implications of these data for Indian youth. We have seen that there is little or no drop in self-esteem scores between the age groups eight to eleven and twelve to fourteen. We have seen that the differences between boys and girls in self-esteem scores do not appear to have any mental health implications.

What, then, do the self-esteem data signify? If the data are reliable and if the data possess validity, we believe that they tell us: How the Indian youth perceives and evaluates his "phenomenological self" and how comfortable the Indian youth feels in his present situation. This feeling is influenced by the support he gets from his age mates; the emotional support he gets from his family and neighbors; and the support he gets from his teachers or employers or other adults with whom he comes into contact.

The self-esteem data reflect the *social adjustment* of Indian youths rather than their *mental health* as a psychiatrist would use the term. We doubt that any paper and pencil test would give valid information about the mental health of Indian adolescents in the psychiatric sense.

Our conclusion is that the self-esteem and self-concept data from our study indicate that the great majority of Indian youths see themselves as fairly competent persons within their own social world. This social world is characterized for the majority of these young people by Indianness and by poverty. If they come into contact with expectations by teachers or others from the social world of the urban-industrial and middle-class society, we should expect them to show some doubts about their competence, and we should expect their self-esteem score to be lowered. One of the most frequent assertions of self-concept theorists is that the level of self-esteem is determined by the social context in which the individual exists. The individual comes to know his "self" as it is defined by "significant others" around him, and once a self-concept is firmly rooted it is evaluated according to the responses the individual receives from the "significant others" he later encounters. The level of so-called "self-esteem" then is based upon the individual's perception of himself in relation to others around him and their responses to him. Soares and Soares[7] used such an explanation to account for the fact that so-called "disadvantaged" youngsters had higher self-esteem ratings than "advantaged" youngsters when they were in elementary school with their "disadvantaged" peers, since the "disadvantaged" students judged themselves in relation to their peers within the homogeneous group. In high school, when the disadvantaged youngsters entered a heterogeneous social environment, the Soareses found that the self-esteem ratings of the disadvantaged students decreased, resulting, they explained, from the change in reference group from the homogeneous disadvantaged environment of early years to the heterogeneous environment of high school years. Such findings led the National Study to test out these notions by checking the self-esteem ratings of the Indian students against their status in school, namely, whether the Indian student was in a homogeneous environment or whether he was part of a small minority within a heterogeneous environment. The hypothesis was that minority group Indian students would have lower self-esteem ratings than majority group Indian students.

To test this hypothesis the data were divided by schools into four groups, two groups where the Indian students were less than 25 per cent of the total school population, urban and rural-small city schools; and two groups where the Indian students were more than 80 per cent of the school population, rural-small city and boarding schools.

The average "combined self" scores for the first two groups are 25.4 and 25.7 respectively, while the score for Indian students when they were in the clear majority is 26.9, thus confirming the hypothesis. However, the average score for Indian students in all-Indian boarding schools is 24.8, the lowest of the four scores. This average is made up of scores from six boarding schools, which differ among themselves in student characteristics. The school with the highest combined self score was Chemawa (Oregon), where most of the students come from Alaska because there were no secondary schools in their home regions. Thus they were a "normal" group of elementary school graduates from Alaska. This school, if treated alone, would confirm the hypothesis. But several of the other boarding schools were mainly composed of students who had not made a good academic adjustment in the local schools, or who had been sent by courts or social agencies because their parents had neglected them, or who had shown behavior problems in their local schools. These students might be expected to show low self-esteem.

The statement that Indian youths suffer from poor mental health has received a limited and ambiguous support from certain studies made with personality tests, which themselves have questionable validity as applied to Indian or other ethnic minority groups. Studies made with the Rorschach test indicate some degree of personality deviation from the average Anglo-American type, on the part of Indian and other groups which have their own cultures and cultural personalities and are under pressure to participate in the surrounding modern industrial culture. This personality deviation is described by some people as poor mental health, while others see it as a form of personality that differs from the standard American form but is not necessarily unhealthy.

Another personality test, the Minnesota Multiphasic Personality Inventory, has been used with Indian adolescents on the Pine Ridge Sioux Reservation by Bryde[8] who concluded that when this group was compared with white adolescents from the same area, "the Indian groups consistently and significantly revealed themselves as feeling more rejected, depressed, withdrawn, paranoid, as well as more socially, emotionally and self-alienated."[9]

There is much doubt concerning the validity of the Minnesota Multiphasic Personality Inventory for use with Indian adolescents as a group. The MMPI was created for use in diagnosing adults who might suffer from psychosis. Then it was applied to normal groups of people as a test of tendencies of groups of people toward various kinds of deviant behavior. Though not designed for use with adolescents, it has been used as a group test to compare various groups of adolescents with respect to delinquency and to other forms of deviant behavior. But its validity and its value for use with adolescents to determine their mental health status has been seriously questioned.

The Minnesota Multiphasic Personality Inventory is especially open to criticism as a measure of the Indian adolescent's feelings about himself because many of the items are expressed in language which is difficult for poor readers to understand. Therefore when given to Indian youths in the eighth or ninth grades, it generally lacks validity. This is seen in the fact that the F-scale, which is designed to discover respondents who (quoting the authors of the test) were "careless or unable to comprehend items," shows many high scores for the Indian adolescents and therefore indicates that the MMPI is not valid for use with these young people.[10]

Suicide is another widely discussed phenomenon. The fact of suicide is so disturbing to most people that they tend to give it more significance as a measure of group mental health than it deserves. Therefore, if two or three suicides take place on or near a given Indian reservation, this fact is given lurid headlines in the newspapers and the inference is drawn, explicitly or implicitly, that the Indian group suffers from poor mental health.

Yet the number of Americans who commit suicide in any given year is 10.8 out of 100,000. If a certain section of the United States shows a suicide rate as high as 22 per 100,000 (which is approximately the rate in the state of California) it hardly seems appropriate to conclude that the mental health of Californians is below that of other Americans. Furthermore, the three countries with highest suicide rates are Denmark, Austria, and Japan, while three countries with very low rates are Egypt, Ireland, and Mexico. Again, this fact hardly seems to justify the proposition that the first group of countries has poorer mental health than the second group.

The report of the U. S. Senate Subcommittee on Indian Education[11] contains several descriptions of suicide among Indian youths, and a number of references to these facts by senators and other commentators which imply that these facts demonstrate a condition of social pathology and poor mental health. Accordingly, we have examined these data, as well as other data on suicide in the United States.

The Public Health Service reports that the suicide rate for Indians of all ages is about 11 per 100,000, little different from that of the total population of the United States.[12] This figure is fairly stable from year to year for the total United States population, but it fluctuates somewhat for Indians, probably because the numbers are small. For the years from 1959 through 1966, the actual number of suicides reported for Indians ranged from 59 to 72, with an average of 63.5. It is this average over an eight-year period which is the basis for the figure given above—11 per 100,000.

Thus, an overall comparison of Indian and non-Indian suicide rates indicates that there is practically no total difference. But there are significant differences between Indians and others with respect to age and sex.

The Indian suicide rates are higher for adolescents and young adults than are the rates for non-Indians; but this is balanced by a lower Indian suicide rate for people aged forty-five or over. This is seen in Table 13.

TABLE 13

SUICIDE RATES FOR INDIANS AND ALL AMERICANS
BY AGE GROUP AND SEX

Source: U. S. Public Health Service. *Vital Statistics, 1965.* Indian data provided by Dr. Michael Ogden, Indian Health Service, U. S. Public Health Service.

Age	Indians* (1963–67)		Suicides per 100,000 persons per year Total U.S. (1965)
	Number	Rate	Rate
10–14	6	1.5	0.5
15–19	44	16.6	4.0
20–24	72	39.0	9.0
25–34	91	31.9	12.4
35–44	61	25.9	16.0
45–54	27	15.0	20.5
55–64	20	16.1	22.6
65 plus	13	10.5	22.9
All ages	*341*	*11.6*	*11.2*
Male		18.1	16.3
	(1959–66)		
Female		3.8	6.1

* The Indian data come from only the 24 states which contain Indian reservations, with probably 90 per cent of the total Indian population.

There are three significant facts here. First, Indian women show only about half the rate of suicide of other American women. Second, Indian males between the ages of fifteen and forty-four show a much higher suicide rate than other American males. Third, after the age of forty-five, Indian suicide rates are substantially lower than the general American rates.

From these facts we see that suicide among Indian men aged fifteen to forty-four is the problem. It is a problem, whether or not it is defined as a problem of Indian mental health.

The suicide rate from age fifteen to nineteen is about four times as high for Indian as for non-Indian young people. Some writers about Indian education have sought to tie this fact to the type of schooling received by Indians. In particular, they have claimed that attendance at federal boarding schools has a bad influence on the mental health of children and youths, and they have implied that the suicide rate is related somehow to boarding-school attendance.

This claim appears to have no basis in fact. The incidence of suicide in boarding schools is very low. In fact, suicides at boarding schools are so infrequent that many experienced boarding-school directors have never known a case throughout their career in boarding-school work.

The history of suicide among young people in various countries points to some cases of a kind of contagious suicide. Small epidemics break out, consisting of two or three or even more cases close together in time and place. This seems to have happened several times among Indian youths, and each episode has been publicized in a way that encourages the reader to believe that this was not an episode, but was a typical recurring phenomenon. For instance, there was such an epidemic at Fort Hall, Idaho, among the Shoshone-Bannock Indians, who numbered about 2600. In the seven years from 1960 through 1966 there were fifteen suicides in this community, thirteen of them being under thirty-five years of age.[13] Dr. Dizmang, who analyzed this phenomenon, found that most of the suicides culminated an experience of family demoralization, death of persons near to the individual, and excessive alcohol consumption. The seven-year record gave a suicide rate of 83 per 100,000. But the Navajo data over a ten-year period give a suicide rate of 10.3 per 100,000, which is close to the national average for whites.

Dr. Dizmang[14] and his associates made a careful comparison of the ten young persons aged fifteen to twenty-four who committed suicide between 1961 and 1968, with a group of forty persons who were matched with them on the basis of age, sex, degree of Indian ancestry, but had no suicidal attempt within their family during this period. The differences were striking between the suicides and the non-suicidal group. Dr. Dizmang concludes as follows:

> The data presented clearly indicate statistically significant differences between individuals who commit suicide and the control group. The subjects in the suicide group were cared for by more than one individual in their developing years, while control subjects were almost always cared for by a single individual. The primary caretakers of the suicide group had significantly more arrests during the time they were the caretakers of the subjects. The suicide group also experienced many more losses by desertion or divorce than the control group.
>
> The individuals who suicided were arrested more times in the years prior to their suicide than were the controls, although the lifetime number of arrests did not distinguish the control and the suicide groups. The individuals who suicided were arrested at a significantly earlier age than the control group. Many of the completed suicides were sent off to boarding school at a significantly earlier age than were the control group, and they were also sent more frequently to boarding school for some period of their life than were the controls. All of the data point to a chaotic and unstable childhood in those who completed suicide compared to the controls.

In a follow-up of the Fort Hall experience, the author inquired of Joyce Hernandez (chairman of the Education Committee, Shoshone-Bannock tribes) concerning suicides at Fort Hall since 1967, who replied, "In the fall of 1967 we had a young youth who hung himself while serving time in jail. It became nationally known, due to the fact that Senator Kennedy made his visit here shortly after it happened. Suicide was determined on another young man who was supposed to have placed himself on the railroad tracks. There has been doubt on this case. This last case was a young man in his thirties who shot himself. Family problems were very evident."[15]

Thus the annual suicide rate in this community for the ten-year period from 1960–69 inclusive is 18/26,000 or 69 per 100,-000 population. This illustrates the fluctuation of the suicide rate when a small population is studied.

Another example of the epidemic quality of suicide data is given in the case of the Quinault Indians, who live partly in a small community on the Olympic Peninsula of Washington. In 1964, Harold Patterson, superintendent of the school district at Taholah, Washington, the Quinault community, presented to the U. S. Senate Subcommittee on Indian Education a memorandum entitled "Suicide Among Youth on the Quinault Indian Reservation."[16] He commenced with this statement: "My interest in this subject is occasioned by the fact that I have been in close contact with three youths who have killed themselves within the past two years (1962–64), and with about 12 others who have either attempted or threatened to do the same." This statement was picked up and used by several writers and speakers as evidence of a high suicide rate in the Quinault area. But Mr. Patterson wrote as follows in 1969: "Contrary to what might be expected, occurrences of suicide have dropped to zero at Taholah. There have been recurrences of attempted suicide, some of which have been very close, but I cannot recall one successful suicide attempt since August, 1965."[17]

He attributed the reduction of suicides to the Quinault Tribal Community Action Program operating under the federal Office of Economic Opportunity. This program provided local recreation facilities; and other programs also came to raise the morale of Quinault youth, such as the Neighborhood Youth Corps, the Educational Counseling program, and the Health Services program.

There is no evidence relating suicide rate directly to the kind of schooling an Indian youth has had. In general, the Indian suicide rates are closely correlated with disorganized family life, alcoholism, and loss of friends and relatives by death.

The relatively low suicide rate among Indian women is an important fact, which has not been explored by mental health specialists. It can hardly be related to their schooling.

The relatively high suicide rate of young Indian men should be taken as a symptom of something seriously wrong with the society in which they live. Probably an improvement in the socioeducational situation of Indians will reduce this symptom. It will require a complex of changes, which include changes in the schools as a necessary part.

Dr. Alexander Leighton, professor of social psychiatry at Harvard University, served as chairman of a symposium on "The Mental Health of the American Indian" at the 1967 meeting of the American Psychiatric Association.[18] Introducing the program, he said about the American Indian society, "Diffuse evidence from many sources suggests the presence of a mental health problem of serious proportions." A psychiatrist serving Indian families in the U. S. Public Health Service says he has the impression that there is a higher proportion of Indian children with personal disturbance than he is accustomed to seeing in a typical white population. There does, indeed, seem to be general agreement among mental hygiene experts that these statements reflect reality, but the evidence is diffuse and somewhat vague. Some psychiatrists have paid brief visits to Indian boarding schools, and come away with the opinion that they are all bad, from the point of view of the mental hygienist. One psychiatrist said, "Boarding schools for elementary age children present a problem. In my opinion there should be no Indian boarding schools for children in the elementary grades. I say this without qualification. These schools do more harm than good. They do not educate, they alienate."[19]

Representing a different point of view in this same symposium, D'Arcy McNickle, an Indian social scientist, writing on "The Sociocultural Setting of Indian Life," says:

> The problem of being Indian, and being obliged to function at two levels of consciousness, for many individuals reduces itself to this: They are aware that their communities, their people, their kinsmen are Indians and are held in low esteem by the general society. The young people especially recognize themselves as Indians, but they do not want the low-status equivalent. They look for some way in which they can share in the status ascribed to middle-class Americans without ceasing to be Indian.

Looking at the Indian boys and girls in thirty varied schools ranging from Alaska to North Carolina, we are impressed by their basic good mental health. The adolescents, who should show symptoms of poor mental health if it is there, have the same level of self-esteem as non-Indians do, they enjoy life, they have an active and rewarding peer group life. *What self-doubt they have is based on a realistic view of their disadvantages in competing for jobs and income.*

They are not depressed, anxious, paranoid, or alienated as a group. They can make use of educational and economic opportunities. However, they do have the same problems that the youth of other low-income groups have, and these problems are complicated to a degree by the fact that they are Indians.

VII

Schools and Schooling
as Seen by Indian Youth
and Their Parents

Although the National Study found that, on the whole, there was mild approval of schools and teachers by Indian students, there are some differences between schools and communities. Certain schools are praised significantly more than others, while other groups are more heavily criticized than the average. How can these be explained?

The schools in the National Study where the students were relatively more favorable than the average were: Bethel, Alaska, and Chemawa Boarding School in Oregon, with a predominance of Alaskan students; a public school on the Papago Reservation in Arizona, and public schools serving Navajo youth in Tuba City, Arizona, and Apache youth in Fort Thomas, Arizona. One thing these schools have in common is a solid enrollment of less acculturated students.

Schools where the students were especially critical are in varied places, but in all these communities the students have more contact with the urban-industrial culture and in most examples the schools have a majority of white pupils. These schools were in Chicago, Minneapolis, Oklahoma, Wisconsin, and Washington.

However, two church-operated schools with 100 per cent Indian enrollment are also included in this group of disfavored schools.

Several hypothetical explanations seem reasonable to account for these differences. One is that the more acculturated students have a better basis for evaluating their schools, for they know more about other Indian and non-Indian schools. They may, consequently, have higher expectations of their schools. Another is that the more critical students tend to be in schools where they are in a minority and are generally doing worse in school than their non-Indian classmates. This may be reflected in their criticisms. Increased contact with non-Indians may give them a more cynical view of the Indian's place in white man's America, and this may be reflected in their attitudes toward their schools. A third possibility is that Indian students, for the most part, prefer all-Indian schools. In such schools Indian students may feel more comfortable and less anxious about discrimination, being accepted by peers, being as well dressed as other students, etc. Moreover, the outstanding students, athletes, etc. have to be Indian in all-Indian schools. Finally, of course, it may be the case that the schools attended by the less acculturated Indians are better in some way. For instance, schools with all-Indian enrollments may have more concern for the education of Indian young people and the special problems they may have, either as Indians or as poor people. Any or all of these four hypotheses seem reasonable.

With some important exceptions, it appears that Indian pupils do not become enthusiastic about their schooling. They do not appear to exert themselves or to feel that school achievement is very important to them. However, they are not hostile to school. They generally speak of their school and their teachers favorably.

This mixture of mildly favorable attitudes toward school with apathy toward academic achievement needs some study. First, to what extent do these two somewhat contrary attitudes exist side by side in Indian students?

In the National Study, interviews were held with students and parents in which they were asked how they felt about the school and the teachers. These interviews were held with approximately fourteen hundred students and seven hundred parents, by a variety of interviewers, nearly all of whom were Indians. Thus we have evidence from a large number of students and parents in approximately thirty communities.

The student and parent interviews[1] were rated on a number of rating scales, two of which are relevant to this particular inquiry. The rating scales originally contained 6 points, but these were collapsed to 4 points for statistical computations as follows:

Points	Meaning	Value
1 and 2	Negative	2
3	Slightly Negative	3
4	Slightly Positive	4
5 and 6	Positive	5

The reliability and validity of these rating scales have been examined carefully[2] and shown to be quite satisfactory.

On the scale which dealt with the student's opinion of the school he was presently attending (Scale K), the majority of students fell at the positive end. Twenty-nine per cent were rated at point 4, and 49 per cent at points 5 or 6 (almost all of these actually were rated at point 5). Eleven per cent were rated at points 1 and 2, and 11 per cent at point 3. The mean rating for the total sample of 1382 students is 4.02; the mode is point 5. A rating of 4 indicates that the student felt that his school was "OK" or about average in relation to other schools. A rating of 5 indicates that the student said that he felt his school was "pretty good" or "better" than other schools. Students rated at points 1 and 2 clearly felt that their school was very poor. Students rated at point 3 seemed slightly more critical than approving of their school.

The most important question on the student Interview Schedule for this rating was: "How does your school compare with other schools you know? Is it better or worse?" Another question about what the student liked best and disliked most also elicited some pertinent information. Some examples of actual responses should help the reader to understand the opinions and attitudes of these students:

MALE: This school is better than the school in New Mexico. You get a better education; they teach you more here. It's harder here, too.

FEMALE: Well, at ——— sometimes kids would hardly talk to me or anything, but here they usually talk to me.

FEMALE: Worse. The teachers aren't very good. Some are "Hippies" or something. Seems like they're out of the bottom of the bag.

FEMALE: Better—because of recess.

FEMALE: It doesn't have as much equipment as schools in the cities.

FEMALE: Well, it's all right but I don't like it. Some of the Indian girls are mad at me. You've got to be around certain people to be accepted. Some of these girls think they are it. One minute you've got a friend and then you turn around and they talk about you. So this school is worse.

FEMALE: I think it rates pretty high overall. About on an even level.

MALE: It's more modern and has better teachers.

FEMALE: I guess it's better because the work is easy.

MALE: I would say it's better because we get to mix with those other kids. I think we learn a lot.

FEMALE: My school is better. The principal, students, and curriculum make it better.

FEMALE: Worse. Sometimes when you go into the lunchroom they holler at you.

Different students clearly give different types of responses. Some say merely, "It's better" or "It's OK." Most praise or criticize one or two specific things, some of which may seem trivial to us. The opinion of the school voiced by some students is a function of how they feel about their peers at the school. Others base their opinion on the learning that goes on there: Some think that their school is better because the work is challenging or "hard," while others prefer their school because it is relatively "easy." Thus, easy generalizations cannot be made, about what students like or dislike in their schools. Clearly, most Indian students have some specific gripes or criticisms about their schools —about a course, certain teachers, rules, poor discipline, overly strict discipline, the way other kids act, etc.—but most feel that their schools are about as good or a little better than other schools they know of.

On the other hand, 22 per cent of the students sampled felt that their schools were not as good as others. Some of these students articulate rather serious criticisms and seem to be quite concerned about them. An example of such a student is the following:

Q: How does this school compare with other schools?

R: Well, when I talked to my girl friend out in California, she had all kinds of electives that they don't have here that I'd love to take . . . And the schools out there—they have more black students and Mexicans and Spanish and all kinds of nationalities, and so they offer—they try to offer everything for each group. I think the school here is too segregated. I think they'd die if a Negro came here to go to school.

Q: What don't you like about this school?

R: Well, let's see—like their guidance and stuff. I don't like the principal, I don't like their electives; I don't like their detention; I don't like the dress code; I don't like the way that—well—they have this late bus that was originally so that Indian students could stay after school for things, and now it's mostly a white bus for white kids that need a ride home after sports. . . .

On the scale dealing with the student's opinion of his teacher (Scale O), students were no more critical of their teachers than they were of their schools in their interviews. The mean rating for the total sample of 1448 students was 4.19; the mode was point 4. Forty-one per cent of the sample were rated at this point and 45 per cent were rated at points 5 and 6. Only 5 per cent were really critical of their teachers (and rated at points 1 or 2); another 10 per cent voiced somewhat more criticism than praise of their teachers and were rated at point 3.

The key question on the interview schedule was: "How well does your teacher do his (her) job?" Students who replied that their teachers were "OK" or "about average," or students who said that some of their teachers were bad and some good were rated at point 4. Students who clearly felt that their teachers were doing well were rated at points 5 or 6. Some examples of student responses to this question are:

MALE: Very well.

MALE: One teacher leaves the room too often. But the rest are all right.

FEMALE: They do a fairly good job, I believe.

FEMALE: Most of them are pretty good.

TABLE 14

COMPARISON OF GROUP SCORES ON
THE SEMANTIC DIFFERENTIAL
INDIAN GROUPS ON "TEACHERS," AGE 12–17

MALES

Group:	Plains	South-west	North-west	Oklahoma	North Caro.	Balti-more	Hoopa	Wis-consin	School C	Chicago
Number:	150	236	129	27	21	23	27	86	21	36
Adjective Pair										
Good-Bad	2.22	1.66	1.72	1.65	1.96	1.87	1.63	2.16	3.24	1.57
Happy-Sad	2.49	1.98	1.76	2.42	2.19	2.22	1.96	2.35	3.05	2.00
Strong-Weak	2.25	2.12	2.02	2.36	2.28	2.00	2.30	2.52	3.43	2.18
Active-Lazy	2.25	1.94	1.98	1.79	2.33	1.74	1.93	2.25	3.19	2.38
Average	2.30	1.92	1.87	2.06	2.19	1.96	1.96	2.32	3.23	2.03

Group:	Plains	South-west	North-west	Oklahoma	North Caro.	Balti-more	Hoopa	Wis-consin	School C	Chicago
				FEMALES						
Number:	160	237	120	14	25	28	21	74	25	33
Good-Bad	2.45	1.65	1.77	2.11	2.35	1.71	1.81	2.55	3.75	2.38
Happy-Sad	2.49	1.84	1.95	2.15	2.40	2.11	1.86	2.85	3.29	1.98
Strong-Weak	2.13	2.32	2.26	2.26	2.35	2.33	1.81	2.68	3.79	2.10
Active-Lazy	2.25	2.22	2.06	2.01	2.20	1.89	1.90	2.24	4.00	1.94
Average	2.33	1.99	2.01	2.13	2.33	2.04	1.85	2.58	3.71	2.10

Note: Low score is the more favorable response.

TABLE 15

COMPARISON OF GROUP SCORES
ON THE SEMANTIC DIFFERENTIAL
NON-INDIAN GROUPS ON "TEACHERS," AGE 12-17

Group:	Anglo-Americans			Latin-Americans	
	Chicago 1961	Chicago-Colorado 1969	Virginia-D.C. 1970	Buenos Aires 1961	Puerto Rico 1968
Number:	50	52	15	50	150
MALES					
Adjective Pair					
Good-Bad	2.04	2.28	2.25	1.52	2.25
Happy-Sad	2.30	2.57	2.69	2.58	2.23
Strong-Weak	3.14	2.37	2.50	2.42	2.41
Active-Lazy	2.38	1.89	2.81	1.78	2.02
Average	2.47	2.28	2.56	2.07	2.23

FEMALES

Group:	Anglo-Americans			Latin-Americans	
	Chicago 1961	Chicago-Colorado 1969	Virginia-D.C. 1970	Buenos Aires 1961	Puerto Rico 1968
Number:	50	52	16	50	150
Good-Bad	1.90	1.79	2.14	1.47	2.22
Happy-Sad	2.40	2.10	3.00	2.50	2.49
Strong-Weak	2.24	2.31	2.93	2.45	2.15
Active-Lazy	1.93	2.22	3.00	1.84	2.30
Average	2.12	2.11	2.77	2.06	2.29

Note: Low score is the more favorable response.

For description of these groups, see paper III, No. 9, "The Indian Self-Image as Evaluated in the Semantic Differential."

Few students elaborated upon their opinion of their teacher(s). On the whole, their reasons for liking or disliking a teacher are little different from the reasons given by other American students. There were some Indian students, however, who did feel that a teacher was prejudiced against Indians.

On the whole, then, Indian students feel that their teachers do an average or better job of teaching. Relatively few voiced serious complaints about their teachers.

The Indian students were also asked to rate the concepts *Teachers* and *This School* on the Semantic Differential.[8] Since the correlation between ratings on *This School* and *Teachers* was high, only the ratings on *Teachers* are reported here. Tables 14 and 15 give detailed data on the SD ratings by boys and girls, from Indian communities and from several non-Indian communities, for comparison. Rather unexpectedly, these tables indicate that Indian adolescents are slightly more favorable toward their teachers than are the Anglo-Americans of approximately the same socioeconomic status. These tables also indicate that Indian girls are slightly more critical of teachers on this instrument than are Indian boys.

As noted in Table 14, the Semantic Differential ratings for "Teachers" are very negative for School C, which is a junior high school in Minneapolis. This school stood apart from others in many respects, and suggested a special inquiry. School C and another junior high school in Minneapolis were scenes of much hostility among students and between students and teachers in the period from 1968 to 1970, when this study was made. Both schools had a minority group of about 20 per cent Indian pupils, and another minority group of black pupils. There was a good deal of hostility between these groups.

There was also a considerable amount of hostility of Indian pupils toward teachers. Students in their interviews frequently singled out teachers by name as ones they thought were prejudiced against Indian pupils. Teachers were asked to comment on the attitudes of a random list of Indian pupils, and they said with respect to the majority on this list that they were "hostile" toward the school and toward teachers. They also mentioned certain ones as having called them names in public and having defied them. Yet the teachers of School C, on the attitude questionnaire to which teachers from all schools in the study responded, were more favorably disposed toward Indian pupils and less authoritarian than the other teachers in the Minnesota-Wisconsin area.

Thus, from the student inventories, from teacher interviews, and from public knowledge, School C presented an unusual degree of conflict and hostility of Indian pupils toward the school and toward teachers.

The situation of Indian adults in Minneapolis is one of greater militancy and greater protest against the Establishment than was true of any other community in the National Study. The Minneapolis Indian group is known to be more militant than any other large city Indian group in recent years. Thus the children may be expected to have heard a good deal of hostile talk and to have observed a good deal of militancy on the part of their parents. This critical attitude of Indian parents showed clearly in the interviews conducted by the study with Minneapolis Indian parents. On the scale which measured the extent to which the parent perceived the school as meeting the needs of his child, the most frequent rating by the eight hundred parents from the thirty communities in the study was 4, which indicated mild approval. But 75 per cent of the School C parent respondents were below 4, expressing degrees of disapproval ranging from mild to extreme. On the scale measuring the parent's opinion of his child's teacher's performance, the most frequent score was 5, indicating definite approval. But 55 per cent of School C parents rated below 4, indicating definite disapproval of the teacher's performance. By comparison, only 15 per cent of the sample of Chicago Indian parents scored below 4 on this scale. On the scale measuring parents' opinion of the school administration, the most frequent scores from the eight hundred parents were 4 or 5. School C had 65 per cent below 4, indicating definite disapproval of the school administration.

Observation of this school in comparison with other urban schools by staff members of the study did not disclose any striking difference visible to neutral observers, except the greater hostility of the students in School C.

Thus it appears that the junior high school pupils to some

extent were reflecting the attitudes of the adult Indian community toward the institutions of Minneapolis.

Further understanding of the School C attitudes is given by a
comparison of pupil attitudes for School C with Chicago Indian
pupils, who were in an urban situation somewhat similar to that
of Minneapolis Indians, but were not exposed to a high degree
of adult and parent militancy at the time the study was made.
Students were asked on the Semantic Differential to rate *Indian
Culture* (average of the ratings on *My Home, Indians* and
Tribe's Way of Life); and *White Culture* (average of ratings
on *This School, Teachers,* and *White People's Way of Life*).
Comparison of these scores shows the following: (The lower
score indicates a more favorable attitude.)

	Teachers	White Culture	Indian Culture
School C	3.47	3.34	1.93
Chicago	2.07	2.20	1.90

Here we see that the School C students are much less favorable
to teachers and to the white culture than they are to Indian
culture, and that they differ from the Chicago Indian students
by being more negative to teachers and white culture.

Reading the interviews with the School C students reveals a
considerable degree of ambivalence on the part of the Indian
pupils toward the life they lead in the city. Nearly all of them
reported that they travel frequently (by bus or automobile) to
the lake country or to the Indian reservations where their grand-
parents or aunts and uncles are today. Weekly or monthly visits
are the rule, and the junior high school youth often make these
trips alone. Some quotations from these interviews illustrate the
ambivalence of some students, and the actual preference of others
for the "Indian way." The most hostile girl (a Chippewa) says,
of the lake area where her forebears lived, "I like it and I would
like to stay there." A boy says, "I go up almost every weekend
to visit my grandfather. I like to hunt and fish up there. I'd
like to stay there all the time because I like to hunt and fish
and the dog can run free." The most frequent kind of comment
is this from a girl, "I like it there. You can do almost anything
you want. But I wouldn't want to stay there all the time. I like

the city and have friends here." A rare comment came from a boy, "I'd rather live down here because some of the adults are funny up there and it's always quiet and a little restricted."

When we consider that the pupils of School C were all in the age range twelve to fifteen, it is not strange that there should be a general romantic feeling about the woods and the lakes and the free life, especially on the part of the boys. It is surprising that the girls of School C are somewhat more negative to the school than the boys are, as measured by the Semantic Differential.

Very few of these young people of either sex can see themselves growing up into a satisfactory future through achievement in school. Most of their parents have not done so and cannot set them an example of rewards gained from schooling. Just at present their parents are actively dissatisfied with employment and housing in Minneapolis, and are setting an example of protest against white institutions.

Parents and students alike at School C are strongly in favor of studying Indian culture. The schools are moving in that direction. It will be interesting to see whether this has any influence on the attitudes of Indian students toward education in that city.

Attitudes of parents were also rated on a number of rating scales.

Students and parents generally agreed in their evaluation of the schools. There were nine schools rated negatively by students, and seven of these schools were among the nine most negatively rated by parents. There were eight schools judged favorably by students, and three of these were among the seven most favorably rated by parents.

Again, it appears that parents in the more isolated all-Indian communities tend to favor the schools, while the more critical parents are in the communities with high contact with the white culture and a predominance of non-Indian students in the schools.

Over 80 per cent of the parents rated on the scale dealing with the parent's perception of how well the school is meeting the needs of his child (Scale II-B) were rated at points 4, 5, or 6 —all positive. The mean was 4.02, and the mode was 4. Fifty-three per cent were rated at point 4. It should be noted that many parents said very little in response to the questions asked them by the interviewer, and very few long conversations in which parents really opened up about their opinions of the school are recorded in the interviews. Parents who said relatively little but who indicated no serious criticisms were inevitably rated at points 4 or 5. Point 4 is defined as: "The parent feels that the school does a fairly good job in meeting the needs of his child, though there is definitely room for improvement." There were two very open-ended questions involved in making the rating: "What do you like about the school your child attends?" and "What don't you like about the school your child attends?" There were also a number of questions pertaining specifically to teachers, curriculum, administration, control of the school, etc.

Those 375 parents (out of seven hundred) who were rated at point 4 indicated general approval of the school, but made a few criticisms. Most common was the suggestion that the schools should pay more attention to the Indian heritage. Other common criticisms were that the school had a few poor teachers, that certain subjects were not offered, that discipline was lax, that some teachers were prejudiced, or that their children were not learning as much as they should.

The two hundred parents rated at point 5 had no serious criticisms of the school and its program. They indicated only their approval of the school and its current program. The fifty parents rated at points 1 and 2 and the seventy-five at point 3, on the other hand, were quite critical of the school or of some important aspect of it. These parents—constituting 18 per cent of our sample—are seriously disappointed in or perturbed about their schools.

Eighty-seven per cent of the 646 parents rated on the scale dealing with the parent's opinion of his child's teacher (Scale VI-A) were rated at points 4, 5, or 6. Two hundred eighty-four were rated at point 4 and 281 at points 5 or 6 (mostly 5). Six per cent were rated at points 1 or 2 and 7 per cent at point 3. The mean rating was 4.24 and point 4 was the mode. Point 4 is defined as follows:

> Slightly positive. Parent thinks that his child's teacher is "OK" or about average in comparison with other teachers. Or he thinks that there

are some good and some poor teachers, but that more of them are good than are poor.

There was one specific question on which this rating was primarily based; it was "How well is the teacher doing?" Other questions about whether or not the parent knew his child's teacher and had visited him, how well his child liked his teacher, how well his child was doing in school, and what a good teacher was like also elicited pertinent responses.

Following are some parent responses—Q indicates where an interviewer asked a question. What follows is a response.

(Q) The teacher does fine. (Q) She usually teaches good. (Q) The teacher treats her (respondent's child) good so she likes the teacher.

(Q) The teachers are nice, and, as far as I know, they're doing fine. (Q) A good teacher is nice and pleased to meet you. (Q) Johnny likes his teachers. He tells me his teachers correct him when he does his schoolwork the wrong way.

(Q) The teacher does fine. (Q) A good teacher is very patient and understanding and is not prejudiced. (Q) My three smallest children like their teachers very much, but the two older ones don't.

(Q) The teachers do as well as they can be expected to. (Q) A good teacher likes children, is strict but can also be easy-going at times. (Q) All my children could be doing better, but it is not all the teacher's fault.

(Q) Teachers at ——— don't pay as much attention to the Indian child as to the white child. They just want to let these kids slide by until they're sixteen. And many of the teachers are milk-toast type. Some are on the border of "man-lovers," and the kids know this. I haven't seen any who present a strong male image, with authority. You need that. Last year the discipline was terrible. (Q) One teacher downgrades Indian ways and Indian people. This causes students to rebel and causes negative feelings about home and community. What happens at home is none of his business if he feels that way. If this teacher were respectful, it would be all right. (Q) A good teacher should be just like one of the gang—they shouldn't stay too much to themselves. They should be accessible, open-minded, and get along with people.

(Q) It seems to me that some teachers aren't really communicating with the students to help them out. They seem to dwell too long on particular points, rather than helping students to move along at their own pace. . . . (Q) The teachers seem to be doing a pretty good job, and the students have to work with the teachers too.

(Q) She's really good. I like her. (Q) A good teacher is stern, but she has a way about her that kids like—they don't think she's being mean. She does special things for them.

(Q) I don't think my children could have any better teachers than they have.

Eighty-six per cent of the 666 parents rated on the scale dealing with the parent's opinion of the curriculum in his child's school were rated at points 4, 5, or 6. Three hundred forty-five of these (52 per cent of the total sample) were rated at point 4 and 230 (34 per cent) at points 5 or 6. Five per cent were severely critical of the curriculum and were rated at points 1 or 2, and 9 per cent were quite critical and were rated at point 3. The mean for the total sample was 4.14.

Point 4 is defined as follows:

> Slightly positive. Parent either thinks that the curriculum is "OK" or he makes both positive and negative evaluations of it, with the positive ones predominating.

Point 5 is defined as positive. A parent rated at point 5 must have said clearly that he felt the curriculum was good and he must have made no serious criticisms of it at all.

There were a number of questions on the interview schedule which dealt with the curriculum. Two were quite general: "What does your child learn at school?" and "What should your child learn in school that he is not now learning?" Several other questions dealt specifically with the incorporation of tribal and/or Indian history, culture, and language into the curriculum. Some examples of Indian parents' responses to these questions are:

> (Q) I'm satisfied with the things she is being taught. (Q) She learns reading and arithmetic and history, and that makes me happy. (Q) I wouldn't mind if she is taught about the Apache history and culture; in fact, I think it would be good. (Q) She already knows her own language so I don't think she should be taught it in school. (Q) I think it would be worthwhile to have some subjects taught in Apache.

> (Q) He learns the usual subjects—reading, math, geography, etc. (Q) They should be teaching more training in different trades to prepare for jobs later. (Q) Yes, they should learn about their culture and history, to preserve their heritage and take pride in it. (Q) Classes could be given in Indian dancing, beadwork, weaving, and basket weaving.

(Q) They learn what the school offers them. (Q) They should learn better penmanship and better study habits that will help them in high school and college. (Q) Yes, they should teach about our tribal history and culture so that the children of today won't lose sight of their Indian heritage and also so they'll learn how much easier life is for the Indian today. (Q) They should be taught all that can be found out about our tribe and set down in a history book as it really happened, not how the white man wants it written. It should be an elective course in high school. (Q) No, the Menominee language is a lost art. There is no one qualified to teach it properly.

(Q) No, they shouldn't teach about the native history and culture at school; this can be done at home.

(Q) My children are learning to accept life in ——— (family just moved to this town). The next important thing they're learning is the academic material. (Is there anything else they should be learning?) They need to learn to plan toward when they will be out of school— toward a broader outlook on life—rather than just for today. They need to realize that there is more to life than just going up to school from year to year—that they have to be prepared for something when they are out of school—college or training for work.

(Q) As to lessons, this school is better than Chilocco or Haskell (BIA boarding schools). A lot of kids going from here to Chilocco have already had the same classes and have to take them over again. (Q) They are learning everything, I suppose. I don't know much about it. My oldest daughter did want to be a nurse, but she found out when she graduated that she couldn't because she hadn't taken the right courses. (Q) Yes, they should learn about their tribe in school. It would be an advantage to the tribe because so many of the younger people have intermarried with whites, that they are losing all of that. Even I don't know anything about the Pawnee tribe.

(Q) They learn what the white way of life and the Indian way of life are like, and how they're different. And they learn how to get along with other people. (Q) The school doesn't have some things like music appreciation and that sort of thing. If they had it in the school they would have more kids going out for band.

Many parents did not know much about what their children learned in school, but approved anyway. Many had definite suggestions for improving the curriculum, usually by adding something (e.g., more vocational training, certain more aesthetic subjects such as art and music, and above all, courses in Indian or tribal history and culture). All parents seem pleased that the standard subjects—reading, writing, arithmetic, history, English, science—were being taught. In short, their attitudes regarding the curriculum were little different from those of other Americans with similar educational backgrounds and in similar social and economic positions, with the one important exception that most of these parents wanted some kind of special attention paid to tribal and Indian history and culture. Curriculum for Indian youth will be examined in detail in a later chapter.

Eighty-four per cent of the 616 parents rated on parent's opinion of the performance of the school administration (Scale VI-C) were rated on the positive side of the scale (points 4, 5, or 6). The modal rating was 4; 260 parents were rated at this point. Ten per cent were rated at points 1 or 2 and 6 per cent at point 3. The mean score was 4.20. Approximately one out of eight parents (16 per cent) had serious complaints about the principal, superintendent, or other administrative official in their children's school(s). But the majority evidently felt that the present school administration was "all right," good, or excellent. Most of those rated at point 4 felt that the administration was "all right" but criticized it on some score or another. The remaining 42 per cent had no real quarrel with the administration, and offered the opinion that it was good or even excellent.

One question on the interview schedule specifically asked: "Is the principal doing a good job?" Other questions concerning the policy making and control of the school, while concerned mainly with local boards of education, occasionally brought out opinions on the school administration. Examples of such questions are: "Who actually sets the policy and makes the decisions regarding the school your child attends?" "Is the school following what the majority of the local parents want for their children?" Responses to these questions were generally brief, such as:

> Yes, he's doing a good job.
>
> She's trying very hard to do her duties as head of the school. She has been helpful to me.
>
> Yes, things seem to be running smooth.
>
> Yes, I never heard no complaints.
>
> I don't know who the principal is. (Q) He seems to do a real good job.
>
> Yes, I've talked to him and he seems to be a real friendly fellow.

Some of these parents appear to know little about the administrators and the administration of the school. Many parents evidently based their opinion on whether "things were running smooth," i.e., whether or not they had heard of any scandals or serious problems. Some parents, however, appeared to be more informed about the administration of the school. A few examples are:

(Q) They need a counselor to work more closely with high school students. Then they could prepare better for college courses. (Q) I know the principal mostly by hearsay. He won't let the kids form clubs; he stopped the homecoming parade, and he doesn't get along with the kids.

(Q) The principal at the high school is new here. What he is doing is best for the kids. Discipline is high compared to last year and B is doing a good job as principal administrator at the elementary school.

(Q) The school is not doing what most parents want. Parents would appreciate more cooperation and less criticism. (Q) I have no voice in deciding what goes on at school. Rules and decisions are only presented after they're made. (Q) Mr. C at C school is good. Mr. D at D school tends to show partiality to town or white children.

Although other studies of Indian education are quite critical of the education provided by public and by federal schools for Indian children, they generally report that Indian students and parents are either favorable or neutral toward these schools.

Bass[4] administered a Semantic Differential and a School Attitude Inventory in 1968 to 2164 Indian high school students in twenty-one high schools ranging from Alaska to Oklahoma. The adjective pairs of his Semantic Differential were similar to, but not identical with, those used in the National Study, and there were other slight differences which do not permit an exact comparison of SD scores from the two studies. However, Bass found a very similar pattern of ratings with the following concepts ranging from *very favorable* to *favorable* in the order given: *Education, School, College, My Future, Indian, Teachers, Myself as a Person, White Man.*

Bass also asked students to mark a number of statements about school as *True* or *False*. He computed the percentage of responses (with some omissions, which makes the percentages add to less than 100) as follows:

	True	False
School is fun	78	19
I am confident of my ability in school	71	27
I would rather stay home than go to school	18	80
I like school	83	15
I would rather be in school than working full-time	73	24
What I learn in school will help very much in earning a living	87	8

In his research in the Pine Ridge Sioux Reservation, Bernard Spilka[5] contrasts the critical views of some researchers on Indian education with the fact that nearly all observers report that many pupils and parents like and value the schools and teachers. He notes that Macgregor thought that "teachers are the important adults as guides and disciplinarians in the lives of the boys . . . (and) . . . teachers appear to have more influence on girls than do their fathers or agemates."[6] Spilka adds, "Considering the rather widely advertised, critical views of Indian education and teachers of Indians, it is difficult to understand the generally positive orientation of Indian children and parents toward teachers and schools on the reservation and the significance of the latter in the lives of Indian pupils."[7]

Using a questionnaire to measure *Attitude Toward School* Spilka asked students to compare teachers with parents in certain respects. He comments, "If this form of testing is valid, we have no evidence of dislike of teachers compared to one's own parents. Conversely, this writer is inclined to feel there is a good bit of respect and admiration for the teachers. It should be noted that one of the most common occupational aspirations listed by students was teacher."[8]

Spilka used an interview with Indian parents to measure the attitudes toward education and toward the local school. He says, "It is immediately evident that the mothers interviewed are over-whelmingly positive toward education in general and the local schools in particular. . . . Actual negativism is less than 15 per cent relative to the local school situation."[9]

In this connection, Wax, Wax and Dumont,[10] who are severe

critics of the educational system as it impinges on Indians in the Sioux area, comment on "a few teachers who develop fine classrooms and teach their pupils a great deal." They also note that, while there is much friction between students and teachers, the students have a rewarding social life within the school.

Since Indian students, on the average, do poorly in the ordinary school subjects, why do they nevertheless approve their schools and their teachers even to a mild degree? Why are they not hostile to a situation in which they do not succeed as well as the non-Indian students?

The best answer to this question seems to lie in the following three propositions:

1. Indian students have a socially rewarding peer group in schools. They enjoy games and sports. They enjoy being with their peer group. Those few who say they do not like school often report unsatisfactory relations with their age mates. Students who are in a minority of Indians in a school are more negative toward their school than those who are in a majority of Indian students.

2. Indian adolescents are "where the action is" as long as they are in school. They get the feeling of being part of something important, with some promise toward the future, which some of them would not get if they were to live in their own villages or families as adolescents, where the community and tribal life is not very rewarding to them.

3. School achievement as such—school grades and positions in school—is not especially important to many Indian students or their parents because they do not see *clearly* how it is related to future opportunity or success, and because it is not stressed as an important aspect of the school program by teachers or students. This proposition emerged from the National Study when school achievement was studied in relation to self-esteem of students.

However, as a policy of economic development under Indian direction goes ahead, with education related to it, Indian youth and their parents may become more concerned with formal education, and education will probably become more attached to self-esteem.

In its study of self-esteem among Indian students, the National Study found at most only a slight relation to achievement in school subjects. This contrasts with what is perhaps the most widely published finding with regard to the self-esteem of young people, that it is positively related to school achievement. It is widely held that a student who does well in school usually has a positive self image and higher self-esteem than others who do less well in school. Similarly, a student who has high self-esteem is likely to have a high level of achievement in school tasks. Rosenberg,[11] for example, states that "Our data show that school grades are clearly related to self-esteem. . . ." To cite only one other example, the Coleman report on *Equal Educational Opportunity*[12] included as part of the student questionnaires self-report items to measure attitudes such as "interest in school . . . pursuit of reading outside school . . . and self-concept," the results of which he stated were that

> These tables show that, whatever measure is chosen, the attitudinal variables have the strongest relation to achievement. It is, of course, reasonable that self-concept should be so closely related to achievement, since it represents the individual's estimate of his own ability. . . . The relation of self-concept to achievement is, from one perspective, merely the accuracy of his estimate of his scholastic skills, and is probably more a consequence than a cause of scholastic achievement. . . .

Since most of these studies that reported the relationship between self-esteem and scholastic achievement were done with white students, the National Study proposed to see if the relationship also held for American Indian students. Initially the large literature supporting the relationship led to an expectation that Indian students would also show a high correlation between their self-esteem ratings and their class ratings; however, one cautionary note regarding the relationship for minority group students was sounded by Coleman that led us to test this expectation carefully.

> . . . of the three attitudinal variables, however, it (self-concept) is the weakest, especially among minority groups, where it shows inconsistent relations to achievement at grades 9 and 12. . . .

The first analysis of our data with regard to self-esteem and scholastic achievement was to study the mean self-esteem scores of the Indian students who were ranked in the top, middle, and bottom thirds of their respective classes in school. Table 16 gives these results.

TABLE 16

AVERAGE SELF-ESTEEM SCORE (COMBINED SELF)
OF INDIAN STUDENTS IN THE TOP, MIDDLE,
AND BOTTOM THIRDS OF THEIR CLASS IN SCHOOL

Area	Top 3rd		Middle 3rd		Bottom 3rd	
	N	Mean	N	Mean	N	Mean
Plains Indians	118	27.4	243	26.0	153	26.2
Southwest Indians	39	25.1	35	27.1	34	24.1
Northwest Indians and Eskimos	51	27.8	111	26.0	167	26.3
Minnesota-Wisconsin Indians	14	28.5	87	26.6	83	24.5
North Carolina Indians	24	31.8	20	29.2	12	29.2
Oklahoma Indians	14	28.9	9	29.8	21	25.6
Total Indians	260	27.7	505	26.4	470	25.8

Note: Assignment of students to top, middle, and bottom thirds of their class was made by the teachers, in most cases. In a very few cases, standardized test data were available, and the field research staff made the assignment. The fact that less than a third of the group were assigned to "top 3rd" indicates that teachers did not perceive one third of their students as belonging in the top third of students as they knew them.

The figures for the total Indian group showed that self-esteem scores did tend to decrease with rank in class, a decrease which was significant from top to middle but not significant from middle to bottom thirds. The figures for the various geographical area groups revealed that three out of six groups showed such a decrease in self-esteem scores from top to middle thirds of the class but little difference between the middle and bottom thirds.

Of the remaining three geographical groups, two showed an increase in self-esteem from top to middle thirds, and one showed a decrease across all thirds of the class. Thus, while there appeared to be a trend in the direction of a positive relationship between self-esteem and class rank, the relationship did not appear to be very strong, nor did it appear to be consistent across all groups.

To explore these facts further, correlation coefficients were computed between self-esteem scores and rank in class for students of various age groups. These correlations ranged from practically zero to .25 and indicate a very low relationship. When the relationship was studied separately for boys and girls, it appeared that boys show it slightly more than girls.

It appears, then, that for Indian students self-esteem and achievement in school subjects are related only slightly. Probably Indian students differ as a group from white students in their motivation for school. However, it appears probable that some of the apparent difference between Indian and white students is due to differences in socioeconomic status rather than ethnic difference. There is some evidence that white students from low-income families also show a rather low relationship between school grades and self-esteem.

Therefore the self-esteem scores of Indian students should be interpreted in relation to their socioeconomic status as well as to their Indianness. While middle-class white students appear to see school achievement as an important part of their total view of themselves, Indian students may view school achievement as a separate activity which does not influence greatly their personal feelings of self-esteem.

The Indian student appears to be psychologically less invested in his school work than middle-class white students, taking as self-evaluation measures his performance in other, non-academic areas of activity. If the Indian youth as a student is to be better understood, it might be by investigating these areas of the orientation toward school and the place which academic achievement has in the thinking of Indian students. It seems clear that commonly held notions about the importance of school performance for the overall "self-concept" of students do not hold for Indian students and that much more needs to be known about the other factors in an Indian student's life, such as his orientation toward his family and Indian society in general, before the "phenomenal self" of Indian students can be accurately assessed and the role of formal education among Indians can be understood.

The majority of Indians, like the majority of Americans, accept the schools that serve them as being adequate or good. The majority also have some complaints, but it appears that, at most, only one in five students and parents has very serious ones. In most schools, it appears that Indian students have little sophistication regarding education; few know much about other schools or other alternatives to the kind of curriculum, teachers, and school program which they have at the school they attend. Indian students in more isolated areas, in particular, have little basis for comparing their school with other schools.

Parents probably would be more critical if they had a wider experience with schools. At present, many seem to know little about even the schools their own children attend. This is understandable in the light of the cultural, social, and economic conditions of life in many Indian communities, and the differences between these conditions and the conditions of life for administrators and teachers in the schools. It does mean, however, that most Indian parents, given this limited experience with schools, have a poor basis for critically evaluating their schools. Thus although Indian parents are generally approving the schools, this does not establish the proposition that the schools are really satisfactory. As Indian parents take more responsibility for schools, their increasing knowledgeability is likely to result in a more critical stance.

Though most students and parents approve of their schools, there are a number of significant exceptions. The more negative criticisms tend to come from Indians and Indian communities which have the greatest interaction with white urban communities, and where Indian students are a minority in the school population. This points to a growing need for concern for the special problems of Indian education in integrated urban settings.

VIII

Indian Education as Seen by Community Leaders

As Indian people are given the opportunity to assume responsibility for the schooling of their children, local community leaders will become the key persons in determining educational policies and practices. They will be elected to school boards of both public and federal schools. They will sit in tribal councils to act on issues of tribal policy with respect to education.

It is important, then, to find out how they perceive the local schools, and how they believe education can be improved. The National Study made a serious effort to get the perceptions of community leaders by means of interviews with them in their homes or places of business. It was important to interview a cross-section of influential people, so as to avoid the bias that comes from seeing only those who volunteer. There are generally a few deeply concerned and vocal people who will write to Washington or to the state capital or will make the trip to appear before an investigating committee. Often they are people with a good deal of influence, and they should be heard; but they do not always "speak for" the entire community.

The field directors in the National Study attempted to get interviews with a cross-section of community leaders, including but not limiting themselves to the more vocal people. For instance, an Indian woman was interviewed in one community who had led a movement to separate an all-Indian elementary school from the local public school district. In contrast, a member of the public school board was interviewed.

The sample of community leaders cannot be considered scientifically representative. There was no list of people who could be defined as community leaders from which a sample could be selected by a random procedure. Community leadership is derived from a variety of traditional and contemporary sources. Some leaders have the voice of authority because of their traditional status such as elder kinsmen and religious leaders. Others are newly developed and more acculturated businessmen, or persons prominent in non-traditional political organizations. However, the field research director in every case did make an informal list of local leaders on the basis of his observations in the community, and he then tried to interview a cross-section of this sample.

A total of 152 community leaders were interviewed—about ninety Indians and sixty non-Indians. In the all-Indian communities the only persons interviewed were Indians—generally members of the tribal council or of the school board. Both sexes were included. Most of these persons at the time did not have children in school, but most of them had some experience with the local schools through children or relatives. Non-Indians were generally business or professional people—members of the school board, pastors of churches, health service workers, women active in the PTA. No school administrators were interviewed as community leaders. The number of persons interviewed in each of the twenty-five communities ranged from two to eighteen, with a median of seven.

The interview was generally conducted by one of the visiting university research staff. This was a contrast with the interviewing of parents, which was generally done by local Indian interviewers. The reason for asking a visiting researcher to interview the community leaders was that the community leader might feel more free to speak frankly on local controversial issues in which he was involved, if he felt that his statements would not be repeated to local people by the interviewer. The interview was read and rated on a number of dimensions which overlapped the dimensions of the interviews with parents, students, and teachers.

In general, it was found that the community leaders were more critical of the schools serving Indians than were the Indian students and parents. Examples of these scales follow. The ratings were made on a 6-point scale, with low ratings signifying unfavorable evaluations, and high ratings indicating favorable attitudes.

Forty per cent of the 152 community leaders rated on their overall evaluation of the school program for Indian students (Scale B) were rated at points 1, 2, or 3—all of which indicate a fairly negative opinion of the schools. Of these 40 per cent, 15 per cent were rated at points 1 and 2, indicating that these individuals were very critical of the schools. This critical stance of the community leaders stands out when it is recalled that only 22 per cent of the student sample and 18 per cent of the parent sample were rated as generally critical of the schools. Still, 37 per cent of the community leaders interviewed were rated at point 4—a "slightly positive" evaluation, and 23 per cent at points 5 or 6. The mean score for the total sample was 3.69.

When asked to comment on their attitudes toward aiming the school's program to assist students to participate in modern society, the overwhelming majority responded affirmatively. Eighteen per cent were rated at point 6, which indicated that they clearly felt the school should prepare students for competence in the non-Indian socioeconomic system, paying no attention to the Indian society and culture; 28 per cent were rated at point 5, which indicated they felt that preparation for the dominant society should be the principal aim of the school, but that this should not be done in such a way as to alienate the Indian student from his culture; and nearly half, 45 per cent, were rated at point 4, indicating that they felt the school should build in a positive way on the ethnic characteristics of the children, but it should also work to make them successful in the modern society. The "man of two cultures" position clearly dominates and the schools are seen as having to participate in this process.

Community leaders were, however, rather critical when asked about how effective the schools actually were in assisting Indian students toward efficient participation in modern society (Scale D). Fifty-three per cent of the 145 individuals rated were placed at points 1, 2, or 3 on this scale. Specifically, 24 per cent were rated at point 3, 26 per cent at point 2, and 3 per cent at point 1. Thirty-five per cent of the respondents were rated at point 4, and 12 per cent at point 5. The definitions of points 2, 3, and 4 on this scale are:

2. Respondent sees the school as ineffective, but not as bad as it could be. This ineffectiveness of the school may be due to attitudes of teachers, or to lacks in the curriculum, or to inadequacies of students and their families.

3. Respondent sees the school as succeeding pretty well with some students, where other things are in their favor, such as family background. But the school does not succeed with the majority of the students.

4. Respondent sees the school as helping most students in the direction of efficient participation in modern society. But the school does not succeed with some students.

Since there might be a difference in attitude on these matters between the Indian and the non-Indian community leaders, the two groups were separated for comparison, as shown in Table 17. There is a small but statistically reliable difference, with the Indian leaders being more critical than the non-Indians.

TABLE 17

COMPARISON OF INDIAN AND NON-INDIAN
COMMUNITY LEADERS ON SCALES INDICATING
APPROVAL-DISAPPROVAL OF SCHOOLS

Scale	Indian Community* Leaders (N=74)	Non-Indian* Community Leaders (N=46)	Total Sample (N=153)
B Overall Approval of the School	3.61	3.98	3.69
D Effectiveness of School in Assisting Pupil Efficiency in Modern Society	3.10	3.59	3.22

(Higher score indicates approval)

* The data in these two columns do not include ratings for community leaders in Chicago, Minnesota, or Wisconsin schools, where there were few Indian community leaders interviewed.

The community leaders were questioned at some length on their attitudes and perceptions of local community influence on the local school program. The central question for this part of the interview was: What degree of responsibility should be held by the parents, the school board, the state board, the tribal council, and the federal authorities? To what extent should the school program be controlled by local people and local organizations? To what extent should it be controlled by the professional staff of the school, which tends to be responsive to non-Indian groups in the community, the state, and the BIA?

Almost all respondents felt that both the local community and the professional school staff should be involved in planning the school's programs and policies. Only 12 per cent were rated at the extremes on the scale—10 per cent saying that "all major policy, program, curriculum, and personnel decisions should be made by the local Indian community through its representatives," and 2 per cent stating that the school should be controlled entirely by the administration and teachers. Thirty-four per cent of the respondents were rated at point 3, which read as follows: R feels that the control of school program and policy should be shared equally by local community representatives and by school professional staff. Equal numbers of respondents (27 per cent of the total sample) balanced themselves around this proposition; both groups being involved but 27 per cent favoring control by the local community, and 27 per cent favoring control by the professional staff.

From all this we gather that most community leaders think that schools for Indians should be set up along the lines of the ideal American model of a school system: a school board working with the administration and teachers to make general policy, personnel, and budget decisions, with the administration and teachers implementing these general policies through the processes of education which they direct. Community leaders generally agreed that the local Indian community had little influence on the programs and policies of the school when queried concerning the actual extent of the local community's influence on the school program (Scale I). Thirty-one per cent of the sample were rated at point 3, 28 per cent at point 2, and 9 per cent at point 1. Point 3 was defined as follows:

> Respondent feels that the local Indian community has some small say in the operation of the school. For example, if it elects a school board or an education committee, these agencies do not function very well, or they do not represent the Indian community well.

Those rated at points 1 and 2 felt that the local community had even less voice.

Less than one third of the community leaders interviewed believed that the local Indian community had some meaningful voice in the operation of the school. It was in only a few towns or districts—roughly one fourth of the areas for which there were interviews with four or more community leaders—that a majority of respondents agreed that such meaningful involvement existed. For the total sample of 141 respondents, 22 per cent were rated at point 4, 9 per cent at point 5, and 1 per cent at point 6. Included in the definition of point 4 is the statement: "For example, the Indian community may elect a school board or an advisory council which is fairly representative of the community's wishes." This third of the sample evidently perceived the relation of the community to the school to be approximately the same as that in the typical American community.

Possible differences between Indian and non-Indian community leaders were examined by comparing the two groups on Scale I. There was no difference between them in their perception of the actual extent of local community influence. However, the Indian leaders favored somewhat greater local Indian control of the schools than did the non-Indian leaders.

The community leaders were overwhelmingly in favor of the school doing something to help Indian students learn about their tribal culture. On the rating scale to measure this attitude, 42 per cent were rated at point 5, and 30 per cent at point 4, as defined:

> 5. R feels that the school should *support* the tribal culture by including it in the school program in some minor way. He mentions class activity such as history, language, or special projects.

4. R says he would like the school to do something about teaching
tribal culture and history, but he does not have ideas as to how this
can or should be done in this particular community.

In addition, 14 per cent of the community leaders were rated
at point 6. The definition of this point states that schools should
give "daily instruction" concerning the local Indian culture and
history. Only 15 per cent of the sample was opposed to teaching about Indian culture in school.

Examples of the attitudes expressed by Indian leaders may
illustrate a variety of views. For instance, here are some of the
statements of an Oklahoma Indian farmer who is regarded by
Indians and whites as an informal leader. He is a former member
of his tribal council. He farms 160 acres and is eternally grateful
to his grandmother for holding on to this land while other
Indians were selling. He has four children, one a graduate of
the state university, now studying law at the University of New
Mexico. He, himself, attended a BIA boarding school. This man
said: "Indian contributions to the growth of this land should
be presented fairly and accurately, not in separate books but as
a part of the treatment of American history. . . . There should
not be an effort to teach the local Indian language in the school.
Indian youngsters today cannot speak the Indian language and
should not. Indians should know about their past but should not
attempt to relive it. They must merge with the white man's
culture. The danger is that the Indian will lose his fundamental
decency and ability to appreciate the simple things, as the white
man has done."

A seventy-year-old Indian woman on an Arizona reservation,
a member of a very small tribe and a member of the tribal
council, looks back on the changes she has observed in the
schools. When asked, "Do you think that Indian life should be
included in the school program?" she said:

I really don't see any sense to it but if they really want it they are
welcome to it. It seems like we have worked all our life to civilize ourselves, so to speak, then they turn right around and want us to do it the
other way. Well, I just don't get the idea, I just don't know what it is. It
just seems like time and money wasted educating the Indians all these
years and now they come to the point where they figure it didn't work. I

know that the main thing is to keep the Indian identified and they don't want us to lose our culture and all that but then I think that we will retain some of these things, I think it is just *in us*. I was away for many years but when I came back I remembered everything. I say if we have to remember, we can.

When questioned: How much and what kind should be included in the school curriculum?" She replied:

Well, we have always had our history within us. But we don't know our tribal history, in a formal way. When my husband was governor of the tribe, he stressed it, he wanted to do many things; but the people don't care about these things. He failed every time he proposed something, and so he just quit. He just couldn't get the support of the people, the tribal council and the BIA. Today they are thinking about it. Language, it should be learned in the home if they know it, but if they want to teach it at school, I don't care.

A more positive attitude about teaching local tribal culture was expressed by a middle-aged Apache man who is close to the school system. He said:

I would say the tribal heritage should be practiced in the classroom, or at least taught. And get away from this Dick and Jane business because a poor child that comes from a wickiup and never had the experience of going off a reservation, how much does he know about the non-Indian? So what I'm saying is try to teach a child within his own world.

Yes, the school should teach the language to a certain extent. We all know that the English language is a second language. We know our language already. Some people say it's fading out, but I didn't see that in my own education. I left my home and was in boarding school for nine years and I came home and I still spoke Apache. I think it could be used at the elementary level; in Head Start and the first grade where these kids don't know any English; some sort of audio-visual machines using Apache language to explain what an apple is in Apache, then translating it into English. This would help a child get his first conversations started.

Community leaders on the reservations and the near-reservation towns are generally representative of the "man of two cultures" philosophy. They look for improvement in the economic position of the Indian people, and they expect the school system to help in realizing this goal. At the same time, they favor increased teaching of Indian culture and history in the schools. Community leaders are more critical of the schools than are the parents, but they do not call for revolutionary change. It is probable that increased responsibility for determining policy and practice in local school systems by these community leaders would support a program of rather conservative change.

IX

Teachers of Indian Children and Youth

There must be about twelve thousand elementary and secondary schoolteachers who work with more than two or three Indian pupils each day. Probably seven thousand of these teachers are in classes with a preponderance of Indian boys and girls in the following types of schools: Bureau of Indian Affairs boarding and day schools—1800 teachers; public schools located on or near Indian reservations—4900 teachers; and mission and other private schools—300 teachers.

Another three thousand are teaching in public schools with five to fifteen pupils in their classes, mainly in towns and rural areas. Another five thousand are teaching in cities over fifty thousand in population, with two to five pupils, enough to make them aware that they work with Indian pupils.

The National Study secured questionnaires from 634 teachers, and 345 of them were interviewed.[1] These teachers were a fairly representative sample of the teachers in the schools that were studied. Before looking at these teachers with some care, we may get some general information by looking at data from a questionnaire study made in 1968 of all of its teachers by the Bureau of Indian Affairs.

There were 1772 teachers who filled out questionnaires, 1209 teaching at the elementary school level, and 563 at the high school level. It is possible to compare these teachers with a national sample of public schoolteachers, described by the National Education Association in 1967. The comparison is shown in Table 18. There is very little difference in the general characteristics between the two groups.

TABLE 18

COMPARISON OF BIA TEACHERS (1968)
WITH A NATIONAL SAMPLE OF
PUBLIC SCHOOL TEACHERS (1965–66)

| | Percentages | |
Characteristics	BIA Teachers	National Sample of Public School Teachers
SEX		
Male	38.8	31.6
Female	61.2	68.9
YEARS OF AGE		
Under 30	37.4	33.9
30–39	21.6	22.8
40–49	15.8	17.5
50–59	14.1	19.2
60 or more	11.1	6.6
LEVEL OF EDUCATION		
Less than Bachelor's degree	4.6	7.0
Bachelor's degree only	76.9	69.6
Degree beyond Bachelor's	18.5	23.3
TYPE OF SCHOOL		
Elementary	68.1	52.5
Secondary	31.9	47.5
YEARS OF TEACHING EXPERIENCE		
Under 3	17.2	18.4
3–9	37.1	36.1
10–19	24.7	24.0
20 or more	21.0	21.5
Number	1772	2344

The BIA teachers differ from the national sample mainly in expected ways. Eleven per cent of the BIA group were Indians. Substantially more of the elementary school teachers are men in the BIA schools than in the national sample, as would be expected, since men are more likely than women to teach in isolated one- or two-room BIA schools.

The BIA teachers are members of the federal civil service. Their salaries are likely to be somewhat higher than the salaries of teachers in neighboring rural and small-town public schools. In 1968, salaries ranged from $6176 to $12,119 depending on length of service and amount of training. These teachers work on a twelve-month basis, with a nine-month school year, and the remaining three months are taken up with in-service training, preparation for the next year, and vacation.

Among 442 educational administrators reported by the BIA in 1968, 26.5 per cent were Indians. The ratio of men to women was 74 to 26.

Information on attitudes held by teachers of Indian youth comes from questionnaires and interviews of the National Study. The questionnaires were intended to be confidential, though it is likely that a few were handed unsealed by the teacher to the school principal, and in these cases the teacher may have expected the principal to look at the teacher's responses. The interview was conducted by a member of the visiting research staff who assured the teacher that what he said would be held in confidence.

The anonymous questionnaire contained the following item:

How do you feel about your present job?
Very favorable—; Favorable—; Neutral—:
Unfavorable—; Very unfavorable—.

This was identical with one used with Chicago public school teachers in 1964; also anonymous. The teachers in the Indian Study rated their jobs more than favorable (average of 1.73 on the five-point scale, which lies between very favorable and favorable). This compares with an average score of 2.17 (less favorable) for the Chicago teachers.

In the questionnaires, teachers were asked to say whether

certain statements about Indian children and parents were true or false. Several statements and responses included:

In class, Indian children are shy and lack confidence.

Fifty per cent of the teachers agreed with this statement, 25 per cent said it was false, and 25 per cent said it was neither true nor false. This opinion was expressed frequently by teachers in group discussions they had with researchers. They spoke of Indian pupils as being reticent, shy, and reluctant to ask questions or recite individually. In the beginning of the year some children would not answer the roll call.

Indian children are well behaved and obey the rules.

Forty-one per cent of the teachers marked this statement as true, 25 per cent indicated it was false, and 35 per cent were undecided. In sum, the typical teacher feels that Indian children are well behaved but that most are shy in class and not eager to learn. They seem both to like and dislike the quietness of Indian children. While they cited reluctance of Indian students to speak in class as a major problem, they also felt that this was one of the desirable features about teaching Indian children. Quiet, unresponsive children provided fewer behavior problems.

Indian parents want to help their children in school.

Fifty-three per cent of the teacher sample said this statement was true and 18 per cent said it was false. A good many teachers felt that parents were indifferent toward the school or perhaps hostile. They felt that only the more educated parents were taking an active interest in the education of their children.

The school's teaching conflicts with the Indian parent's teaching.

Forty-one per cent of the teacher sample said this was true, and 39 per cent said it was false. It is clear that about half of the teachers had a rather negative picture of Indian parents, while the other half were positive.

This conclusion can be checked against the ratings from the interview. On the teacher's degree of understanding of and sympathy for the problems of the local Indian people (Scale B), 30 per cent of the teachers were rated at a point on the scale which indicated that they were "sympathetic" toward Indian people as being "disadvantaged" but that they had a poor conception of the problems Indians actually face. Twenty-nine per cent were rated at point 3. Such teachers expressed some understanding and sympathy for certain aspects of the situation in which their Indian pupils were living without really understanding the total situation of the Indian people in the community. Twenty-five per cent of the teachers were rated at point 4, suggesting that they have a good understanding of and considerable sympathy for the problems of the local Indian people.

In addition, 6 per cent of our teacher sample evinced no understanding of the Indian people in their communities. At the other end of the scale, 10 per cent of the teachers seemed to have a very good understanding of the Indian community and a real sensitivity to and respect for it.

Thus, approximately one third of our teacher sample had a good basis for forming their attitudes toward Indians. Two thirds did not appear to know and understand their Indian "clients" as well as they could have.

Given these attitudes we may ask how these teachers felt about teaching Indian children.

On teacher's attitude toward teaching Indian children (Scale F), nearly half of the teachers (46 per cent) were rated at point 4, indicating that they liked teaching Indian children. These teachers were not necessarily enthusiastic about Indian children, but they certainly had no serious complaints about their teaching situation. Another 35 per cent of our sample were rated at point 3, suggesting that they saw teaching Indian children as no different from teaching non-Indian children. They expressed no positive or negative feelings about this. On the other hand, 16 per cent of the teachers rated on this scale found the experience of teaching Indians to be unique and clearly preferred it to other teaching situations. Finally, 4 per cent of our sample expressed negative feelings about teaching Indian children. Thus, with few exceptions, teachers of Indians in the schools we studied appear to feel neutral to positive about teaching Indians as opposed to teaching non-Indians.

There is a tendency for schools which are most criticized by parents and students to be the ones where teachers have more negative attitudes toward students and parents. This is seen in Table 19.

TABLE 19

COMPARISON OF ATTITUDES OF TEACHERS WITH
ATTITUDES OF PARENTS AND STUDENTS

Seven Schools Most Criticized by:		Schools in Which Teachers Have Relatively Negative Attitudes Toward:	
Students	Parents	Students	Parents
A	A	–	A
–	B	B	B
C	C	–	–
D	D	–	–
–	E	E	E
F	F	F	F
–	–	G	G
H	H	H	H
J	–	J	J

Note: Since there were about twenty-five schools with all four sets of data, the correspondence between the two halves of the table is clearly beyond what might have occurred by chance. Each letter stands for a particular school.

In the National Study there were four different measures of attitudes and perceptions on the issue of assimilation *into the dominant white culture* versus *maintenance of a separate Indian culture.* In the interviews, the majority of teachers tend to take the "man of two cultures" position. They believe that Indians should acquire the skills and attitudes that make for success in modern society, but they should also maintain some of their tribal or Indian culture. On the questionnaire, they were asked to indicate their own schools' policy in this respect, and they tend to see their school as more Anglo oriented than their own preference would suggest. On the questionnaire item "There is conflict between what most Indian parents teach their children and what this school tries to teach," they average right at the mid-point or "undecided" point on the scale. On the item "The Indian people should become completely assimilated with the larger American society," the average of the teachers' marks is at the "disagree" point.

Summing up, the teachers' position on assimilation is moderate and cautious, not Anglo oriented, but also not inclined to see the teaching of tribal or Indian culture as a major objective for them in school.

The 11 per cent of Indian teachers in the National Study sample differ in many not unexpected ways from their non-Indian colleagues. Their knowledge about and contact with the Indian community are considerably higher. They tend to teach in schools with a high percentage of Indian students and have more contact with parents and students outside of school. They have more positive attitudes toward Indian students. With regard to their position on assimilation, the only difference, if any, to the non-Indian group, is a slight inclination toward an Anglo orientation.

The Indian teachers, then, seem to be characterized as a group with close contacts to the Indian communities and a firm Anglo orientation for themselves and in their view on the role of the school.

Comparing the two groups of teachers whose interview ratings show the most versus the least involvement with the lives of their students outside of school, we note that teachers with a great amount of contact rate considerably higher in their sympathy for their Indian pupils, see them significantly more interested in the academic aspects of school, and tend to make more positive judgments about Indians in general than their colleagues with little contact.

Against this background it is puzzling to see that with regard to the position on assimilation through education, the group with the highest out-of-school involvement holds a position considerably more Anglo oriented than both the group with low student contacts and the total teacher sample.

This group, then, with a very positive overall attitude toward their Indian students sees a better future for them only in less

Indian-oriented schools. This position could be due either to their analysis of the situation and their resulting realistic conviction that the individual Indian, in order to get ahead in today's American society, has to have a good Anglo school training, or, since this group of teachers is not particularly critical of their school's administration, it could be just a going-along with the school's policy on that matter.

Perceptions of Teachers by Parents and Students

In Chapter VII, we reported that parents and students were mildly favorable toward their teachers. Still, there were differences in level of approval between various communities, and it is possible to compare teachers in schools with high approval of schools to teachers of schools that were given only low approval ratings.

In schools where teachers are highly approved by students, the teachers are well above average in their enthusiasm for teaching Indians, know more about the Indian community, have more contact with Indian students outside of school, rate higher on understanding and sympathy, and show more favorable attitudes toward Indians than the average teacher or the teacher in the schools with lower teacher approval scores.

The parents differ somewhat from the students in their evaluation of teachers. They favor teachers who are more authoritarian and more Anglo oriented with respect to assimilation policy. Also, these teachers have slightly lower ratings for perception and sympathy for pupils.

Teachers who work in schools which receive high approval by students can also be compared with teachers in schools which receive low approval. The schools the Indian students like best are the ones with the highest percentage of Indian students. This factor may be more important to students than the actual qualities of the teachers in these schools. The teachers in these schools had generally positive attitudes toward Indian students. On the other hand, teachers in the less favored schools are more authoritarian than teachers in the other group, and are more critical of the school administration. Their critical attitude toward their administrators may be due to qualities in the teachers themselves, or on the other hand, to faults among the administrators.

Teachers in all schools agreed that tribal or Indian culture and history should be taught in the schools. On the questionnaire item "There should be courses in the curriculum which teach the local Indian history and culture," practically every teacher indicated "agreement" or "strong agreement."

Few teachers of Indian children overtly express bigotry, and most have a favorable attitude toward their pupils. But observers of Indian schools were often impressed by a view prevalent among many—that they did not treat their Indian pupils differently than others, that they saw children, not Indians. While this appears as an expression of egalitarianism, it does reflect an absence of sensitivity to the actual differences among pupil populations and a denial of Indian identity. Even where teachers expressed deep concern for their Indian pupils and were aware of cultural conflicts, they—especially the more sensitive teachers—were aware of their inadequate preparation for cross-cultural education and their inability to work effectively. They also expressed conflicts over appropriate goals for their students.

It would be easy to oversimplify the task of learning how to teach Indian children. For example, the following excerpt from a letter written by an Indian woman probably does this. The woman, now the mother of three high-school-age children, attended a boarding school from the age of seven to fifteen. She says she was homesick a good deal of the time, but none of the matrons in the dormitory bothered to "mother" her. "There was one Indian teacher I remember. She used to take us in her arms and laugh with us. She really cared for us and loved us." No doubt this was *very important* for the young children in that boarding school. That quality of motherliness plus qualities of patience and sympathy are important.

Beyond being humane, loving teachers, however, there is the need to know a good deal about the local tribal culture and history, not only to be able to teach about them, but also to know and respect their unique elements, to understand the tribe's system of rewards and problems of culture change. And in schools where several different tribes are represented, it is important for teachers to have in addition a general knowledge of the Indian peoples, their histories, and conditions.

One practicable procedure for learning these things is for teachers to participate in some form of in-service education that is focused in Indian culture and history, problems in cross-cultural education, and linguistics. This can be done in summer school, where courses are offered just for this purpose in many southwestern and western colleges. Also in areas such as Arizona, New Mexico, South Dakota, and Alaska, where there are relatively large numbers of native Americans, the state department of public instruction or the BIA could provide specialists to visit teachers in their classrooms, discuss their work, and suggest reading and other experiences to help them get a better understanding of the local Indian culture, history, and community.

The Indian communities too, however, have an important role to play in helping teachers understand their pupils better. As Indian representation on the boards of public schools and BIA schools increase, Indians may help teachers develop better ways of teaching. Almost all observers of Indian schools express their belief in the importance of communication between school staffs and the communities in which they work.

Ways of Improving the Work of Teachers

Teachers of Indian children and youth, who appear in general to be about average or above average in the characteristics and qualities of American teachers, nevertheless present several problems of policy and practice. One of them is that of housing or living arrangements. Slightly over half of the teachers who answered questionnaires lived in compounds more or less separated from the surrounding community. Approximately 15 per cent of the teachers lived in cities, where they would normally never see the families of their pupils except at school.

This fact is not surprising, for in the relatively isolated areas where most Indian schools are located, there is little or no rental housing available, and the school must provide housing for the staff, which it generally does by building one or more houses on the school grounds. This tendency for teachers to be housed in a fenced-in compound has been characteristic of many BIA schools, and is also fairly common in the case of rural public schools. In their spare time, teachers tend to visit other teachers within the compound, to watch TV, or to read. Important to them is the weekly long-distance shopping and fun visit to the nearest city.

One of the principal problems is the relatively high degree of mobility of teachers. Even those in the BIA service tend to move from one school to another quite frequently, while those in rural and small-town public schools generally stay only about two years. It is a general fact that a large proportion of teachers, both in BIA schools and in rural or small-town public schools, quit their jobs after one or two years of work. A study made by the BIA showed that slightly over half of the teachers in BIA schools who quit work during the 1964–67 period were people with less than two years of teaching experience. When asked why they were leaving, 38 per cent of the "leavers" said it was because of the geographical isolation of the school to which they were assigned. The mobility of those in public schools is due partly to the fact that salaries are seldom increased regularly in relation to years of service in these schools, and therefore a teacher who wants a salary increase must move to a larger community. Thus a good many promising young teachers simply move on after the first couple of years, when they might prefer to make a career of teaching Indians, and seek in-service training on Indian culture, etc.

In group discussions, teachers often spoke of other reasons for the high mobility. Isolation from the mainstream of society seemed to be a major cause. Some locations did not have television reception. Unmarried teachers expressed dissatisfaction with the lack of social life. Generally their living conditions were the major cause of moving, rather than the school organization or the nature of the students.

There are some obvious things that might be done to encourage teachers to stay longer with Indian schools. One is a regular salary increase, from a state or federal fund, as long as the teacher stayed in a given school system. Another is an extra or "hardship" payment, made to teachers in BIA schools which are quite isolated. Still another would be the opportunity to purchase or lease land and to build their own homes.

While improved conditions are essential, they may not by themselves insure teacher retention. This is illustrated by the case of

Alaska. The last frontier for teachers is Alaska, where village schools are maintained by the Bureau of Indian Affairs or by the Alaska State Department of Education serving about twenty thousand Eskimo, Aleut, or Indian pupils. There are about eighty village schools operated by the BIA, enrolling twenty to two hundred pupils, with some seven thousand enrollment, and about twelve thousand students in schools operated by the state or by local school districts, generally in larger communities or in the archipelago of southeastern Alaska. Teachers recruited by the Bureau of Indian Affairs are paid 25 per cent more than the regular BIA salaries, because the cost of living and the conditions of life make the job more difficult. In 1967, there were twenty-nine one-teacher and thirty-four two-teacher schools, in small, isolated villages.

The schools and teacher residences in the isolated villages are made of prefabricated parts that come by ship during the few ice-free months. Most of the food comes in cans. They have sophisticated heating and cooking plants—diesel motors, space heaters, stoves and lighting plants, with radio, mainly operating with oil as fuel. They arrive at their villages generally by a "bush" plane from the metropolis of Anchorage or from a smaller sea or river port of twenty-five hundred to ten thousand population. With some sophistication they arrange with a grocer or butcher in Anchorage, Fairbanks, or Nome to ship their occasional supplies of fresh meat, fruit, and vegetables by plane. In case of emergency, they can usually get medical aid by bush plane within an hour. Mails come once or twice a week.[2] But the conditions of isolation encourage even the most committed teachers to move from their posts within a very few years.

The requirement for the college degree for teaching certification has prevented Indians from entering the profession in large numbers. With the recent rapid increase in numbers of Indian college students, it seems very likely that the numbers of certified Indian teachers could be increased to a thousand or even two thousand in a very short time, thus reaching a proportion of 25 or 30 per cent among teachers in schools with predominant Indian enrollment. Until then, more Indian teaching assistants should be included on school staffs. More Indian teachers and assistants in schools would have three principal advantages. First, Indian students would see "role models" among young Indian men and women in their own schools, and thus would be encouraged to go on further with their own high school and college education. Second, Indian teachers would generally have more empathy with Indian culture and history than would white teachers. Third, the teaching profession would offer many jobs to young Indians.

In general, the research evidence supports very strongly the proposition that teachers in schools with a preponderance of Indian pupils are fairly competent people, well disposed toward Indians in general, middle-of-the-road on policy about assimilation of Indians into white culture and on the authoritarian-permissive dimension of classroom management.

The following statement about teachers in Alaska by John Collier, Jr., who has been critical of the schools for Indians and for Alaskan natives, is an illustration of our findings: "We found few 'inferior' teachers. The vast majority of school personnel in Alaska appear to be dedicated teachers, often with excellent educational training. The material quality of the schools and the general excellence of staff—as evaluated within white educational standards—leave us with no villains, no clear-cut default, no run-down school plants. Yet, by some reverse process, it appears that the better the school is by white standards, the more erosive becomes the educational experience."[3] It may be that a school, which is conducted in the orderly and systematic way that is desired by a white community, is not well adapted at present to an Eskimo culture.

Teachers and schools are in the position of teaching boys and girls who are caught between two conflicting cultures. The conflict is perhaps most serious with the Eskimos of Alaska, where the white culture has almost destroyed the pre-1940 economy of the natives of northwest Alaska. But the conflict is present in all Indian communities, whether they be relatively isolated or immersed in a big city.

This conflict is being worked out by the Indian people, in situations where the government and other agencies of white culture both help and hinder. Schools and teachers cannot "solve" this problem, but they can be helpful in its solution. For this, they need a better knowledge and understanding of the Indian communities and the cultures in which they work. They need to apply themselves systematically and patiently to the specific tasks of teaching a given age level in a given type of community with goals that are approved and supported by the Indian community. Fundamental to the search for improvement of the educational environment for Indian children and their teachers is an examination of curriculum.

X

The School Curriculum

In its most traditional sense, curriculum refers to the content of subject matter presented to pupils. The larger, more contemporary usage refers not only to content but also to the services provided children by the school, including the social climate for learning.

With occasional exceptions, curriculum for Indian children in both BIA and public schools parallels the curriculum provided others in the public schools of the various states in the nation. This is due to the influence of accrediting agencies, state guidelines, availability of texts, the influence of teacher education institutions, and to the prevailing educational fashions of the day.

The National Study of American Indian Education has documented a broad consensus among parents, students, teachers, and influential persons that the most important role of the schools is to prepare Indian students for employment in the dominant economy and for successful lives in modern society. Thus there is virtually no quarrel with the principle that the curriculum for Indian youth should include the very best curriculum provided the non-Indian youth of the country.

This does not mean, however, that the present curriculum is without criticism or escapes controversy over focus. Several major areas stand out as issues of concern. Among these are whether or not tribal culture and history should be included in school instruction; language instruction; vocational or academic emphasis; and most important—attention to the dignity of Indian identity.

Through the first three decades of this century, curriculum duplicated that of other American schools, but with considerably more emphasis placed on vocational subjects and institutional work in the boarding schools, and attention to English instruction.

Although it continued to view assimilation as a goal, the Meriam Report of 1928 did mark the point of departure from the deliberate anti-tribal language policies of the past. During the subsequent administration of John Collier as Commissioner of Indian Affairs, between 1935 and World War II, a conscious effort was made to encourage bilingual education and to establish day schools. An effort to fill the void left by conventional teacher-training institutes and prevailing curriculum was made by encouraging the writing of materials in several Indian languages. World War II interrupted this formidable task of restoring recognition to Indian languages and cultures.

The educational policies supported by John Collier continued in part until the 1950s when the federal policy of termination of the reservation system saw many Indian children moved into public school systems which had no special language or Indian culture programs for them. Since that time, there has been a growing interest in BIA schools in special programs of language instruction and a growing interest in public schools, especially in areas of heavy Indian concentration, on special language programs.

By now the goals for Indian education have moved toward maintaining respect for Indian culture and the dignity of Indian peoples, while maximizing the capabilities of students in the larger American society and economy. However, curriculum efforts to support such goals have yet to be made on a large scale, and as yet there is no agreement on what the curriculum should include.

Language and Culture

No question is receiving more serious attention today in discussions on curriculum than the matter of language instruction for Indian children. As the National Study findings indicate, it is clear that the Indian pupils as well as their parents accept the need to learn and study in English. For example, only four students out of twelve hundred interviewed indicated that they believed that knowledge of their native language was more important than knowledge of English.

Although recognizing the necessity for English competency, those interviewed held strong positive attitudes toward the tribal language as well. Three fourths of the students indicated an interest in learning their tribal language, and 68 per cent of the parents thought it would be nice or important for the schools to offer instruction in the native language.

In a radical shift from the earlier period when the use of Indian languages was forbidden, the Bureau of Indian Affairs now is developing a new curriculum designed to bring to Indian children a fuller appreciation of their origins and an understanding of their own importance in the history of the country. As stated in 1968:

> Teaching of Indian languages is being encouraged as rapidly as possible beginning with a search for Indian teachers, encouragement of Indian youth to enter the teaching profession, and the use of Indian speaking adult teacher-aides . . . confidence and trust are being placed with Indian people.[2]

Commenting on vacillating Bureau policy, one Indian Sioux elder has said:

> I see we have made a complete circle . . . I know during my time when the police picked me up and took me to the boarding school, the first thing they did was cut my hair. At the time I didn't know how to speak English, but they had a very strict rule if we were caught talking Indian, we got a spanking. Now the circle is complete. They now want to teach the kids the Sioux language without a spanking.[3]

Despite the shift in official policy toward permitting children to use their home language without fear of punishment, stress continues to be placed on the teaching of English. In all public, BIA and mission schools, with the recent exception of some schools engaged in experimental and innovating programs, the child is expected to study and respond in the English language, a language in which many have limited competency.

There are no clear data on the numbers of Indian children entering school with little or no English. The BIA estimates that two thirds of children attending its schools do speak another language. The percentage for public school is unknown but is probably much lower. Particularly many Alaskan native children and many Navajo children enter school with little or no command of the English language. How best to teach English has been of considerable interest in recent years and has resulted in growing interest in linguistic approaches. Currently, approaches to language instruction include:

1. Using linguistic techniques to teach English as a second language, moving the children from their use of the native language to the use of English as the language of instruction.

2. Bilingual education, which employs two languages as the medium of instruction for a child in a given school in any or all of the school curriculum except the actual study of the languages themselves.

3. The teaching of the native language as a separate subject.

Using linguistic techniques to teach English is encouraged by the BIA through use of ESL (English as a Second Language) in all its schools. Teachers, most of whom have no linguistic pre-service training, have been encouraged to attend linguistic institutes sponsored by USOE, NDEA, and EPDA programs. The BIA also conducts workshops in ESL methodology. In addition the BIA sponsors a newsletter, *English for American Indians,* initiated in 1968-69.[4]

Recent years have seen considerable emphasis upon testing and evaluation of the ESL program. An English language proficiency test is being devised for the BIA. Preliminary data from the test indicate that 63 per cent of the children enrolled in BIA schools speak English as a second language. Currently, a study by TESOL (Teachers of English to Speakers of Other Languages), a professional organization, has been commissioned by BIA to evaluate the English language program of the Navajo area office.

Teaching of English as a second language program assumes that a major cause of school failure is an inadequate grasp of the English language and therefore concentrates on language training, pattern drills, pronunciation, using aural-oral methods.

Somewhat critical of this approach are advocates of bilingual-bicultural educational programs. They argue that the methods of ESL are too mechanistic. Also accepting the hypothesis that school failure is related strongly to inadequate command of English, they go further in arguing that the teaching of literacy in English to those who do not have adequate command of the language is a major part of the educational problem faced by Indian youths. They therefore urge that instruction in reading be given in the home language of the child first.

Proponents of bilingual education also argue that it is a more humane approach to instruction, avoiding the frightening, frustrating experiences of the non-English speaking child in an all-English environment. They argue further that there is evidence that bilingual instruction makes for improved intellectual functioning; that it indicates respect for the native culture and helps retain pride. Proponents also argue that bilingual programs provide employment for native speakers as teachers, consultants, and in curriculum development; and that community and parental involvement with the school is more likely to occur with a bilingual program. Bilingual education is proposed not simply as a bridge to the past, but for its positive value in providing familiarity and skill in the handling of different cognitive systems. In a multinational, multiethnic world, language is seen as a key to identity and protection against alienation and disorientation.[5]

Several bilingual education programs for Indian students were instituted in recent years. Among these are programs at several schools in Arizona: the Toyei Boarding School (BIA), which has a bilingual elementary program for 671 Navajo children, the Rock Point Boarding School (BIA), and the Rough Rock Demonstration School (a BIA school contracted to Dine, Inc.).

The Rough Rock Demonstration School has attracted a great deal of national attention for its work in bilingual, bicultural education. Navajo is the main language of instruction for the younger children, supplemented by a continuous program in Navajo culture and language for all grades. The schedule is arranged to provide four hours of spoken Navajo and two of English in the preschool; four hours of spoken and written Navajo, and two hours of spoken English in the kindergarten to second grade; and two hours spoken and written Navajo and four hours spoken and written English in grades three to nine.

Six BIA kindergarten classrooms had bilingual programs in

1968–69, and the program was extended to the first grade for 1970–71. In addition, the BIA is conducting a bilingual program in isolated day schools in the Bethel region of Alaska.

The Department of Health, Education, and Welfare has sponsored bilingual education programs in several Head Start classes. There are no large-scale bilingual programs in state schools, other than those Head Start classes and a few programs financed under the Bilingual Education Act and administered by H.E.W.

Many difficulties stand in the way of the development of bilingual programs. Perhaps the most important is that many Indian languages have no standard orthography. In addition, although the theoretical problems involved in bilingual education have been explored, the practical experience with the day-to-day problems of teaching remain to be examined and reviewed.

The dearth of relevant teaching materials also remains a problem. The serious lack of materials available at present for bilingual programs for Indians is understandable when it is remembered that education for American Indians has for most of its history concentrated on the eradication of Indian languages and traditions in the name of Americanizing, or assimilating, the Indian child. The reversal of this policy between 1935 and World War II, under the then Commissioner of Indian Affairs John Collier, did encourage the production of preprimers, primer readers, dictionaries, grammars, and secondary materials in several Indian languages. Among the materials produced were eleven bilingual readers for Teton Dakota, and two in English and Hopi.[6] In addition, teachers were stimulated to develop materials, and many Indian teachers were recruited into BIA service.

Conventional teacher training then, as is still true today, and conventional curriculums were unconcerned with the special problems posed by cultural linguistic minorities, and the Collier administration made an effort to fill the void.

The Collier educational policy was not fully implemented after World War II and critical problems today still include the shortage of teachers trained to work in bilingual situations, dearth of materials, and the lack of adequate funding.

Several relatively new experimental schools such as Ramah School in New Mexico and Rough Rock School in Arizona have employed local people with expertise in traditional language, culture, and history to teach. The use of this primary source of personnel sometimes runs into the problem of teacher certification usually necessary in order for schools to be accredited. One way of dealing with the problem is the use of teacher aide, but this places the teacher of Indian languages and cultures in lower positions.

Among those who are working on the development of curriculum materials for bilingual, bicultural programs are the Southwest Cooperative Regional Laboratory in New Mexico, the University of Texas, the TTT program of the University of Washington which is developing Navajo curriculum, the Rough Rock Demonstration School, and the Navajo Studies Program of the new Navajo Community College in Arizona.

Much of the materials for the Navajo curriculum at Rough Rock are being developed at the Navajo Curriculum Center, associated with the school. Books and classroom materials; recording of oral histories by Navajo elders and medicine men; *Coyote Stories, Black Mountain Boy* and *Grandfather Stories* have been translated, as well, into English. Dr. Oswald Werner of Northwestern University has developed an orthography which is the basis for the written language. Craftsmen and artists give talks and demonstrations.

Although Indian languages are no longer being stamped out as a matter of official policy, there remains a resistance to bilingualism on the part of many educators committed to English-only policies and acting out an implicit melting-pot philosophy which assumes the assimilation of Indian pupils in a one-way direction. Members of the non-English speaking communities themselves, having been taught that English is utilitarian in the school setting are not always convinced of the need for bilingual programs. Evidence from the National Study of American Indian Education, however, points out that a majority of parents interviewed wanted some recognition of tribal language and culture by the school. The value of bilingual education as the most effective route to an excellent education may be increasingly accepted given the success of model programs. Certainly, despite all the problems inherent in bilingual education, it would seem practical in the near future to have such programs in communities where the native language is the home language and to concentrate efforts in this direction in the early grades. Careful planning with local communities is an essential ingredient in the success of bilingual programs and such programs should not be imposed without community approval and support.

Whether or not Indian cultures and Indian languages, as subjects, should be taught as part of the regular school curriculum for Indian children has become a subject of debate in recent years. The question becomes particularly significant when it is a matter of whether or not a particular tribe's culture or language should be taught in the school. Disagreements are related to different tribal needs, local conditions, and to differences between more traditional and more progressive factions within tribes.

The viewpoints of two leading Indian educators points up the controversy. Joe Sando, speaking for the All Pueblo Tribal Council, has said:

> In the Pueblo system, the learning of language and culture is the responsibility of the families. Each Pueblo student living in the village generally speaks in the vernacular. And if the student speaks the correct language, he or she is more than likely to have learned the culture or be aware of its customs. Consequently, we would not or could not justify teaching Indian languages or culture in the classroom. An exception would be if the student were a preschooler as in Head Start . . . And this would be only until the child has learned to be a student, and begun to learn English as a second language.[7]

Thus, interestingly enough, there is strong sentiment among the more traditional Pueblos for retaining the indigenous system for the teaching of traditional custom and language. The school is viewed primarily as the mechanism for learning English and the skills to deal with the non-Indian world.

Articulating another point of view, Dillon Platero, director of the Rough Rock Demonstration School, argues:

> In addition to what is demonstrably sound in a typical non-Navajo oriented curriculum, the People (the Navajo) would like to add courses in both Navajo culture and history. By making these indigenous subjects an integral part of the curriculum and giving them an importance equal to any other subject, we would accomplish the task of reinforcing a positive self-image and assisting learners to optimal self-realization. To

encourage children to be proud of being a Navajo is not enough. We must show them traits both Navajo and worthy of pride before sincere accomplishment is produced.[8]

In interviews conducted by the National Study with over one thousand Indian students and over five hundred Indian parents, it is clear that the overwhelming majority of Indian students and parents have positive feelings about their tribal language and culture. The largest numbers expressed interest in learning about culture and language in the schools, although few expressed very militant feelings about Indian curriculum, and a small but significant minority (especially of students) appears to feel that this would be better done at home, many giving as their reason the fact that there were no teachers at school who knew anything about the tribal culture.

The overwhelming majority of parents made the realistic appraisal that the school is not doing anything to teach their children about their tribe's history or culture. However, very few believe that the school is attacking or downgrading it either. Most seem to feel that Indian culture is simply ignored at school.

Despite lack of unanimity, the National Study found considerable support among Indian youths and their parents for instruction in the native languages themselves, as subjects of study, within the schools, both at the elementary and secondary level. Even in the most acculturated situations, for example, Chicago, children interviewed expressed an interest in the Indian languages. In areas where there is a large concentration of native speakers, and where there is this interest, schools could make provision for the teaching of a course in an Indian language, at least on an elective basis. This is valuable not only for its general cultural and cognitive aspects and the recognition it accords the Indian community, but also in providing interested students with the necessary skills to function more effectively as potential teachers, administrators, scholars, in reservation development, etc. Teachers of these courses can be recruited from the community or from among the graduates of the growing number of university native American studies programs.

As more Indians take active roles in local public school boards, support for Indian language and culture programs grows. Recently the Gallup-McKinley Board of Education in Arizona became predominantly Navajo. One newly elected member was Abe Plummer, deputy director of the Ramah Navajo High School. Mr. Plummer campaigned for the inclusion of more Indian culture included in the curriculum of the public schools, along with the culture of other minority groups—the Mexican-Americans and Blacks. *The Navajo Times,* the official newspaper of the Navajo tribe, commenting on the election, also called for the inclusion of the teaching of the Navajo language as an elective subject in any school system in which the Navajo predominates.

> We would also like to see the Navajo language taught in the public schools as an elective subject. The Navajo language is very difficult to learn, but it holds the key to the complex and fascinating Navajo culture and should be included in any school system in which the Navajo predominates.[9]

The all-Indian school board in Taholah, Washington, has developed curriculum including instruction in the Quinault language, culture, and history. And the Indian advisory board to the Intermountain Boarding school in Utah has called for the teaching of the Navajo clan system to the students.

Recently, the desire to revive a language nearly lost has stimulated the local school boards on the Yakima Reservation in Washington to add to the school curriculum Sahapten, a language spoken by the Yakima, Umatilla, and Warm Springs Indians.

Again, despite the absence of official policy deliberately seeking to stamp out Indian cultures, curriculum materials and programs incorporating tribal history, culture, contemporary issues including tribal government and politics were generally absent in the schools studied by the National Study. Exceptions do of course appear. Among those are the St. Francis Mission School in South Dakota, which includes curriculum materials on Indian culture; the Taholah public school in Washington which has developed curriculum including instruction in Quinault language, culture, and history; the BIA has sponsored a course in Indian psychology developed by Dr. John Bryde; the BIA initiated Project Necessities (no longer BIA sponsored), an effort to develop curriculum materials based on the local experiences of Indian children and including the training of teachers to develop their own materials relevant to local conditions; the Alaska Reading Series is used in many Alaskan schools, incorporating illustrations and experiences of Alaska and Alaskans as text in pre-primers and primers. In addition, many teachers have made individual efforts to introduce Indian-oriented materials in their teaching.

Teachers interviewed by the National Study often expressed a desire to teach more accurately about Indian culture, history, and current affairs, but felt severely handicapped by a lack of information and a lack of materials.

Curriculum innovation has been stimulated by several sources, but primarily federal funding has provided the impetus for the major programs.

Through the BIA itself, in its school system the thrust has been primarily in support of ESL. Although the curriculum office of BIA has supported bilingual programs, psychology courses, and Project Necessities, these have been more controversial and have received limited support.

The major impetus to innovation has been the Elementary and Secondary Education Act of 1965. The Bilingual Education Act has stimulated public school districts and community agencies to develop special programs for Indian children. Many of these programs emphasize local Indian cultures and language instruction.

Indian History

Textbook studies by a number of states, historical societies, and individual scholars indicate that misconceptions, myths, inaccuracies, and stereotypes about Indians are common to the curriculum of most schools. In the words of the Senate Subcommittee report *Indian Education: A National Tragedy—A National Challenge:*

> It is a history which calls an Indian victory a massacre and a U.S. victory an heroic defeat. It is a history which makes heroes and pioneers of gold miners who seized Indian land, killed whole bands and families and ruthlessly took what they wanted. It is a history which equates Indians and wild animals, and uses the term "savages" as a synonym for Indians.[10]

The evidence that our textbooks have neglected the Indians or distorted their roles, characteristics, and relationships with the Americans is overwhelming. One author, after examining more than a hundred history texts, concluded that the American Indians have been obliterated, defamed, disparaged, and disembodied. The notion of the blood-curdling, perilous, massacring savage is common.[11]

A report prepared by the University of Alaska showed that twenty widely used texts contained no mention of Alaskan natives at all, and in some cases no mention of Alaska; although some textbooks mention Alaskan Eskimos, very few mention Indians; and many texts at the elementary and secondary level contain serious and often demeaning inaccuracies in the treatment of the Alaskan native.

A study made by the University of Idaho found similar results —with Indians presented as inarticulate, backward, unable to adjust to modern Euro-American culture, sly, vicious, barbaric, superstitious, and destined to extinction. California found in a study of fourth, fifth, and eighth grades that, in the forty-three texts used, hardly any mention was made of the American Indian's contribution or his role in the colonial period, gold rush, or mission periods of California history, and when mentioned, was usually distorted or misinterpreted.[12]

After studying three hundred textbooks in use in public and federal schools, the American Indian Historical Society, an all-Indian organization of scholars and native historians, commented, "Not one could be approved as a dependable source of knowledge about the history and culture of the Indian people in America. Most of the books were, in one way or another, derogatory to the Native Americans. Most contained misinformation, distortions, or omissions of important history."[13]

Their study considered the textbooks to be degrading and insulting to the Indian student. The president of the American Indian Historical Society has said, "There is not one Indian child who has not come home in shame and tears after one of those sessions [in school] in which he is taught that his people were dirty, animal-like, something less than a human being."[14]

Indian children are of course not the only ones affected by

this situation. An effort to assess the thinking of white suburban children about Indians was made by the University of Minnesota's Training Center for Community Programs, and is part of the Final Report of the NSAIE.[15] Grade-school children were asked to write essays on "What I Know About Indians." The results indicated a wide variety of ideas about Indians, ranging from the romantic and recognizing the injustices inflicted by white people to "if I saw an Indian, I'd be scared stiff." The authors of the report concluded that, on the whole, the generalizations made by the white children about Indians were negative enough to validate the conclusions of the U.S. Senate Indian Education Subcommittee's study which contends that: "To thousands of Americans, the American Indian is, and always will be, dirty, lazy, and drunk. That is the way they picture him; that's the way they treat him."[16]

The authors of the Minnesota study point out a situation observed by NSAIE in almost all schools visited:

> . . . precious little *contemporary* information about living, breathing American Indians is apparently being provided in schools. . . . It is this absence of contemporary materials, which, combined with over-generalized, often demeaning, and under-elaborated historical materials which sets the stage for a new round in the old cycle of myth creation and maintenance about the American Indian. When the problems of poor teacher preparation, or inadequate teacher attitudes are added, together with the often negative influences of family, media, and peer groups, the picture becomes generally depressing. . . .[17]

The research, writing, and production of scrupulously honest textbooks are necessary steps to be taken. Without accurate materials, schools will be hampered in their efforts to correct the distortions that continue to feed ignorance and distrust.

But textbooks alone are not likely to make for significant change. As the Minnesota study points out: "*. . . even where every effective classroom resource exists for the teaching of American Indian history and culture, the benefits of these resources will be sadly undermined by other forces operating to diminish the impact of the classroom.*"[18]

The informal climate of the school regarding intergroup relations, radio, television, commercial films, comic books, weekly magazines, local newspapers, all impinge on the learning environment of the child. And influences beyond the control of the formal curriculum of the school, such as peer groups and families, will continue to affect social attitudes. If anti-Indian sentiment persists in the society, children will continue to learn the attitudes appropriate to it. If educators wish to make a serious effort to counteract ignorance about Indians, they at least must be sensitive to the materials used for instruction.

In its study the Indian Historical Society also accused the BIA of having the most outdated textbooks. It is difficult to compile comparable statistics for public schools, but the BIA itself has studied the textbook situation and reports that 37 per cent of its texts are up to five years old, 40 per cent are six to ten years old, and 18 per cent are eleven to fifteen years old, 4.75 per cent are sixteen to twenty years old, and .25 per cent are twenty years or more old.[19]

As scholarship and writing in this area improve and as more accurate portrayal of the role of American Indians in the history and development of this country becomes available, more effort will have to be made to feed these materials into the schools. The age of texts is important in matters pertaining to American Indian materials. Equally important is the need to make available in schools attended by Indian youths the most current educational resources in all subject areas.

The concern of Indian scholars for the development of greater accuracy in the content of the curriculum is growing. Their influence upon publishing companies, state boards, etc. will be increasingly felt in this decade. The dearth of accurate textbook treatment of native Americans requires the encouragement and support of Indian scholarship to re-evaluate content and to write.

Concerning Indian cultural traditions in the curriculum, it is important to note that historically and at present the school is an agent of transmission of non-Indian culture to Indians. In only a very few exceptional cases, e.g., Rough Rock, is the transmission of traditional Indian culture viewed as a goal of the school to be worked out through the curriculum. There is little quarrel, even among the stanchest supporters of bicultural programs, with the view that the schools should prepare Indian youngsters to deal with the larger society. However, the absence of Indian cultural and historical materials are viewed as a denigrating, one-sided version of the real world. The absence of instruction in current affairs and tribal government is not realistic preparation for dealing with the larger society. Recognition of the Indian presence is valued and is to be encouraged.

Throughout most of the history of Indian education, there was a strong vocational emphasis. In recent decades, most high schools attended by Indian youngsters have paralleled the educational trend throughout the nation with its growing emphasis upon a comprehensive education, including academic courses that would qualify successful graduates for college entrance while providing commercial and vocational course offerings as well. Special programs such as the 1950s crash literacy program for Navajos who entered school late have been phased out and replaced by curriculums that generally meet state certification. Vocational emphasis continues to be high, however, especially in BIA boarding schools.

Proponents of academic training see in vocational education a limitation on career choice; others see vocational training as realistic preparation for jobs. Increasingly, however, vocational training has been postponed to post-high school programs.

Work-study programs, career development programs, job training programs can be of great value to Indian youngsters before high school graduation. The despised outing system and the institutional labor required of pupils in the old boarding schools should not be allowed to stand in the way of modern programs that can provide the opportunity to earn money, acquire skills, as well as provide useful roles for youth while attending school, whether they are preparing for advanced academic work or not. One of the criticisms directed against some schools for Indian children is that their isolation, both physical and cultural, inhibits the goals and aspirations of Indian youth. Conscious attention to career opportunities in both the Indian and non-Indian communities should be included in the curriculum offered.

It is difficult for school counselors, especially in the public schools, to have access to vocational and educational scholarship information for Indian youngsters. In states with large Indian populations in the public school it would be useful to have a central office which can act to disseminate information to school counselors.

Curriculum in the broader sense includes more than the content of course offerings. It may be thought of as including all the services provided children as well as the total social atmosphere of the school. Many factors influence the learning environment. Some of these come from outside the school itself—job opportunities, accrediting agencies, curriculum trends in the universities, etc. Within the school, attention to the Indian presence is essential to a positive learning environment. Too often, educators, believing themselves democratic, prefer to view all children as alike. Children differ not only as individuals, but as members of different groups. Respectful recognition of their identity as Indians will help open the way to a search for better communication between teachers and pupils.

Education for Indians, with infrequent exceptions, has been designed without reference to their particular interests and needs. It has been the same curriculum designed for non-Indian children, sometimes a more punitive and moralistic version, and where it has not succeeded, the Indian child has been criticized for not fitting the curriculum, rather than the curriculum criticized for not fitting the needs of the Indian child.

Most schools conduct their business with little reference to the Indian community about them. Calendars do not coincide with local customs—the Indians having to adjust their life style to meet the demands of the school for a five-day week, nine- or ten-month school year. School holidays to coincide with the rice gathering in Minnesota, for example, or harvesting seasons, etc. would seem to be desirable. Calendar conflicts, such as the need to pack salmon in Alaska, often cause pupils to drop out of school because they are regarded as truants. The schools blame the "truancy" on the Indians and Eskimos, whereas it would seem not impossible for schools, in conjunction with community leaders and parents, to work out a calendar that is less conflicting. (At Rough Rock this summer, the school has moved into brush shelters on top of the mesa, near the summer camps of the families.)

Schooling often requires enormous amounts of family adjustment—the school has been inflexible in terms of both its calendar and its location. Coercion in the form of a single alternative begets rejection . . . example and choice are more likely to achieve change.

Similarly, styles of learning must be accepted. Group cooperation, rather than being labeled cheating, for example, can be utilized constructively by sensitive educators.

Respect for their history, traditions, and cultures is given lip service by everyone dealing with Indian education at the present time. No longer are there blatant, overt attempts to force Indian children into mechanistic models of white men. However, many educators in practice do not carry through on stated goals either because they are themselves prejudiced or carry on habitual ethnocentrism despite their sincerity in wishing to help. But, perhaps most important, they are not quite sure how to best educate Indian youngsters and find their pupils performing at unsatisfactory levels.

Indian control and the presence of more Indian teachers and aides in schools are likely to improve the climate of trust and concern. The curriculum to be taught, however, and the best ways in which to do this are not so easily determined, and even with increased Indian influence there is likely to be no unanimity concerning curriculum and the goals of education.

Analysis of the literature on Indian education indicates that discussion of the curriculum for Indian students does not loom large.[20] The field studies of the National Study confirm this. In general, curriculum in BIA schools has followed that of the Anglo culture, and the curriculum in public schools is the same for Indians as non-Indians. Curiously, curriculum is taken as given and is rarely analyzed. Despite this, it is unlikely that Indian parents will want anything less for their children than the same curriculum offered to other Americans. The most outstanding difference, however, is that they would like the schools to give respectful recognition to their identity.

XI

Boarding Schools

No aspect of Indian education is without controversy, but the severest criticisms of all are those directed at the fact that most Indian children attending schools run by the Bureau of Indian Affairs have to leave home for their education. Presently, some thirty-five thousand American Indian children are enrolled in seventy-seven BIA boarding schools, more than twice the number attending BIA day schools, and nearly four thousand are living in BIA dormitories close to reservations, while attending classes in local public schools.

Critics of the boarding schools have been adamant and evoke considerable passion. One, Dr. Robert Leon, a psychiatrist, categorically states:

> . . . in my opinion there should be no Indian boarding schools for children in the elementary grades. I say this without qualifications. These schools do more harm than good. They do not educate, they alienate. Those children who have families should remain with their families, and those children who are so unfortunate as to not have families should be placed in adequate foster homes.[1]

That these sentiments are not shared unanimously is made evident by the declaration of the Navajo Tribal Council which in 1969, alarmed by a rising tide of boarding school critics, stated:

> BIA boarding schools on the Navajo Reservation were built and are operated through the close cooperation of the Navajo Tribe, the parents

of Indian children and the Bureau of Indian Affairs. If there is a better
way to educate children, we think it should be discussed with the Navajo
Tribe and the Navajo people. Until that time it is the request of the
Navajo people that the boarding school program on the Navajo Reservation be expanded by the Bureau of Indian Affairs, working closely
with the Navajo Tribe and the Navajo people, and we request that this
be continued until concrete evidence is submitted and that no precipitous
action be taken without complete information.[2]

The question of where best to educate Indians goes back to
the earliest contacts between native Americans and Western
education and is inextricably interwoven with education goals
and philosophy.

Even before the founding of the nation, the Society for the
Propagation of the Gospel in Foreign Parts argued for schools
located in Indian communities, noting:

> Very few of the Indians can be prevailed upon to let their Children go to
> any great Distance for Instruction, and when they are persuaded to it,
> the Children always go with Reluctance. They are continually anxious to
> return to their Parents and Brethren, which is an Obstruction to their
> literary Progress.

With considerable wisdom and striking modernity, the Society
argued that

> . . . It is therefore a mistaken Notion that Seminaries at a Distance
> from the Indians and only among Christians are fittest for the Education
> of Indian Youths . . . the Indian Country is evidently the properest
> Place to fix such a Seminary for this Purpose, where the Parents can
> frequently see their Children; by which all Uneasiness would be re-
> moved from both . . . It would also be pleasing to the Indians in gen-
> eral. They would look upon it as a Mark of our Regard and Confi-
> dence in them.[3]

The policies of the early missionaries were continued during
the early years of the new republic, federal subsidies were
provided Indian schools located among the frontier tribes.

Many of these schools were missionary boarding and day
schools, although in 1833, the Choctaws started a comprehensive
school system of their own with twelve schoolhouses and non-
Indian teachers, supported by tribal, missionary, and federal
funds.

The westward expansion of white Americans beyond the

Mississippi led to much conflict with resisting Indian peoples. During this time the one-room local schoolhouse, its calender related to the farming cycle, became the education pattern for white rural Americans. But for Indians, the boarding school, accompanied by student labor, developed.

The boarding school style was related only in part to the vicissitudes of the frontier. More significant was the evolution of the view that reservation confinement and education for assimilation were more humane and less costly than military control and extermination of those native Americans standing in the way of uncontrolled westward expansion. Extinction by force or extinction by assimilation were the alternatives presented the people whose language and cultures were ignored except as subjects for romance, entertainment, or contempt.

In 1865, a congressional committee investigating conditions among the western tribes recommended "boarding schools remote from the Indian communities" where stress would be placed on agricultural pursuits. President Grant stated as the goal of this process "the civilization and the ultimate citizenship" of Indians. In short, removal from home and tribe was viewed as necessary for the elimination of Indian identity and, therefore, the Indian "problem."[4]

It was not long before a federal boarding school system developed, beginning with the founding of the Carlisle Indian School in Carlisle, Pennsylvania, in 1878 by General Richard Henry Pratt.

The Carlisle Indian School enrolled children from the Midwestern and Western tribes and taught them to speak, read and write English, to dress and live like white people, and to perform various tasks which would prepare them for certain trades. One of the most significant aspects of the Carlisle School was its "outing system," which Pratt referred to as the "right arm" of the school, the supreme Americanizer.

Under this system, students were placed with a white family for three years after completing school. The government paid fifty dollars a year for each student's medical care and clothing, and his labor was to compensate for the benefits derived from the home situation.

Paying little attention to the multitude of linguistic and other cultural differences among the tribes, and the varied traditions of child rearing in preparation for adulthood in the tribal communities, the package deal that accompanied literacy included continuing efforts to "civilize the natives." To Pratt, the essential process of making American citizens out of Indians was immersing the Indians in our own civilization, and after getting them under, holding them there until they were thoroughly soaked.

Between 1889 and 1892, twelve such boarding schools were opened. Abandoned army forts were converted into boarding schools; children were removed, sometimes forcibly long distances from their homes; the use of Indian languages by children was forbidden under threats of corporal punishment; students were boarded out to white families during vacation times, and native religions were suppressed. These practices were rationalized by the notion that the removal from the influence of home and tribe was the most effective means of preparing the Indian child to become an American. Indian agents were held responsible for keeping the school filled, by persuasion if possible, by force if necessary; and rations and annuities were withheld from reluctant parents.

The ignominious beginnings of the boarding school system, rooted in forced assimilation, paradoxically grounded in white humanitarianism, have left a legacy of unpleasant memories that affect attitudes and policies today.

It was not long, however, before critics of boarding schools caused a shift in government policy toward Indian education, and after 1890, attendance in public schools and BIA day schools was supported as official policy. The reasons for this shift are many and not always based upon humanitarian concern or tolerance for cultural diversity. The non-reservation boarding schools were costly; they did not succeed in their goal of total assimilation; and, perhaps most important, politically there was resistance to continuing federal responsibility for Indian welfare. Commissioner Francis Leupp (1904–09), for example, referred to boarding schools as "an educational almshouse" and, looking forward toward a time when Indian parents would support their children without government assistance, he championed the day school—an inexpensive version fitted out simply like a white rural school. By 1901, the Commissioner of Indian Affairs called for a policy to "abolish rations and annuities, throw the educated Indian on his own resources, and the settlement of the Indian question is the natural sequence."[5]

The day schools were seen as the means of gradually withdrawing support from the Indians, giving them little or no aid in clothing and subsistence. In addition, the day schools were viewed as carrying "civilization" to the great mass of Indian homes, the boarding schools viewed as not affording this opportunity as well.

Implementing the thrust away from boarding schools, the first contracts for the coeducation of Indians and whites in state and territory schools were made in 1891. Soon, California, Idaho, Michigan, Montana, Nebraska, Nevada, Oklahoma, Oregon, South Dakota, and Wisconsin had such federal contracts. By 1920, more Indians were in public schools than in federal schools.

However, boarding schools did continue as part of the BIA educational program, with a curriculum emphasizing industrial training and military discipline. But morale and the general quality in most BIA schools were extremely low—and in 1927, personnel turnover in Indian schools reached 48 per cent. By then, humanitarian concern for Indians had turned toward criticism of the boarding schools.

In 1926, at the height of public outrage over the state of Indian education, the Brookings Institute launched an investigation of Indian affairs for the federal government. Under the direction of Lewis Meriam, the education sections of the resulting report were written by W. Carson Ryan, Jr., professor of education at Swarthmore College. Looking at Indian education from a Deweyan perspective, he argued for individualistic, non-authoritarian, decentralized education in which the focus would be on the whole child and his relationship to his family and community.

> The most fundamental need in Indian education is a change in point of view. Whatever may have been the official governmental attitude, education for the Indian in the past has proceeded largely on the theory that it is necessary to remove the Indian child as far as possible from his home environment; whereas the modern point of view in education and social work lays stress on upbringing in the natural setting of home and family life.[6]

The Meriam Report recommended improvement in existing boarding schools; bedrooms for three or four students, smaller classes, less regimentation, better qualified teachers and matrons.

At the time of the report, nearly 70,000 Indian children were enrolled in schools; 26,700 of these were in government schools, and over 22,000 were in boarding schools, half on and half off the reservations. In the light of these figures, the report recommended:

> As quickly as possible the non-reservation boarding schools should be reserved for pupils above sixth grade, and probably soon thereafter for pupils of ninth grade and above. This would leave local schools—public schools wherever possible, government day schools or even small boarding schools where no other arrangement can be made—to take care of all elementary schooling.[7]

The report further suggested that certain off-reservation schools might specialize in particular fields and in caring for special kinds of problem students.

Changes in the education of Indians were instituted soon after the publication of the Meriam Report. By 1932, several boarding schools had been converted to day schools, and a few others simply were closed. High school grades were added in the remaining boarding schools, and improvements were made in the academic curriculum and vocational training. The qualifications necessary for teaching were raised; student labor was curtailed; and the care of students improved.

The trend away from boarding school continued during the period of the New Deal. John Collier supported day schools as an aid to community development. It was during this period that firm commitment to public education with continued federal financial responsibility was made. The Johnson-O'Malley Act of 1934 (amended in 1936) provided for federal aid to states which had Indian students enrolled in public schools, and federal boarding schools decreased in number from forty to thirty-one.

But boarding school attendance received an impetus after World War II when there was renewed effort to provide formal education for large numbers of Indians who previously had had little or none.

One of the more dramatic efforts was the Navajo Special

Education Program. This was primarily a crash program developed to meet the basic requirements of Indian people between the ages of twelve and twenty who had had little or no previous schooling, and a concerted federal effort was made to create places in schools for all Navajo youth.

The main objectives of the Special Program were a basic knowledge of written and spoken English, as well as the development of vocational and other skills necessary to successful living in communities off the reservation. The program began as a pilot project at Sherman Institute in 1945, enrolling 245 Navajo students, and by 1956, 5000 students were enrolled in ten schools. The program has since been phased out. As schooling became available to all Navajo children there was a declining need for this particular program for adolescents.

During the 1950s, official policy confirmed the view that in order not to separate children from their parents, Indian children should be educated, when possible, within their home environment, at least through the elementary grades. Educational opportunities were to be made available in public schools wherever local conditions permitted. The BIA often cooperated with state authorities to make school plants available for public instruction. However, in practice, boarding school attendance continued to grow.

Currently, official policy continues to encourage the attendance of Indian children in public schools. Despite this, more than forty years since the Meriam Report, the numbers of Indian children in boarding schools have risen rather than declined. Of the 52,000 children for whom the BIA has direct responsibility in the federal school system, over 35,000 are in boarding schools. Between 1959 and 1967, for example, enrollment in BIA boarding high schools doubled, rising from 5600 to 11,600. Over 23,000 children attended BIA elementary boarding schools.

The BIA also sponsors a dormitory program in towns or cities bordering on the reservations where children are housed while attending public schools. This border-town program has been used most widely in Arizona, New Mexico, Oklahoma, and Utah. In 1956, twenty-one hundred Indian students lived in these dormitories. Ten years later, the number doubled to over four thousand.[8]

The increase in boarding school attendance is due to several factors. Among them are the rapidly growing Indian population, the larger percentages of Indian children attending school and persisting into higher grades, continuing isolation, and a road and school construction program which has not kept pace with requirements for day school attendance, as well as the continuing social service functions of many of the boarding schools.

Selection of students for admission to federal boarding schools reflects these conditions. Eligible for admission are Indians living on trust lands (reservations) for whom there is no other day or public school available; pupils with severe academic retardation—three years or more; pupils from severely disorganized or problem homes; and pupils with severe emotional problems. Significantly, non-reservation Indians are not eligible for admission, thus urbanization often carries with it loss of the right to attend the federal school system.

Examination of the criteria for admission points up the major difficulties faced by most of these schools. They combine academic, remedial, disciplinarian, psychiatric, and social service functions. Whether or not they actually perform these functions and how well are subjects of considerable debate.

Elementary Schools

As noted above, BIA boarding schools are of two types: secondary schools and elementary schools. Elementary schools have been a particular target of concern. Except for Indians and a small section of the upper class, separating young children from their parents for their formal education for more than several hours a day has not been part of the American education tradition and is viewed with some suspicion. Few outside of Indians and the BIA are familiar with conditions and life in these institutions.

Physical plant and location vary widely from place to place. Some schools like Theodore Roosevelt Boarding School at Fort Apache, New Mexico, are still housed in old army forts, others such as Shonto, Toyei, or Rock Point in Arizona are large, very modern school plants designed to deliver a wide variety of enriched programs.

It must be emphasized that the overwhelming majority of children attending such schools are Navajo. Approximately twenty thousand Navajo children attend forty-eight federal boarding schools. Almost eight thousand of these children are under the age of ten. Thus it can be seen that the BIA elementary boarding schools primarily serve the Navajo Reservation.

The most frequently advanced argument for these schools is that isolation on the vast Navajo Reservation precludes the children attending BIA day schools.

Navajo families do live scattered over a large, rugged area with very few all-weather roads. Currently the policy of the Bureau of Indian Affairs which requires that in order for a child to attend a day school, he must live within one and one-half miles of a school bus line and the bus ride is not to exceed one hour each way, makes many Navajo children ineligible for busing to a day school. Some argue that were the BIA to advance a comprehensive program of road building on the Navajo Reservation, they could eliminate the need for most of the elementary boarding schools. Since BIA data indicate that 64 per cent of the Navajo children in boarding schools live within twenty-five miles of the boarding school they attend, it could be argued that more and better roads would accomplish this.[9]

Unfortunately there is no simple agreement that roads would solve the problem.

Allan Yazzie, chairman of the Navajo Education Committee, stated in 1968, "Recent surveys have shown that it would take one mile of road to pick up four or five students,"[10] and the director of the Navajo area estimated "a total of 1689 miles of road could be built at the cost of $84,450,000; these roads would allow students to be bused daily to and from presently existing boarding schools." However, ". . . there is no assurance the Indian families would continue to live along these routes for any length of time."[11]

Whatever the educational need for boarding schools may be, it is clear that these institutions perform social welfare functions.

While the children are at the boarding schools, they are assured of clothing, sufficient food, laundry services, a warm place to sleep and work, etc. A great number of families whose children attend would have difficulty providing for their children throughout the entire year. A Public Health Service study has demonstrated, for example, that the incidence of nutritional anemia in Navajo children rises over the summer, but that by midwinter this condition has been corrected in children in the boarding schools.[12] Furthermore, studies of Navajo preschool children show more of them to be below the third percentile in height and weight than that of school-age children, suggesting that the older children were possibly better nourished because of the school feeding program.[13] Indian parents and leaders are aware of these problems, and this influences support for the continued existence of boarding schools.

Paradoxically, the modernization of school plants, leading to the closing of small schools and the opening of large consolidated institutions capable of providing more complete programs, has also led to the rise of boarding school attendance. Added to this has been rising public school attendance—over eighteen thousand Navajos, ages six to twenty, attend public schools. In order to fill the new consolidated BIA plants, students are recruited from longer distances, making busing difficult and boarding more necessary.

Thus, while actual isolation may be of decreasing significance, relative isolation re consolidated schools, continuing welfare dependency, and a boarding school tradition combine to retain the system for the Navajo.

Among the most outspoken critics of continuing boarding school for elementary school children, the psychiatrist Dr. Robert Leon cautions against psychological damage caused children as a result of separation of the child from his family.

> The damage caused to the child by his separation is directly related to the child's age and the length of time that he is separated from the parents. I am aware that most of the children in the Indian boarding schools are of school age. As far as I can determine from studying the literature, there is no serious irreversible damage which can occur to the adolescent as a result of separation from his parents. Separation

can, however, produce some serious effects on elementary school age
children, particularly those children age five to eight. . . . There is no
doubt that all elementary school age children are tremendously unhappy when separated from their parents and show many emotional
symptoms which may or may not be irreversible.[14]

Dr. Leon argues that young children sent to boarding schools
are lonely and feel rejected. He thinks that many symptoms of
regression will be found among such children, including crying
and striving for attention. More serious problems might include
childhood schizophrenia and severe neuroses, particularly withdrawal.

Other psychiatrists agree that young children are apt to suffer
psychological damage in boarding schools. Dr. Robert L. Bergman
believes that though the incidence of psychosis in Indian boarding
school youngsters seems no higher than it is in the urban middle-
class population, the incidence of less severe behavior disorders
is probably higher. For the most part, these disorders seem to
be "patterns of passive resistance," which the children have
adopted. Such children are often suspected by their teachers of
being mentally retarded, for they learn nothing in school, yet
Bergman finds that they can perform non-scholastic tasks—especially Navajo ones—very well. It is quite possible that these
patterns of passive resistance may be a function of limited comprehension in English and consequent failure to understand
rather than any deliberate or "cultural" resistance.

In actuality, however, the extent of separation of the child
from his parents varies considerably, depending partly on the
location of the school, the nature of the surrounding community,
and upon the attitudes of the administrators at the different
schools. Children at Theodore Roosevelt, for example, coming
from the Pima and Papago tribes in distant southern Arizona
are unlikely to see their families often during the school year.
On the other hand, at Shonto, Rough Rock, or Rock Point on
the Navajo Reservation the school is the social center for most
of the young people, and many community events either take
place at the school or are sponsored in part by the school.
Weekly movies and athletic events are attended by many parents.
Some school administrators encourage weekly home visits,

others do not, reflecting official anxiety about runaways—children who might not return. It is clear, however, that the pickup truck and official encouragement make it possible for children on the Navajo Reservation to board without prolonged separation from families, and, indeed, siblings and clan relatives are usually in attendance in the same school. Children from severely disorganized families are more likely to have difficulties in relation to home visits as are children sent long distances away from home.

Conditions of dormitory life also vary. Some are impersonal institutions with stark, uncomfortable facilities and little or no privacy. A few, particularly Rough Rock and Rock Point, are more favorable in terms of physical plant and atmosphere. Nevertheless, it does appear that most dormitories are understaffed, and that most aides have little training for their jobs and are likely to perpetuate the harsh practices they experienced in boarding schools as children. The overall ratio of students to aides in the elementary boarding schools approximates 60 to 1, and when one considers that fewer than half of these are on duty at any one time, the ratio becomes 120 or more students to 1 aide. In some schools aides are discouraged from counseling or becoming personally involved with the children. Though official policy, as set out in the *BIA Handbook for Teacher and Dormitory Aides* (1968), states that aides should try to create a family atmosphere in the dormitory, observers have noted at more than one school that this goal is not accomplished. Moreover, aides in most schools must devote considerable time to housekeeping chores. As a consequence, regimentation is severe and children may have no adult to whom they relate and with whom they can share their troubles or achievements.[15]

Given the likelihood that elementary boarding schools will not be immediately phased out, Dr. Bergman maintains that a very significant improvement would be made by increasing and improving the staffing of dormitories. The Indian Health Committee of the American Academy of Pediatrics has recommended that at least one dormitory attendant be on duty for every fifteen children in the dorms at any time. Dr. Bergman feels that if the number of aides was increased by a factor of four, and if all were encouraged to work closely with the children, life would be much improved for the children involved.

The Toyei Boarding School on the Navajo Reservation is, in addition to conducting a bilingual program, instituting a larger adult-child ratio in the light of Dr. Bergman's recommendations. At Rough Rock a dormitory-parent system was instituted whereby parents served as dormitory aides for six-week periods in an effort to provide more adult relationships in the dormitories.

A major problem that remains, as illustrated by Theodore Roosevelt Boarding School, is the absence in some dormitories of speakers of the home language of isolated, less acculturated children who do not speak English when they first come to school.

Secondary Schools

A similar set of conditions exists for the boarding high schools. The location of these varies considerably; many of the modern institutions having developed out of a mixed heritage of old army forts and available federal land. Phoenix Indian School, in Arizona, looks out on downtown Phoenix, and is only yards away from a bustling drive-in shopping strip typical of western cities. The Institute of Indian Arts at Santa Fe, New Mexico, is located on a major highway leading into town, and views the abundant motels and restaurants that have arisen to accommodate the many attracted to the thriving tourist center of Santa Fe. Chilocco, in Oklahoma, on the other hand, is in a more isolated rural area and critics have argued that this precludes desirable experience with the larger community.

Physical distance from local communities constitutes but a part of the picture as regards isolation of students in boarding school. Social isolation is a factor and varies according to the administrative practices in the various schools. Critics of Chilocco, for example, have argued that students are restricted from going into town or seeing movies on weekends. At Flandreau Indian School in South Dakota there are rules that allow town visits only under supervision on specified days. At Albuquerque, on the other hand, students are free to participate in various community activities and to visit local friends at their homes.

Phoenix Indian School has rules which permit students to leave the campus after their classes on school days, requiring them to return by five-thirty. During the school week, students may leave again for the evening, signing out at the dormitories, and must return by 8 P.M. On Saturdays, students can leave at noon with the stipulation that underclassmen return at 10 P.M. and seniors at midnight. On Sundays, all students must return to the dormitories at six o'clock. Parents may check out students for the weekend. Over six hundred of the students engage in part-time work in the local community during the weekends, many as household workers.

Practice varies considerably and changes with different administrations at the various schools. In good measure, many of the more restrictive practices are reminiscent of most boarding school or dormitory situations in colleges of the past, where the school, acting *in loco parentis,* was anxious in regard to safety and town conflicts. Given the radical shift toward greater permissiveness in the schools and campuses of this country in general, and public concern for the civil rights of young people, the more restrictive schools appear coercive, and as student bodies become more sophisticated, their rules are likely to be resisted increasingly.

The boarding high schools also vary considerably in regard to their physical condition. Some, like Flandreau are quite new and comparable in their plant with the best public high schools. Others, such as Chilocco in Oklahoma and Oglala in South Dakota, are inadequate and in need of repair.

The school plants represent an impressive investment. For example, Phoenix Indian School houses one thousand students, ages twelve to twenty-one, from the Navajo, Papago, Hopi, Apache, Pima, Hualapai, and other tribes, in grades seven to twelve. It contains an administration building; twenty-six classrooms; eleven home economics classrooms; shop, and trade facilities; gymnasium; dining hall; auditorium; eight dormitories, seven of which have been built since 1963; a library; maintenance buildings; and a clinic which is operated by public health personnel. The library, classrooms, and administrative buildings are relatively new, having been built since 1966. These buildings are located in a strikingly attractive "L" complex of concrete block construction, painted off white with yellow trim, blending nicely with a landscape of grass-covered campus dotted with orange, olive, and palm trees.

Most boarding schools serve a very diverse student population. At Flandreau, seven relatively distinct categories of pupils have been identified: individuals of average intelligence having relatively stable home backgrounds and capable of doing academic high school work; individuals of average intelligence having relatively stable backgrounds and seeking vocational training to enable them to become skilled artisans; individuals of average intelligence having relatively unstable backgrounds, causing them to be socially dependent and/or neglected; individuals having physical handicaps which interfere with learning; individuals who are mentally retarded and incapable of actively participating with members of the preceding four groups; individuals who are socially maladjusted and pose special problems in the repetitive conflicts with authority; and individuals having severe emotional conflict, who develop psychoneurotic, psychosomatic, or psychotic reactions.[16]

Although the percentage of students in each of these categories varies from school to school, heterogeneity is characteristic of all and is a logical outgrowth of the criteria for admission established by the BIA. To some, the mixed nature of these institutions is viewed as a major problem. The Special Subcommittee on Indian Education of the Committee on Labor and Public Welfare, U. S. Senate, concluded after intensive hearings that:

> . . . off-reservation boarding schools have generally become dumping grounds for Indian students with severe social and emotional problems. Unfortunately there are also some students who are enrolled simply because there is no other school available to them. It is highly questionable whether or not these two groups of students should be without any plan, mixed together.[17]

A recent study prepared for the Far West Laboratory for Education Research and Development recommended that until Indian education is transferred to the control of local communities:

> . . . *we recommend that a definite statement of goals and purposes be made for each of the boarding schools operated by the Bureau of Indian Affairs.*
>
> We recommend that the boarding schools be converted to special-purpose institutions such as terminal vocational centers, academic high schools, remedial, and special education centers, junior colleges, special subject schools (such as the Santa Fe Institute for American Indian Art) or regional schools rather than maintain their confused and archaic status as mixed academic, remedial, and disciplinary institutions.[18]

In defense of current policy against grouping in separate schools according to distinct needs, the BIA has noted several problems. One question raised is on what basis or by what criteria will a student's attitude and emotional, physical, and mental well-being be measured for placement? Another is the problem of distance from home and how transportation and contact with the home, which is all too often minimal, would be accomplished. Also, in an argument familiar to proponents of comprehensive schools, the segregation of the present situation would be heightened to the point that students might seldom encounter much individual diversity in interests, abilities, etc.

School programs and difficulties reflect their diversified nature. Clearly, however, whether the federal boarding schools remain comprehensive institutions, or change their policy to develop into schools with special functions—remedial, social, or academic and vocational, it will be necessary for appropriate program planning, staffing, and commitment to be made in order to ensure constructive functioning.

Curriculum and School Life

Currently, in keeping with national education trends, BIA high schools are comprehensive institutions offering an academic and prevocational curriculum. In contrast to the terminal vocational emphasis typical of boarding schools of the past, the policy of BIA since 1963 has been to provide only prevocational education, on the assumption that graduating students could go on to post-secondary vocational training schools.

Although official policy has led to a trend toward an academic curriculum in most schools, large numbers of students are academically retarded, and large numbers participate in vocational work.

Phoenix Indian School illustrates this. Here the curriculum materials used are those adopted by the state of Arizona for public schools and high schools. In addition, some local subject matter is used to meet the special needs of the Indian children in attendance. Three levels of course content are offered. These consist of an academic high school curriculum for the more advanced 20 per cent of the student body, an elementary curriculum for the lower 20 per cent, and a diversified prevocational oriented program for the remainder. The student is provided an opportunity to move from one level to another and to participate in certain common courses such as social studies. Every student is required to take four years of English, four of social studies, two of mathematics, two of science, two of physical education, and two of home economics or practical arts. Some thirty vocational electives are offered along with a course in American Indian heritage.

One boarding school which provides a unique focus is the Institute of American Indian Arts in Santa Fe, New Mexico. Created in 1962 and using the remodeled facilities of the Santa Fe Indian Boarding School, the purpose of the school is to provide an accredited high school program with emphasis on the arts, as well as a post-high school vocational arts program. Both of these programs prepare students for college, technical schools, or arts-related vocations.

The curriculum of the Institute of American Indian Arts does not stress the revival and re-creation of native American handicrafts. Rather, it encourages a contemporary interpretation and application of Indian art traditions.

Young people from all over the country, including Alaska, attend. At the end of the school year the students hold a festival, re-creating the house styles, customs, and foods of their regions, sharing their heritage in an atmosphere of mutual respect.

Another special program has been that of the Concho Demonstration School in Oklahoma, operated in 1968 to work with students who had special educational problems. Here the school staff focused on a remedial program designed to reorient the student to the school he left or to a school more in keeping with his needs and objectives. This school however, has a capacity of only forty-four pupils.

Achievement in school by Indian youth has been discussed in an earlier chapter. On the whole, achievement levels on standardized tests are low, and pupils are below average in grade. In the boarding schools, 48 per cent of the children in grades one to eight are two years above expected age compared with 36 per cent in day schools. Sixty per cent of those in grades nine to twelve are two years above expected age compared with 33 per cent in day schools.[19]

The data for the elementary grades suggest that there is a tendency for Indian parents not to send children to off-reservation boarding schools while the children are still very young. In the higher grades, children who are above age in federal day or public schools—an indication of school difficulties either because of language or social problems—move into the BIA off-reservation boarding school system.

Despite the trend toward an academic curriculum, at some schools, such as Stewart Indian School, vocational emphasis remains high. At Stewart Indian School the academic curriculum is definitely second in importance; girls take four years of home economics and boys four years of practical arts. In the earlier grades students are rotated from one vocational specialty to another. In the junior and senior year, they spend one half of each school day in one vocation—either wood shop, painting, or farm work. The girls may choose from only two fields: general and home service (domestic work) or "hospital ward attendant" training, which the girls considered a degrading farce, a euphemism (they say) for more domestic work.

BIA schools are still criticized for stressing vocational training too highly at the expense of college preparation and, in addition, the vocational training programs are often criticized for being inadequate and/or poorly designed.

Another question of curriculum concerns the importance of remedial and special education programs. Many students enter the boarding schools considerably below the expected academic level. At Pierre and at Flandreau in South Dakota, for instance, first-year students average two and one-half years behind national norms in most subjects. This is not unusual. As noted above, any Indian student living on federal trust land who is three years or more retarded in his academic work may be admitted to a Bureau boarding school. Dr. Glen Nimnicht, in his report on the Stewart Boarding School, stated:

> Their (the Indian students) basic problem is that they come to Stewart with academic problems requiring intensive remedial work. Instead of this they get a watered-down, "easy" curriculum.[20]

It appears that this is the case in many federal boarding schools.

The needs of Indian youngsters with serious emotional difficulties are met only minimally in the boarding schools. Most schools do not have professional psychiatrists in residence. All have some counseling and guidance personnel. There are two categories of counselors: regular school counselors and "instructional" or dormitory aides. Unfortunately, most of these people have had no training to engage in personal counseling. There are also supervisory aides who oversee the dormitory programs; some of these may be qualified to counsel.

Boarding schools themselves have been criticized for creating problems for their students, especially in regard to their dormitory programs. The dormitory is the student's home away from home, and he spends a good deal of time there. At the Oglala Community Boarding School:

> The dormitories have a typical institutional atmosphere. Children sleep in barracks-type rooms which in some cases are overcrowded. Furniture is badly needed. Two main problems are evident in the dorms. First, there is an almost complete lack of privacy which is a major cause of dissatisfaction among the older students. Secondly, provisions for study are very poor, particularly in the boys' dorm.[21]

Although somewhat better facilities seem to exist at Intermountain in Utah and Chemawa in Oregon, the lack of privacy and the regimented, institutional atmosphere are common complaints about Bureau boarding school dormitories.

Most schools attempt to provide recreational activities for their students, though a few have difficulties doing so due to lack of staff and funds. At Pierre, South Dakota, investigators observed that despite severe winters which limited outdoor activities only two old television sets and a few paperback books were available for students' amusement. The aides tried to hold hobby sessions for small groups of pupils each week, but most of the materials had to be bought by the aides themselves. At the Stewart School things seemed somewhat better. Students have two hours of "leisure time" scheduled for each evening. Ping-pong and similar games are available in the dormitories; band, 4-H Club, student newspaper, yearbook, athletic teams, home economics clubs, and other activities meet at this time. Opportunities for recreation vary from school to school. It is certain, however, that at every school, students who are accustomed to fewer restrictions at home have some difficulty adjusting to the more confined life of the boarding school.

There are many rules and regulations governing student behavior at the boarding schools which invite friction. One important set of restrictions covers male-female interaction. At off-reservation boarding schools the sexes are pretty well kept separate most of the time, and even casual contact between them is looked on with some suspicion by school officials anxious about possible scandal. The psychiatrist Dr. Bergman suggests that students are apt to get in trouble because they must develop and carry on heterosexual relationships on the sly. Students at Chemawa complained to interviewers that they were not even allowed to hold hands with their girl friends and boy friends on campus. When it is remembered that many of these students are in their late teens and at home would be considered adult, the rules seem unrealistic.

Feelings about the regimentation and consequent lack of independence were expressed by students at the Albuquerque Indian School in a discussion about dormitory life:

> (1) The senior students resented turning out the lights at 9:30 P.M., particularly when they had been assigned by teachers to observe a given television presentation, (2) girls particularly objected to being "marched" across campus at night when they were going to and from one place or activity to another, (3) both boys and girls objected to people entering their room without knocking—the people to whom they were referring were the dormitory aides and department heads, (4) students reacted negatively to "collective" punishment . . .[22]

There is little doubt that many aspects of the dormitory situation should be changed. Improving the physical surroundings, increasing the number of aides, training the aides in a new philosophy of the residential school, and relaxing some restrictions are a large order, but one that should be filled as soon as possible. Increased appropriations for such a program are a necessity.

How the boarding school experience affects the psychosocial adjustment of Indian adults who attended is of considerable interest, but is not a question easy to answer. It is very difficult to determine to what extent particular psychosocial problems are due to the educational experience of Indian children and to what extent they are due to other economic, political, cultural, and social factors.

The relation of adult emotional and social adjustment to school experience is poorly understood. Moreover, many adult Navajos, for example, were educated in the Navajo Special Education Program, which provided a five-to-eight-year vocational program for adolescents between the ages of twelve and twenty. Thus, it is not the case that all of these young adults were put in boarding schools at a very young age. The effects of this kind of early experience on psychological and social adjustment, therefore, are still not clear.

It should be noted that many Indian leaders are favorably disposed toward BIA boarding schools at this time. Several reasons account for this position. Among them are jobs which the boarding schools provide for Indian people, fears over the termination of federal services which the closing of boarding schools would stimulate, and the familiarity with the boarding school system which many Indians have. In addition, many leaders are concerned about the problems which will face those families for whom boarding schools provide assistance in the form of food and shelter for their children.

Several Indian leaders in addition to the Navajo Tribal Council have spoken out in favor of boarding schools. Enos Poorbear, president of the Oglala Sioux, in appraising the education program on Pine Ridge, Sioux Reservation, South Dakota, has stressed that his tribal executive committee felt that measurable progress is being made in solving the educational problems of the reservation:

> In other words, efforts at Pine Ridge Agency to improve the quality of
> education for Indian children have not been totally ineffective, considering the social and economic status of many of the parents of our
> students . . . If improvements are made to alleviate some of the more
> serious problems stemming from socioeconomic conditions, the education program could then institute effectively changes. . . .[23]

The Pine Ridge Tribal Executive Committee recommended increased involvement of parents, including establishing and training advisory school boards, and the improvement and expansion of boarding facilities to serve students in isolated areas of the reservation and students from broken homes.

Domingo Montoya, chairman of the All-Indian Pueblo Council, has stated that he preferred federal schools to public schools for young Indian children because they need special language instruction. The Navajo Social Action Group, while recognizing the many negative experiences that affect young people in boarding schools, nevertheless stressed the necessity of these schools at the present time.

The National Study report on the Chemawa Boarding School in Oregon also found sentiment to retain the BIA boarding school:

> The Chemawa School and its staff have come through two programs
> (the Navajo Program and the Alaska Program) with students who have
> come to the school from relatively small, isolated, and relatively unsophisticated backgrounds with respect to the broader society. In the
> new setting of incredible diversity, the young students were viewed as
> children, counseled as children, supervised as children by adults who
> seemingly had no notion of the adult roles played by these young people
> in their home communities. The behavioral orientations of institutional
> personnel are very often demonstrated in trivial edicts and regulations
> formulated upon "appearance of things" rather than the substance of
> things. For students from isolated, small communities confronting a new,
> bewildering, complex life experience, the school strictures may be low-level irritants and inconveniences, but they also insinuate a degree and
> kind of Indian inadequacy and incompetency. Students do perceive the
> institution's self-concern about how they appear to outsiders.
> Now that the enrollment of Chemawa is shifting to receive more
> students from the Northwest, rather than those from Alaska, the in-

stitution will be required to make new adjustments. It is to be anticipated that the future student population will be coming predominantly from experiences of discontent and frustration with public schools and urban experiences. This will require severe changes of attitudinal and operational approaches in both instruction and guidance.

There will probably be a greater number of students who do not speak a native language but have had poor and negative experiences with language arts curriculum areas of schools. There will probably be a number of applicants from urban areas where families have suffered socioeconomic problems both in school and community life. Students may be expected to have a greater amount of experience with the larger society, much of it negative. In most instances, the earlier Navajo and Alaskan students did not encounter television until they arrived at Chemawa; Northwest students, for the most part, have had it all their lives. In many respects, students from the Northwest may be expected to have had a more realistic and intense experience in some areas of the general society than do their teachers and counselors. The school will be hard pressed in making adjustments from programs geared to rural students, to programs for students more mobile and more urban in their experiences and views.

Despite the long history of criticism leveled against boarding schools, there is prevalent in the Northwest the feeling that Indians should ". . . recapture Chemawa for the Northwest," to have it provide all that has been viewed as valuable, eliminate all that has been disturbing, and add much of what should or could have been.[24]

Many Indian leaders recognize the many problems associated with the federal boarding schools, and they have suggested many changes in curriculums, teacher training, pupil personnel services, dormitory arrangements, and location of the schools. But they are also aware that these schools serve several important functions, including the provision of some special programs for the special needs of many Indian children, employment of many Indian people, and the provision of food, clothing, medical care, and shelter to many children whose families would have great difficulty in providing for them. They are also concerned that federal commitment to education continue, and the federal schools stand as a symbolic representation of this obligation.

Currently, efforts are being made to extend the influence of Indian communities in the boarding schools attended by their children. The history of boarding schools' attendance has for the most part represented estrangement from the home community—the contacts by children with family and friends possible during the school year affected by administrative policies toward home visits, some more lenient than others; distance; lack of money; and absence of political involvement in school administration by Indian communities.

The BIA administers Indian Affairs through eleven area offices. At present, each off-reservation school remains under the jurisdiction of one of these area offices. On-reservation schools are responsible to the BIA agency superintendent.

In a departure from past policy, the BIA now encourages the formation of school advisory boards made up of representatives from the home communities of the children. These have mainly advisory functions, but the system now provides an opportunity to view the schools, visit officially, and make recommendations.

Given the current views held in Indian communities concerning boarding schools and their functions, no decisions to retain, close, expand, or retrench the federal boarding school system should be made without the involvement of the Indian parents and groups whose children attend.

XII

Toward New Approaches

It is as though the whites were in a grassy canyon and there they have wagons, plows, and plenty of food. We Navajos are upon the dry mesa. We can hear them talking but we cannot get to them. My grandchild, education is the ladder . . .

MANUELITO, Navajo leader, 1893

We want our children to be proud of being Navajos. We want them to know who they are . . . In the future they will have to be able to make many choices and do many different things. They need a modern education to make their way, but they have to know both worlds—and being Navajo will give them strength.

JOHN DICK, Navajo School Board member, Rough Rock, 1968

Though nearly a century has passed since Manuelito expressed awareness of the chasm which separates Indian and white traditions, cultural difference is still viewed as a problem in Indian education. Education has not proved to be a ladder which can be traversed in either direction. Historically, schools have been agents for assimilation away from Indian life and they have ordinarily paid little attention to the functions of the existing Indian subcultures in the educative process.

This is in part due to ethnocentrism—the phenomenon of being so rooted in one's own culture that it is simple to move on to a disdain for others. Even more, this can lead to the view that Indian children are without any culture, a concept termed "vacuum ideology" by one observer, and expressed in our folk language as "wild Indian," "savage," "uncivilized."

Enforced assimilation has not led, however, to complete suppression of the vitality and community life of America's native peoples. Commenting on the tenacity of Indian differences, Brewton Berry states:

> He [the Indian] has succeeded thus far to everyone's surprise, in resisting the efforts of the white man to destroy that culture and to supplant it with his own brand of civilization. The school, the Indian rightly suspects, is a device for hastening his assimilation, and he resists it as best he can by withdrawal, indifference, and non-cooperation.[1]

It is extremely difficult to generalize accurately about all Indian peoples—the degrees of culture change, adaptation, loss, assimilation vary from group to group and within groups. Nor is it possible to generalize accurately about the conflict of values with those of the dominant society. Values themselves in American life are undergoing evaluation and change. However, major themes such as achievement and success, work and activity, efficiency and practicality, progress, material comfort, freedom and equality, humanitarianism, conformity, nationalism, science and secular rationality are powerful forces in the dominant culture and are taught as ideals in our schools.[2]

Indians, on the other hand, have usually been regarded as valuing reserve, generosity, individual autonomy, bravery and courage, fear of the world as dangerous, a practical joker strain, attention to the concrete realities of the present, and dependence on supernatural power.[3]

These generalizations, while interesting, do not provide us with enough insights concerning the ongoing conflicts as experienced by schools and communities and within classrooms, and should not be applied to particular situations without caution.

In their study of the Oglala Sioux, Wax, Wax, and Dumont examine the public school as an agent of acculturation representing the domination of one group by another. They suggest several causes for the educational problem of Sioux youth. These include, in addition to cultural disharmony, the extent to which Indians feel the schools are punitively directed against them, the influ-

ence of the peer society, unfamiliarity with careers and the necessary educational prerequisites for them arising from the provincial
character of their environment, and their isolation from the mainstream of the dominant society.[4]

In a study of dropouts, Rosalie Wax more explicitly focused on
the cultural disharmony between country Sioux life and the school
expectations. Among the country Sioux of the Pine Ridge Reservation in South Dakota, large numbers of youths become high school
dropouts. According to Dr. Wax, many of their problems parallel
those faced by other American minorities, namely, dissimilarity
between the values of the minority subculture and that of the
middle-class, white-citizen-oriented schools, and a seeming inability of the school system to respond with flexibility and insight
to adapt the instruction and the facilities of the school to the
needs of the youths. She writes:

> . . . on the Pine Ridge Reservation, a majority of the young men arrive
> at adolescence valuing *elan,* bravery, generosity, passion, and luck, and
> admiring outstanding talent in athletics, singing, and dancing. While
> capable of wider relations and reciprocities, they function at their social
> best as members of small groups of peers or relatives. Yet to obtain even
> modest employment in the greater society, they must graduate from high
> school. And in order to graduate from high school, they are told that
> they must develop exactly opposite qualities to those they possess: a
> respect for humdrum diligence and routine, for "discipline" (in the sense
> of not smoking in toilets, not cutting classes, and not getting drunk),
> and for government property. In addition, they are expected to compete
> scholastically on a highly privatized and individualistic level, while
> living in large dormitories, surrounded by strangers who make privacy of
> any type impossible.[5]

Because their adjustment problem is further complicated by de-
ficiency in English, cultural misunderstandings and loneliness, Dr.
Wax concludes the end result for many of the youth is that they
drop out.

In their studies the Waxes also stress the importance of the
peer-group influence in schools, which makes it difficult for Indian
youth to function as individuals in a competitive school environment. They attribute this more to the separation between the
school and the Indian community than they do to cultural differences.

With most children the peer group reaches the zenith of its power in school. In middle class neighborhoods, independent children can usually seek and secure support from parents, teachers, or adult society as a whole. But when, as in an urban slum or Indian reservation, the teachers stay aloof from parents, and parents feel that teachers are a breed apart, the peer group may become so powerful that the children literally take over the school. Then group activities are carried on in class —jokes, notes, intrigues, teasing, mock-combat, comic book reading, courtship—all without the teacher's knowledge and often without grossly interfering with the learning process.

Competent and experienced teachers can come to terms with the peer group and manage to teach a fair amount of reading, writing and arithmetic. But teachers who are incompetent, overwhelmed by large classes, or sometimes merely inexperienced may be faced with groups of children who refuse even to listen.

We marveled at the variety and efficiency of the devices developed by Indian children to frustrate formal learning—unanimous inattention, refusal to go to the board, writing on the board in letters less than an inch high, inarticulate responses, and whispered or pantomime teasing of victims called on to recite. In some seventh and eighth grade classes there was a withdrawal so uncompromising that no voice could be heard for hours except the teacher's, plaintively asking questions or giving instructions.[6]

Similar conditions have also been noted in Cherokee classrooms in eastern Oklahoma.[7] An observer in an Oklahoma Cherokee school writes:

Observing the upper-grade classroom, I concluded that the students regard it as their own place, the locus of their own society, in which the teacher is an unwelcome intruder, introducing irrelevant demands. It is rather as though a group of mutinous sailors had agreed to the efficient manning of "their" ship while ignoring the captain and the captain's navigational goals.[8]

Observations in eastern Oklahoma classrooms also indicated that the children do not tolerate an individual show of superior knowledge. Often a teacher cannot find any pupil who will volunteer an answer to a question that several of them know. In oral reading, the whole class tends to read together in audible whispers, so that the child who is supposed to be reciting can simply wait when he comes to a difficult word until he hears it said by his classmates. Generally, pupils like to work together and to help each other. Consequently, the weak students are carried along by the stronger ones, and the stronger ones do not exert themselves to excel the weaker ones. This same kind of behavior was noted by H. Wolcott in his study of Kwakiutl children in British Columbia.

The Indian children may appear to be either apathetic or sullen to a teacher who does not understand this cultural characteristic. Dumont says that Indian children "learn to be silent" in the classroom of the ordinary well-meaning teacher, who expects them to be individualistic, competitive, and anxious to win the teacher's approval. He compares two classrooms which he observed. One took on the pattern of silent resistance to a male teacher who pushed and hammered at them, while the other became an active, cooperative learning group under another male teacher who skillfully turned his class into a "team" of which he was a member. He became a kind of coach who helped them find ways of working together to learn to speak English with some sophistication. In explaining his method to an observer, he said, "The difference with Cherokee kids is their power to associate different things. You got to find out what interests them and run with it. . . . I kind of teach by ear."

Whatever method of teaching is indicated here, it is not simply following a set of rigid techniques, but a flexible style of interacting with the subculture of the Indian group in such a way as to steer it toward the desirable educational outcome.

Many teachers interviewed in the National Study were concerned about what seems to them to be apathy or even silent resistance to learning on the part of some of their pupils. Some of their comments follow, taken from interviews in many different schools:

> It is easier to work with Indian children because of the quiet way they have. They are very agreeable and this helps. And they are very good listeners.

> The kids need to learn to carry more responsibility—they are too dependent on others to make decisions.

> If they are in groups together, they tend to work together quite well; they seem to stick up for each other.

> Indian pupils need more individual attention. They need the motivation, the spark. If I had a smaller class, I could help them much more.

They are very well-mannered children. And they talk to the teacher with respect. But it's hard for them to really express themselves, so, rather than just blunder around, they just don't answer at all.

Most of them have very good dispositions. They tend to be rather slow and deliberate in their decisions. They are rather quiet and don't tend to be a disturbing influence in a group. But they need more self-confidence. [This teacher is an Indian.]

This situation might lead teachers insensitive to the cultural barriers between themselves and their pupils to neglect their Indian students, to act as though these students could not learn much, and to be content with low-level achievement as long as the students did not cause trouble.

Wax, Wax, and Dumont have also called attention to isolation as a major factor in school failure—isolation for the teachers between themselves and other teachers at the school, within the classroom resulting from mutual rejection between teachers and pupils, isolation of teachers from parents in the Indian community, and isolation of teachers from their own metropolitan society. These conditions were also evident in the schools and communities observed in the National Study.

Education of Indian pupils viewed as a cross-cultural exchange bridging the many cultural worlds in which people live requires efforts by the school to teach the dominant culture, while recognizing the subcultures as real and viable. For such a task teachers clearly need preparation in cultural awareness and understanding, combined with attitudes of respect for their pupils and their parents.

One set of proposals for educators which seeks to respond to the different cultures and conditions in varied ethnic communities has been presented by Jack D. Forbes:

Each school must be responsive to the needs and interests of the total community which it serves.

All sectors of the community must have a voice in educational planning and policy making.

The school must concentrate upon essential learning and dispense with irrelevant attacks upon the cultural values of minority groups.

Freedom, tolerance, and cosmopolitanism must above all be exhibited by school people as an example for the youth and adults of the community.

The cultural assets of the total community and the skills of minority group persons be utilized as a positive educational force by the school . . .

The curricula of our schools should vary from region to region in order to reflect the rich diversity of American life.

Bilingualism should be regarded as not merely an asset, but as a necessity in the twentieth century, and all pupils should be expected to master at least two languages in the elementary grades . . .

All teachers and administrators be required to receive training of an anthropological-sociological nature and be expected to possess or acquire the linguistic skills necessary for communication with local students and their parents.[9]

Recent innovations designed to help bridge the gap between schools and Indian communities have included those changes in curriculum discussed in Chapter X. In addition to these, however, new schools, structured to permit Indian adults to participate in a closer, more responsible relationship to the education of their children and the management of schools, have developed. These schools represent a move toward Indian control and Indian administration of the schools their children attend.

Rough Rock School

The most famous of the efforts to create a new form of school, more responsive to the Indian community it serves and more successful at educating Indian children, is the Rough Rock Demonstration School, at Chinle, Arizona, on the Navajo Reservation. Funded by the Bureau of Indian Affairs and the Office of Economic Opportunity in 1966, the school provides for the education of more than 250 Navajo children from Head Start through grade ten, and has stirred up enormous interest during the years it has been in operation.

To receive the funds, the Navajo tribe organized DINE, Inc., a private non-profit corporation. Symbolically, DINE, Inc. (Demonstration in Navajo Education) also stands for the Navajo name for themselves, *Dine*—"The People." In a radical move, the corporation in turn handed over the operational control of the Rough Rock School to a board of education, consisting of five middle-aged Navajos, only one of whom had even a few years of schooling, who were elected by the Rough Rock community. Robert Roessel was recruited as director and the Rough Rock Demonstration School was on its way.

Rough Rock itself is a community of one thousand persons living in family groups scattered widely through an area of some fifteen miles' radius. Here among the eroded washlands and the rugged terrain of Black Mesa, more than six thousand feet above sea level, live some of the most traditional members of the Navajo Reservation. The area has both the advantages and disadvantages of sheer physical isolation. Sixteen miles of unpaved roads separate the community from the nearest hard-surfaced road. The nearest hospital is at Ganado some eighty miles away, and the closest sizable town is Gallup, New Mexico, one hundred miles distant. The absence of surfaced roads in the Rough Rock area makes its fifteen-mile radius appear to stretch endlessly. Sudden seasonal rains turn roads into veritable seas of mud, making even those that exist impassable.

The Navajos of this region, like those at Shonto, are sheepherders and practice the traditional crafts of blanket weaving and silver work. Their average annual income of $700 places them among the lowest income levels of the American population. Their homes or "camps" consist of the traditional hogan or cabin, a sheep corral, and a lean-to for horses set among the family grazing lands. To some of these homes, water must be hauled from miles distant; there is no electricity or plumbing.

The school has been committed to developing a bicultural, bilingual program. Expressed in the words of John Dick, one of the first school board members:

> We want our children to be proud of being Navajos. We want them to know who they are . . . In the future they will have to be able to make many choices and do many different things. They need a modern education to make their way, but they have to know both worlds—and being Navajo will give them strength.

In addition to its pioneering approach to local Indian control of schools, and bicultural curriculum development, the school developed a parent dormitory program bringing local persons to live in the dormitories with the children; an open door policy, encouraging visits by community members to the corridors and classrooms; and provided a center for recording and developing Navajo cultural materials.

Because it received part of its funding from the Office of Economic Opportunity, Department of Health, Education, and Welfare, Rough Rock was subject to an evaluation by that agency. A report on the school, made by a team of investigators headed by Donald A. Erickson of the University of Chicago, has aroused much controversy, a controversy which sheds light on the complexities and passions which permeate all discussions of Indian education programs.[10]

The study agreed with some of the critics of the Rough Rock experiment that the publicity surrounding the school tended to exaggerate its promise and obscure its realities; that the innovations at Rough Rock were already occurring within Bureau schools, and could easily be extended throughout the existing federal school system; that emphasis on traditional Navajo life was not what pupils wanted; that the Navajo school board was concerned mainly with non-professional matters such as job allotments, leaving many of the major professional considerations to the director; and that academic achievement was no higher there than at other schools with similar populations. Comparing Rough Rock with Rock Point, a BIA school also on the Navajo Reservation, but part of the regular federal school system run by an able director knowledgeable in Navajo matters, the Bureau-run school in many particulars, including dormitory supervision, appeared equal to or more favorable than the conditions at the well-funded, highly advertised contract school at Rough Rock.

Although the report recommended the refunding of the Rough Rock School to the Office of Economic Opportunity, its less than enthusiastic tone aroused criticism, some of it prior to the report's publication. One group of anthropologists, with deep commitment to self-determination in Indian affairs, contended that the authors of the report had suffered from "culture shock," their negative response to many matters resulting from a misunderstanding of Navajo culture.[11]

Many of those who support the Rough Rock experiment maintain that it is unrealistic to expect local Indian school boards to be thoroughly involved with the professional concerns of the school—leaving such matters to hired administrators. They point to the value of local control in involving Indians in the educational enterprise, largely through jobs; opening the school to greater visibility; and changing power relationship which give parents a greater influence as compared with the educators—this, it is expected, leading to more concerned and respectful treatment of the children. That extraordinary academic achievements do not occur in a relatively short period of years is viewed as the result of the difficulties engendered in starting from nearly scratch in the development of new curriculum and teaching techniques, and from the fact that the school population is drawn largely from an area of limited exposure to the reading and English language skills associated with academic achievement as ordinarily measured.

There is a tendency in Indian education for the proponents of public schools, federal schools, or contract schools to see their particular solution as mutually excluding all others. Rough Rock does present one possible model, useful and viable for communities that prefer this arrangement. There are other communities that may prefer a less parochial kind of education for their children as well as those communities that prefer not to involve themselves in politics around school control and may prefer that the schools remain part of the regular public school or federal school systems.

Because Rough Rock does not necessarily represent the *sine qua non* of Indian education does not mean that its existence is not important, nor very significant, nor that it does not influence the course of Indian education. Pointing out that the responsibility for the education of Indian children has now been diffused through dozens of public school districts and religious schools besides the federal system itself, Philleo Nash, former Commissioner of Indian Affairs and himself an anthropologist, states:

> Improving the delivery of education in public and religious systems can only come about through the application of federal funds and setting of standards. The significance of Rough Rock is that it provides a model for certain kinds of standard setting. It has already had this effect within the Federal Indian system. More Rough Rocks will lead to more Rock Points. Eventually we hope that improved models will be available

and that increased Indian participation will be accomplished by Indian demands that the Rough Rock and Rock Point models be recognized in public school systems. It is in this sense that Rough Rock is a landmark.[12]

Dillon Platero, currently director of the Rough Rock Demonstration School, maintains:

> Rough Rock does matter; it will not be shrugged off. Although little referred to, probably one of our most important accomplishments has been to infuse into Indian education in general, and Navajo education in particular, a refreshing spirit that has so long been missing. Rough Rock's very existence fosters the hope of inspiring other tribal groups to attempt to realize greater control of their own destinies. The presence of our school on the reservation has already made its influence felt in securing the extension of school facilities to the secondary and junior college levels, in establishing an organization (*Dine Biolta* Association) through which Navajo people can bring their expertise to bear on the problems of Navajo education, and in housing development.[13]

Although criticized for the enormous publicity and public relations efforts made by the Rough Rock School, that experiment in Navajo education was designed to be a demonstration project; its experiences and attendant publicity aimed at encouraging the stimulation of new approaches in Indian education, both curricular and administrative.

Rocky Boy School

Twelve years ago, the BIA school on the Rocky Boy Reservation, a small thousand-member reservation of Chippewa and Cree Indians in Montana, was attached to a public school district thirty miles away. Rocky Boy children were bused to a predominantly white community of fifteen thousand, and Indians had no policy-making roles in the new school. After several years of effort, the reservation Indians were able to get established a restructured school district. The Rocky Boy Reservation then became an independent public school district with separate funding, and controlled by a five-member, all-Indian Board of Education. This board hired an Indian from the reservation as superintendent.

Funding the school was initially the major problem for the new district. Currently the Rocky Boy School is supported primarily by funds from Impact Aid (P.L. 874). In addition, private funds and monies awarded through both HEW and BIA have been secured.

The school district is very new and is still developing its programs. Impressive beginnings have been made in the refurbishing of the school plant. Cree language instruction for children and parents is given in the evenings. There is a bilingual program for five-year-olds. Adult education classes in school law and finances are provided for members of the community.

Schools on the model of Rocky Boy must contend with problems not only of getting their full share of federal funding for Indian programs, but also their share of general state revenues for education. This kind of local control ensures that education funds operate directly for the benefit of Indian children and also as a source of income for those local people employed by the schools. Since their children did not succeed adequately in the larger integrated schools outside the reservation, the supporters of Rocky Boy are hopeful that they will do as well, if not better, in their own school district.

Ramah School

The Ramah High School is the first Indian-controlled high school since the close of the Cherokee and Choctaw school systems. Ramah owes a debt to the Demonstration in Navajo Education at Rough Rock, for it was that project which laid the groundwork in the federal establishment for the legal concept of the right to give funds directly to local Indian communities to run their schools.

In 1968, the small public high school serving the Ramah Navajo community in New Mexico was closed. Although busing to another school was provided the white students of the area, the Indians who lived in more remote locations found themselves without transportation to high school; the only alternative open to them was to attend distant federal boarding schools. Aided by legal and financial support from private foundations, the Ramah Navajos drew up plans for a local high school to be funded by the BIA and OEO. By the spring of 1970, they raised $600,000 from OEO and private foundations, as well as $300,000 from the BIA with a promise of BIA funding for four more years. The grant by the BIA to the Ramah school board was not a privilege, it was a result of legal precedent giving the local community the right to receive funds to run its own schools—a precedent established by the Rough Rock experience.

Ramah developed with the grass-roots participation of local Navajo Indians and the legal advice of outsiders.

The school in 1970–71 had about 140 students, with a 10 to 1 student-faculty ratio. One of the advantages of programs such as that at Ramah is that it tends to attract staff from a wide range of backgrounds. One half of the faculty is Navajo; all teachers but one have B.A. degrees and several have advanced degrees. One teacher is an L.L.D. from Yale, and there is a Harvard M.A. in education. The faculty includes one local Navajo from Ramah who never attended school, but who knows four languages and teaches Navajo history, language, and culture.

The school is run by an all-Indian school board, three members of whom do not speak English, none of whom have high school diplomas. The school points with pride that it stayed open all winter and had excellent attendance though the temperature at times dropped to below 0° F.

Ramah is not experimental in the sense that Rough Rock was and the terms of its grants do not require that it run anything but a traditional school with a standard curriculum. The inclusion of Navajo culture is its major curricular difference from that of the New Mexico public high schools. Its major innovation for the Ramah community has been the infusion of excitement and interest as well as the encouragement of formal, active involvement of parents, teachers, children, and school board members in the development of their own community school, which makes it possible for students to continue to live at home.

Ramah received tremendous political support from the federal government and liberal interpretation of policy from the BIA, which made it possible for them to educate their children in a day high school near home in lieu of sending them off to a federal boarding school. When it opened, President Nixon sent a message to the Ramah community in which he stated that the establishment of the Ramah school "represents an important new direction in Indian education . . . which my administration will actively encourage."

The Ramah experience with the state of New Mexico was less fortunate. The parents early faced threats of suit by the New Mexico Board of Education for violation of the compulsory attendance laws by sending their children to a non-accredited school. New Mexico, requiring private schools to conform to the standards of the public schools was interpreting its regulations in a way which left little room for educational alternatives. The Ramah community was successful in generating enough support to allow it to survive—the model presented by Rough Rock set the stage for direct funding by the federal government with no state jurisdiction over them. This is in part due to interpretation of a federal law by which the states can enforce education law on reservations only with the permission of the tribes.

Rough Rock, Rocky Boy, and Ramah, examples of innovation in Indian education, have significance in several directions. Most important, they provide experience for Indian control and administration of educational programs in place of the paternalistic, bureaucratic administration of programs *for* Indians. They encourage Indian involvement in schools and act as a stimulus to community innovations in curriculum programs. In addition, they represent techniques for infusing federal aid to Indian communities, directly, through the funding of schools. This is likely to engender great political controversy. Huge sums of federal monies, allocated through the Johnson-O'Malley Act, Impact Aid, and OEO grants as well as other BIA funds are involved. Indian communities will find themselves in competition with state systems for these funds. It is also likely to raise the question of states' responsibilities in relation to funding education for their Indian citizens along with others.

Whether or not contract schooling will result in superior pedagogy and improved academic achievement remains to be seen. As Philleo Nash points out:

> The public schools tend to treat the Indian child like any other rural American, which often placed the Indian child at a disadvantage. The BIA schools tend to have curricula which ignores those who have no desire to enter the middle class. The contract school has many social advantages. Its educational performance is as yet undemonstrated.[14]

XIII

Post-High School Education for Indians

Post-high school education has grown very rapidly for Indian young people since 1960. This is due partly to the rapid increase of high school graduates, and partly to increase in the proportion of high school graduates who go on to college or to some other form of post-secondary school.

In 1957, some crude figures support an estimate that there were about two thousand Indian students in colleges and other post-secondary school institutions. For 1970, somewhat better data indicate that this number had increased to about ten thousand.

It is estimated that about three thousand Indian high school graduates entered college or some other post-high school education institution in 1970 and that about one fourth of this number will graduate from a four-year course. This indicates that approximately 18 per cent of an age cohort are entering college, compared with about 40 per cent of the age group of all American youth; and that 4 per cent are graduating from a four-year college course, compared with about 22 per cent of the total American age cohort.

The numbers of Indian high school graduates can be estimated with a fair degree of accuracy at about ten thousand as of 1970. This is 55 per cent of the number of Indians and Eskimos who reached the age of eighteen that year, which was approximately eighteen thousand. Thus it appears that there has been something like a five-fold or 500 per cent increase of post-secondary students during the twelve years before 1970, while the age group from which these students came increased 80 per cent in numbers.

Among post-secondary school students, the ratio between those going to college and those going to technical-vocational schools that require high school graduation for entrance is about 3 to 4. That is, 42 per cent are attending colleges and taking academic courses, while the other 58 per cent are taking vocational-technical courses which require from one to three years of training. About one thousand of this latter group of students are in Haskell Institute at Lawrence, Kansas. A small but growing number are post-secondary students at the Institute of American Indian Arts at Santa Fe. The ratio of men to women among post-secondary students is approximately 55 to 45.

The Bureau of Indian Affairs, since 1956, has operated an Employment Assistance Program which helps Indian adults get training of various kinds and to find employment. This program assists five to seven thousand persons each year, at centers in Chicago, Cleveland, Dallas, Denver, Los Angeles, Oakland, and San Jose. About one third of these people are high school graduates who receive a cost-of-living stipend while they study courses training them to be stenographers, typists, cosmetologists, nurses, welders, autobody and fender repair men, electronic technicians, and diesel mechanics.[1]

College Students

It is clear that Indian youth have a relatively high proportion participating in post-secondary schooling, compared with the youth of other low-income groups, including low-income whites. One reason for the relatively good record of Indian youth is that some scholarship funds are available to them. Many Indian tribes have placed some of their money in scholarship funds. Also, the BIA has provided scholarship money. In 1969, the BIA made scholarship grants to 3432 Indian students, with an average of $868. Also, the United Scholarship Service, Inc., of Denver secures funds from private foundations and other sources, and in 1969–70 aided about eighty Indian college students and twenty graduate students. Scholarship money for graduate studies is not so readily available.

Fairly detailed information on Indian college students was obtained in two parallel studies of high school graduates of June 1962. The Northwest Regional Educational Laboratory[2] and the Southwest Cooperative Educational Laboratory[3] identified high school graduates in these two regions, and studied these young people in 1968. About 70 per cent of these high school graduates continued their formal education beyond high school, and 32 per cent entered college for an academic program.

Some data on the colleges which have the larger Indian enrollment have been brought together by Aurbach and Fuchs.[4] Most of these are state colleges. The following all had fifty or more Indian students in the period 1966 to 1970: University of Alaska, Northern Arizona University (Flagstaff), Fort Lewis College (Colorado), University of New Mexico, Phoenix Community College, Pembroke State University (North Carolina), University of Montana, Northern Montana College, Central Washington State College, Northeastern State College of Oklahoma, Brigham Young University (Utah), and the Navajo Community College, the first Indian college founded by Indians on a reservation.

Over three hundred Indian students from forty-three different tribes attend Brigham Young University, in Provo, Utah. This impressive number is the result of a deliberate effort being made by the Church of Jesus Christ of Latter-day Saints (Mormon or LDS), sponsors of the university, to recruit and educate Indian students—an endeavor viewed as a religious mission.

The school has developed an extensive, carefully organized program, especially designed to give educational, social, and financial support to Indian students in order to ensure successful completion of the college course. Encouragement is given to prepare for the highest professional levels.

Over one third of the students are Navajos. Many of them had been taken as children into Mormon households in preparation for their years at Brigham Young. Because the program for Indians at Brigham Young is part of the proselyting of the LDS

Church and has assimilationist goals for the students, it is viewed critically by those who value the Indian heritage.

By 1969, a number of state universities set up Indian studies programs which were aimed to attract Indian students. An article in the *Stanford Observer* in 1970 states as follows:

> Working closely with University officers, Stanford's six American Indian students are quietly moving to expand total enrollment of native Americans here to 25 next fall.
>
> Only with a group of two dozen or more, students and staffers agree, will Indians be able to overcome the isolation on campus which all too often has been their lot in American society.

Something quite similar has been done at the following places: University of California at Los Angeles, Sacramento State College, University of Washington, University of Minnesota, University of Illinois at Chicago, and the University of Oregon. In some cases, Indian students are encouraged to spend their first college year almost entirely in course work in Indian studies. Sometimes these courses are designed to help the students ease into traditional college work. In some cases this has the advantage of helping the student to get used to the campus, to improve his study habits, and his facility with English, before he comes up against the "tough" courses in English composition and certain other departments that cause a good many students with only average high school preparation to drop out of college. In other cases the course work in Indian studies is designed to develop scholarship in matters pertaining to Indian history, culture, language, etc. The Bureau of Indian Affairs had a record of forty-eight Indian studies programs in as many colleges and universities in 1971.

In a critical discussion of such programs, an Indian anthropologist, Dr. Beatrice Medicine,[5] suggests that they have not yet adequately solved the problem of selecting and presenting material on North American Indian cultures. Also, she has the following comments on the Indian students who have enrolled in such courses. Since a number of these programs were started at about the same time, in 1969 and 1970, they required a strenuous effort to find and recruit students.

> Eventually, a wide range of Native American students were collected. These students reflected the entire gamut of life styles of the varied

tribal groups in urban areas. A polyglot of tribal backgrounds also appeared. There were students who were not far removed from predominantly monolingual families. In contrast, there were students, products of the relocatees and voluntary urban dwellers, who often did not know to what tribes they belonged. They only knew they were Indian. These students presented an interesting, and in some cases, pathetic search for identity. There were some older students who represented the transient life so typical of some Indian males—travels to urban cities, life on "skid rows" and transactions in Indian bars.

Although Native American studies programs are still in their formative stage, it can be predicted with confidence that the development of these programs in a number of universities will produce Indian scholars who will become major scholars and participants in university life.

Also, there are a number of Indian teachers pursuing graduate programs in fields related to education. For example, the Harvard University Graduate School of Education and Pennsylvania State College recruited a small group of Indian college graduates for a Master's degree program, in 1970–71, financed by the Office of Economic Opportunity. Currently, the BIA does not provide scholarships for graduate education. Also, terminated or urban Indians do not receive federal assistance through the BIA.

Navajo Community College

As larger numbers of Indian students enter the colleges, many find themselves faced with the need to resolve the demands of these institutions with the obligations, values, and life styles of their home communities. Higher education has often represented estrangement from their roots. With growing opportunities for using higher education accomplishments in the service of Indian communities, alternatives to the alienation higher education represented in the past are becoming available.

The colleges and their staffs, as has been true for the lower schools, have not ordinarily been prepared to respond appropriately to the special needs of Indian students. The U. S. Office of Education and several universities have begun to sponsor institutes in which Indians and college staffs meet to explore the financial, curricular, and counseling areas as viewed by Indians.[6]

Near Tsaile Lake in northeastern Arizona, amid sage brush,

piñon, and juniper trees, with the Luckachukai Mountains in the background, work is progressing on construction of a college campus which symbolizes a major change of focus in Indian education. Here will be located the new building of the Navajo Community College—the first Indian organized and controlled institution of higher education on an Indian reservation, founded in 1968.

The Navajo Community College represents several significant breakthroughs in Indian education. It is, first of all, an example of Indian responsibility and control of education which historically has been managed by outsiders *for* Indians; it is potentially the source of needed assistance as the Navajo Reservation moves in the direction of economic development; and it provides a learning environment which respects the integrity, values, and heritage of the Indian peoples.

Today, an air of hope and excitement permeates the reservation as a surge of national pride and a massive educational and economic effort by the Navajos themselves moves toward Indian control over their own affairs within the context of federal support. A vigorous tribal government has declared itself the Navajo Nation and is seeking to implement current federal policy which, as stated in the President's message to the Congress, July 8, 1970, reads ". . . *The time has come to break decisively with the past and to create the conditions for a new era in which the Indian future is determined by Indian acts and Indian decisions.*"

Navajo Community College accepts and recognizes the reality of and the persistence of Indian culture and Indian institutions. It holds that uniquely Indian values, skills, and insights are highly functional in the modern world today, and just as Indian knowledge contributed to the survival of European settlers in the New World, so today, Indians have much to contribute to the survival of American and world society. Navajo Community College is based upon the assumption that not only is it possible for Navajos to direct and control their own institutions, but that this is the only way they ever will be able to assume total responsibility and self-support, at least as a group.

Unlike the two earlier efforts at Navajo control of schools, the Rough Rock Demonstration School and the Ramah High School, both of which have given the tribe added confidence in the administration of educational programs, NCC receives no BIA monies. This is a Navajo college established by the Navajo Tribal Council, the governing body of the Navajo tribe, which delegated to the Board of Regents the authority to operate and control the college. There are ten Navajos on the Board, one from each of the agencies (federal administrative units) on the Navajo Reservation, two members elected at large and appointed by the tribal chairman, and three members who serve by virtue of the position they hold, the chairman of the tribe, the chairman of the Navajo Education Committee, and the president of the college student body.

The need for a college had become apparent for many reasons. Currently there are more than 130,000 Navajos living on the reservation. They represent a vital, growing group increasing at a rate twice as fast as the American population. Some 55,000 children are of school age (five to eighteen) and, since this is a young population, the numbers are expected to increase. At present some 1700 Navajos are being graduated from high school yearly. There are 1400 Navajos attending colleges throughout the country, but especially in the Southwest, under tribal and federal grants. Even today, however, the average number of years of schooling for Navajos over twenty-five years of age is just three. Now, increasing numbers of adults are participating in adult education programs.

Viewed against a past history of paucity of educational opportunity, federal paternalism, and Navajo resistance to schools, which demanded forced assimilation, this marks a radical shift in attitudes and accomplishments as more Navajos, both young and old, now turn to schools for education.

Part of this is due to the reality that traditional Navajo economy, which consists of sheepherding and subsistence farming, is clearly unable to support this growing population or provide employment for increasing numbers of educated young people. The extent of distance between the Navajo and the cash economy of the larger society is made evident by the fact that the average annual family income is less than $800 a year and that over 60 per cent of the Navajos are unemployed.

Thus tribal leaders have seen the need to educate for new occupations in conjunction with economic development programs. They need educated youth to assume responsibility for the tasks, among them education, which have been controlled and administered by federal agencies.

Despite these great needs, the reservation has until now been the largest contiguous area in the continental United States without an institution of higher learning. But much of the off-reservation higher education has not been satisfactory. More than $500,-000 in tribal scholarship money given to the top 10 per cent of high school graduates has not paid off; 90 per cent did not complete their college studies. The extensive education needs are emphasized by the fact that after a century of federal education programs, the Navajos have produced only one doctor, one lawyer, one Ph.D., and several engineers. With education as the largest business on the reservation, over 90 per cent of the teachers are non-Navajo. To the tribe, a Navajo college designed for Navajo needs was clearly a priority.

Although Navajo control of education has its real and significant economic and political implications, it also has important philosophical and pedagogical questions to resolve. While they have resisted forced assimilation, the Navajos have not been unwilling to adapt and change. As they gain political and economic control over reservation affairs, the major issue which has arisen is how to develop a generation of educated people with the skills to manage reservation development, to be able to take on jobs on and off the reservation in a technologically oriented, advanced industrial economy without losing those values of Navajo life which have sustained the people over the centuries.

A Navajo college is logically the place for searching out a philosophy of life for the present-day needs of the Navajo people, consonant with their distinct cultural tradition. It is one of the most exciting and heroic undertakings of the school that this search is being conducted in partnership between Western educated Navajos and the traditional learned men of the reservation. To this end, the Indian faculty members have organized a Curriculum Committee to search for a Navajo philosophy of education, in which the present and the future are rooted in the values of the traditional past, in which Western education and Navajo learning are combined.

"If we can blend these and come up with a philosophy this would be a stepping stone for the Navajo tribe. There is something good in Navajo values, in their way of rearing children. The Navajo have existed for centuries and we have seen the growth of the people. Medicine men, the elders, are helping us search for the things that have sustained the Navajo," says Dr. Ned A. Hatathli, president of the college.

And as Jack Jackson, the young Navajo dean of students and active on the Curriculum Committee puts it, "We are searching for how to change without destroying ourselves."

Close to seven hundred students attend NCC, three hundred in on-campus programs, the others in the various service programs conducted by the school on the reservation. The students are not all Navajo or even all Indian. Approximately 20 per cent of the student body has been non-Navajo, including about 10 per cent from other tribes, as well as some Anglos, Chicanos, Orientals, and Blacks.

Students come here for a variety of reasons. Mostly they have heard about the school by word of mouth and are attracted by the small classes, and the reservation location which, particularly for the Navajo students, gives them a chance to become accustomed to college life before leaving for larger institutions off the reservation. Some, including several veterans of the Vietnam war have returned because they wish both a higher education and an opportunity to be close to their homes and among their people. For others, NCC represents the only possibility for college attendance because of their financial or academic limitations. Several students with extensive off-reservation experiences at other colleges, or relocation find at the college a comfortable, accepting atmosphere compared with unfavorable impressions of the outside world.

Students are encouraged to continue their education elsewhere after NCC and to return to the reservation to contribute their skills later if they so wish. Neither the tribe nor the administration of the school suggests that NCC is the only path for Navajo higher education, and the tribe does not seek to channel all high school graduates into NCC even after its capacity expands. Tribal Chairman Peter MacDonald says, "I am suggesting that there are students who want and need to attend the college. Others will go elsewhere."

The faculty is drawn from a wide variety of backgrounds; about one third of the teaching staff is Navajo. For the Navajo faculty members, the college has provided opportunity for educated Navajos to return to the reservation and work in Navajo institutions.

As manpower needs become more clear and college facilities expand, the tribe anticipates that the college will perform an important function in developing skilled manpower resources. Currently, the school vocation offerings include nursing, auto mechanics, welding, commercial art, drafting, design, and secretarial studies.

Although NCC was originally envisioned as providing mainly a vocational-technical program, the number of students in the transfer program, designed to grant an Associate of Arts degree, is at present greater. Students graduating from this program can transfer to four-year institutions and tend to plan to become teachers, social workers, managers, executives, or other professionals.

Courses here include those usually offered in the first two years of college elsewhere. However, the curriculum does depart from those at other schools for it includes attention to fulfilling its commitment to the Indian heritage. Thus the very heart of the academic program at NCC is the Navajo Studies Program, aimed at developing pride in Navajo culture and history, and understanding of the history and current issues affecting the Navajo and other Indians, as well as the development of publications about Indians and for Indians written by Indians.

But the Navajo Studies Program is not without its critics and problems. Many students are concerned that their credits be transferable, although the universities and colleges of Arizona and New Mexico have already accepted several graduates and NCC is moving toward accreditation. The novelty of the courses has aroused doubts on the reservation as to whether or not they are really "college" courses. And misunderstandings about their content and intent among the high schools on the reservation lead some critics to think that all that goes on at NCC is arts and crafts.

But, in addition to making its work understood by the reservation community and others, the Navajo Studies Program has important tasks before it. It has been charged by the Board of Regents to develop Navajo curriculum, which would be useful in the education programs being planned for the entire reservation. To this end there is much use of community resource people, including especially older, traditional Navajo whose experiences and knowledge are being recorded.

In addition to its Associate of Arts and regular vocational offerings, NCC provides many community services. One of these is the Pre-College Program, in which students are prepared to take the GED, the nationally recognized high school equivalency diploma.

The college serves still another purpose, that of sponsoring agency for special programs such as those that are funded by the federal government. The college is a source of professional consultant help, it maintains a visual learning center which is at the disposal of its program, and the expertise to assist in program development and grant applications. One special program, the Navajo Adult Basic Education program, is designed primarily to reach people with no knowledge of English. Among the kinds of things that have been requested by groups of Navajo have been instruction in animal husbandry, building trades, and driver education. And many people want help in child care and how to keep children in school. English instruction is given when people request it and feel they need it. In some of the more remote areas where all trade is carried on in the traditional trading posts, English is not absolutely essential. But use of the pickup truck, and increasing use of supermarkets require English and some consumer education.

NCC's financial worries would overwhelm a less determined and hopeful enterprise. It must be remembered that NCC is building a campus from scratch, has no alumni endowments, no income producing property, and that although tuition fees are moderate ($1200, including board and books), 99 per cent of the student body has no money at all; so scholarship funds for practically everyone must be raised in addition to everything else.

To date there has been no support from the states of Arizona, Utah, and New Mexico, which include portions of the Navajo Reservation. The position of the states is that NCC is a federal responsibility and the states cannot accept any of it. Without some funds which can be counted on on a regular basis, the future of NCC is seriously clouded.

The Navajo Tribal Council has been generous in its support of the college. The Navajo tribe has contributed over $2,000,000, including 1200 acres of land for the new campus. In addition, it has guaranteed loans totaling over $3,000,000. But the resources of the tribe are limited, and, clearly, other sources of income are essential. There has been some response from industry on the reservation, including the El Paso Natural Gas Co. and the Salt River Project, and several foundations including the Andrew Mellon, Ford, Donner, and Charles E. Merrill Trust. Several traders have also sponsored scholarships for students from their areas.

The college looks mainly to the federal government to provide basis sustaining financial support. With limited exception, in the past, the federal government has financed Indian higher education through a system of scholarship grants to students to be used in existing, off-reservation institutions. A move in the direction of financing the cost of construction and operation of an Indian college has been facilitated by authorizing legislation which makes it possible for the Department of the Interior, through the BIA, to provide funds.

Legislation entitled Navajo Community College Bill, was passed in Congress 1971–72. This bill gives construction funds of $5.5 million to the college. The bill also authorizes BIA support on a per-student basis equivalent to the sum the BIA already spends in its own post high school institutions.

The direction NCC takes in the future depends on many factors; its financial stability for one, economic development on the reservation, for another. Some would like to see NCC develop into a four-year institution or even a great Indian university. Others prefer it to remain small and to provide only local services. There remains the serious question as to how the school can effectively adapt to unique Navajo needs while being required to prepare people to meet certification standards imposed from outside. Most important, the Navajos are engaged in a heroic effort to make education meaningful and useful in terms of Navajo-defined needs under Navajo direction.

The very rapid increase of Indian college students and college graduates is likely to be reflected almost immediately in the schools for Indian boys and girls, since many Indian college graduates are planning to teach.

Other areas which will see increased numbers of Indian college graduates are law, economics, history, and anthropology.

The field of Indian socioeconomic development calls for competence in such areas as management, forestry, building construction, plant and animal husbandry, factory management, health services, and cooperative and small business enterprise. Both the BIA and tribal scholarship funds as well as universities with large numbers of Indian students should provide students with career opportunity information.

As more Indian youth acquire higher education, their options for employment both off and on reservations will be greater. In the past, little opportunity existed on reservations for Indian college graduates. Today, increasing numbers of young adults wish to use their education in reservation development. If employment opportunities become available to Indian college graduates who wish to work among their people, this is likely to provide a tremendous stimulus to education in general in their home communities.

XIV

Indians in Big Cities

Indians have migrated to the cities in relatively large numbers during the 1960s. Their reasons for migration have been similar to the reasons of other low-income families for crowding into the cities since 1950. They wanted employment and better living conditions.

In 1928, the Meriam Report observed that small numbers of Indians were living in cities in 1926, most of them close to reservations (Winslow, Gallup, Needles, Phoenix, Albuquerque, Santa Fe) and only a few in the large cities some distance from reservations, such as Los Angeles, Minneapolis, and Milwaukee. It was estimated that less than ten thousand Indians lived in urban communities.[1] In the 1960 U. S. Census of Population, about 160,000, or over 30 per cent of all Indians, were reported to be living in urban areas.

In 1970, according to U. S. Census reports, there were forty cities of 50,000 or more which contained at least 1000 Indian people, and made a total of 120,000 Indians in all (see Table 20). It is anticipated that the 1970 census will show that approximately 280,000 or 35 per cent of all Indians were living in places of 2500 population or over.

Canadian Indians and Eskimos have migrated to the cities for much the same reasons. A recent interview study in Toronto found the three most frequent reasons given by Indians to be

TABLE 20

CITIES WITH 1000 OR MORE INDIANS IN 1970
in Cities with Total Population
of 50,000 or More

Source: U. S. Census, 1970

Albuquerque, N.M.	3,351
Anchorage, Alaska	2,808
Baltimore, Md.	1,740
Boston, Mass.	1,047
Buffalo, N.Y.	2,189
Chicago, Ill.	6,575
Cleveland, Ohio	1,183
Dallas, Tex.	3,437
Denver, Colo.	2,635
Detroit, Mich.	2,914
Great Falls, Mont.	1,161
Houston, Tex.	2,406
Kansas City, Mo.	1,128
Lawrence, Kans.	1,213
Lawton, Okla.	1,928
Long Beach, Calif.	1,172
Los Angeles, Calif.	9,172
Midwest City, Okla.	1,002
Milwaukee, Wis.	3,300
Minneapolis-St. Paul	7,735
New York City	9,921
Oakland, Calif.	2,890
Oklahoma City	7,360
Omaha, Neb.	1,131
Philadelphia, Pa.	1,961
Phoenix, Ariz.	5,893
Portland, Oreg.	1,967
Rapid City, S.D.	2,112
Sacramento, Calif.	1,227
San Diego, Calif.	2,259
San Francisco, Calif.	2,900
San Jose, Calif.	1,941
Seattle, Wash.	4,123
Spokane, Wash.	1,419
Syracuse, N.Y.	1,067
Tacoma, Wash.	1,703
Tucson, Ariz.	1,926
Tulsa, Okla.	8,510
Wichita, Kans.	1,549

employment, education, and "excitement."[2] Census data for 1951 and 1961 in Canada showed the Indian population of Toronto increasing tenfold; Winnipeg, fivefold; and Montreal, twofold during this ten-year period.

The largest urban Indian population in the United States is in the Los Angeles area, where about twenty-five thousand Indians are living and about two thousand children and youth are in school. Next largest is probably Minneapolis-St. Paul with approximately eight thousand Indians and seventeen hundred Indian school pupils in the twin cities. There are some twelve thousand Indians in the San Francisco Bay Area, and six to ten thousand in each of Oklahoma City, Tulsa, Phoenix, and Chicago.

In nearly all of these cities a large proportion of the urban population consists of young men and women who were sent at BIA expense to be trained for an occupation.

Although many Indians have also moved to cities on their own to search for work and experience outside the reservations, many have been encouraged to move off the reservations by the Bureau of Indian Affairs, following the urbanization policy of the post-World War II period. The BIA has maintained a program of Employment Assistance to qualified Indians. Direct Job Placement, also known as "relocation," is the oldest of these activities. In this program, Indians participating were usually placed in a location remote from the reservations. Recent emphasis is now placed less on relocation and more on self-support. Financial help, while in training or adjusting to a new job, is provided.

The BIA maintains relocation centers in Chicago, Cleveland, Dallas, Denver, Los Angeles, Oakland, and San Jose, accounting for the rapid growth in the Indian populations of these cities. In Seattle and in Oakland, the BIA also maintains "halfway houses" to assist those relocating away from traditional home areas to adjust to life in urban settings. Most of those relocating under this program are young people under the age of thirty. Whether or not those who have arrived in cities under BIA programs have an advantage in maintaining themselves in the cities is not known. As one writer states,

> It seems important to note that Indians, whether they arrive in the urban environment through the Employment Assistance or Relocation Pro-

grams, or whether they come without Federal assistance, often tend to
end up in the same socioeconomic boat . . . both assisted and unas-
sisted relocation movements by American Indians have had the effect
in most cases of removing reservation ghetto residents from their rural
surroundings and transplanting them in the ghettos of large American
cities.[3]

When Meriam wrote on urban Indians in 1928, movement
into the cities was just starting. The contemporary picture seems
to suggest larger numbers of migrants to the city, many of whom
are at the lower end of the economic continuum and are evolving
new life styles around urban life and Indian identity.

The urbanization of Indians may be seen in all its diversity in
the Los Angeles city and metropolitan area. The process has
been most active since 1950, and more so in the '60s than in the
'50s. The census showed approximately four thousand Indians in
Los Angeles and its metropolitan area in 1950, and 12,400 in
1960. Between 1960 and 1970, the numbers of Indians in the
area doubled. The 1970 census showed 24,500 living in Los
Angeles County, including over 9000 in the city of Los Angeles.

The characteristics of the Indian population may be seen with
the aid of some interview and questionnaires studies made in
1965 and 1966.[4] Indian individuals studied were generally members or participants of social centers or churches that are operated mainly for and by Indians. The largest number of persons
(adults and children) for whom data were given is 2945. Consequently, the data can hardly be considered representative. Two
principal groups were overlooked. One is the very large group
with the lowest incomes, the least stable employment and family
structure—possibly a third of the total Indian population. The
other is the quite small group of relatively high-income, white-
collar people who have merged into the conglomerate of middle-
class life in a large city. Therefore, the Indian community as
pictured here is the 60 per cent who are most stable in residence,
occupation, and Indianness.

The present Indian population of the Los Angeles area consists
almost entirely of people who have migrated into the area in the
last thirty-five years, with their children born in this area. These
people are mostly from outside California, although a few Indian

people have come into the area from the several small reservations in southern California.

Several hundred Indians, at least, came to Los Angeles during the 1930s and early 1940s from Oklahoma, as part of the great migration of poor people from Oklahoma and neighboring areas during the Depression years. Many of their families have fared well, economically, and are settled in the various suburban areas of Los Angeles.

The postwar in-migration was stimulated by the decision made under the Eisenhower administration to encourage and assist Indians to leave the reservations for employment in urban centers. Between 1953 and 1968, the Los Angeles office of the BIA Field Employment Assistance helped eight thousand heads of families or unmarried young adults to locate in the Los Angeles area. With their family members, this meant an annual in-migration of about thirteen hundred per year. Not all of these people stayed. Perhaps a third of them left Los Angeles. A study made by the Navajo Tribal Agency found that between 1952 and 1961 3273 Navajos were "relocated" by the BIA, but 37 per cent returned to the reservation.

Beginning in 1958, the Bureau of Indian Affairs operated a program of vocational training of Indian adults, with subsistence grants for as much as a year or two, while the individual was in training. This program in Los Angeles involved an average of 550 adults per year since 1965. These people, with their families, numbered about six thousand between 1958 and 1968. Many of them remained in Los Angeles to live after completing their training.

The people relocated and trained were largely Navajo, Pueblo, Sioux, Cheyenne, Chippewa, Blackfeet, and Apache. This is reflected in the data from the survey on the proportions who came first to Los Angeles on the BIA programs: approximately 50 per cent of the respondents came from Arizona, New Mexico, Montana, North Dakota, and South Dakota, while 30 per cent of the Oklahoma Indians came under these programs.

Area of Residence. The map (Figure 11) shows the places in the Los Angeles area where most of the Indian families live. They are quite widely distributed. Wherever an X shows on the map, there were at least thirty people from the sample survey, which included only 8 to 10 per cent of the Indians in Los Angeles. The shaded areas are places of relatively high concentration, though there are no areas as large as a city block which contain a majority of Indians.

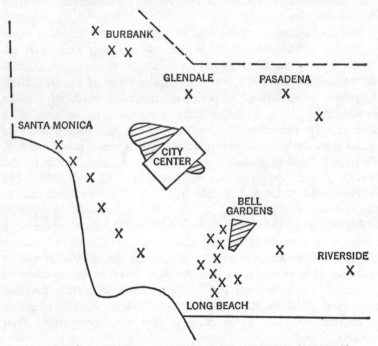

INDIANS ARE CONCENTRATED IN AREAS SHADED OR MARKED X

FIGURE 11. *Location of Indian residence in the Los Angeles area*

The map shows two principal areas of residence. One is a low-rent area of approximately four square miles just west of the city center. This area is bounded by Western Avenue, Beverly Boulevard, Figueroa Street, and Pico Boulevard. This is a kind of "port of entry." It has a number of old two- and three-story wooden houses which have been cut up into small dwelling units. In this area were located several "Indian churches," and several "Indian bars."

The other area of relatively concentrated residence is the small city of Bell Gardens, several miles south and east of the city center. This area was originally, and still is, largely populated by Anglos from Oklahoma, Arkansas, and Texas. Nine per cent of the sample resided in Bell Gardens. Two Indian churches are located there, including the Indian Revival Center (Assembly of God), which is the largest and most active Indian congregation in the Los Angeles area. This is the most stable residential area. It is a working-class community, with small bungalows ten to thirty years old, and a few trailer courts and one-story court-apartment complexes. The Oklahoma-Anglo character is still well preserved, as is indicated by the abundance of fundamentalist Protestant churches.

There is a good deal of transiency in this area. The schools report about a 50 per cent change in the school population in a given year. There is some in-migration of Mexican-Americans, but Anglos are also coming into the community. The Indian population has come partly because of BIA relocation practice, but also because the churches attract a stable working-class Indian group from other parts of the area.

In addition to these areas of relative concentration, the sample survey showed a wide distribution of Indian families in many other community areas. One per cent or more of the sample were residing in: Compton, Cudahy, Norwalk, Huntington Park, Maywood, Paramount, Whittier, Glendale, Pasadena, El Monte, Burbank, Inglewood, Hawthorne, Artesia, Gardena. On the map, the locations of most of these communities are marked with an X.

A total of 101 tribes were named in the survey, but the majority of these were represented only by one to ten persons. On the other hand, there were larger numbers of Navajo, Sioux, Cherokee, Creek, Pueblo, Choctaw, with the following percentages, respectively: 14, 12, 6, 6, 5, 5.

From a sample of 681 households, the following occupational data were obtained, for males: professional, 5 per cent; skilled, 32 per cent; unskilled, 40 per cent; unemployed, 10 per cent;

student, 9 per cent. This is similar to the occupational distribution of a sample studied in Chicago. Probably a truly representative sample would increase the proportion of unskilled and unemployed men. Many of the adults in this sample (40 per cent were under twenty-five) were too young to have school-age children.

The adult Indian population is relatively young, due to the in-migration of many young people since 1960. The sample of 319 married persons reported 3.2 children per family, which is slightly higher than the figure for white families in the western states. (These, of course, are not completed families in most cases.)

The youthfulness of the population is due to the large number of young adults who have come for training and employment. These young adults are having children, most of whom are now of elementary school age or younger. There is a relatively large number of young adults in the twenty to thirty range, and relatively few people over thirty. This is a result of the BIA training and relocation programs.

An especially interesting fact about Los Angeles Indians is the large number of churches which serve Indians almost exclusively. There were in 1966 ten predominantly Indian churches, nine of them Protestant fundamentalist and one Mormon. The church preferences noted in the survey were as follows:

Catholic	29 per cent
None	18 per cent
Baptist	14 per cent
Indian Revival Center	7 per cent
Latter-day Saints	5 per cent
Methodist	5 per cent
Presbyterian	3 per cent
Assembly of God	3 per cent
Episcopal	2 per cent
Native American	1 per cent
Congregational	1 per cent

In any program for improvement of social and family life, it appears that the churches may be more important than they might be in other cities. Most of them have active youth programs, which tend to keep the young people "out of trouble." The churches probably give strength to the stable working-class structure of the population.

The Los Angeles city schools serve the majority of Indian children, but there are a number of suburban school districts which also have considerable Indian enrollments. The Bell Gardens area is in the Montebello school district.

The public schools make an annual "ethnic count," in which the teachers report the numbers of children of various ethnic groups, *as judged by the teachers.* Teachers are instructed not to ask children their race. The data for the Los Angeles city schools are summarized in Table 21. When data are collected in this way, the Indian group is likely to be undercounted, since a number of children who identify as Indians have blue eyes and fair skin color. The Mexican Americans are differentiated from Indians by the classroom teacher by counting all those with Spanish surnames. This also leads to errors in counting Indian children, who are often confused with Mexican Americans because of similar appearance, and in some cases, similar names.

As Table 21 shows, the Los Angeles city school system reported 1192 Indian pupils in 1968 and 1014 in 1969. Most of them are attending one or another of twelve elementary schools, seven junior high, and three senior high schools. The Bell Gardens schools have perhaps 250 Indian pupils. The apparent decrease in the Los Angeles Indian enrollment from 1968 to 1969 may not be a true one. The ethnic count is obviously uncertain for Indians, who may be difficult for teachers to identify.

Examination of the ethnic data indicates that there are more pupils with Spanish surnames than there are Indian pupils in every school attended by Indians. Thus the problems of educating Indian children in Los Angeles (and probably other southwestern cities) are interlaced with the problems of educating Chicano children.

Brief interviews with six school principals and several classroom teachers indicated that the principals and teachers have a generally favorable view of Indian pupils. They regard these children as quite obedient and well-behaved, and possibly too passive in the classroom. They report that Chicano children and their parents are likely to be more aggressive about school matters, and to have something of a "chip on the shoulder" attitude, a reflection in part of a more militant stance than that taken by Indians.

The Los Angeles principals and teachers reported that their Indian pupils were about average, with some very bright children

TABLE 21

INDIAN STUDENTS IN LOS ANGELES
AND BELL GARDENS CITY SCHOOLS (1968–69)

Source: Los Angeles Public Schools, *Racial and Ethnic Survey,* Fall 1968, 1969. Montebello Unified School District, Private Communication.

Level	No. of Schools with 8 or more Indian Pupils	Indian	Negro	Oriental	Spanish Surnames	Total
LOS ANGELES CITY SCHOOLS						
1968						
Elementary	12	711	90,773	12,982	75,546	370,903
Junior Hi.	5	216	31,981	4,982	24,509	143,354
Senior Hi.	9	265	23,932	5,177	25,336	134,320
1969						
Elementary	9	631	90,552	11,441	82,698	363,792
Junior Hi.	7	179	33,502	5,030	26,906	145,135
Senior Hi.	3	204	28,259	5,366	25,854	141,397
BELL GARDENS, MONTEBELLO SCHOOL DISTRICT						
1968						
Elementary	5	159		31	872	5,036
Junior Hi.	1	46		7	232	1,593
Senior Hi.*	2	26		215	1,915	4,662
1969						
Elementary	5	170		32	1,121	5,167
Junior Hi.	1	58		4	241	1,634
Senior Hi.*	2	46		193	2,152	4,749

* Bell Gardens Senior High and Montebello Senior High Schools

and some slow ones. They also reported that art is a favorite subject with Indian children, and some of them do very well in high school elective art courses.

There was not much interest on the part of the Los Angeles and Montebello teachers in curriculum materials dealing explicitly with Indian history and culture. They generally felt that units now in use in social studies, history, and literature present an adequate picture of the American Indian and his adaptation to white culture. Los Angeles teachers, then, are similar to teachers of Indian children generally, as seen in Chapter IX, in regard to their perception of and attitudes toward Indian children.

Several people spoke of the adjustment problems of Indian young adults who come for training or for their first steady employment. Some of these young people frequent the Indian bars at Third and Main, and in the Alvorado section, west of the city center, and tend to get in trouble. Others of them become attached to church groups. The school system does not seem to attract them to its adult education program, though Los Angeles has one of the better programs of adult education in the country. Since so many of the young Indians are there for vocational training, they do not care for more schooling after their training sessions.

Although Los Angeles illustrates the diversity of urbanization, not every city provides the same kind of environment to newly arrived Indians—some are more hospitable than others. Reasons probably vary from the cosmopolitan or provincial nature of a particular city and its housing and employment problems through the historical encounters with Indians and history of conflict which is maintained in some areas.

In Yankton and Rapid City, South Dakota, for example, considerable prejudice and discrimination have been found to operate against the Sioux.[5] The San Francisco Bay area, while it presents problems, is more cosmopolitan, more accepting of varied life styles.

Harkins and Woods suggest that Indian Americans in St. Paul are engaged in an urban adjustment pattern quite different from that of Minneapolis Indians (or Chicago or Los Angeles or

Baltimore) and more akin to urban experiences in Duluth, Minnesota. It is evident that, aside from tribal and related differences, the characteristics of each city are of crucial importance to creating differences in adjustment. These studies suggest that residential patterns and absence of prejudice are important. Most significantly, the host city has responsibilities and can affect the experiences of newly arrived Indians.[6]

In addition to the differences in the cities to which Indians come, there are differences which result from the particular experiences which different groups of Indians bring to cities, as well as different styles of life which develop to meet conditions in the urban environment. Indian-white relations in Minneapolis, for example, have been affected by the particularly militant stance of Indians there:

> Recent severe criticism of Indian education at the national and local levels, while thoroughly justified, seems to have had the effect of reinforcing the alienation of some Minneapolis Indian adults, notably the militants, from educational institutions. While many Indian adults appear to value education as a means to a better future, some militants seem bent upon persuading the young that education is not "the Indian way" and upon "raising hell" with teachers and administrators. Unfortunately, these confrontations often seem to occur for their own sake, and viable alternative approaches to Indian education are not proposed by these militants, perhaps because they are not capable of doing so. The community of Indians in Minneapolis, then, is further divided on the issue of the meaning and importance of formal education to the American Indian.[7]

During 1968–69, the Committee on Urban Affairs of the National Council on Indian Opportunity, an all-Indian council under the Vice-President's office in Washington, D.C., held hearings on urban Indians. Among the cities included were Los Angeles, San Francisco, Minneapolis, St. Paul, and Dallas.

Serious problems which relocated Indians reported were those of employment at low-level jobs with low wages and housing difficulties. Many also reported that they did not know when relocated that their particular tribes had laws concerning residence, which meant that after a number of years away they might lose their tribal membership, or that in some cases their children born away from the reservation would not be enrolled as members of the tribe.

A major concern expressed in the hearings was that relocation for some was synonymous with termination. Indians in cities often have difficulty relating to municipal, state, and federal agencies not specifically directed at Indians. At the same time they've been cut off from BIA assistance. Testimony given at the hearings before the Committee on Urban Affairs of the National Council on Indian Opportunity illustrates this:

> Whenever I was going to College I went to the agency at Andarko and tried to get help. I didn't live on the reservation they told me, and I've been back to look for that reservation, and I haven't found it yet. (Applause) I didn't qualify because I didn't live on this reservation and so I think there is certainly a great need for change. In this way, we are penalizing our Indians who move to the city to try to do better, to be the ideal of the BIA and then they don't qualify . . .[8]

Several Indian organizations, including the California Indian Education Association, Inc., and the National Indian Education Association are actively concerned with the educational problems faced by Indians off reservations.

As noted above, a search for jobs, for improved economic conditions, is probably the major reason Indians come to cities. Chicago illustrates some of the problems Indians face:

> Several factors impede the Indian as he seeks to utilize the economic opportunities of the city. City jobs make unusual demands on rural Indians and they find difficulty achieving steady employment. Most workers are unskilled or semiskilled. Skilled workmen are rare and white collar workers are almost absent from the Indian population of the North Side which is the "Port of Entry" into the city. To this lack of preparation for the requirements of many city jobs is added unfamiliarity with the procedures involved in securing employment. The newly arrived migrant, in particular, is made uncomfortable by the array of application blanks, forms, and interviews entailed in getting a job. The tendency is to avoid the complexities and to seek the most convenient ways of getting employment, even though these do not lead to the best jobs. In addition, there is unfamiliarity with the various agencies, public and private, which can assist him.
>
> The single men, in particular, seem to prefer casual labor that requires working two or three days out of the week. Piecework jobs which enable them to earn higher wages by increased productivity in an abbreviated

work week are more appealing than hourly wages. Low level jobs are typical even for those who seek more stable employment and greater integration into the economic life of the city.

LIFE STYLES

Life styles appear associated with employment status which range from that of the derelict through those employed in a manner similar to the white middle class.

At the lower end of the economic continuum might be a drunk lying in a Clark Street gutter, unable to do anything but beg. When the panhandling gives out he may work for a day for a day labor contractor. He will often first try for a "going south." This consists of getting a job on the far south side of the city through an employment agency, collecting the dollar travel money, and then buying a jug with it. This is considered a great sport and much skill is developed in carrying it out. The day labor contractors are not sure that Indians invented this game, but they are considered most skillful at playing it. Accounts of various "going south" coups are recited endlessly in a manner often seemingly an unconscious parody of the old warrior boasting. But neither the most skillful pantomime nor the most appreciative audience can hide the fact that it is a shallow victory indeed, that the warrior has lost his self-respect.

Further up the scale are those who work more or less continuously at day labor, although with frequent stretches of unemployment for one reason or other. Employment is obtained easily and with a minimum of involvement on the part of the worker. Here is where the day labor offices with placement and bus rides to and from work come in handy. Indians in this category will frequently be unable to peruse the want ads and come up with an improved working situation. They know that their pay scale is low and that the contractor gets the difference, but they are often unable to better their working situation.

Language usage may be related to this. Persons with an exceedingly limited vocabulary of slang expressions can appear to be extremely fluent. "Reservation English," along with other ethnic subdialects, has a restricted vocabulary as well as nuances of meaning that differ from standard English. Thus a fluent speaker of "Reservation English" will often experience a great deal of difficulty, especially at first, in understanding English as it is spoken in the city. People will "talk too fast" or "use too many big words," the latter often being taken as a "put down." Personal interaction in most Indian communities depends on a great many subtle cues; the brusque manner in which life goes on in the big city is interpreted by many Indians as downright hostility.

Employers are usually surprised that Indians are such good workers. They seem to prefer jobs where they are left alone with some degree of responsibility.

For this group of day laborers, consisting largely of unmarried young men, wages are strictly for current living expenses. A person will find that he can live comfortably on two or three days' wages a week and will work no more. There are occasional binges, but with nothing like the frequency seen among derelicts. With some individuals this will be a weekend affair, with others it may consist of a three- or four-day drunk once or twice a month. There are often spontaneous decisions to go back home for a visit, usually a matter of many hundred miles.

A third group presents a different picture in several respects. While some may work only through day labor contractors, they are less transient, usually working four or five days a week. Those who do work at a steady job have often found it themselves, or through friends or kin. This group will have steady work habits for most of the year, but will then take off for two or three months, usually during the summer, to go back home. For them the city is often a place of refuge for the winter months; men with families will often take their wife and children back to their home communities as soon as school is out. They will return to the city and work for a time. If any problems develop at work concerning taking time off, they will often quit on the spot or, more frequently, just not report the next day. Persons in this group seem to have confidence in their ability to secure and hold a job for as long as they will need one.

At the other end of the continuum, are those Indians who are employed in much the same manner as other working-class or middle-class city dwellers. They work steadily at the same job, often with retirement benefits in mind, or they attempt to be mobile upward in their job changes. Contact is still maintained with the home community but not to the extent seen before. Vacations will often be arranged to enable the family to attend their own tribal gatherings, although frequently only some of the children will spend the entire summer with relatives in the home community. At the very end of this continuum are those individuals who have come closest to severing ties with their rural homes and with their extended kin groups.

THE CIRCLE OF FRIENDSHIP

To persons used to small folk communities, with the primary ties those of kinship, the seething mass of humanity in the city is intimidating. The sheer numbers are something that take many people a long time to get used to and even then they may feel uncomfortable.

To people from a folk community neighbors are frequently kin. To those from an Indian community any neighbors who are not blood kin share a common tribal identity. The city is inhabited by strangers, and every stranger is a potential enemy. The very real threat of physical violence that exists in many inner city areas cannot help but strengthen the natural fears of many Indians.

Indians in cities tend to maintain social contacts with other Indians. In Chicago, for example, the majority of American Indians in the city have few or no white friends. Interpersonal contacts are often confined to a quite limited number of kinsmen, old friends from the home community, or Indian neighbors. However, there is extensive visiting among them.

Children often have white friends at school, with whom they play, but many shift, as they grow older, to more exclusively Indian friendships. In a great many cases a pattern evolves of increased activity in Indian Center activities with several close Indian friends. Many Indian children go to the Indian Center to work on their schoolwork, although many parents express worry over the distance that they walk. Some have to take public transportation.

Taken in the context of almost exclusive Indian friendships, the use of an Indian language is very interesting. Except when older persons are present, Indian languages are generally not spoken at home. However, many middle-aged couples are able to speak their native tongue and in fact do so when they are visiting back home. When asked why they didn't speak Indian in the home, many were genuinely perplexed. While there are those who do not speak Indian around their children, for example, for a definite reason, many seem to have never really thought about it. The answers of those who could verbalize their thoughts seemed to revolve around "talking with old people" (who theoretically could not speak English) and "talking Indian when you are talking about Indian things." At any rate, many persons had a definite idea of white-world English and Indian-world Indian. Attempts to start up Indian language classes in the city are by and large unsuccessful. The lack of printed material in a usable form and interpersonal conflicts over correct word forms are major disadvantages.

Children often develop strong desires to learn their tribal language as they grow older. Sometimes children pressure their parents to let them move back to their home communities so they can learn their language and traditions.[9]

Indian Centers

Strangers to the city, Indians tend to organize Indian centers— a local rallying point, a place to share experiences and concerns. Chicago has such a center as do other cities. The following Indian Center charter, drawn up by Indians in Omaha, Nebraska, is illustrative of the purposes for which these centers are organized.

The Indian Center Industries Association is a charitable organization operating in Omaha, Douglas County, Nebraska, whose purposes are

(1) to help the American Indians to help themselves

(2) to help them adapt to urban life;

(3) to make them aware of the available services in

    a. the fields of education

    b. the fields of employment

    c. housing

    d. hospitalization

(4) to create jobs through the center for Indians

(5) to help in any way we can the American Indian both on and off the reservations;

(6) to help combat juvenile delinquency by establishing and providing and assisting in a recreation and sport program among the young teen-age Indian children, such as baseball, football, track, and boxing.

(7) to help to eliminate prejudice and discrimination, and

(8) to defend human rights, secured by law.[10]

Indian centers have constant problems of financing and housing and uniting native Americans of various tribal and nontribal backgrounds, and they tend to rise and fall rather quickly.

Many do not attend ceremonial dances at the centers because they are accustomed to their own tribal ceremonial cycle in its own particular context. Others do not because of religious scruples. Many of the Catholic Indians, for example, are more or less forbidden to participate in "pagan ceremonies" back home. This often carries over into their behavior in the city. In some cases, however, the restraints are removed by moving away from the home community. Indians who never danced before learn and become regular active attenders of Indian ceremonies held in the city.

Indian centers attract persons from many tribes and may be conducive to developing pan-Indianism or Indian nationalism, uniting persons around issues concerning all native Americans. Who attends varies from place to place. Whether or not they can perform the function of the *landsmannschaften* for the European migrant in evolving a life style for the city remains to be seen.

Many of the newcomers to cities have had schooling. Almost all early studies showed no advantage to high school diploma for adjustment to city life. The evidence remains unclear.[11]

A recent study of relief recipients in Minneapolis offers evidence that there is some advantage to a high school diploma but only in that those who are graduated from high school go on relief more slowly. The National Study did suggest some correlation between education and income in Chicago.

Although urban Indians are increasingly the subject of attention of many studies, the urban schooling experience of their children has received relatively little attention.

Many of the new migrants do not yet have many school-age children. In most cities, the ratio of children to adults is quite small. But in another ten years the Indian school-age population in the cities will be several times as large as it is today.

A conservative estimate of the number of school-age Indian children and youth in urban places today is approximately sixteen thousand. In another ten years the present group of young adults will have many children, and the numbers of school-age children may reach seventy-five thousand.

At present the Indian adolescents appear to have special difficulty adapting to urban conditions. They drop out of school in large numbers after reaching the eighth grade. Many of them become chronically truant at ages fourteen and fifteen, and then are officially dropped from the school rolls when they reach sixteen.

The urban schools that Indian children attend differ from most other schools serving Indian children in that the number of Indian children attending are relatively small—indeed sometimes not even noticed by the school authorities. The Indian children tend to be merged into the ranks of the "disadvantaged," attend predominantly lower class schools in the inner city, and little attention is paid to their unique characteristics as Indians.

As part of a study of the education of Cherokee Indians in eastern Oklahoma, Patrick Petit and Murray L. Wax report on an elementary school in Tulsa.[12] This school, containing some 10 per cent Indian pupils, is considered by the investigators as illustrative of the kind of school to which rural northeast Oklahoma Indians, migrating to Tulsa, might send their children.

Their description is striking in its replication of many of the conditions critics have described for urban schools in lower-class areas. Although smaller—this elementary school contained four hundred pupils—the Tulsa school, like those in Chicago, was little affected by the Indianness of the small Indian clientele. The school shared the problems of many inner city schools elsewhere—older plant, poor tax base creating continued financial difficulties, central administration of hiring and firing. The pupils were in a state of motion—the high transiency rate making for marked change in the membership of the school population over the year, without any additional supplies or money needed to cope with an enrollment that, due to turnover, far exceeded four hundred. There was preoccupation with discipline and order. Many teachers were newcomers, and there was a high turnover rate among teachers.

Teachers argued that they had not been prepared for working in a lower-class, polyethnic school. The general absence of cross-cultural sensitivity was reported:

> An occasional teacher explicitly stated that he would have been benefited by training in understanding the cultures of the various groups whose children entered his classes, but this was usually expressed in the managerial sense, namely that with such background knowledge, he could handle the children more expeditiously and train them into becoming better citizens. No one revealed any consciousness of the intimate relationships among language, culture, personality, and mode of learning that would have been basic to assisting these children toward educational achievement.[13]

A particularly frustrating aspect of the urban school, the authors note, is its tempo of activities—short-time schedules which have been imposed on the basis of a theory of brief span of childhood attention. The Cherokee child often works more slowly. This is not a reflection of slowness of thought or of learning, but the deliberativeness of someone who takes seriously an unfamiliar task and wishes to make certain that it is performed to a high level of precision.

A study of a Minneapolis junior high school attended by Indian children reported similar conditions. The investigators maintained that Indian parents have minimal contact with the school, and that there was an absence of human and professional concern for Indian students on the part of a significant number of classroom teachers. Many teachers appeared to them to be ignorant of Indian life styles and showed little evidence that they were willing to make human contact with their Indian students.[14]

It is another travail in the history of America's native population that Indians should be taking an active part in the movement to cities at a time when the urban centers are confronted with the most difficult crisis in their histories. Coming for employment, the Indians face growing unemployment; coming for education, their children face the crisis of the inner city schools; finding housing, they are hounded by the encroachment of urban renewal—necessary, to be sure, to remove blight and decay, but at the same time, affecting the traditional neighborhood useful for the introduction of the new migrant to city life.

Disappointment with urban living and schools is likely to affect many Indian youngsters. The continued existence of the BIA boarding-school system represents a possible alternative for those seeking special programs and an environment different from that of urban schools.

During the coming ten years, the National Study recommended that the federal and state governments devote monies to a special program in all cities with one hundred or more Indian children and youth of school age to improve the educational environment for Indian children.

This program should deal with two groups. One is the group from twelve to eighteen years of age. For these there should be special educational programs, as far as possible staffed by Indian teachers and community aides, which provide the equivalent of a high school course, including special courses in Indian arts and crafts, Indian history and culture, and work experience which leads to employment and income. This program could be concentrated in one or two junior and senior high schools, and could be chosen by Indian students as an alternative to the regular program in their neighborhood school. This kind of program could also be located in Indian centers, through rental by the school board, and assignment of staff to work at these centers. Urban Indian education organized this way provides potential for Indian parent participation in schools affairs if they wish.

The other target group should be kindergarten and primary grade children and their mothers. Community aides could visit the mothers and encourage them to come to school and to mothers' club meetings. A special teacher could be employed in every school with as many as forty pupils in these grades, to assist the regular classroom teachers in their work with Indian pupils and their mothers.

With a fund available through the state Departments of Education for these and other programs, a variety of innovations could be tried out, stimulated by a supervisor from the state department or from the central school administration when numbers of students are great enough to support this kind of staff work.

Financing could be arranged through federal appropriations under the Johnson-O'Malley Act. Congress might appropriate funds sufficient to pay $100 per Indian pupil per year to school districts with one hundred or more Indian pupils. With the estimated numbers given above, this would mean an appropriation of $1,600,000 for the first year, increasing to $7,500,000 at the close of the decade, plus administrative expenses of approximately 10 per cent.

The decade of the '70s will be crucial for the school adjustment of Indian pupils in urban schools, since their numbers will be increasing rapidly and their problems will be new to their parents and to the schools.

XV

Criticisms of Indian Education

It is an understatement to say that Indian education recently has had a "bad press." Consider the following lead paragraph of an article on Indian education by a staff member of one of the more prestigious universities. We shall not give names, because this kind of statement could be duplicated twenty times in published reports of the period since 1965, and therefore it represents a position taken by a group of critics of American governmental and social policies—not merely by one person in one institution.

> By every standard, Indian children receive the worst education of any group in this country. Indians are largely taught by non-Indian teachers who are untrained, unprepared, and often unwilling to deal sympathetically with their problems and needs. The average Indian child is two to three years behind his white counterpart in school achievement. The percentage of Indians who drop out of school is twice that for all other children. Fully two-thirds of Indian adults have not gone beyond elementary school, and one-quarter of the Indian population is functionally illiterate. Beyond these tragic if not surprising statistics, there lies a more profound problem. Public schools have alienated Indian children from their culture while failing to provide them with the type of education which would enable them to function effectively in the majority culture. The economic result of this pattern is that Indian families have an average income of only $1500 per year, and that nearly half of the Indian labor force is unemployed. The psychological result is that Indian children, more than any other group, believe themselves to be of inferior intelligence.

This paragraph contains eleven declarative statements, which presumably are meant to be regarded as considered statements of fact, resulting from objective research. Three of them are demonstrably false. Three are demonstrably true, and five are ambiguous—partly true and partly false. The first two sentences are obviously false if tested against the facts about schooling for other low-income minority groups. More misleading, but ambiguous, are such statements as the last sentence: "Indian children more than any other group, believe themselves to be of inferior intelligence." This statement is based, presumably, on the table in the Coleman study of *Equality of Educational Opportunity*,[1] which reports the proportions of pupils in various ethnic groups who indicated agreement with certain statements:

	Per Cent Responding:				
	MA	*PR*	*IA*	*Neg.*	*Maj.*
Sometimes I feel that I just can't learn.	38	37	44	27	39
How bright do you think you are in comparison with other students in your grade? *Brighter than average.*	31	37	31	40	49
I would do better in school if teachers didn't go so fast.	28	31	26	21	24
People like me don't have much chance to be successful in life.	12	19	14	12	6

Note: MA—Mexican American; PR—Puerto Rican; IA—Indian American; Neg.—Negro; Maj.—white majority.

Comparing the data on Indian pupils with those of other ethnic minorities, it becomes clear that the differences between the Indians and the other low-ranking groups are negligible. With respect to the statement, "Sometimes I feel that I just can't learn," the proportion of Indian students who agreed with this statement was 44 per cent, while 39 per cent of the white majority also agreed with this statement. It is difficult to understand how a person seeking to report objectivity on these data could make the statement cited above, which implies to the reader that the Indian children are substantially below other minority groups in their feelings of self-assurance. Furthermore, the maker of this statement could have found other studies of the self-concept of Indian youth, such as the study by Willard Bass of the Southwestern Cooperative Educational Laboratory in Albuquerque, who gave social-psychological tests to 3375 Indian high school students in seven states.[2] He asked them to mark as true or false the following statements:

	Per Cent	
	True	False
I am confident of my ability in school	71	27
I like school.	83	15

Bass's sample was more representative of Indian students than was the *Equality of Educational Opportunity* study, which involved only 380 twelfth-grade students in BIA schools plus a number not given of twelfth-grade students in public schools. The 380 Indian twelfth graders in BIA schools were nearly all from six boarding schools which are known to have a student body made up largely of students who have been sent to these schools because they did not adjust well to day schools in their own home areas.

Thus there is grave doubt that the Indian data in the *Equality of Educational Opportunity* study are representative of Indian students, and Coleman does not claim that they are representative.

It would seem that a competent scientific study of the self-concept of Indian students would hardly take the data from the Coleman study as a valid report on Indian high school students. The National Study of American Indian Education presents data (Chapter VI) which indicate that the self-concept of Indian adolescents is at least as favorable as that of non-Indian boys and girls in the same geographical areas.

These considerations throw light on the problem of objective evaluation of Indian education. An expectation that things should be bad for Indians leads to the uncritical use of dubious data that point in this direction. When such data are then published in what purports to be a judicious analysis of the situation, the truth suffers.

The quotation with which this chapter begins gains support

from the United States Senate report entitled *Indian Education: A National Tragedy—A National Challenge,* published in 1969 as the conclusion of an eighteen-month investigation made by a Special Subcommittee on Indian Education, headed first by Senator Robert Kennedy and later, after his death, by Senator Edward Kennedy. The life of the investigation was first set at nine months, but in January 1968, Robert Kennedy asked for an extension so as to make a more thorough study. He said:

> To a substantial extent, the quality and effectiveness of Indian education is a test of this Government's understanding and commitment. The few statistics we have are the most eloquent evidence of our own failure: Approximately 16,000 children are not in school at all; drop-out rates are twice the national average; the level of formal education is half the national average; Indian children, more than any other group, believe themselves to be "below average" in intelligence; Indian children in the 12th grade have the poorest self-concept of all minority groups tested; the average Indian income is $1,500—75 per cent below the national average; his unemployment rate is 10 times the national average. . . .
>
> These facts are the cold statistics which illuminate a national tragedy and a national disgrace. They demonstrate that the "First American" had become the last American with the opportunity for employment, education, a decent income, and the chance for a fulfilling and rewarding life.
>
> This subcommittee does not expect to unveil any quick and easy answers to this dilemma. But, clearly, effective education lies at the heart of any lasting solution. And it must be an education that no longer presumes that cultural differences mean cultural inferiority.[3]

It is important to note that the Kennedy subcommittee was part of the Senate Committee on Labor and Public Welfare, while the Bureau of Indian Affairs is administered by the U. S. Department of the Interior, whose affairs are largely the concern of a different Senate committee—the Committee on Interior and Insular Affairs. Thus there was here a basis for internal political rivalry in the Senate, with one committee which had no authority over the Bureau of Indian Affairs undertaking to "investigate" the BIA. On the other hand, since only one third of Indian pupils are in BIA schools, the Senate Committee on Labor and Public Welfare, which is responsible for reviewing education legislation, had a legitimate interest in Indian education.

The aim of an evaluation of the present status of Indian education, admittedly unsatisfactory, is to collect all the principal relevant facts, analyze them coolly, find out the causes of the unsatisfactory condition, and to propose improvements that are feasible.

Objectivity is peculiarly hard to achieve in relation to Indian affairs, because knowledgeable people generally believe that Indians have been mistreated by the dominant American society, and we are under moral obligation to make up as far as possible for past mistakes and mistreatment. The authors of this book share this belief. With this set of feelings and convictions, it is easy to oversimplify the present situation and its problems, and to propose solutions that depend only on the dominant society's recognition of the errors it has made in the past and its disposition to "buy its way" out of the present problem by money payments.

Money is necessary, and more money than has been appropriated by government agencies in the past, but money alone will not solve the problem. There is need for a *complete* consideration of the many-sided problem, and especially of factors that do not reside in the schools, and over which educational institutions have little control.

The problem of Indian education has a good deal in common with the problems of education of other economically disadvantaged minorities, and we are just beginning to grasp the complexity of this problem. More than five years of a massive federal government supplement to local school expenditures on the education of children of low-income families has not produced the results that were anticipated, in terms of improved reading and arithmetic skills. Some improvement has taken place, but not so much in relation to the added expenditure of money as in the development of better methods of teaching these children in a few school districts. Thus, although the education of Indian children has demonstrably received less support from the federal Elementary and Secondary Education Act money than they were entitled to, merely spending more money on them in their present schools in traditional programs is not likely to make much improvement in their educational performance.

A large part of the school achievement of boys and girls depends upon factors other than the school. Formal schooling is only a part of the education that teaches children to read and to use numbers; the school is just one segment of the community.

Many Indian children live in homes and communities where the cultural expectations are different and discontinuous from the expectations held by schoolteachers and school authorities. The average Indian family teaches its children valuable attitudes and skills, but conditions of poverty, isolation, nonparticipation in the urban-industrial society, and language differences are conducive to lower performance on the usual measurements of academic achievement.

The complexity of the situation is beginning to be apparent to many people who themselves are in a position to influence social policy in educational matters, and also to some social scientists who are making evaluative studies of schools. For example, in evaluating the very significant experiment in local Indian responsibility for the school at Rough Rock, the level of success should be judged and measured in other ways as well as in the children's performance on tests of reading and arithmetic. To consider the school unsuccessful because it does not produce dramatic leaps in academic areas is to ignore the complexity of the problems involved.

One reason that some people resist consideration of the influence of family and of minority culture is that they feel that they are somehow *blaming* parents who are illiterate or poor, or harassed by poverty and bad living conditions for the poor school performance of their children. Since they know that these parents are not intentionally hurting their children, they tend to shift the blame to the schools, and in effect, to demand that the schools produce *equality of educational performance* among all groups, regardless of other factors. These people become victims of the fallacy in the following syllogism:

1. The level of reading and arithmetic competence in a country or a social group depends entirely on the schools which their children attend.

2. Any definable or visible group whose children average below the national average in reading and arithmetic is either
   (a) inferior by inheritance, or
   (b) mistreated by the school system.
3. Since Indian children average below the national average, and since they are not inferior by biological inheritance, they must be mistreated by the school system.

This "logic" has also been applied to evaluate the schools in their service to other minority groups which are disadvantaged in the socioeconomic sense—Puerto Ricans, Spanish Americans of the Southwest, Blacks, Appalachian, and Ozarkan whites. Although appealing, it ignores the complex problems of poverty, peer influence, isolation, lack of political power, cultural discontinuity, and historical influence on alienation between schools and communities, all of which impinge on school performance. While criticism of schools has called public attention to important concerns, attacking the schools as a primary cause of educational failure oversimplifies the issues and, more important, diverts attention from the basic economic and political problems of ethnic minorities.

It would of course be futile to argue that the school system can do nothing for children who are handicapped by poverty and cultural differences in relation to their performance in the school skills. The schools *must* do a better job than they are now doing. But how to do a better job is a question with no easy answers.

Robert Kennedy may have sensed this problem when he wrote that his subcommittee did not expect to unveil any quick and easy answers to the dilemma. The plan for the investigation of the Kennedy subcommittee was to take into consideration the following facts:

1. The failure of Indian education has deep historical roots and is closely interrelated with a general failure of national policy.

2. The failure of Indian education must be examined in the context of the most severe poverty confronting any minority group in the United States.

3. Indian education is a cross-cultural transaction. The failure must be examined in terms of its complexity of causes and psychological and social effects.

4. Indian education has evolved a controversial and unique institution —the Federal Boarding School—which deserves special attention and concern.

5. Indian education takes place in a great diversity of geographical and cultural settings.[4]

XVI

Global Evaluation
of Indian Education

In the following pages we shall try to make an objective global evaluation of Indian education, based on such facts as are now available. This evaluation should satisfy the following criteria:

A. Evaluation should recognize the existence of three broad types of schools for Indian children and youth, and should be applied appropriately to each type.
  1. Federal (BIA) schools, mostly boarding schools, with all-Indian enrollment.
  2. Rural and small-city public school systems, in which Indians make up 5 to 100 per cent of the enrollment.
  3. City public school systems, in which Indian students make up less than 5 per cent of the enrollment, though they may reach 25 per cent in certain school buildings.

B. Evaluation should take account of the non-school factors which tend to determine the direction of development and to set boundaries to what the schools can accomplish with respect to the mental skills of reading and mathematics. Major determining factors are:
  Poverty.

Geographical isolation from centers of employment and of non-Indian culture.

Lack of English, or very limited English in the home.

Lack of facilities for reading and study in the home.

A variety of Indian and Eskimo cultures with life styles that at present do not work positively for school achievement.

C. Evaluation should be based on adequate samples of schools and of Indian families and students.

D. Evaluation should be made with research methods and research instruments which have proven reliability and proven validity, or, at least, which use two or more different instruments or two or more different researchers to establish the truth of a particular proposition.

E. Evaluation should compare Indian education and its results not only with the educational norms and achievements of the white majority, but also with other disadvantaged minority groups.

F. Evaluation should be relevant to the goals of education for Indians as these are stated and developed by Indian leaders and by Indian parents.

G. Evaluation should be applied critically to:
1. Amount of money, and efficiency of use of money for Indian education.
2. Competence of teachers and administrators.
3. New methods and special methods that may compensate for educational disadvantages of Indian children, such as:
   a. Head Start or preschool classes.
   b. TESL (Teaching English as a School Language).
   c. Bilingual procedures in the school.
   d. Teaching of Indian culture and history.
4. Forms of local community school government that increase the participation of Indian people.

Nobody in possession of the facts could reasonably argue that Indian education is either satisfactory or even as good as it can be, under the present circumstances. There is room for improvement and need for improvement. In the following pages we shall attempt to describe a practicable program which is based on the present reality and promises to make real improvement, but does not promise miracles.

The program has two essential bases: Indian self-determination in education and Indian economic development.

I. Types of Schools

The three broad groups of schools named above will continue throughout this century to serve large numbers of Indian boys and girls. Each can be improved in relation to its own peculiar nature.

Boarding Schools. Since sparse populations and travel difficulties will continue to make it necessary to provide boarding schools for an important fraction of Indian children and youth, there should be major improvements of facilities, curriculcums, pupil services, and Indian influence. Several new schools must be built, to take the place of current quarters which are no longer usable. The locations of these new schools should be considered carefully together with the communities whose children will be served. Probably several of the Oklahoma schools should be closed and new schools built closer to the Navajo area and in Alaska, where the bulk of boarding school students will live. In situations where Indian communities wish to run their own school—both boarding and day schools—they should have the right to do so under contract with the BIA.

Rural and Small-City Day Schools. These schools are mostly state or local public schools, with proportions of Indian pupils ranging from 5 to 100 per cent. BIA day schools are also in this category. These schools will continue to educate at least 50 per cent of Indian youth for the next ten or twenty years. It is here that substantial improvements can be made—in the quality of teaching and in the curriculum, by teachers who have learned to work effectively with Indian children.

City School Systems. The next frontier for Indian education lies in the cities of one hundred thousand and over, which are gaining Indian population rapidly. Some special assistance to Indian pupils and Indian families with small children should be organized through the school system, and financed with funds voted by Congress under the Johnson-O'Malley Act.

II. Relating the Program to Poverty and Indian Cultures

Sharing a position of poverty, the performance of Indian students is very similar to that of other low income minority groups. Further, the many Indian cultures may have some things in common which impede the child's success in schools if schools are conducted in the usual way. Wax *et al.* have presented evidence that this is so.[1] Dumont[2] has argued that teachers can help Indian children to learn more efficiently if they take account of the social characteristics of Indian children, and learn to work *with* these characteristics, rather than *against* them.

These considerations suggest that teachers of Indian children should be systematically trained to take account of the sociocultural processes operating in the communities and classrooms where they work.

With respect to the *poverty conditions* in which most Indian families are submerged, the most important thing is to assist the Indian people to work themselves out of this status. In the meantime, the best of preschool and Head Start methods should be used with young Indian children to help them to develop the linguistic skills useful for school success.

III. Comparison of Indian Education with the Education of Other Minority Groups

It is not enough to compare the educational achievement of Indian youth with that of other disadvantaged minority groups, such as Blacks, Mexican Americans, and Puerto Ricans. These other groups are much more fully committed to participate in the dominant culture, albeit a variation or different version of the dominant culture. Most Indians, however, are members of tribes which have now or had until recently a many-sided and non-Western culture, modified to be sure over years of contact with others, but not as fully committed to assimilation as most minority groups in this nation.

Most Indian tribes are now trying to participate successfully in the economy of the dominant culture, and at the same time trying to maintain part of their traditional culture. Their children grow up in this ambiguous situation, which makes it impossible for them to throw themselves fully into an educational program designed only to help them become more successful earners than their parents.

Since Indian youth do just about as well in school achievement as the other disadvantaged minorities do, this might be taken as a sign of successful education, except for the fact that none of these groups does well in the dominant economy. But the Indian adults also want their children to learn to be "good Indians," and most Indian adults hope that the schools will help in this process.

IV. The Goals of Education for Indian Youth as Indians

It is difficult and perhaps impossible to state what Indians want their children to get from the schools *as Indians*. In the first place, various Indian groups have different desires in this respect. For example, the thirty thousand Lumbees of North Carolina have lost their traditional language and now use English. They do not practice a traditional culture although they have pride in being Indian. They contrast enormously with the Navajo, who have a living language, living myths and religious ceremonies, and a vital tribal life which they wish their children to retain.

Secondly, many tribes are divided among themselves concerning their expectations of the school as a teacher of Indian culture and history. Among the Hopi, for instance, one faction would limit the school to teaching the English language and other skills necessary to do business in the outer world, while the tribe teaches the children their culture. Another faction would use the schools more fully to carry on the Hopi culture.

White people cannot usefully help to settle this kind of problem. Indians will work it out, and the schools, especially those on and near reservations, should follow the Indian voice.

V. Financing Indian Education

In Chapter I it was shown that the vast majority of Indian children and youth are in the public schools, which means that the amount of money spent on their schooling is about the same as the amount spent on white children's schooling in the same schools. For the 15 to 20 per cent of Indian pupils in federal boarding schools, the expenditures seem high, since the full cost of their living must be paid. But proposals for improving conditions in boarding schools require increased expenditure.

There are two general questions to be answered concerning the financing of Indian education. One is whether the money that is intended for the education of Indian students is actually used for this purpose. The other is whether the level of expenditure on Indian education is as high as it should be.

In an effort to answer the first question, the Legal Defense and Educational Fund, sponsored by the National Association for the Advancement of Colored People, has examined the use and distribution of federal funds for Indian children in public school districts.[3] In the course of interviewing state and local educational officers in sixty school districts in eight states, this project found little Indian representation and a number of specific inequities and inadequacies in the administration and distribution of these funds.

The conclusion of this study was that these funds were *not* being administered for the maximum benefit of the Indian students for which they were intended. Major improvements in administration of these funds should be made by the U. S. Office of Education and by the Bureau of Indian Affairs. One way of speeding up this process would be to bring Indian leaders into a position where they could examine the administrative procedures with respect to federal funds for Indian education, and where they could make changes in policy and administrative organization.

It is clear, from the study made by the Legal Defense and Educational Fund, that there are some irregularities in the expenditure of federal funds for Indian education in public schools. Other critical studies of the use of funds under Title I of the

Elementary and Secondary Education Act have indicated that this money, which is intended to increase the amount spent on the education of children from low-income families, is not always used efficiently for this purpose. This criticism applies to the use of Title I funds for all children of poor families, not simply for children of poor Indian families. These irregularities are now being cleared up by the work of the staff of the U. S. Office of Education.

Criticisms of inefficient use of Johnson-O'Malley funds have been made frequently, and it seems mandatory for the BIA to review its contracts with various states and school districts, and probably to work out a set of guidelines for the more effective use of these funds. Also, it would be wise for the Congress to appropriate some money under the Johnson-O'Malley Act to improve the services of the public schools to Indian students in the large cities.

The broader question of whether the public expenditures on Indian education should be substantially increased is not easy to answer. The BIA has proposed that the funds for BIA schools be more than doubled. A report of a management consultant to the BIA says: "BIA schools are at this time insufficiently funded to overcome the students' initial difficulties resulting from poverty and cultural barriers. The price of this economy is ultimately paid in high welfare payments and reduced revenues. Annual per pupil expenditures, now around $1000, should be greatly increased on the basis of conserving future welfare costs and income tax collections."[4]

This argument is seldom used seriously in 1971. It assumes that the child of a poor family (Indian or any other low-income group) will learn economically valuable skills which he can use in getting employment and better paying jobs if substantially more money is put now into his education. But the experience of the post-1965 period with substantially increased expenditure on education for poor children and with Job Corps programs for adolescents who have dropped out of school throws doubt on the validity of this assumption. It appears likely now that the same extra money spent on improving the economic situation of Indian adults through tribal economic development and public works on the reservations is more likely to be reflected in increased earnings of the present and the following generations of adults.

Furthermore, the argument that increased expenditure on Indian education will increase the earning power of Indians is based on the assumption that this education will be aimed at the assimilation of Indian youth into the labor force of the dominant society. But this assumption should not be made unless and until it becomes official policy for Indian education, stated by spokesmen for Indian people.

We recommend an appropriate increase of educational expenditure for Indians with the federal government paying for the increase. Probably a sensible and generally acceptable beginning could be made by providing a 10 per cent increase in real dollars devoted to education under the BIA, with the expenditures allocated by a National Indian Education Commission composed of Indian leaders.

VI. Teachers and Administrators

In Chapter IX, we noted that the teachers of Indian children are a cross-section of the teachers who work in the rural and small-city school systems. Their attitudes toward their work are favorable. The vast majority of them like to teach Indian children. They would like to see more Indian history and culture in the curriculum. Therefore it would not improve the teaching personnel very much if a rigorous screening was imposed on the schools with many Indian students, so as to eliminate those who detest their jobs and those who dislike Indians. There are probably just as many teachers who dislike their jobs in the non-Indian schools, and just as many who dislike white children or black children.

Nevertheless, the quality of teaching for Indian children could be improved if the turnover of young teachers was reduced, and if new teachers had systematic in-service training in cultural awareness linguistics, and in the study of Indian history and culture. More than this, there may be some teaching methods which are especially well adapted to Indian children because

Indian children react somewhat differently to classroom teaching than children of other minority or majority groups. These methods should be brought out more clearly in experimental classes, and teachers in service should be shown how to use these methods.

Finally, it seems desirable to encourage more Indian men and women to go into teaching of Indian children; and this is feasible, due to the recent rapid increase in Indian college students.

Teacher aides and other paraprofessionals should be recruited and trained among Indian and Eskimo adults. This is especially important where the children come to school without knowledge of English and the teacher does not know the local native language.

VII. Special Methods and Curriculum for Indian Students

The most basic evaluation of any school system in the modern world focuses on two periods in the pupil's life. First, how successful is the process of learning the basic mental skills of reading, writing, and calculating? Second, how successful is the last phase of general education in helping the student to move into adult roles? In the case of Indian education, this evaluation must be made against a definition of success which is vague, in view of the fact that there is no general agreement on the importance of assimilation into the economic system as a major goal.

The first phase of formal education for all children is that of learning the basic mental skills so that these, in turn, become tools for further education. In the case of reading, the goal is to master the mechanics of reading to the point where one can read new material to *learn that material,* not to learn *how to read.* In the average case of a child growing up in an English-speaking household where the adults read freely, this goal is achieved by the third or fourth grade. From that point on, children can take books from the school or town library and read on their own, adding new words to their reading vocabulary as these words appear with some regularity. Spelling follows along, as the child writes in order to convey his meaning to other people. Arithmetic up through the multiplication table enables the child to do the ordinary business of thinking and talking quantitatively about the affairs of everyday life.

The fact that speaking English is learned in the family and the neighborhood gives the young child a speaking vocabulary which is always ahead of his school vocabulary.

Since the majority of Indian and Eskimo children come to school with little or no spoken English, the school must cope with this basic fact. No schools anywhere in the world have found it easy to solve this problem. There appear to be two general approaches. One is to conduct the school entirely in English, teaching English speech and English reading and writing together, and holding off all other instruction until this is far enough along to permit the use of English in the teaching of arithmetic. This method is a slow, laborious process, and seldom brings an Indian child to the level of fifth-grade fluency according to national norms until the Indian child is twelve or thirteen years old.

At present, at least half of Indian and Eskimo children are in this situation. They are fluent in speaking their native language, and they have great difficulty in learning to speak and read in English. The other half—those Indian children who live in the cities and those in the more acculturated tribes—generally have English as their basic language and can follow the normal school curriculum.

For those children who do not come to school speaking English, some form of bilingual education appears to be indicated. These have been described in Chapter X. The approach to English is through the spoken language. Children learn to speak English in school a part of each day, but they also speak and learn to read in their native language a part of each day. Their progress in school is not limited by their progress in English. This approach appears to be the most promising procedure at present.

The problem of a high school curriculum for Indian young people has not even been well formulated yet. Clearly, the high school is likely to terminate the formal education of more than half of Indian youth as it does for more than half of all American youth. At present, getting past the tenth grade of the high school or completion of the high school does not lead ordinarily to an adult role as a worker in many Indian communities. With a large segment of the adult group unemployed or underemployed, the labor market does not readily absorb young people aged sixteen to twenty.

Economic conditions in the Indian and Eskimo communities will probably develop to the point where there will be a need for young workers. Then the high schools will be able to help the majority of boys and girls to move into a role of economic competence. How this can be done most effectively will have to be determined as a part of the solution of the problem of Indian economic development.

There is widespread agreement on the desirability of teaching Indian culture and history. It has not been done adequately in the past, but there is much activity in this area now. Consequently, it appears that no evaluation can now be made of the effectiveness of this curriculum emphasis. There is bound to be improvement. By the mid-1970s, a wide variety of books and other teaching materials are likely to be used in classes with Indian students. Some will deal with the local Indian or Eskimo culture. Others will deal broadly with the history of the Native Americans and their relations with the foreigners who have preempted most of the land and resources of this continent.

VIII. Indian Influence on the Education of Indian Youth

In the public schools of rural and small-city school districts with substantial numbers of Indian pupils, the Indian influence will develop rapidly where the schools serve an all-Indian community, and probably more slowly where the Indians are in a minority. Progress will depend very much on the establishment of effective machinery in the Bureau of Indian Affairs and the U. S. Office of Education to bring representative Indians into positions of influence over the distribution of Johnson-O'Malley and other federal funds that are intended to serve Indian education.

The goal of substantial Indian influence on the education of Indian boys and girls is now within reach, in principle, though not in fact. Presidents Nixon and Johnson both affirmed it. The Bureau of Indian Affairs has been officially working toward this goal through its program of contracting education to the tribes. Advisory boards are now operating for practically all BIA schools. The scene is set. It remains for the policy to be put into effective practice.

XVII

The Indian Voice in Education

Indian education is an essential part of the complex process by which the Indian peoples make progress toward their own goals as individuals and as social groups. For this, they must secure a higher material standard of living, and more *real* options for themselves as individuals, families, and tribes.[1]

This complex process of development requires the dominant society to act in good faith, mainly through the federal government. Indians are skeptical of the white man, for they have experienced over two centuries of broken treaties, poorly kept promises and depredation of their lands. Furthermore, the 1953–58 policy of termination of reservation status, with its bad consequences for several tribes who gave up their reservations, has produced in some Indian leaders what has been called a "termination psychosis"—a suspicion that every government policy, program, or action may have termination as a hidden goal.

For over a century most Indian tribes have been in special relationship with the federal government, which has given them certain rights and claims that other residents of the country do not have. At the same time, however, they have been denied the power to govern themselves on many matters, to administer programs, or to make agreements and transact important business without the approval of a white man representing the federal government.

From this status to the status of full self-determination is a long journey which may be made in various ways. Today Indians themselves and their supporters are making plans and starting actions that are moving in the general direction of greater self-government, while revising and improving strategy as conditions change.

A major component of this policy is that the Indian voice should grow stronger with respect to education and on this issue there is a broad consensus.

There are several strategies whereby an increased influence by Indians over the education of their youth may be effected. One is at the local level, the others are at the state and national levels.

The idea of local control of schools by the Indian people grew to be a major concern during the 1960s. The idea is not a new one; the Meriam Report recommended in 1928:

> The whole task of community participation, so important for the Indian, has to be consciously worked at; for example, the Indians should be serving on school committees in the day school as a means of enlisting their general interest in all that involves the child's education and development, and also as a gradual preparation for service on boards of education.[2]

Private investigators, educators, and others have been recommending various forms of local control for many years. The Waxes concluded that the crucial factor in the problem of education for Indians on the Pine Ridge Reservation is the lack of communication between the Sioux community and the mainstream of national life, between educators and the Sioux people, and between pupils and their teachers. They present recommendations for remedying this. Their most basic suggestion is that the Sioux be closely involved in the schooling of their children. To implement this, they suggest:

> Neither resolutions from Area and Washington offices nor P.T.A. type organizations can bridge the gulf between Indian community and federal schools. Only an organizational change, such as transferring some authority and responsibility to community representatives, offers the

probability of being effective—namely, transferring control of the elementary school system to a board elected or otherwise selected by the Indians themselves. Funds would continue to be advanced by the federal government under Johnson-O'Malley or parallel legislation and would be subjected to the same types of budgetary and auditing controls as are routinely applied when agencies or institutions receive financial support from the federal government in return for performance of specific services.[3]

The Waxes admit that the "process of transition may be awkward unless there is careful preparation and unless the Sioux population has some period of time to discuss the change." They suggest that "more temperate proposals . . . involving joint boards of Bureau officials, Tribal representatives, and outside parties" should be considered if the Sioux resist the idea of taking over complete control.

Another long-time proponent of local control for Indians is Dr. Robert Roessel, former director of the Rough Rock Demonstration School. In testimony before the Senate Subcommittee on Indian Education he said:

> The Number One need, in my estimation, can be characterized by the problem of local control. The Indian people today enjoy most rights to which other citizens of this great Nation are entitled. However, they have in almost every instance been denied the right to be wrong . . . The professionals and the expert are the ones . . . who determine the character as well as the objectives of Indian education.[4]

Roessel does note that there will be problems in bringing about local control. The Navajos, for instance, are apt to defer to professionals in making decisions about schools. He believes that "a real effort must be made on the part of the professional school administrators to educate all school board members into their responsibilities and functions."

Another advocate of local control is Dr. Herbert Striner, a member of the 1967 presidential Task Force on Indian Affairs. In a paper on training and employment for American Indians, Striner recommended the following:

> An all-Indian school board should be established for each Federally operated Indian school. The basic purpose of establishing such school boards would be: (1) to give Indian parents an important voice in shaping the educational experiences of their children; this is a *sine qua*

non for obtaining affirmative parental involvement, which in turn is essential for any school to operate effectively; (2) to stimulate use of the schools as centers for adult education and community development; (3) to ensure that the school administrations and teachers remain attuned to the attitudes and values of the local community they serve . . .[5]

The idea of much greater self-government and self-determination by Indians has received strong support in the Congress during the past decade. In 1966, Senator George McGovern of South Dakota introduced in the Senate a Concurrent Resolution which gave full support to the idea of Indian self-determination. At about the same time, President Johnson appointed a Task Force on Indian Affairs consisting of several university professors who had been students of Indian affairs, one or two educators, and one or two men of business and political experience who had some Indian ancestry. Although the report of this Task Force was not officially published, the essence of it was given limited distribution by Herbert E. Striner, an economist on the staff of the W. E. Upjohn Institute for Employment Research.[6]

This report devoted about three fourths of its space to problems of economic development and government administration of Indian affairs, and about one fourth to education. It proposed that the federal government should create an Indian Development Corporation to finance a variety of programs by which Indian-owned and tribal business and industry would be aided, and public works projects would be financed on Indian reservations. For instance, it was recommended that a vast public housing program be initiated with Indians doing most of the work. This and other public-financed projects would pay for sixty thousand *new jobs* on reservations by 1977. These recommendations were different from previous ones more through the size of the funds involved than through the ideas involved. The report says: "A solution to the Indian 'problem' calls for efforts in education, training, housing, welfare, and health at a level of funding never properly understood." However, this Task Force argued that the Indian "problem" was not a simple one. "What makes the problem formidable is not its size, but its nature. For it is made up of generous portions of just about every major social problem of the day: self-sustaining rural poverty, slum diseases, chronic unemployment of almost 50 per cent of the adult male population, race prejudice, an imperfectly adapted school system, and very little available socioeconomic data on which to build programs to alleviate or remedy these situations."[7]

Except for relatively small financial inputs by the Office of Economic Opportunity into economic development on or near Indian reservations, the recommendations for substantial economic assistance have not been acted upon by Congress. However, the recommendation for a stronger Indian voice in educational matters has been heeded.

President Johnson on March 6, 1968, delivered a message on Indian affairs which began:

> I propose a new goal for our Indian programs: a goal that ends the debate about "termination" of Indian programs and stresses self-determination; a goal that erases old attitudes of paternalism and promotes partnership self-help.[8]

The President went on to say:

> To help make the Indian school a vital part of the Indian community, I am directing the Secretary of the Interior to establish Indian school boards for Federal Indian schools. School board members—selected by the communities—will receive whatever training is necessary to enable them to carry out their responsibilities.[9]

In its final report, *Indian Education: A National Tragedy—A National Challenge,* the Special Subcommittee on Indian Education of the Committee on Labor and Public Welfare of the U. S. Senate also expressed strong support for Indian boards of education and increased parental and community influence at the local level.

The President's directive for Indian school boards was put into effect by the BIA. As of May 1969, one hundred and seventy-four of the Bureau's two hundred and twenty-two schools (most of which are in Alaska and on the Navajo Reservation) had selected advisory boards. The BIA felt that such advisory boards might function as follows:

> 1) Assisting with curriculum improvement, particularly by suggesting and providing cultural materials for inclusion; 2) consultation concern-

ing the selection of employees; 3) consultation in setting up campus and school rules and regulations; 4) inspection of the school's physical plant; 5) encouragement of parents to enroll children in school; 6) regular visitation of the school; 7) facilitation of information between school and community; and 8) consultation concerning the budgeting and use of funds.[10]

Under this arrangement, of course, the Indians do not really have control; they can only offer advice and give or refuse assent. Perhaps most importantly, they cannot employ and discharge school personnel.

Recognizing this, the BIA has also issued guidelines to the tribes on how they may proceed to take almost complete control of the operation of the schools. This plan has been designated "Project TRIBE." The BIA described this project for the Senate subcommittee:

> In brief, this plan provides for a tribal governing body to initiate a request that under a contract with the Bureau of Indian Affairs the Indian community be authorized to assume the responsibility for operation of a Bureau school under the direction and management of a local school board. Full funding would be provided by the Bureau and the school board would be responsible for providing an educational program which meets the standards of the State in which it operates. Evidence of approval of tribal operation of the school by a majority of the qualified voters of the community would be required.
>
> Such an arrangement would mean that teachers would become Tribal rather than federal employees, and the local school board would have "hiring and firing" authority, as well as authority for making other decisions regarding the school program and operation.[11]

To facilitate the process of establishing school boards, the BIA assembled a collection of materials on school boards, state boards of education, how to conduct a school board meeting, etc. They prepared the *BIA School Board Handbook*,[12] in which they described the importance of a consistent philosophy of educational objectives for the school, the legal framework for both advisory and contracting school boards, the financing of the educational program, the way to run meetings, how to work with superintendents, establishing good relations with the community, evaluating the school program, etc. In June 1968, the BIA sponsored a School Board Workshop at the University of New Mexico. In December 1968, they sent out their guidelines for Project

TRIBE. In March 1969, they arranged for the First National Indian Workshop on School Affairs, at which Indian tribal and community leaders discussed parental involvement, school board training, and other matters. This workshop was designed to provide training for Indians serving on advisory school boards. Thus, some effort has been made to encourage Indian people to take over the control of their schools and to make preparations for this to happen.

There may be a great difference between the creation of an advisory board by a school director and the exercise of influence or control by the local Indian or Eskimo people. For example, a staff member of the National Study reported on a meeting of the advisory board of a day school in an Eskimo village. Those attending the board meeting were all Eskimo women, and the school director was a Caucasian woman. The Eskimo women had great difficulty in comprehending the English language used by the school director in explaining the functions of the board. Their own schooling was limited, and they had never before been in a position of influence or authority over the school or its director. They hardly spoke during the meeting, except to give assent to statements worded for them by the director in response to questions sent to the school by the area office concerning school policies. They did not ask questions.

Even where the situation is more favorable to Indian understanding and control of the school, actual movement toward the goal is slow and uncertain. As was noted in Chapter XII, the evaluators studying the Rough Rock School concluded that the white director tended to dominate the school board. However, there is evidence that the Indian school board by 1969 was taking more responsibility. This is not very different from the situation of most public school boards in small American communities, which generally acquiesce to the proposals of their school administrators in evaluating teachers and managing the day-to-day operation of the school, and limit themselves to establishing general policies.

In addition to Indian school boards in BIA schools, the number of Indian school board members of local public school districts has increased since 1965. For example, when the former BIA school on the Rosebud Sioux Reservation was taken over by the Todd County Public School District, an Indian was elected to the Todd County School Board. Also, Indians have been elected to the board for the Gallup-McKinley School District in New Mexico, and in Montana, state support was given for the public school district organized by the Rocky Boy Reservation.

A problem which may be encountered in certain communities is that some Indian people simply may not wish to be responsible for their own schools. Many Indians feel that the Bureau—or other—schools are quite adequate and may not wish to change. There may be several reasons for this. At the Whiteriver Education Conference of Apache citizens and parents, one of the participants, an Apache advisory school board member, spoke as follows:

> With respect to our BIA school in Cedar Creek . . . some white people have been seeing us about the feasibility of making it a "contract school" (e.g., like Rough Rock). As far as I am concerned, I stated that my education was very limited and that I have very little, if any, experience in doing "paper work." Therefore, I invited some of my best friends and local people to help out with this decision. The decision that the people arrived at was the school would remain under the auspices of the BIA. The feelings of the people were that if the contracting took place, politics probably would enter the picture and relatives of the politicians would take over the various positions. In addition, it was felt that although many of our people have been to college, they were not qualified to assume teaching and administrative positions. In short, we were not ready to take over the school.[13]

The question of politics is a significant one. Many Indian communities are deeply divided by factions. In these communities, Indians are understandably reluctant to have education and the schools become a political issue. Moreover, if and when a system of local control is instituted, problems may develop from the conflict of various factions, as one group advocates one policy or program and another supports another one. For instance, many Indian communities are divided along lines of relatively more "traditional" and relatively more "acculturated"; conceivably, conflicts might well develop between these two groups concerning the curriculum.

The possibilities of effective control also vary from place to place. Schools which are located in relatively small, all-Indian communities present problems different from schools where Indians are a small minority in an urban school setting.

Important, too, is the long history of Indian-government relations which cause many Indian groups to view direct federal administration of schools as symbolic of the government's continuing acceptance of its traditional and legal responsibilities.

The broad movement toward local control of local schools is now very popular among non-Indian social scientists and educators. They have done most of the relevant research. Along with congressmen, commissioners, and Presidents of the United States, they have made most of the recommendations concerning local control. Their efforts support Indian wishes in this direction. Lacking money and power, Indians are not in a position to easily establish or to operate their own schools without outside legal and financial assistance. The support of concerned persons in positions of political influence in state and federal governments, as well as support by educators, social scientists, and citizens is needed to effect a change in the current control of schools.

It must be emphasized that the difficulties and possibilities for local Indian control of the schools their children attend vary from community to community. Implementation of this policy must respond to the wishes and concerns of the community affected. Flexibility and responsiveness to the heterogeneity of Indian community life in this country are essential.

Local control of schools within the federal school system operated by the BIA is but one part of the whole picture. Most Indian children attend public schools. It is through public school systems, operating under state law, that over one hundred thousand children are educated at federal expense, with funds distributed by the BIA. In addition, many Indian children attending public schools have been cut off from special BIA funding, at times receiving assistance through federal programs designed to augment education funds for disadvantaged populations generally. Active Indian participation in the decisions concerning the expenditures of funds and development of programs designed for Indian children requires a many pronged approach. Important is increased Indian participation on local public school boards. Increasing watchfulness over the use of funds and development of programs has also led to legal efforts seeking to make schools more accountable in regard to their programs for Indian children.

However, the divided responsibilities for Indian education between state and federal governments, between the BIA of the Department of the Interior, and the programs of the Department of Health, Education, and Welfare through its Office of Education and Office of Economic Opportunity, all point to the need for a national Indian group or groups to oversee Indian education.

A National Commission on Indian Education

One way to move on the national level toward greater authority and responsibility by Indians for the education of their children is through new congressional legislation that sets up an Indian Education Commission, composed entirely or mainly by Indians, with substantial power and money. However, the general tendency for congressional legislation to move slowly points to the possibility of a more rapid action under existing legislation and organization.

There are two Indian education groups which are already in existence and could undertake the role of overseeing Indian education. These groups are made up entirely of Indian members. They are the National Indian Education Advisory Committee to the Commissioner of Indian Affairs and the Subcommittee on Indian Education of the National Council on Indian Opportunity.

The National Indian Education Advisory Committee to the Commissioner of Indian Affairs has been operating since 1967. It could usefully assume more responsibility for assistance in policy making and administration of BIA programs and establish criteria and set standards for federal schools.

The National Council on Indian Opportunity was established by the President in 1968 and reports to the Vice-President. It consists of Cabinet officers whose departments have Indian interests, plus an Indian advisory group. The Subcommittee on Indian Education is an all-Indian body which has been charged by the White House with implementing a program for Indian control of education. This committee is in a position to advise not only BIA, but also other federal departments.

To be effective, these or any other groups set up by the federal government to oversee Indian education require adequate staff and money to employ service by contract. Both committees would be in a good position to help the BIA and the U. S. Office of Education to deal more efficiently with local school districts and local communities which have a major concern with Indian education. They would be in a position to give special attention to helping the various state departments of education to develop programs and administer funds entrusted to them for the education of Indian children and youth, as well as to offer information to states which have assumed full financial responsibility for educating Indian children. In addition, these committees would be in a position to be concerned with the growing need by city school systems for assistance as the numbers of urban Indians increase.

In addition to the official government advisory committees or commissions that have been recommended, it appears important to create and maintain with non-governmental funds a National Commission on Indian Education. Such a commission could maintain a continuous evaluative survey of the quality of education for Indians. It could make special studies of various aspects of Indian education, and recommend policies for government and private-operated education of Indians. A field staff of Indians who will work with local Indian communities to help them use their growing autonomy effectively through self-studies and through school boards and school advisory councils could be developed.

The major effect of such a commission would come from its continual determined and rational pressure on public and private organizations to improve the quality of education for Indians.

The commission should be composed of Indians, or at least a majority of its members should be Indians. They should be men and women characteristic of the variety of Indian interests and points of view.

The commission should be guaranteed at least a five-year life and should leave funds for a competent staff.

Three bills scheduled to come up in Congress in the spring of 1972 would provide more federal government money for Indian education in public and BIA schools. The Jackson bill (S. 1401) would establish a National Board of Regents to assume full responsibility for Indian education that is controlled by the federal government. At least a substantial number of the Board of Regents would be Indians. The Kennedy-Mondale bill (S. 2482) would provide federal funds for Indian children in public schools, based on the number of Indian children within a school district. The Montoya bill (S. 2416) gives Indian education a higher status within the Department of the Interior.

From now on the decision making about Indian education and the execution of these decisions should be increasingly in the hands of Indians. It appears to us that the basic questions of Indian education cannot be answered unless definite steps are immediately taken in this direction.

It seems likely that this movement toward Indian control over education will succeed most effectively if it is a part of a national and state policy for economic development as well as educational development of Indian people. The Indian policy of the federal government will constitute the basic decision. If this policy determines to finance Indian economic development at an adequate level, and if this policy places Indians in major policy-making and administrative posts in the federal government, the education of Indian children and youth will come increasingly under Indian control and decision-making activity.

It is important to recognize that the efforts to involve Indian people in the formal education of their children as part of a broad policy of economic development and elimination of poverty lead toward participation of Indians in the democratic-urban-industrial society of America. On the whole, present evidence indicates that Indian participation in control of schooling is likely to be aimed at increasing the motivation of Indian students to perform well in a system of formal education which has been developed by and is oriented primarily to the dominant society. Although some communities may develop a different direction, this increased motivation should lead students to get more education and, eventually, better jobs, both of which involve one more deeply in institutions of the dominant society.

The encouragement of Indian economic and educational development under increasing Indian self-determination is not pointed in the direction of a return to past traditional life; neither is it designed to deliberately remove Indian peoples from retaining identification with their particular heritage. It does open the possibilities for Indian peoples to play an active role in evolving modes of life they consider necessary for being Indian in the world of today and tomorrow.

Overview of the National Study of American Indian Education

A considerable amount of the data in this book came from the National Study of American Indian Education, conducted in 1968–70 under the direction of the authors and supported financially by the United States Office of Education. This brief description of the study is intended to provide information that will make it easy for the reader to understand the nature of the study and its background.

EVENTS LEADING TO THE STUDY

Social scientists have been officially asked to study the education of American Indians several times during the past forty-five years. The first major study, made under the direction of Lewis Meriam at the request of the Secretary of the Interior, was commenced in 1926 and the report was published in 1928. Since that time a number of studies of Indian children and youth have been made by anthropologists, sociologists, and psychologists. Most of them have been done on the private initiative of individual scholars or university departments, but some have been made by researchers on the staff of the Bureau of Indian Affairs and some have been commissioned and paid for by the Bureau of Indian Affairs or the United States Office of Education.

When the 1926–28 study was made with the aid of W. Carson Ryan, professor of education at Swarthmore College, and Mary Louise Mark, professor of sociology at Ohio State University, the census indicated that there were 325,000 Indians in the country, plus some 25,000 Eskimos in Alaska. The officially estimated birth rate in 1925 for Indians was 31.5 per 1000 population, against a death rate of 25.6, thus supporting a natural increase at the rate of 0.6 per cent per year. There were approximately 69,000 Indian children and youth in school, and a large and unknown number not in school.

By 1967 the birth rate for Indians had gone up to 37.4 per 1000, and the death rate had gone down to approximately 13 per 1000. Thus the rate of natural increase was more than 2 per cent a year, and the Indians were the fastest growing ethnic group in the country. The Indian population was twice what it had been forty years earlier, and the number of Indian children and youth in school was approximately 180,000.

Meanwhile the administration of the schools attended by Indian students had changed, due to a government policy of reducing the educational responsibility of the Bureau of Indian Affairs. Approximately 63 per cent of Indian students are now in public schools, operated by local district or county school boards. Some 31 per cent are in schools operated by the Bureau of Indian Affairs, and about 6 per cent are in mission schools.

By the mid-'60s, there was a growing interest in the problems of disadvantaged minority groups, and it was natural for attention to be turned again to the state of Indian education. The call for the present study came from the National Research Conference on Indian Education, held at Pennsylvania State University, May 24–27, 1967. This conference was organized by the Society for the Study of Social Problems, together with Pennsylvania State University, with Herbert Aurbach of the university as project director. Financial support was given by the U. S. Office of Education through its research branch, Division of Elementary and Secondary Education. Staff members Howard Hjelm, Ronald Corwin, and Michael Bohleber assisted in planning the conference and in getting the subsequent study organized. Participation of the Bureau of Indian Affairs was arranged through Carl Marburger, then Assistant Commissioner for Indian Education and later to become Commissioner for Education of the state of New Jersey.

The National Conference called for a national fact-finding study, and stated the following guidelines for such a study:

1. Provide Indian leadership with systematic and objective information about the attitudes, aspirations, and expectations of a cross-section of their peoples regarding education.

2. Provide Indian leadership and the officials of governmental and nongovernmental educational agencies which serve Indian children with basic information to assist in planning more effectively for the educational needs of the Indian populace.

3. Provide governmental agencies with information for arriving at a more adequate basis for the allocation of demonstration and research funds for Indian education.

4. Provide base line data so that experimental and demonstration programs can be more adequately and systematically compared longitudinally, over time with each other, and with current ongoing programs.

5. Systematically draw together, summarize, and evaluate the results of past and current research on Indian education so as to articulate the results of those studies with current and future educational programs and research studies.

6. Not do much testing of school achievement or of intelligence. It was felt that enough information of this sort is already available.

7. Include an adequate cross-section of Indian children in the various kinds of school settings in which they are presently being educated. This should include Bureau of Indian Affairs schools, public schools, and mission schools and should include schools located in various settings (e.g., res-

ervations, rural non-reservation locales, and urban areas) and should include institutions of higher education and vocational as well as academic schools. This cross-section should include some representation of the various broad types of cultural patterns found among the over three hundred Indian tribal groups located in various geographic regions of the nation. For this purpose it would seem that the major unit of study should be the school as a sociocultural institution.

8. Probably involve in its field operations a number of research institutions located centrally to areas where sizable numbers of Indians are located. The overall planning, direction, and coordination, however, should be located in a single research organization.

The major recommendation of the conference, one that was supported unanimously in a resolution passed by the participants attending the concluding session, was that Indian leadership must be involved in all the major decisions leading to the development and implementation of such a study. Indian leadership should have a major voice in selecting the director of the study and auspices under which it is conducted. It was further recommended that the mechanism for involving Indian leadership in this decision-making process should be the National Indian Education Advisory Committee recently established by Assistant Commissioner for Education, Bureau of Indian Affairs, and representing the leaders of seventeen major tribal groups. There was also general agreement that Indians should be involved in the study in the following ways:

a. Engaging to the fullest extent possible, Indians who are professionally trained researchers in the design and direction of the study;

b. training and utilizing Indians to the fullest extent possible in data collection and analysis;

c. presenting the research results in such a manner as to be of maximum use to Indian leadership in the development of educational policies for Indians and in recommending more effective educational programs to serve Indian peoples.

The U. S. Office of Education offered to finance the study under its Basic Research Program.

An executive committee of the National Conference was appointed, with power to select a director in consultation with USOE officers. This committee consisted of the following:

Wendell Chino, chairman, National Indian Education Advisory Committee

Vine Deloria, National Congress of American Indians

Flore Lekanof, Alaska Federation of Native Association

Melvin Thom, National Indian Youth Council

James Wilson, Indian Division, United States Government, Office of Economic Opportunity

Herbert Aurbach, coordinator of the National Conference, Pennsylvania State University

Ozzie Simmons, professor of sociology, University of Colorado

Edward Spicer, professor of anthropology, University of Arizona

Sol Tax, professor of anthropology, University of Chicago

Through this committee and the staff of the U. S. Office of Education, Professor Robert J. Havighurst of the University of Chicago was asked to become director of the proposed study and to work out the plan for the study.

Professor Havighurst then worked during the autumn of 1967 to design the study. This design was accepted by the U. S. Office of Education with a budget totaling $515,000. From January to September 1968, the plans for the study were worked out, so that field work could commence in the autumn of 1968. Mr. Havighurst conferred with Indian leaders, with university professors, and researchers who were interested in Indian education, and with officials of the state Departments of Education in states where there were large numbers of Indian students.

ADVISORY COMMITTEE

During this period an Advisory Committee was appointed, to advise Mr. Havighurst and the staff concerning the conduct of the study and concerning the final report with recommendations.

This committee consisted of six Indians and six non-Indians who are interested in education and Indian affairs. The Indians on the committee were delegates from the National Indian Education Advisory Committee to the Commissioner of Indian Affairs, and they in turn were representatives of various Indian organizations—national and tribal.

Members of the Advisory Committee to the National Study were:
Daniel Honahni, education coordinator, Hopi Tribal Council
Ronnie Lupe, chairman, White Mountain Apache Tribal Council
Domingo Montoya, chairman, All Pueblo Council
Melvin Thom, Walker River Paiute Tribal Council
James Wilson, Indian Desk, U. S. Office of Economic Opportunity
John Woodenlegs, chairman, Tribal Council of the Northern Cheyenne
Robert L. Chisholm, superintendent, Albuquerque public schools
Leslie Dunbar, executive director, The Field Foundation
Mary Kohler, director, National Commission on Resources for Youth
Edward Spicer, professor of anthropology, University of Arizona
James Officer, professor of anthropology, University of Arizona (substituting for Professor Spicer when the latter was out of the country)
Sol Tax, professor of anthropology, University of Chicago
Ralph W. Tyler, director emeritus, Center for Advanced Study in the Behavioral Sciences

CONDUCT OF THE STUDY

The broad outlines of the study were formulated at a meeting of the Advisory Committee in June 1968. It was agreed that an intensive field study should be conducted from September 1968 to the end of 1969, with further data analysis and a final report to be completed at the end of 1970. The field study would be carried through by working groups located at six universities in addition to the central staff at the University of Chicago. The six universities and their research directors are listed below.

The field research was planned at a two-week research conference in

Boulder, Colorado, in August 1968. The major decisions made at the time were:

1. To study intensively the educational systems of twenty-five to thirty communities selected so as to include the larger tribal groups and the various types of schools attended by Indian children, including schools in cities where Indian and white children are together.

2. The field work would be done by a team consisting of two to five persons who would spend ten to fifteen weeks in each community. They would make arrangements in advance with the leaders of the community and the director of the schools and do the following:

a. Collect information on a sample of pupils, probably in grades one, five, eight or nine, and eleven to twelve.
b. Interview the sample of pupils to learn about their vocational goals, their feelings about the school, their attitudes toward the local community and the larger society, etc.
c. Observe systematically in the school.
d. Interview parents of the sample of pupils, to learn about their attitudes toward the school, their expectations about the careers of their children, etc.
e. Interview local community leaders concerning their expectations of the school, their view of the future of their community, and the ways by which the school does or could serve effectively.
f. Interview teachers to learn their attitudes toward their jobs and their expectations of what Indian children should learn.

The Sample of Communities and School Systems. The sample had to be chosen so as to get a reasonably good geographic spread and to include the most numerous Indian tribes. It was also desirable to include the four major types of schools for Indian youth—public day schools, Bureau of Indian Affairs day schools, BIA boarding schools, and mission schools.

Another consideration was the degree of contact between the Indian community and the surrounding white community; and another was the "strength of the Indian voice" in the administration and policy making of the school system.

The schools and communities actually studied are listed in Table 1, in categories that refer roughly to degree of contact between Indians and whites in the school and community.

NATURE OF THE FIELD RESEARCH

The field research was planned to secure the following kinds of data in each of the communities that were studied:

Community background data, based on previous studies and on observation by field research staff.
Observation of the school and its relation to the community, by field research staff.
Interviews with students, parents, teachers, and influential persons in the community.
Data from social-psychological questionnaires on attitudes, from students and teachers.

Data on mental alertness, with the Draw-A-Man Test, for younger students.

It was agreed that the research instruments and the field work procedures should all be given a thorough tryout before they were put into final shape. The tryout period was the autumn and early winter of 1968–69. Some centers did as much as one third of their field work during this initial period, while others barely got started.

A second research conference was held at Tucson, Arizona, during the week of January 1, 1969. At this time the final decisions were made concerning field work, interview schedules and questionnaires were revised, and some tentative plans were made for analysis of the field data.

At this time it was decided to emphasize the study of Indian students in big cities more than had been originally intended.

The field work was completed approximately as planned. Local situations prompted adaptations, but the sampling procedure within a community and school was carried out substantially as called for in the design. The actual numbers of interviews, inventories, and tests completed are listed in Table 2.

DATA ANALYSIS AND CONCLUSIONS

The final phase of the study started in January 1970 and ran through that year. It consisted of five parts:

a. Systematic analysis of the field research data, with conclusions about the quality of education in the schools studied.
b. Conferences of field center directors with Advisory Committee on the conclusions and recommendations of the study.
c. Conferences of Chicago and Field Center staff with Indian leaders and with other interested citizens, to discuss tentative findings of the study.
d. Writing the conclusions and recommendations of the study.
e. Dissemination of the report, through publications.

RESEARCH PERSONNEL

There were approximately two hundred people engaged to work full time or part time in the study. Their numbers and roles are indicated in Table 3. More than half of these people were Indians. Almost all of the Indians served on a part-time basis as field research assistants. Their principal assignment was to interview parents and students.

The Field Center directors and their seconds in command are listed here. A complete roster of research assistants is given in the Final Report of the study, Series IV, No. 1.

CHICAGO OFFICE

Director—Robert J. Havighurst
Associate Director—Estelle Fuchs
Associate Director—Herbert A. Aurbach

Research Assistants: Bruce Birchard, Philip Dreyer, Kay Levensky, Camille Numrich, George Scott, John K. White, Gary Witherspoon, Carol Ziegler

UNIVERSITY OF ARIZONA

Center Director—John H. Chilcott
Field Director—Ned Anderson

UNIVERSITY OF COLORADO

Center Director—Gottfried O. Lang
Associate Director—Bryan P. Michener
Research Assistants—Theodore Humphrey, Georg Krause, Wolfgang Mueller

NORTH CAROLINA STATE UNIVERSITY

Center Director—John Gregory Peck
Assistant Directors—Robert Birchfield, Mrs. Kolman R. Hettleman

OKLAHOMA STATE UNIVERSITY

Center Director—Larry M. Perkins
Research Assistant—Arrahwannah Moreland

SAN FRANCISCO STATE COLLEGE

Center Director—John C. Connelly
Research Associates—Ray Barnhardt, John Collier, Jr., James Myers (Chico State College)

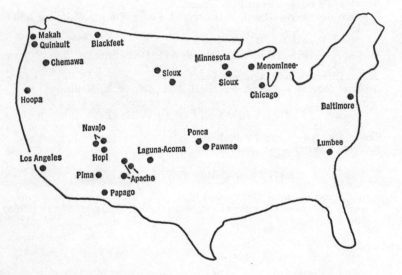

FIGURE 12. *Location of Indian communities studied in the National Study of American Indian Education*

APPENDIX TABLE 1

COMMUNITIES AND SCHOOLS IN THE NATIONAL STUDY

	Grades	Per Cent Indian	
1. Urban with low proportions of Indian students, up to 25 per cent Indian			
Baltimore Elementary and Secondary schools	K–12	1–5	P
Chicago Elementary and Secondary schools	K–12	1–5	P
Minneapolis Elementary and Junior High schools	K–9	6–22	P
2. Rural and Small City with low proportions of Indian students, up to 25 per cent Indian			
Red Wing (Minnesota) Elementary and High schools	K–12	1–5	P
Cut Bank (Montana) Elementary and High schools	K–12	7–8	P
Shawano Senior High School (Wisconsin)	9–12	16	P
Shawano Junior High School	6–8	25	P
Pawnee (Oklahoma) Elementary and High School	1–12	19	P
Moclips (Washington) Junior and Senior High School	7–12	20	P
Ponca City High School (Oklahoma)	7–12	5	P
3. Rural and Small City with proportions of Indian Students between 30–70 per cent Indian			
Hoopa Elementary School (California)	K–6	57	P
Hoopa High School	7–12	33	P
Neah Bay Elementary and Secondary School (Washington)	1–12	66	P
4. Rural and Small City with proportions of Indian Students, 70–100 per cent Indian			
Cheyenne-Eagle Butte (South Dakota)	K–12	80	BIA & P
Browning (Montana) Elementary and Secondary School	K–12	83–88	P
Keshena (Wisconsin) Elementary	1–5	95	P
Todd County (South Dakota) Elementary and Secondary School	1–5	95	BIA & P
St. Joseph (Wisconsin) Elementary	1–8	100	Catholic
Neopit (Wisconsin) Elementary	1–5	100	P
Magnolia (North Carolina) Elementary and Secondary	K–12	100	P

	Grades	Per Cent Indian	
4. Rural and Small City with proportions of Indian Students, 70–100 per cent Indian (CONT'D)			
Pembroke (North Carolina) Elementary and Secondary	1–12	95	P
Ponca City (Oklahoma) White Eagle Elementary	1–6	100	P
5. Relatively Modern but essentially Indian communities			
Taholah (Washington) Elementary	K–6	100	P
Laguna-Acoma (New Mex.) Junior and Senior High Schools	7–12	80	P
Tuba City (Arizona) High School	9–12	95	P
Angoon Elementary (Alaska)	1–8	100	P
Fort Thomas (Ariz.) Elementary and Secondary	1–12	100	P
Pima Central and Blackwater Elementary (Arizona)	1–8	100	P
Indian Oasis (Ariz.) Elementary and High Schools	1–11	100	P
6. Isolated and relatively non-acculturated Indian communities			
Cibecue (Arizona) Elementary	1–8	100	P
Topawa (Arizona) Elementary School	1–8	95	P
Hopi Second Mesa (Arizona) Elementary	K–6	100	BIA
Bethel (Alaska) Elementary and High Schools	K–12	90	P
7. Boarding Schools (High to Low Acculturation)			
St. Francis (South Dakota) Mission	K–12	100	Catholic
Phoenix (Arizona) Indian School	7–12	100	BIA
Flagstaff (Arizona) Dormitory	3–12	100	BIA
Chemawa (Oregon) Boarding School	9–12	100	BIA
Theodore Roosevelt (Arizona)	3–8	100	BIA
Shonto (Arizona)	3–8	100	BIA

Note: P=Public School, BIA=Federal Government School

NATIONAL STUDY OF AMERICAN INDIAN EDUCATION

APPENDIX TABLE 2

NUMBER OF INTERVIEWS AND INSTRUMENTS REPORTED

Center	DAM	Student Inventory	Student Interview	Teacher Q'naire	Teacher Interview	Parent Interview	Influential Person Interview
Arizona							
Papago	60	66	44	29	11	15	
Pima	73	0	37	8	3		8
Apache							
Ft. Thomas, Cibecue	190	88	73	23	16	31	1
T. Roosevelt (B.S.)	42	93	43	10	8	0	2
Flagstaff (B.S.)	7	29	40	0	0	0	0
Phoenix (B.S.)	0	108	53	11	12	0	0
Pueblo							
Hopi Second Mesa	86	18	19	3	5		2
Laguna-Acoma	0	109	39	17	9	17	5
Tuba City	0	86	48	11	10	8	9
Total	458	597	396	112	74	71	27
Colorado							
Blackfeet							
Browning	60	108	154	50	16	33	18
Cut Bank	34	32	41	9	9	16	2
Sioux							
St. Francis (B.S.)	22	81	103	16	19	23	3
Todd County	29	77	144	53	10	28	5
Cheyenne-Eagle					11	36	13
Butte	30	111	143	51			
Navajo							
Shonto (B.S.)	60	75	88	31	9	38	7
Total	235	484	673	210	74	174	48
Minnesota							
Redwing	14		19	45	40	7	14
Menominee							
Keshena, Neopit, St. Joseph	269	29	151	12	25	98	20
Shawano	0	151	173	40	46	43	
Minneapolis	61	48	71	35	33	43	12
St. Paul	51	0	44	16	9	13	0
Total	395	228	458	148	153	204	46

APPENDIX TABLE 2

NUMBER OF INTERVIEWS AND INSTRUMENTS REPORTED
(Cont'd)

Center	DAM	Student Inventory	Student Interview	Teacher Q'naire	Teacher Interview	Parent Interview	Influential Person Interview
North Carolina							
Baltimore	0	58	58	0	5	51	0
Robeson County							
Magnolia	100	127	159	13	13	40	4
Pembroke	77	113	165	17	21	39	4
Total	177	298	382	30	39	130	8
Oklahoma							
Pawnee	30	31	38	8	14	13	2
Ponca							
White Eagle	16	10	12	2	3	4	1
Ponca City	0	30	38	5	7	7	1
Total	46	71	88	15	24	24	4
San Francisco							
Taholah							
Taholah El.	28	55	17	7	7	6	8
Moclips	0	97	40	14	7	11	3
Neah Bay	18	111	25	15	13	19	18
Chemawa (B.S.)	0	42	100	34	14	0	0
Bethel	121	24	55	37	26	21	18
Angoon	40	34	26	8	7	21	0
Hoopa	28	76	76	10	10	17	7
Total	235	439	339	125	84	95	54
Chicago							
Chicago Schools	108	115	86	19	20	37	3
GRAND TOTAL	1654	2232	2422	659	468	735	190

APPENDIX TABLE 3

SUMMARY OF PERSONNEL

Role	Number	Number of Indians
Center Director	7	0
Associate	3	0
Field Director	8	1
Research Assistant		
Arizona	4	2
Chicago	8	2
Colorado	3	0
Minnesota	2	0
North Carolina	5	0
Oklahoma	1	1
San Francisco	5	0
	28	5
Field Research Assistant		
Arizona	40	40
Chicago	4	4
Colorado	14	14
Minnesota	27	17
North Carolina	15	15
	100	90
Research Analyst		
Arizona	2	0
Chicago	5	0
Colorado	10	0
North Carolina	2	0
Oklahoma	3	0
	22	0
Secretarial Staff		
Arizona	6	2
Chicago	4	1
Colorado	4	0
Minnesota	1	0
North Carolina	2	0
San Francisco	2	0
	19	3
TOTAL	187	99

APPENDIX TABLE 4

ESTIMATES OF INDIAN SCHOOL-AGE POPULATION (5 TO 17 INCLUSIVE) BY STATE, 1968a

Source: Unpublished data from Office of Program Coordination, Bureau of Indian Affairs, February 1969.

States with Federal Reservations		States with no Federal Reservations	
Alaska	20,600	Alabama	500
Arizona	39,900	Arkansas	200
California	15,900	Connecticut	300
Colorado	2,000	Delaware	200
Florida	1,300	Georgia	300
Idaho	2,100	Hawaii	100
Iowa	700	Illinois	2,400
Kansas	1,800	Indiana	400
Louisiana	1,600	Kentucky	100
Michigan	3,300	Maine	700
Minnesota	7,400	Maryland	600
Mississippi	1,400	Massachusetts	700
Montana	10,600	Missouri	700
Nebraska	2,500	New Hampshire	100
Nevada	2,400	New Jersey	600
New Mexico	25,800	New York	6,400
North Carolina	16,500	Ohio	800
North Dakota	5,800	Pennsylvania	700
Oklahoma	23,100	Rhode Island	300
Oregon	3,500	South Carolina	400
South Dakota	11,500	Tennessee	200
Utah	3,400	Texas	2,200
Washington	9,500	Vermont	100
Wisconsin	6,000	Virginia	800
Wyoming	2,000	West Virginia	100
		District of Columbia	200
Total	220,600	Total	20,100

United States, Totalb   240,700

a Indians as defined by the Bureau of the Census, including Alaskan natives. California estimates are probably low because of considerable immigration of Indians. Many off-reservation Indians in North Carolina and other southern states may be misclassified as Negroes in other surveys.

b Corresponding figure in 1960 was 179,100.

APPENDIX I 341

APPENDIX TABLE 5
NUMBER AND PERCENTAGE OF INDIAN CHILDREN IN
PUBLIC SCHOOLS RECEIVING FEDERAL SUPPORT
IN SELECTED STATES, KINDERGARTEN THROUGH
GRADE 12, BY STATE AND BY ELEMENTARY AND
SECONDARY ENROLLMENT, 1967–68

Source: Data from state departments of education reporting school enrollment on questionnaires distributed by the National Study of American Indian Education, 1968–69.

State	Total Enrollment Number	Elementary School Enrollment Number	%	Secondary School Enrollment Number	%	Other[a] Number	%
Alaska	11,534	9,146	79.3	2,388	20.7	—	—
Arizona	11,207	8,877	79.2	2,275	20.3	55	0.5
Colorado	692	513	74.1	173	25.0	6	0.9
Idaho	1,444	1,097	76.0	342	23.7	5	0.3
Michigan	4,561	3,142	68.9	962	21.1	457	10.0
Minnesota	2,123	1,944	89.5	70	3.2	109	7.3
Montana	2,296	1,910	83.2	386	16.8	—	—
Nevada	1,535	1,218	79.3	317	20.7	—	—
New Mexico	10,692	7,919	74.1	2,196	20.5	577	5.4
N. Carolina	11,754	8,978	76.4	2,776	23.6	—	—
N. Dakota	1,633	1,262	77.3	349	21.4	22	1.3
Oklahoma	15,096	11,408	75.6	3,688	24.4	—	—
S. Dakota	4,177	3,306	79.1	871	20.8	—	—
Washington	9,172	7,112	77.5	1,714	18.7	346	3.8
Wisconsin	966	692	71.6	270	28.0	4	0.4
Wyoming	1,038	832	80.2	206	19.8	—	—
Total	89,920[b]	69,356	77.1	18,983	21.1	1,581	1.8

[a] "Other" includes children identified as handicapped or in special education, in ungraded programs, and for whom grade level is unknown.

[b] There were 2617 Indian children reported enrolled in New York and at least 12,000 in California. Both of these estimates are probably quite low because they are based on ethnic surveys in which teachers were asked to identify their pupils' ethnic groups. A personal communication from the Bureau of Intergroup Relations, California State Department of Education, indicated that the official count in California may have been well over 20,000 Indian school children in 1966.

APPENDIX TABLE 6

NUMBER AND PERCENTAGE DISTRIBUTION OF
INDIAN CHILDREN, AGE 6–18, REPORTED IN
ANNUAL SCHOOL CENSUS BY TYPE OF SCHOOL
AND BY STATE OF REPORTING AGENCY,
SCHOOL YEAR 1967–68[a]

State	Enumerated Number	Federal Schools Number	%	Public Schools Number	%
Alaska	19,792	7,094	35.8	11,534	58.3
Arizona	39,368	16,616	42.2	16,804	42.7
Colorado	670	19	2.8	595	88.8
Florida	391	109	27.9	255	65.2
Iowa	194	64	33.0	126	64.9
Kansas	1,010	14	1.4	979	96.9
Mississippi	1,312	1,160	88.4	126	9.6
Montana	9,590	867	9.0	7,511	78.3
Nevada	1,669	1,215	72.8	343	20.5
New Mexico	29,244	8,835	30.2	16,627	56.8
N. Carolina	1,524	950	62.3	494	32.4
N. Dakota	8,502	3,273	38.5	3,293	38.7
Oklahoma	23,316	990	4.2	21,282	91.3
S. Dakota	11,712	4,397	37.5	5,167	44.1
Utah	2,359	1,058	44.8	1,125	47.7
Wyoming	1,435	64	4.4	1,100	76.6

APPENDIX TABLE 6 (*Cont'd*)

Mission and Other Private Schools		Total, All Schools		Not Enrolled		Information Not Availablec	
Number	%	Number	%	Number	%	Number	%
842	4.2	19,470	98.4	72	0.4	250	1.3
2,544	6.5	35,964	91.4	2,923b	7.4	481	1.2
17	2.5	631	94.2	39	5.8	—	—
6	1.5	370	94.6	21	5.4	—	—
2	1.0	192	99.0	2	1.0	—	—
4	0.4	997	98.7	13	1.3	—	—
4	0.3	1,290	98.3	22	1.7	—	—
779	8.1	9,157	95.5	216	2.2	217	2.3
86	5.2	1,644	98.5	25	1.5	—	—
1,847	6.3	27,309	93.4	59	3.9	—	—
21	1.4	1,465	96.1	1,664b	5.7	271	0.9
798	9.4	7,364	86.6	257	3.0	881	10.4
22	0.1	22,294	95.6	683	2.9	339	1.4
1,380	11.8	10,944	93.4	402	3.4	366	3.1
38	1.6	2,221	94.2	134	5.7	4	0.2
154	10.7	1,318	91.8	84	5.8	33	2.3

a Data are for children for whom the Bureau of Indian Affairs has educational responsibility as enumerated by BIA agencies in its Annual Census of Indian Children. These data do not include Indian children for whom the BIA does not have direct responsibility in those states.

b Mostly Navajo children living in isolated rural areas.

c Indian mobility accounts for most children in this category.

APPENDIX TABLE 7
ENROLLMENT BY TRIBE IN SCHOOLS OPERATED
BY THE BUREAU OF INDIAN AFFAIRS,
FISCAL YEAR 1968

Source: Division of Education, Bureau of Indian Affairs, *Statistics Concerning Indian Education, Fiscal Year 1968* (Washington, D.C.: Bureau of Indian Affairs, U. S. Department of the Interior, 1968), Table 8.

Tribe	Total
Aleuts, Eskimos, and Indians[b]	7,940
Apache	1,094
Arapaho	114
Blackfeet	129
Cherokee	1,481
Cheyenne	378
Chippewa	1,827
Choctaw	1,320
Colville	107
Creek	275
Crow	182
Hopi	1,390
Navajo	23,591
Papago	773
Pima	1,042
Pueblo	1,597
Seminole	126
Shoshone	133
Sioux	5,441
Three Affiliated Tribes[c]	744
Ute	124
Yakima	125
All Other Tribes[d]	1,625
Grand Total	51,558[a]

[a] Exclusive of enrollment of 37 at Concho Demonstration School and 4204 living in federal dormitories and attending public schools.

[b] Alaska natives.

[c] Includes Arikara, Gros Ventre, and Mandan tribes of the Fort Berthold Reservation.

[d] Includes 80 tribes represented by 1 to 99 members.

Summary and Critique
of Research Methods for
Study of Indian Education

Research on Indian education may have either one of two quite different purposes. One purpose may be to report factually and fully the actual operation of education in schools attended by Indian pupils, without making judgments of good or bad. The other is to find out what is being done well and what is being done poorly, to serve as a basis for improvement of education. Neither purpose has been very well achieved, partly because over the years relatively little time or money has been spent on Indian education research, and partly because Indian education is a complex set of operations taking place in a variety of settings with a variety of goals, some goals being in conflict with other goals.

Non-evaluative research on the *status* of Indian education is important for an understanding of problems of Indian education. This usually consists of the collection and presentation of data on types of schools, numbers of pupils in the various types of schools and levels of education, financial data, information about legislation and administration of Indian education, information about teachers of Indian children.

Evaluative research on Indian education is more complex and tends to be controversial. The authors of this book have attempted to minimize controversy in their own research and in their reports on the research of others. They have tried to be objective, and to report the objective basis for any judgments or conclusions they state about Indian education.

There are four broad categories of research methods which have been used to study the education of Indians or of other social groups. They are:

TESTS OF SCHOOL ACHIEVEMENT
AND DATA ON EDUCATIONAL ATTAINMENT

If the tests are carefully administered and scored, and used with representative samples of pupils, the results are reliable, as has been noted in Chapter V. Data in grade level in relation to age are available in a number of states, where departments of public instruction keep records on Indian students. Two examples of careful objective research on educational attainment are seen in the school dropout studies of Bass and Selinger, reported in Chapter V.

It is clear, however, that test scores and data on educational level are not fully adequate for evaluation of Indian education, since the various Indian tribes have values and life styles different from the Caucasian majority.

SOCIAL-PSYCHOLOGICAL TESTS
OF PERSONALITY, ATTITUDES, AND ADJUSTMENT

Paper and pencil instruments to measure aspects of personality must be used with the greatest caution in the study of people who have a different culture or life style from the people for whom the instrument was originally devised. There have been a good many mistaken interpretations and conclusions drawn from such tests when these precautions were not observed.[1]

Nevertheless, such tests may be useful as a means of understanding Indian students and their educational needs and problems. The use of a Self-Esteem Inventory or a Semantic Differential as reported in Chapters VI and VII, may provide valuable information.

But the validity of these tests and their interpretation are always open to question. Conclusions drawn from a single test used with a single group such as Indians are always questionable. Generally two ways of validating such conclusions should be used: (1) Another test purporting to measure the same thing should also be used, and the results from the two tests compared. If the results are quite similar, this is evidence for their validity. (2) A test should be applied to two or more groups which have certain common characteristics, but may differ in the characteristic to be studied. For instance, an attitude or personality test used with Indian adolescents should also be used with non-Indians of the same socioeconomic status, or the same level of school achievement. Thus the results that are due to Indianness can be separated from results due to socioeconomic status or level of school achievement.

In any case, the evaluation of schools with such tests is questionable, since so many other things than schooling enter into the formation of attitudes and the personal-social adjustment of the individual. Such data are more useful to help discover needs and conditions which might be met at least partially through education than they are for the direct evaluation of a school program.

OBSERVATION BY TRAINED OBSERVERS

Persons who have been trained as social anthropologists and as educators may make systematic observations which they record. If their observations are extensive enough to cover the variety of the community or the school they are studying, their reports are likely to be valuable sources of factual information. Such is the case with the reports by Harry Wolcott[2] and A. R. King[3] on Indian schools and communities in British Columbia and Northwest Canada. These men, trained in anthropology, lived and taught school for a year in the communities they were studying. As long as they report actual events with some indication of the frequency of these events, the reader is left to make his own judgments of how good or how bad the situation is. The researcher may also express his own judgment, but this should be separated as far as possible from his reported observations.

INTERVIEWS AND QUESTIONNAIRES

Useful factual and evaluative information can be obtained through interviews and questionnaires with people who are involved in Indian education in roles of student, parent, teacher, and community leader. This is the method which was used mainly in the National Study, as a means of seeing schools and education through the eyes of the people most concerned. The research staff took as neutral a stance as possible, expressing interest in any aspect of education that seemed to be of importance to the respondent. At the same time, the research staff used an interview guide or a questionnaire which systematically explored the aspects of education that were considered important from the point of view of the research.

This method gets information on how the school is evaluated by the respondent, but does not give a necessarily accurate or useful evaluation of the school from the point of view of the research. To be successful, this method must be used with a representative sample of the people whose perceptions and evaluations are being studied, and the data from the interview or questionnaire must be analyzed and organized in a reliable, valid, and relevant way.

Sampling. Adequate sampling of respondents can be defined by the usual criteria of sampling, but the actual conduct of the research often fails to live up to the criteria. Interviews are costly; some people refuse to be interviewed; some people are not at home when the interviewer calls; some people try to give the interviewer the answers that seem to be socially desirable. In the National Study, the criteria for interviewing an adequate sample and for interviewing objectively were probably met as well or better than they have been met in any field research on education. The samples were drawn to be representative; there were few refusals; the interviews were carefully recorded; the interviewers were trained to be neutral in manner; for interviews with parents the interviewer was generally a local person who spoke the local language and had no personal interest in the school system.

The Interview Instrument. The National Study used an interview instrument and a method of analysis which is described in the following paragraphs.

In order to discover and record and report the perceptions and evaluations that people have of the educational system, we must have a flexible procedure which encourages people to respond fully and freely, to express their attitudes in their own ways, and to clarify and expand their first brief answers to questions that have some depth. Furthermore, we are seeking information from people on a topic they have not generally talked about or read about. We are dealing with adults and youth who, on the average, have had little formal education and little opportunity to observe a variety of schools.

For this purpose, we have used an "open-ended interview." That is, we have asked the respondent a series of predesigned questions which he may answer either briefly, with a "yes," "no," "I don't know," or with a long statement. If his answer is very brief or unclear, the interviewer asks further questions to bring out the respondent's ideas. The interviewer is an important element of the method. His job is to ask the questions, translated into the local language if necessary, and amplified so as to help the respondent make full answers; to record the answers in writing or with a tape recorder; and to encourage the respondent to speak fully and freely. Interviewers were trained by the field directors, usually through an initial discussion of the interview schedule, and then through conferences on their first one or two interview reports.

The interview schedule itself was a product of preliminary work and trial interviewing by various members of the research staff. Those who had the most experience with Indian parents and Indian schools took the lead in this work.

This kind of interview clearly would not give many clear-cut yes-no responses to such questions as "Do you think your child's teacher is doing a good job?" Rather, the respondent was encouraged to talk about the teacher, to say what was good or bad about the teacher, and to say what he likes or dislikes about teachers in general. Thus, the data from the interview can seldom be placed in *yes* or *no* boxes and counted. Rather they should be placed on some sort of scale varying from *good* to *bad,* or from *a great deal* to *very little,* or from *I like it very much* to *I don't like it at all.*

The Rating Procedure. Each interview item was designed to get information on the respondent's attitude, or knowledge, or customary behavior on some topic or problem. From reading the interview as reported, a reader can conclude that Respondent A is quite favorable to the school or quite unfavorable; that the respondent knows a great deal or very little about the school; that the respondent would very much or not much like to have a certain subject taught in school, etc.

Such data, provided by the interview, can be placed on *rating scales,* and the resulting scores can be analyzed and interpreted like scores on a test or on a questionnaire.

The rating procedure, to be used scientifically, requires:

1. A set of rating scales, appropriate to the data of the interviews.
2. A reliable procedure for applying the scales to interviews.
3. A statistical procedure for analyzing the ratings.

The rating scales were made by the following procedure. A list of *dimensions* covered by the interview was drawn up by the research staff. A tentative rating scale was then constructed for each dimension. There were always between five and seven steps or points on a rating scale—generally six. The group who created the scale first read a number of interviews, then defined the steps or points on the scale, with illustrations of responses from the interviews which fitted the various scale points. For each type of interview there was a committee consisting of members of several field center staffs. Thus the whole range of interviews came into use.

The tentative set of rating scales was then applied by at least four or five people from different centers to a number of their interviews. They made note of any problems they met and made revisions of the wording of the rating scales. Finally they came together for an intensive work period, to produce the final rating scale.

The final rating scales were put together into manuals and given to every field center. Each field center then read and rated its own interviews, tabulated the ratings, and sent them to the Chicago Center for integrated and comparative analysis. Each center used its own ratings for study of its own schools and communities.

Validity and Reliability of the Ratings. There are two basic questions which must be answered positively if we can have faith in the findings from our interview studies. They are:

1. Do the rating scales actually report the "real" attitudes, perceptions, and behaviors of the respondent? In other words, are the interviews and their rating scales *valid?*

2. Are the rating scales being applied consistently by various judges or raters from the various field centers, so that comparisons may be made between communities, and so that various judges or raters give equal ratings to a given interview? In other words, is the rating procedure *reliable?*

List of Dimensions Rated from Parent Interview. As an example of the analysis of an interview, the following list of twenty-three dimensions was used with the Parent Interview. It was found that some of these dimensions could be rated more reliably than others, and these were used in drawing conclusions about parental knowledge and attitudes toward schools and teachers. They are marked with an asterisk.

INTERVIEW WITH PARENTS
N=735

I. *Parent's Knowledge of the School*
   *A. Parent's Factual Knowledge of the School's Program and Policy

II. *Parent's Ideas and Attitudes Concerning the Education of His Child*
   A. Extent and Clarity of the Parent's Ideas Concerning His Child's Educational Needs
   *B. Parent's Perception of How Well the School Is Meeting the Needs of His Child
   *C. Parent's Attitude Toward Formal Education
   D. Parent's Perception of the Relation of School to His Child's Adult Life

III. *Student's Home Background*
   A. Extent of the Child's Participation in Family Activities
   B. Extent and Quality of Adult Instruction
   C. Parent's Involvement and Interest in the Life and Concerns of His Child

IV. *Personal and Community Involvement in the School*
   *A. Parent's Actual Involvement in School Affairs
   B. The Parent's Perception of His Influence as an Individual Over the School Program and Policy
   C. Parent's Perception of the Community's Actual Involvement in the Affairs of the School
   D. Parent's View of How Much Control the Community Should Have Over School Program and Policy

V. *Parental Attitudes and Practices Regarding Tribal Culture and Language*
   A. Parent's Attitude Toward Tribal Culture as Expressed in His
      Concern for Child's Socialization into Tribal Culture (Excluding
      Language)
   B. Parent's Actual Practice Directed Toward Enhancing the Child's
      Socialization into the Tribal Culture
   *C. Parent's Attitude Concerning the School's Relationship to Tribal
       Culture
   D. Parent's Perception of School's Actual Relationship to Tribal
      Culture
   E. Parent's Attitude Concerning the Child's Learning of Tribal
      Language

VI. *Parent's Opinions Concerning Various Aspects of the School*
    *A. Parent's Opinion of His Child's Teacher's Performance
    *B. Parent's Opinion of the Curriculum in His Child's School
    *C. Parent's Opinion of the Performance of the School Administration
    D. Parent's Opinion of the Performance of the School Board

VII. *Parent's Perception of the School's Relationship to Himself and the
     Community*
     A. Parent's Perception of the Teacher's Efforts to Talk to Him
        About His Child's Life in School
     B. Parent's Knowledge of and Opinion Concerning the School's
        Programs for Adults

Reliability of the Rating Scales. The interviews may be used simply to evaluate a particular school, in which case it is important to establish that the ratings given by a particular judge who reads and analyzes the interviews are similar or equivalent to the ratings given by another judge, in which case it can be said that the procedure is *reliable* or consistent. The situation becomes more complex if the rating scales are used to compare two or more schools, or to compare the perceptions and attitudes of parents with students, of parents with teachers, etc.

In this latter case it is necessary to show that the judges or raters in one community or one research center assign the same ratings on a particular interview as the judges or raters of another community or research center. Thus the problem of inter-rater reliability or consistency of the first case becomes a problem of inter-center reliability. This problem has been worked out in the National Study at considerable cost in time and communication between centers.

There are a number of sources of error or disagreements by judges or raters. Some of these are:

Halo effect—rating the interviews favorably or unfavorably because the judge sees the situation himself favorably or unfavorably.

Leniency—rating the interviews favorably through giving the interview the "benefit of the doubt" because the judge knows the situation being rated and supposes that the respondent would see things that way if he knew more about the situation.

Clustering ratings near the center of the scale—tendency of some judges to be very conservative about giving very high or very low ratings.

Logical error—giving the same rating for traits or dimensions that seem to the judge to be logically related, though this fact has not been established.

Some of these errors can be reduced by skillful construction of rating scales. Others can be reduced by training raters or judges to be more careful and more objective in their ratings.

In the scales developed for this study, some time and effort were spent to reduce the probability of errors:

1. Members of several center staffs worked together in constructing the rating scales; discussing the meanings of the various dimensions and the various scale points on a given dimension.
2. Sample interviews were studied in constructing rating scales.
3. Sample interviews were rated with preliminary rating scales. The judges or raters compared these ratings, and then revised the rating scales to clear up ambiguities where they had disagreed in their ratings.

In the end, each rating scale was examined and revised at least once by two or more people using the procedures noted above.

Reliability of the Revised Scales. When the rating scales had finally been sent out for use by the various centers, the time had come to study the reliability or consistency of the ratings from any one center, and also to study the cross-center reliability.

Basically, this process required a statistical comparison of the ratings of two or more judges on a number of interviews which were rated by these judges.

The procedure we adopted was a two-stage process:

(1) Testing reliability of the scales and raters within a field center;
(2) Testing reliability of the scales and raters between field centers.

Since there were seven field centers which conducted interviews and made ratings, it was necessary to test the reliability of the scales and raters between all seven field centers. This procedure has been described in a technical paper by Havighurst.[4] It resulted in the establishment of a high or medium reliability (far beyond chance agreement) of the judges of the seven centers on well over half of the sixty-three rating scales that were developed from the four types of interview.

Validity of the Interview and Rating Procedure. Having established the reliability or consistency of the rating procedure, it remains to establish the *validity* of the interview and rating procedure as a means of getting the "truth" or the "reality" about the school or community that is being studied. In the usual situation where interviews are made and studied, with good interviewers and a representative sample of respondents, it is customary to assume that the respondents are telling the truth as they see it, and the interviews are a valid basis for drawing conclusions. However, the interviews could be unsatisfactory as a means of getting at truth for a number of reasons, including the possibility that the "right questions" were not asked, or there was a silent consensus among respondents that they would give no information or false information in certain delicate areas of questioning.

If the interview procedure suffers from such disadvantages or errors, the fact might be disclosed by checking the interviews against the careful observations of trained observers. And since the research associates and assistants in the National Study were trained observers, and since they spent at least several weeks in any given community, it was possible to compare their conclusions based on their field observations with the conclusions based on interview ratings. One could assume that the observations of field workers and their resultant conclusions were the best approach to reality, or one could assume that the interview ratings were superior. In any case, if the interview ratings agreed with the conclusions of the field workers from their observations, the two procedures would mutually support one another, and we would have a case of "concurrent validity."

This test of concurrent validity was worked out between the San Francisco team of field workers (John Connelly, Ray Barnhardt, and Carol Barnhardt) and a team of interview raters at Chicago, headed by Bruce Birchard.[5] The Chicago team began the test by analyzing student, parent, teacher, and community leader interviews (using the rating scales), several items from the Semantic Differential for students, and several items from the Teacher Questionnaire. They did this for three communities and school systems that were studied by the San Francisco State team in the field: Bethel, Alaska, and Neah Bay and Taholah, Washington. There were four schools involved, since the Taholah pupils transferred at the beginning of the seventh grade to Moclips High School, where the majority of pupils were non-Indians. After completing this analysis, the Chicago team drew up a list of questions designed to elicit answers from our field investigators which could be compared with the results of the rating scale and questionnaire analysis. This list of questions was sent to Dr. Connelly and to the Barnhardts without their having seen the results. These two parties replied separately to the questions and returned their responses to Chicago. The Chicago team then read and closely compared the results of the rating scale and questionnaire analysis with the analysis they had made of their observations.

It was particularly important to know how the field workers ranked the four schools on a number of key variables or dimensions, since this was intended as a basis for comparisons of the total sample of schools in the study.

With some significant exceptions, agreement between the rating scale and questionnaire analysis and the field workers' observations on ranking and comparing the four schools was good. The main exceptions were: (1) In evaluating parental opinions of the school administration in the four schools, the field team was in marked disagreement with the scale results; (2) In ranking the four schools according to the teachers' "understanding of the local Indian community," there was no agreement on the ranking of three of the four schools; (3) The scales sometimes failed to differentiate between schools where the field workers felt they could; and (4) The field workers sometimes felt that no meaningful differentiation between or ranking of schools could be done where the scale results did indicate differences.

The more important area of disagreement between the analysis of the interviews and questionnaires and the field workers' observations was in the interpretation of what each "saw." For example, the members of the field team felt that, though many teachers voiced support for a policy of "cultural pluralism" and wanted a course in Indian history and culture, few if any understood the native culture or the idea of "bicultural education." Another major difference in interpretations was in evaluating the degree of dissatisfaction in the native community (students and parents), the school (teachers and administrators), and among influential persons in the community. The scale results were interpreted as indicating that students and parents voiced few serious criticisms of the schools while teachers and community leaders were seen as more critical and more apt to institute changes. The field team members felt that meaningful changes would only come as a result of agitation from the native community, and this they believed was possible.

In answer to the original question "Are the differences in interview ratings between schools consistent with observations of the field team?" the answer was a qualified Yes. The qualification is that the differences must be quite large to be considered valid. Even then, a small percentage of the interview ratings may not be in accord with observations by the field team. In such cases, a field team that is experienced and essentially objective in making judgments is probably to be favored. The reason for this is that skilled field observers have a better basis for interpreting data on a school or community than do strangers who simply read and rate the interviews. However, field observers sometimes go into a situation with such pronounced prejudices or blind spots that their judgments are less valid than the ratings from interviews made by neutral interviewers and neutral judges.

CONCLUSION

The broad conclusion concerning methods to be used in studying Indian education is that both the quality of research and the quantity of research falls short of being satisfactory. Still, a thorough and cautious use of the available data provides a firm basis for a number of general conclusions about the status of Indian education, but a less firm basis for conclusions about the good or bad qualities of Indian education.

In making judgments about the quality of the education of Indians, researchers are frustrated by the fact that the goals of Indian education are not clearly stated or clearly agreed upon. One goal is competence in the contemporary economy; another goal is self-respect and self-confidence; another is a secure attachment to an Indian culture. To move closer to all three goals at once requires a kind of education which cannot be clearly defined.

Selected Bibliography

Adams, Evelyn C., *American Indian Education*. New York: King's Crown Press, 1946.

American Indian Chicago Conference. *The Voice of the American Indian: Declaration of Indian Purpose*. Chicago: AICC, University of Chicago Press, 1961, 49 pp.

Annals of the American Academy of Political and Social Science, "American Indians and American Life," Vol. 311, May 1957.

Aurbach, Herbert; Fuchs, Estelle; with Macgregor, Gordon, *An Extensive Survey of American Indian Education*. Pennsylvania State University, 1969.

Beatty, Willard W., *Education for Cultural Change*. Chilocco, Okla.: U. S. Department of Interior, Bureau of Indian Affairs, 1953.

Berkhofer, Robert F., Jr., *Salvation and the Savage: An Analysis of Protestant Missions and American Indian Response, 1787–1862*. Lexington: University of Kentucky Press, 1965.

Berry, Brewton, *The Education of American Indians: A Survey of the Literature*. Washington, D.C.: U. S. Government Printing Office, 1969.

Brophy, William, and Aberle, Sophie, *The Indian, America's Unfinished Business*. Norman, Okla.: University of Oklahoma Press, 1966.

Brown, Dee, *Bury My Heart at Wounded Knee*. New York: Holt, Rinehart & Winston, Inc., 1970.

Cahn, Edgar (ed.), *Our Brother's Keeper: The Indian in White America*. New York and Cleveland: New Community Press, World Publishing Company, 1969.

Chafe, Wallace L., "Estimates regarding the present speakers of North American Indian languages." *International Journal of American Linguistics*, Vol. 28, No. 3, 1962, pp. 162–71.

———— "Corrected estimates regarding speakers of Indian languages." *International Journal of American Linguistics*, Vol. 31, No. 4, 1965, pp. 345–46.

Colson, Elizabeth, *The Makah Indians*. Minneapolis: University of Minnesota Press, 1953.

Coombs, L. Madison *et al.*, *The Indian Child Goes to School: A Study of Interracial Differences*. Washington, D.C.: U. S. Department of the Interior, Bureau of Indian Affairs, 1958.

Costo, Rupert (ed.), and Henry, Jeanette, *Textbooks and the American Indian*. Berkeley: Indian Historian Press, Inc., 1970.

Crawford, Dean A. *et al.*, *Minnesota Chippewa Indians. A Handbook for Teachers*. St. Paul, Minn.: Upper Midwest Regional Educational Laboratory, 1967.

Deloria, Vine, Jr., *Custer Died for Your Sins*. New York: The Macmillan Company, 1969.

Driver, Harold E., *Indians of North America*. Chicago: University of Chicago Press, 2nd ed., 1969.

Erikson, Erik, *Childhood and Society*. New York: W. W. Norton, 1950.

Farb, Peter, *Man's Rise to Civilization as Shown by the Indians of North America from Primeval Times to the Coming of the Industrial State*. New York: E. P. Dutton & Co., Inc., 1968.

Fey, Harold E., and McNickle, D'Arcy, *Indians and Other Americans*. New York: Harper & Row, Publishers, Inc., 1959.

Forbes, Jack D. (ed.), *California Indian Education. Report of the First All-Indian Statewide Conference on California Indian Education*. Ad Hoc Committee on California Indian Education, November 20, 1967. ERIC No. ED 017 391.

Forbes, Jack D., *A Model for the Improvement of Indian Education: The California Indian Education Association*. Berkeley: Far West Laboratory for Educational Research and Development, 1968.

Gridley, Marion E. (ed.), *Indians of Today*. Chicago: Indian Council Fire, 1960.

Hagan, William T., *American Indians*. Chicago: University of Chicago Press, 1961.

Havighurst, Robert J., and Neugarten, Bernice L., *American Indian and White Children*. Chicago: University of Chicago Press, 1955.

Hawthorn, Harry B. (ed.), *A Survey of Contemporary Indians of Canada: Economic, Political, Educational Needs and Policies*. Ottawa: Queen's Printer, Vol. 2, 1967.

King, A. Richard, *The School at Mopass: a problem of identity*. New York: Holt, Rinehart & Winston, Inc., 1967.

La Flesche, Frances, *The Middle Five: Indian Schoolboys of the Omaha Tribe*. Madison: University of Wisconsin Press, 1963 (originally published in 1900).

Leacock, Eleanor Burke, and Lurie, Nancy Oestrich, eds., *North American Indians in Historical Perspective*. New York: Random House, Inc., 1971.

Lurie, Nancy O., "The Voice of the American Indian: Report on the American Indian Chicago Conference." *Current Anthropology*, Vol. 2, No. 5, 1961, pp. 428–500.

———and Levine, Stuart (eds.), *The American Indian Today*. Deland, Fla.: Everett/Edwards Inc., 1968.

Macgregor, Gordon, *Warriors Without Weapons*. Chicago: University of Chicago Press, 1946.

McKinley, Francis; Bayne, Stephen; and Nimnicht, Glen, *Who Should Control Indian Education?* Berkeley: Far West Laboratory for Educational Research and Development, February 1970.

Meriam, Lewis (ed.), *The Problem of Indian Administration*. Baltimore: Johns Hopkins Press, 1928.

National Association for the Advancement of Colored People, Legal Defense and Educational Fund, *An Even Chance: A Report on Federal Funds for Indian Children in Public School Districts*. New York, 1971.

National Study of American Indian Education: The Education of Indian Children and Youth, Project No. 8-0147. United States Office of Education, OEC-0-8-08147-2805.

Owens, Charles S., and Bass, Willard P., *The American Indian High School Dropout in the Southwest*. Albuquerque, N. Mex.: Southwestern Cooperative Educational Laboratory, January 1969. ERIC No. ED 026 195.

Parmee, Edward A., *Formal Education and Culture Change, a Modern Apache Indian Community and Government Education Program*. Tucson: University of Arizona Press, 1968.

Pettitt, George A., *Primitive Education in North America*. Berkeley: University of California Publications in Archaeology and Ethnology, Vol. 48, No. 1, 1960.

Ray, Charles K.; Ryan, Joan; and Parker, Seymour, *Alaska Native Secondary School Dropouts*. College, Alaska: University of Alaska, 1962.

Roessel, Robert A., Jr., and Nicholas, Lee (eds.), *Indian Education Workshops*. Part 1—Education of Indian Adults. Part II—Community Development in Indian Education. Tempe, Ariz.: Arizona State University, Indian Education Center, 1962. ERIC No. ED 017 855.

Schusky, E., *The Right to Be Indian*. San Francisco: Indian Historian Press, Inc., 1970.

Selby, Suzanne R., comp., *Bibliography on Materials in the Field of Indian Education*. Saskatchewan, Canada: University of Saskatchewan, Institute for Northern Studies, 1968.

Selinger, Alphonse D., *The American Indian Graduate: After High School, What?* Portland, Oreg.: Northwest Regional Educational Laboratory, 1968. ERIC No. ED 026 165.

———*The American Indian High School Dropout: The Magnitude of the Problem*. Portland, Oreg.: Northwest Regional Educational Laboratory, 1968. ERIC No. ED 026 164.

Smith, Anne M., *Indian Education in New Mexico*. Albuquerque, N. Mex.: University of New Mexico, July 1968. ERIC No. ED 025 346.

Spicer, Edward H. (ed.), *Perspectives in American Indian Culture Change*. Chicago: University of Chicago Press, 1961.

———*Cycles of Conquest: The Impact of Spain, Mexico, and the United States on the Indians of the Southwest, 1553–1960*. Tucson: University of Arizona Press, 1962.

Spindler, George D. (ed.), *Education and Culture: Anthropological Approaches*. New York: Holt, Rinehart & Winston, Inc., 1963.

Steiner, Stan., *The New Indians*. New York: Harper & Row, Publishers, Inc., 1968.

Stern, Theodore, *The Klamath Tribe, a People and Their Reservation*. Monograph No. 41. American Ethnological Society, 1965.

Striner, H. E., *Toward a Fundamental Program for the Training, Employment, and Economic Equality of the American Indian*. Kalamazoo, Mich.: W. E. Upjohn Institute, 1968.

Styles of Learning Among American Indians: An Outline for Research. Report and Recommendations of a Conference Held at Stanford University, August 8–10, 1968. Washington, D.C.: Center for Applied Linguistics, February 1969. ERIC No. ED 026 638.

Thompson, Hildegard, and associates, *Education for Cross-Cultural Enrichment*. Washington, D.C.: U. S. Department of Interior, Bureau of Indian Affairs, Branch of Education, 1964.

Thompson, Laura, and Joseph, Alice, *The Hopi Way*. Chicago: University of Chicago Press, 1944.

Underhill, Ruth, *Red Man's America*. Chicago: University of Chicago Press, 1953.

United States Congress Hearings before the Special Subcommittee on Indian Education of the Committee on Labor and Public Welfare, Ninetieth Congress, Parts 1–5. Washington, D.C.: U. S. Government Printing Office, 1968.

The Education of American Indians. Subcommittee on Indian Education of the Committee on Labor and Public Welfare, United States Senate, Ninety-first Congress, Washington, D.C.: U. S. Government Printing Office, Vol. 1–5, 1969.

Indian Education: A National Tragedy—A National Challenge. Special Subcommittee on Indian Education of the Committee on Labor and Public Welfare, United States Senate, Ninety-first Congress, Senate Report No. 91–501. Washington, D.C.: U. S. Government Printing Office, 1969.

U. S. Department of Interior, Bureau of Indian Affairs, Branch of Education. Annual Statistics Concerning Indian Education.

Vanstone, James V., *Point Hope: An Eskimo Village in Transition*. American Ethnological Society, 1962.

Wahrhaftig, Albert L., "The Tribal Cherokee Population of Eastern Oklahoma." *Current Anthropology*, Vol. 9, No. 5, 1968, pp. 510–18.

Walker, Deward E., Jr., *Conflict and Schism in Nez Perce Acculturation. A Study in Religion and Politics.* Washington State University Press, 1968.

Wax, Murray L.; Wax, Rosalie H.; and Dumont, Robert V., Jr., *Formal Education in an American Indian Community.* Monograph No. 1, the Society for the Study of Social Problems, 1964.

Wax, Murray L., and Wax, Rosalie H., *Summary and Observations in the Dakotas and Minnesota, Indian Communities and Project Head Start.* Report No. 010–520, September 15, 1965. ERIC No. ED 013 670.

Wax, Murray L., *Indian Americans: Unity and Diversity.* Englewood Cliffs, N.J.: Prentice-Hall, Inc., 1971.

Wilson, Edmund, *Apologies to the Iroquois.* New York: Random House, Inc., Vintage Books, 1966.

Wolcott, Harry F., *A Kwakiutl Village and School.* New York: Holt, Rinehart & Winston, Inc., 1967.

Notes

CHAPTER I

1. Good discussions of Indian education history are to be found in Adams, Evelyn C., *American Indian Education*, New York: King's Crown Press, 1946; Berry, Brewton, *The Education of American Indians: A Survey of the Literature*, Washington, D.C.: U. S. Government Printing Office, 1969; Orata, Pedro T., *Democracy and Indian Education*, Washington, D.C.: U. S. Department of Interior, Office of Indian Affairs, 1938.

2. Franklin, Benjamin, *Two Tracts, Information to Those Who Would Remove to America and Remarks Concerning the Savages of North America*, 3rd ed., London: 1794, pp. 28–29; also described in *The Papers of Benjamin Franklin*, Labaree, Leonard W., *et al.*, eds., New Haven: Yale University Press, 1961, Vol. IV, pp. 481–83.

3. Aurbach, Herbert; Fuchs, Estelle; with Macgregor, Gordon, "The Status of American Indian Education." NSAIE, Final Report, Series V, U.S.O.E., O.E.C.-0-8-080147-2805, p. 6.

4. Annual Report of the Department of the Interior, 1901, Indian Affairs, Part 1, Report of Commissioner, and Appendixes, Washington, D.C.: U. S. Government Printing Office, p. 3.

5. Annual Report of the Department of the Interior, 1901, Indian Affairs, Part 1, pp. 1–2.

6. Ibid., p. 26.

7. Report of the Commissioner of Indian Affairs to the Secretary of the Interior for the Fiscal Year ended June 30, 1916. Washington, D.C.: U. S. Government Printing Office, pp. 22–23.

8. Ibid., p. 23.

9. Annual Report of the Commissioner of Indian Affairs of the Department of Interior. Washington, D.C.: U. S. Government Printing Office, 1929, p. 38.

10. The right to purchase liquor was not extended to Indians at this time. This right was granted in 1953. Some reservations maintain dry laws, however, to the present date.

11. Meriam, Lewis (ed.), *The Problem of Indian Administration*. Baltimore: Johns Hopkins Press, 1928.

12. Ibid., p. 403.

13. Ibid., p. 415.

14. Ibid.

15. Ibid., p. 21.

16. Ibid., p. 51.

17. Quoted in *Indian Education: A National Tragedy—A National Challenge*, 91st Cong., 1st Sess., Report of the Committee on Labor and Public Welfare, Special Subcommittee on Indian Education, U. S. Senate. Washington, D.C.: U. S. Government Printing Office, 1969, p. 157.

18. Ibid., p. 157.

19. Aurbach, Herbert; Fuchs, Estelle; with Macgregor, Gordon, "The Status of American Indian Education." NSAIE, Final Report, Series V, p. 14.

20. Striner, Herbert E., *Towards a Fundamental Program for the Training, Employment, and Economic Equality of the American*. Mimeographed. Washington, D.C.: W. E. Upjohn Institute for Employment Research, 1968.

21. Ibid.

22. *Indian Education: A National Tragedy—A National Challenge*, op. cit.

23. Message from President Richard Nixon, Recommendations for Indian Policy. 91st Cong., 2nd Sess. Document No. 91–363. July 8, 1970.

24. The New York *Times*, September 22, 1971.

25. American Indian Chicago Conference, *Declaration of Indian Purpose*. Chicago: University of Chicago, Department of Anthropology, 1961, p. 4.

26. Ibid.

27. Communication to National Study of American Indian Education.

28. Whiteriver Education Conference, April 12, 1969. NSAIE, Final Report, Series I, No. 25.

CHAPTER II

1. Census count of Indians is widely recognized to be subject to inaccuracy. Recent estimates of the aboriginal population of the United States prior to 1492 run around 2,500,000. There was a rapid decline in population until about 1850 when there were about 250,000. After a period of about 50 years the numbers began to rise again. Prior to 1960, the Census Bureau defined an Indian as any person of mixed white and Indian blood (*sic*) if enrolled in an Indian agency or reservation roll, or if of one fourth Indian blood (*sic*) or if regarded as an Indian where he lived. In 1970, self-declaration or enumerator judgment constituted the criteria. Even this relatively straightforward identification has not neces-

sarily produced an accurate count. Particularly in rural areas and small towns distant from reservations, and in the inner cities of large urban centers, persons who consider themselves Indian may have been classified otherwise by enumerators.

2. Aurbach, Herbert; Fuchs, Estelle; with Macgregor, Gordon, "The Status of American Indian Education." NSAIE, Final Report, Series V.

CHAPTER III

1. Based on Michener, Bryan P., "Shonto Boarding School and Community, Arizona." NSAIE, Final Report, Series I, No. 9.

2. Kelly, William H., *A Study of Southern Arizona School-Age Children.* Tucson: Bureau of Ethnic Research, Department of Anthropology, University of Arizona, 1968, p. 9.

3. Based on Connelly, John, and Barnhardt, Ray, "Bethel, Alaska." NSAIE, Final Report, Series I, No. 11, 1970.

4. Collier, John, Jr., "Film Evaluation of Eskimo Education." NSAIE, Final Report, Series III, No. 4, 1970, p. 30.

5. Ibid., pp. 19–20.

6. Ibid., p. 136.

7. Ibid., p. 123.

8. Based on Chilcott, John H., and Mackett, Robert, "Papago Reservation, Sells, Arizona." NSAIE, Final Report, Series I, No. 17.

9. Based on Fuchs, Estelle, "Theodore Roosevelt Indian Boarding School." NSAIE, Final Report, Series I, No. 15.

10. Based on Mueller, Wolfgang, "The Cheyenne River Sioux Reservation." NSAIE, Final Report, Series 1, No. 6.

11. Cooperative Agreement, Cheyenne River Agency and Independent School District No. 3, 1968.

12. Balliet, Henry, "The Sioux Benefit and Its Effect on the Education and Future of the Sioux Youth." Mimeo., 1954 (reissued, Cheyenne-Eagle Butte School, 1969), p. 2.

13. Based on Perkins, Larry M., "Ponca City and White Eagle, Oklahoma." NSAIE, Final Report, Series 1, No. 4, 1970.

14. A full discussion of the political controversy over the White Eagle Community Action Programs is in McKinley, Francis; Bayne, Stephen; and Nimnicht, Glen, *Who Should Control Indian Education?* Berkeley, Calif.: Far West Laboratory for Educational Research and Development, February 1970.

15. Based on Peck, J. Gregory, "Robeson County, North Carolina." NSAIE, Final Report, Series I, No. 1; and "Indians and Their Education in Baltimore." NSAIE, Series II, No. 3, U.S.O.E. Project No. OEC-0-8-080147-2805.

16. Based on Fuchs, Estelle; Scott, George D.; White, John K.; Numrich, Camille; and Havighurst, Robert J., "Indians and Their Education in Chicago." NSAIE, Final Report, Series II, No. 2.

CHAPTER IV

1. Coombs, L. Madison, *The Educational Disadvantage of the Indian American Student*. New Mexico State University, Educational Resources Improvement Center (ERIC), Las Cruces, New Mexico, 1970.

2. Levensky, Kay, "The Performance of American Indian Children on the Draw-A-Man Test." NSAIE, Final Report, Series III, No. 2, 1970.

3. Havighurst, Robert J.; Gunther, Minna K.; and Pratt, Inez Ellis, "Environment and the Draw-A-Man Test: The Performance of Indian Children." *Journal of Abnormal and Social Psychology*, 41:50–63, 1946.

4. Anderson, H. Dewey, and Eells, Walter Crosby, *Alaskan Natives: A Survey of Their Sociological and Educational Status*. Stanford, Calif.: Stanford University Press, 1935.

5. Havighurst, Robert J., and Hilkevitch, Rhea R., "The Intelligence of Indian Children as Measured by a Performance Scale." *Journal of Abnormal and Social Psychology*, 39:419–33, 1944.

6. Voyat, Gilbert, "Sioux Children: A Study of Their Cognitive Development." Unpublished paper presented at annual meeting of American Educational Research Association in Minneapolis, 1970. Department of Psychology. Yeshiva University.

7. Kleinfeld, Judith, "Cognitive Strengths of Eskimos and Implications for Education." Occasional Paper, No. 3, University of Alaska, Institute of Social, Economic, and Government Research, Fairbanks, Alaska, 1970.

CHAPTER V

1. Coleman, James S. *et al.*, *Equality of Educational Opportunity*. Washington, D.C.: U. S. Government Printing Office, 1966.

2. Coombs, L. Madison; Kron, Ralph E.; Collister, E. Gordon; and Anderson, Kenneth F., *The Indian Child Goes to School*. Lawrence, Kans.: U. S. Bureau of Indian Affairs, Haskell Institute, 1958.

3. Bryde, John S., *The Sioux Indian Student: A Study of Scholastic Failure and Personality Conflict*. Vermillion, S. Dak.: Dakota Press, 1970.

4. Spilka, Bernard, "Alienation and Achievement Among Oglala Sioux Secondary School Students." Report on research project to the National Institute of Mental Health, August 1970.

5. U. S. Senate Special Subcommittee on Indian Education, *Indian Education*. Part 2, Appendix. Washington, D.C.: U. S. Government Printing Office, 1969, p. 1623.

6. Ibid., p. 1169.

7. Ibid., p. 1340.

CHAPTER VI

1. The technical papers from which this section is drawn can be obtained from the Educational Research Information Clearinghouse. They are: "The Extent and Significance of Suicide Among American Indians Today," Robert J. Havighurst; "The Meaning and Validity of the 'Phenomenal Self' for American Indian Students," Philip H. Dreyer; "The Indian Self-Image as Evaluated with the Semantic Differential," Robert J. Havighurst; "The Self-Esteem of American Indian Youth," Philip H. Dreyer and Robert J. Havighurst; and "The Relation of Self-Esteem to Personal-Social Adjustment Among Indian Students," Philip H. Dreyer.

2. For technical data on the reliability and validity of these tests and for a description of the samples of Indian youth, see the technical papers previously referred to.

3. Havighurst, Robert J. et al., A Cross-National Survey of Buenos Aires and Chicago Adolescents (Bibliotheca "Vita Humana" Fasc. 3). New York and Basel (Switzerland): S. Karger, 1965.

4. Ibid.

5. Ahlstrom, Winton, and Havighurst, Robert J., Four Hundred Losers: Delinquent Boys in High School. San Francisco: Jossey-Bass, 1971.

6. In evaluating this evidence concerning the "adolescent crisis" hypothesis, it should be remembered that the subjects in this study were all students in school. Since only 60 per cent who are in 8th grade stay on to finish high school, school attendance itself tended to act as a selective force, suggesting that Indian young people who attended school were more likely to be "better adjusted," higher in achievement, and commanding higher respect in their communities than their non-school attending peers. Thus the fact that the "self-esteem" scores do not decrease at adolescence may be accounted for by either of two contrasting explanations. One is the students' awareness of their relatively better position than the dropouts in the community. The other is that schooling in the more traditional communities is not regarded as having much significance, and consequently students in such communities do not feel that their self-esteem has anything to do with school attendance.

7. Soares, Anthony T., and Soares, Louise M., "Self-Perceptions of Culturally Disadvantaged Children." American Educational Research Journal, 1969, 6, 31–45.

———, "Interpersonal and Self-Perceptions of Disadvantaged and Advantaged High School Students." Proceedings, American Psychological Association, 1970, 457–58.

———, "Self-Concepts of Disadvantaged and Advantaged Students." Proceedings, American Psychological Association, 1970, 655–56.

8. Bryde, John F., The Indian Student: A Study of Scholastic Failure and Personality Conflict. Vermillion, S. Dak.: Dakota Press, 1970.

9. Ibid., p. 140.

10. It is for these reasons that we find it necessary to disagree with the claim by Bryde that the Sioux Indian adolescents he studied suffered from severe personality deviation. The F-scale consists of 64 items which are answered *true* or *false* with extremely low frequencies by the main group of respondents. According to the authors of the test, when as many as 16 of these items are answered in the "unusual" way, this is a sign that the entire test is not valid because the respondent was careless or unable to comprehend the items. Starke R. Hathaway and E. D. Monachesi (*Analyzing and Predicting Juvenile Delinquency with the MMPI,* Minneapolis: University of Minnesota Press, 1953, p. 16) say, concerning the F-score, "one will obtain a high score for persons who cannot read well enough to make discriminating responses and, what is more significant for high school use of the Inventory, this scale will be high when the student answers carelessly, making random or facetious responses to the items. A third source of moderately high F-scores is general maladjustment of a severe sort." Later, when discussing the use of the Inventory with adolescents, these authors write (*Adolescent Personality and Behavior,* University of Minnesota Press, 1963, p. 26), "Whatever the reason for a high F-score, such a profile is of doubtful value. We have arbitrarily called invalid all profiles with F greater than a raw score of 15 items." Bryde reports for eighth-grade Indians a mean F-score of 14.61 with a standard deviation of 6.53. This means that approximately 42 per cent of these students scored 16 or over on the F-scale. According to Hathaway and Monachesi, these should have been excluded as not valid; but Bryde keeps them in his computations and discussions. For the ninth grade Indian sample the mean F-score was 13.26, which means that some 35 per cent of those students scored 16 or over, and their MMPI scores were technically invalid. Only when he reaches the twelfth grade, where the Indian youth no doubt read much better than the eighth or ninth graders, does the mean F-score drop to 8.56. But for the twelfth-grade Indian students the mean F-score was not significantly different from the mean F-score of the white students whom Bryde tested.

Furthermore, on page 53 of Bryde's book he refers to Hathaway and Monachesi (*Analyzing and Predicting Juvenile Delinquency with the MMPI,* p. 23) to support the notion that "High F-scores are to be expected with adolescents and particularly with young people who feel rejected." The reference in H. and M. says, "Normal people, young and old, however, tend to become depressed and show high scale 2 values when they are in trouble or feel that they are rejected." The problem here seems to be some confusion on the numbering of the MMPI scales. Bryde numbers these scales so that scale 2 is the F-scale; but Hathaway and Monachesi number the scales so that their scale 2 is the D, or Depression scale, while they do not number the F-scale at all but treat it separately as a validity index. Hence Bryde appears to be using his F-scale values to stand for Depression. When Indian students get high F scores, he interprets this as meaning that they are depressed.

11. U. S. Senate Special Subcommittee on Indian Education. Hearings, Part 5, 1968. Pages 2016–21, 2134, 2177–81, 2279–2304, 2351–55, 2367–71.

12. Rabeau, Irwin S. (Chief of Indian Health, U. S. Public Health Service), Testimony before the U. S. Senate Committee on Appropriations, March 1968. Senate Hearings, 90th Cong., 2nd Sess., Part 2, pp. 1685–87.

13. U. S. Senate Special Subcommittee on Indian Education, op. cit.

14. Dizmang, Larry H.; Watson, Jane; May, Philip A.; and Bopp, John, "Adolescent Suicide at Fort Hall Reservation." Paper presented at annual meeting of the American Psychiatric Association, May 1970.

15. Personal communication, Dec. 10, 1969.

16. U. S. Senate Special Subcommittee on Indian Education, op. cit.

17. Personal communication, Aug. 21, 1969.

18. Leighton, Alexander H. et al., "The Mental Health of the American Indian: Symposium." American Journal of Psychiatry, 125:217–36 (1968).

19. Leon, Robert L., M.D., U. S. Senate Special Subcommittee on Indian Education. Hearings, Part 5, 1968, p. 2153.

CHAPTER VII

1. Birchard, Bruce, "How Indian Students and Parents Evaluate Their Schools." NSAIE, Final Report, Series IV, No. 11, 1970.

2. Birchard, Bruce, "The Validity of Rating Scales and Interviews for Evaluating Indian Education." NSAIE, Final Report, Series IV, No. 8, 1970. Havighurst, Robert J., "The Reliability of Rating Scales Used in Analyzing Interviews with Parents, Students, Teachers, and Community Leaders." NSAIE, Final Report, Series IV, No. 9, 1970.

3. Havighurst, Robert J., "The Indian Self-Image as Evaluated with the Semantic Differential." NSAIE, Final Report, Series III, No. 9, 1970.

4. Bass, Willard P., "An Analysis of Academic Achievement of Indian High School Students in Federal and Public Schools—A Second Year Progress Report." Southwestern Cooperative Regional Educational Laboratory, Albuquerque, N. Mex., 1969.

5. Spilka, Bernard, "Alienation and Achievement Among Oglala Sioux Secondary School Students." Report on research project to the National Institute of Mental Health, August 1970.

6. Macgregor, Gordon, Warriors Without Weapons. Chicago: University of Chicago Press, 1946.

7. Spilka, Bernard, op. cit., p. 77.

8. Ibid., p. 277.

9. Ibid., p. 355.

10. Wax, Murray L.; Wax, Rosalie H.; and Dumont, Robert V., Jr., Formal Education in an American Indian Community. Monograph No. 1, Chapter "Within the School." The Society for the Study of Social Problems. Supplement to Social Problems Vol. 11, No. 4. Spring 1964, p. 75.

11. Rosenberg, M., *Society and the Adolescent Self-Image*. Princeton: Princeton University Press, 1965.

12. Coleman, James S., *Equality of Educational Opportunity*. Washington, D.C.: U. S. Government Printing Office, 1966.

CHAPTER IX

1. Krause, Georg; Ziegler, Carol; and Havighurst, Robert J., "Teachers of American Indian Youth." NSAIE, Final Report, Series IV, No. 5, 1970.

2. Logan, Eunice, and Johnson, Dorothy Nadeau, "We Teach in Alaska." Bureau of Indian Affairs, Juneau Area Office, 1965.

3. Collier, John, Jr., "The Challenge of Eskimo Education." Unpublished paper presented at 1970 annual meeting of the American Anthropological Association.

CHAPTER X

1. Fuchs, Estelle, "Curriculum for American Indian Youth." NSAIE, Final Report, Series IV, No. 4.

2. Annual Report, Bureau of Indian Affairs, 1968.

3. Report of Annual Conference on Indian Affairs, Pierre Boarding School. Pierre, S. Dak., Oct. 29–30, 1969, pp. 40–41.

4. Bureau of Indian Affairs, U. S. Department of Interior, *English for American Indians*, a newsletter of the Division of Education.

5. Hearings on Bilingual Education, 90th Cong., 1st Sess.: Hearings on S. 428, May 18, 19, 26, 29, 31, June 24, July 21, 1967; Hearings on H.R. 9840 and H.R. 10224, June 28, 29, 1967. Washington, D.C.: U. S. Government Printing Office.

6. The most complete set of bilingual works developed during the 1930s and 1940s are to be found at the Instructional Services Center of the Bureau of Indian Affairs, Brigham City, Utah.

7. Burger, Henry G., ed., *Ethnics on Education*. Albuquerque, N. Mex.: Southwestern Cooperative Educational Laboratory, Inc., p. 18.

8. Ibid.

9. *The Navajo Times*, Feb. 18, 1971.

10. *Indian Education: A National Tragedy—A National Challenge*. Washington, D.C.: U. S. Government Printing Office, 1969, p. 22.

11. Vogel, Virgil J., "The American Indian in American History Textbooks." *Integrated Education*, Vol. 3, May–June 1968, pp. 16–32.

12. Ibid., p. 17.

13. Costo, Rupert, and Henry, Jeannette, *Textbooks and the American Indian*. American Indian Historical Society, 1970.

14. *Indian Education: A National Tragedy—A National Challenge*, op. cit.

15. Hanson, Lorie; Harkins, Arthur M.; Sheracts, Karen I.; and Wood, Richard G., "Suburban School Children and American Indians: A Survey of Impressions." NSAIE, Series III, No. 5.

16. *Indian Education: A National Tragedy—A National Challenge,* op. cit., p. 22.

17. Hanson, Lorie, *et al.,* "Suburban School Children and American Indians: A Survey of Impressions." Training Center for Community Programs, University of Minnesota, 1970, p. 37. See also: Cavender, Chris. C., *An Unbalanced Perspective: Two Minnesota Textbooks Examined by an American Indian,* 1970.

18. Ibid., p. 36.

19. Unpublished report, U. S. Bureau of Indian Affairs, 1968–69.

20. Berry, Brewton, op. cit., p. 64.

CHAPTER XI

1. Leon, Robert L., Statement to the Special Subcommittee on Indian Education, Oct. 1, 1968, as printed in Special Subcommittee on Indian Education, *Indian Education,* Part 5, Washington, D.C.: U. S. Government Printing Office, 1969, pp. 2153–54.

2. Nakai, Raymond, Letters to Chairman, Special Subcommittee on Indian Education, printed in *Indian Education,* Part 5, 1969, p. 2184.

3. "Memorial to the English Government, 1771" printed in William Webb Kemp, *The Support of Schools in Colonial New York by the Society for the Propagation of the Gospel in Foreign Parts.* Newkerk, 1913, pp. 231–33.

4. Adams, Evelyn C., *American Indian Education, Government Schools and Economic Progress.* New York: King's Crown Press, 1946, pp. 27–30.

5. Annual Report of the Department of the Interior, 1901. Indian Affairs, Part I, Report of Commissioner and appendixes, p. 41.

6. Meriam, Lewis, *et al., The Problem of American Administration.* Baltimore: Johns Hopkins Press, 1928, p. 346.

7. Ibid., p. 403.

8. Aurbach, Herbert; Fuchs, Estelle; with Macgregor, Gordon, "The Status of American Indian Education." NSAIE, Series V.

9. Special Subcommittee on Indian Education of the Committee on Labor and Public Welfare, U. S. Senate, Field Investigation and Research Reports. Washington, D.C.: U. S. Government Printing Office, Oct. 1969, p. 55.

10. Ibid., p. 56.

11. Ibid., p. 57.

12. Fredericksen, Michael J., and McDonald, Barbara S., "Anemia in Na-

vajo Indian Children." Mimeographed Research Paper, U. S. Public Health Service, Window Rock, Ariz., 1967.

13. Van Drizen, Jean, *et al.*, "Protein and Calorie Malnutrition Among Preschool Navajo Indian Children." *American Journal of Clinical Nutrition*, Vol. 22, Oct. 1969, p. 1369.

14. Leon, Robert L., op. cit., p. 2205.

15. Field Investigations and Research Reports, op. cit., pp. 61–64.

16. Krush, Thaddeus P., and Bjork, John, "Mental Health Factors in an Indian Boarding School." *Mental Hygiene,* Jan. 1965, as reprinted in *Indian Education,* Part 5, 1969, pp. 2212–13.

17. *Indian Education,* Report of the Committee on Labor and Public Welfare, U. S. Senate, made by its Special Subcommittee on Indian Education. Washington, D.C.: U. S. Government Printing Office, Nov. 3, 1969, p. 123.

18. McKinley, Francis; Bayne, Stephen; and Nimnicht, Glen, *Who Should Control Indian Education?* Berkeley, Calif.: Far West Laboratory for Educational Research and Development, Feb. 1970, p. 52.

19. "The Status of American Indian Education," op. cit.

20. Nimnicht, Glen; McKinley, Francis; and Bayne, Stephen, "A Report to the Senate Subcommittee on the Stewart Boarding School," in Special Subcommittee on Indian Education, *A Compendium of Federal Boarding School Evaluations.* Washington, D.C.: U. S. Government Printing Office, 1969, p. 418.

21. Koch, Harold, and Spuce, Bert, "Evaluation of Oglala Community Boarding School," in *A Compendium of Federal Boarding School Evaluations,* ibid., p. 391.

22. *A Compendium of Federal Boarding School Evaluations,* op. cit.

23. Pine Ridge Agency, Branch of Education, BIA. "An Appraisal of the Pine Ridge Education Program," Pine Ridge, S. Dak., n.d. as reprinted in *Indian Education,* op. cit., pp. 1269–70.

24. Connelly, John, and Barnhardt, Ray, "Chemawa Indian Schools." NSAIE, Series 1, No. 15, Part C, p. 2.

CHAPTER XII

1. Berry, Brewton, *The Education of American Indians.* Washington, D.C.: U. S. Government Printing Office, 1969, p. 50.

2. Ibid., p. 53.

3. Spindler, George D., and Spindler, Louise S., "American Indian Personality Types and Their Sociocultural Roots." *The Annals of the American Academy of Political and Social Science,* CCCXI, 147, May 1957.

4. Wax, Murray L.; Wax, Rosalie H.; and Dumont, Robert V., Jr., "Formal Education in an American Indian Community." Monograph No. 1, The Society for the Study of Social Problems, Supplement, *Social Problems,* Vol. II, No. 4.

5. Wax, Rosalie H., "The Warrior Dropouts." *TRANS-action*, Vol. 4, No. 6, May 1967, p. 45.

6. Ibid., p. 40.

7. Dumont, Robert V., Jr., and Wax, Murray L., "The Cherokee School Society and the Intercultural Classroom." *Human Organization*, Vol. 28, 1969, pp. 217–26.

8. Wax, Murray L., "Indian Education in Eastern Oklahoma." Final Report on Research Project No. OE6-10-260, Washington, D.C.: U. S. Office of Education, 1969, p. 101.

9. Forbes, Jack D., *Education of the Culturally Different: A Multi-Cultural Approach, A Handbook for Educators.* Berkeley, Calif.: Far West Laboratory for Educational Research and Development, p. 22.

10. Erickson, Donald A., and Schwartz, Henrietta, "Community School at Rough Rock." Document PB 184571, Springfield, Va.: U. S. Department of Commerce, 1969.

11. Bergman, Robert; Muskrat, Joseph; Tax, Sol; Werner, Oswald; and Witherspoon, Gary, "Problems of Cross-Cultural Educational Research and Evaluation," Mimeo 1969. Quoted in *School Review*, Vol. 79, No. 1, Nov. 1970, p. 108.

12. Quoted in *School Review*, ibid.

13. Platero, Dillon, "Let's Do It Ourselves!" *School Review*, Vol. 79, No. 1, Nov. 1970, p. 58.

14. Quoted in *School Review*, ibid., pp. 107–8.

CHAPTER XIII

1. Bureau of Indian Affairs, "A Follow-up Study of 1963 Recipients of the Services of the Employment Assistance Program." Washington, D.C.: Bureau of Indian Affairs, Oct. 1966.

2. Selinger, Alphonse D., "The American Indian Graduate: After High School, What?" Senate Subcommittee on Indian Education, *Indian Education*, 1969, Part 2—Appendix, Washington, D.C.: U. S. Government Printing Office, 1969, pp. 1189–1315.

3. Bass, Willard P., *The American Indian High School Graduate in the Southwest.* Albuquerque, N. Mex.: Southwestern Cooperative Educational Laboratory, 1969.

4. Aurbach, Herbert A.; and Fuchs, Estelle; with Macgregor, Gordon, "The Status of American Indian Education." NSAIE, Chicago, 1970, Chapter 7.

5. Medicine, Beatrice, "The Anthropologist and American Indian Studies Programs." *The Indian Historian*, 1971, pp. 15–18.

6. "Educating the Educators," a report of the Institute on the American Indian Students in Higher Education, St. Lawrence University, July 12–30, 1971.

CHAPTER XIV

1. Meriam, Lewis, *et al., The Problem of Indian Administration.* Baltimore: Johns Hopkins Press, 1928, p. 346.

2. Nagler, Mark, *Indians in the City: A Study of the Urbanization of Indians in Toronto.* Ottawa: Canadian Research Center for Anthropology, St. Paul University, 1970.

3. Harkins, Arthur M., and Woods, Richard G., "Indian Americans in Duluth." Minneapolis, Minn.: Training Center for Community Programs in Coordination with Office of Community Programs Center for Urban and Regional Affairs, May 1970, page 42.

4. Price, John A., "The Migration of American Indians to Los Angeles." *Human Organization,* 27:168–75, 1968.

5. Hurt, Wesley R. J., "The Urbanization of Yankton Indians." *Human Organization,* XX: 4:Winter 1961–62, pp. 226–31.

6. Harkins, Arthur M., and Woods, Richard G., "Indian Americans in St. Paul: an Interim Report." NSAIE, Series II, No. 4, 1970, p. 26.

7. Harkins, *et al.,* "Indian Education in Minneapolis: an Interim Report." Minneapolis, Minn.: University of Minnesota Training Center for Community Programs, Dec. 1969, p. 27.

8. National Council in Indian Opportunity, "Public Forum before the Committee on Urban Affairs." Mimeo., March 18, April 18, 1969, p. 101.

9. Fuchs, Estelle; Scott, George D.; White, John K.; Numrich, Camille; and Havighurst, Robert J., "Indians and Their Education in Chicago." NSAIE, Series II, No. 2, 1970.

10. Harkins, Arthur M.; Zemyan, Mary C.; and Woods, Richard G., "Indian Americans in Omaha and Lincoln." Minneapolis, Minn.: University of Minnesota Training Center for Community Programs in Coordination with Office of Community Programs Center for Urban and Regional Affairs, Aug. 1970, p. 19.

11. Drilling, Laverne; Harkins, Arthur M.; and Woods, Richard G., "The Indian Relief Recipient in Minneapolis: An Exploratory Study." Minneapolis, Minn.: University of Minnesota Training Center for Community Programs, Center for Urban and Regional Affairs, Aug. 1969, pp. 16–17.

12. Wax, Murray L., *et al.,* "Indian Education in Eastern Oklahoma." U. S. Department of Health, Education, and Welfare, USOE, Bureau of Research, Part III, Jan. 1969.

13. Ibid., p. 227.

14. Harkins, Arthur M., *et al.,* "Junior High School Children in Minneapolis: A Study of One Problem School." Minneapolis, Minn.: University of Minnesota Training Center for Community Programs, July 1970, p. 53.

CHAPTER XV

1. Coleman, James S. *et al.,* "Equality of Educational Opportunity." Washington, D.C.: U. S. Government Printing Office, 1966. Table 10.

2. Bass, Willard, "Analysis of Academic Achievement of Indian High School Students in Federal and Public Schools: A Progress Report." Albuquerque, N. Mex.: Southwestern Cooperative Regional Educational Laboratory, 1969, p. 25.

3. *Indian Education: A National Tragedy—A National Challenge.* Washington, D.C.: U. S. Government Printing Office, 1969, p. 3.

4. Ibid., pp. 3–4.

CHAPTER XVI

1. Wax, Murray, *et al.,* "Formal Education in an American Indian Community." *Social Problems,* Vol. 11, No. 4, Spring 1964.

2. Dumont, Robert V., Jr., "Learning English and How to Be Silent: Studies in American Indian Classrooms," in *Functions of Language in the Classroom,* ed. by Dell Hymes, Courtney Cazden and Vera John. New York: Teachers College Press, 1971.

3. National Association for the Advancement of Colored People, Legal Defense and Educational Fund, "An Even Chance: A Report on Federal Funds for Indian Children in Public School Districts." New York, 1971.

4. *Indian Education: A National Tragedy—A National Challenge.* Washington, D.C.: U. S. Government Printing Office, 1969, p. 57.

CHAPTER XVII

1. This chapter draws heavily on a working paper entitled "The Control of Education for American Indians" by Bruce Birchard, research assistant, National Study of American Indian Education.

2. Meriam, Lewis, *et al., The Problem of Indian Administration.* Baltimore: Johns Hopkins Press, 1928, p. 414.

3. Wax, Murray L., *et. al.,* "Formal Education in an American Indian Community." *Social Problems,* Vol. 11, No. 4, Spring 1964, p. 106.

4. Roessel, Robert, Statement at Hearings of Subcommittee on Indian Education, U. S. Senate, Part 1. Washington, D.C.: U. S. Government Printing Office, 1968, pp. 12–14.

5. Striner, Herbert E., "A Program for the Training, Employment, and Economic Equality of the American Indian," unpublished paper. Washington, D.C.: W. E. Upjohn Institute for Employment Research, 1968, p. 27.

6. Ibid.

7. Ibid., p. 3.

8. Josephy, Alvin M., Jr., "The American Indian and the Bureau of Indian Affairs—1969." A study prepared for the Office of the President, pp. 1421–59 in Part 2—Appendix of Hearings Before the Subcommittee on Indian Education, U. S. Senate. Washington, D.C.: U. S. Government Printing Office, 1969, p. 1442.

9. Ibid., p. 1500.

10. Bennett, Robert L., Commissioner of Indian Affairs, "Memorandum in Response to Questions from Senator Mondale Concerning Indian Advisory School Boards," pp. 1500–18 in Part 2—Appendix of Hearings Before the Subcommittee on Indian Education, U. S. Senate. Washington, D.C.: U. S. Government Printing Office, 1969, p. 1501.

11. Ibid.

12. Educational Consultant Services, Inc., *BIA School Board Handbook.* Albuquerque, New Mex.: 1968.

13. Anderson, Ned, and Chilcott, John H., "Formal Education on the White Mountain Apache Reservation," report of a self-study conference. NSAIE, Series I, No. 25, 1970, p. 37.

APPENDIX II

1. Manaster, Guy, and Havighurst, Robert J., *Cross-National Research: Social Psychological Methods and Problems.* Boston: Houghton-Mifflin, 1971.

2. Wolcott, Harry, *A Kwakiutl Village and School.* Englewood Cliffs, N.J.: Holt, Rinehart & Winston, Inc., 1967.

3. King, A. R., *The School at Mopass.* Englewood Cliffs, N.J.: Holt, Rinehart & Winston, Inc., 1969.

4. Havighurst, Robert J., "The Reliability of Rating Scales Used in Analyzing Interviews with Parents, Students, Teachers, and Community Leaders." NSAIE, Final Report, Series IV, No. 9, 1970.

5. Birchard, Bruce A., "The Validity of Rating Scales and Interviews for Evaluating Indian Education." NSAIE, Final Report, Series IV, No. 8, 1970.

Index

Academic curriculum in board-
    ing schools, 237–39
Achievement, see Scholastic
    achievement
Adjustment problem, 147–48
    boarding schools and, 242
    of Sioux students, 247–48
    of urban Indian students, 283
Adolescent crisis, 144
Adult education programs, 45,
    49, 90–91, 283
Age
    average, of urban Indians, 276
    school attendance by
        Indian Oasis School, 72
        1970, 34–35
        at Theodore Roosevelt School,
        79
    suicide rates by, 151–52
Alaska Reading Series, 215
Alaskan Native Association, 56
Albuquerque   Indian   School
    (N.M.), 241
Aleut Indians, 23, 26, 35
Alienation, scholastic achieve-
    ment and, 133
All Pueblo Tribal Council, 212,
    243
American Indian Arts, Institute
    of (Santa Fe, N.M.), 238–
    39, 261
American Indian Center (Chi-
    cago, Ill.), 109, 114, 288
American Indian Chicago Con-
    ference (1961), 20
American Indian Historical So-
    ciety, 216, 218
Anderson, H. Dewey, 120

Anglo-American students
    attitude of, toward teachers,
    164–65
    IQ of, 120
    mental development of, 122
    self-concept of, 140–44, 147
Apache Indians, 9, 28, 118, 277,
    321
Apache students, see Theodore
    Roosevelt School
Arizona, Indian population of,
    26, 28
Assimilation
    in boarding schools, 224–25
    through education, 9, 11, 19–
    20, 246–47
Assiniboin Indians, 30
Attendance
    at Bethel public school, 59
    compulsory (1890s), 8
    at Indian Oasis School, 72–73
    at Navajo Community College,
    268
    in 1901, 8–9
    in 1930s, 12
    1970, 34–35
    Navajo students, 35, 39–40, 45,
    268
    Ramah High School, 258
    in Shonto Boarding School, 39,
    40, 45
    by urban Indian students, 110–
    11
Aurbach, Herbert, 262

Baltimore public schools (Md.),
    Lumbee students in, 105–6
Bass, Willard, 175, 296

Beatty, Willard, 12
Bell Gardens city schools (Calif.), 281–83
Bennett, Robert, 19
Bergman, Robert L., 232, 233, 241
Berry, Brewster, 247
Bethel (*Mulreknlagamiut*, Alaska), 53–59
 life in, 57–59
 location and characteristics of, 53–55
 socioeconomic conditions in, 56
Bethel High School (Alaska), 60, 63–64
Bethel public school (Alaska)
 alternatives to, 61–63
 attendance at, 35, 59
 student attitudes toward, 157
 teachers of, 60, 201–3
BIA, *see* Indian Affairs, Bureau of
BIA Handbook for Teacher and Dormitory Aides, 233
BIA School Board Handbook, 319
Bilingual education, 208–13
 favored, 208–9, 311
 at Rocky Boy School, 257
 at Rough Rock Demonstration School, 253–54
 teachers for, 210–11
 views on, 212–13
 See also Two-culture education
Bilingual Education Act, 215
Birth rate, Indian (1967 data), 32
Black Mountain Boy (reader), 211
Black students
 achievement of, 305–6
 test scores of, 125
Blackfeet Indians, 29, 30, 277
Blackwater School (Ariz.), 35
Blessing Way (Navajo religious ritual), 45

Boarding schools, 222–45
 BIA operated, 8–10, 33, 97
 attendance, 34
 enrollment (1968), 344
 evaluated, 303, 304
 termination policy and, 14–15
 See also specific schools; for example: Shonto Boarding School; Theodore Roosevelt School
 curriculum in, 237–45
 elementary schools, 229–34
 enrollment in
 1926, 227
 1959–67, 228–29
 present-day, 222
 evaluated, 304
 high schools, 234–37
 historical background of, 223–26
 trend away from, 226–27
Bruce, Louis R., 19
Bryde, John, 126, 127, 149, 214

California, Indian population of, 26, 28, 275–79
California Achievement Test, 127
California Indian Education Association, Inc., 285
Canadian Indians migrate to cities, 273–75
CAP (Community Action Program), 66, 85
Carlisle Indian School (Pa.), 224
Chemawa Boarding School (Ore.), 157, 240, 243–44
Cherokee Indians
 areas of residence of, 30, 97
 school system developed by, 6–7
 urbanization of, 279
Cherokee students
 characteristics of, 249–50
 in city schools, 290–92

Cheyenne-Eagle Butte School (S.D.),
  adult education programs of, 90–91
  budget of, 87
  curriculum at, 89
  ethnic composition of students at, 82
  location of, 86
  teachers of, 87–88
Cheyenne Indians, 30
Cheyenne River Reservation (S.D.), 82–86
Cheyenne River Sioux Tribal Council, 86
Chicago (Ill.), 109–17, 285–88
Chickasaw Indians, 7
Chilocco Indian School (Ponca City, Okla.), 94, 234, 235
Chippewa Indians, 9, 30, 107, 277
Chippewa students, 256–57
Choctaw Indians, 6, 31, 97, 223, 279
Cities, see Urban Indian population
Citizenship, Indians granted, 10
City schools
  adult education programs in, 283
  Baltimore, 105–6
  Bell Gardens, 281–83
  characteristics of, 290–92
  evaluated, 304
  Los Angeles, 281–83
  Ponca City, 94
  See also Urban Indian students
Coleman, James S., 123, 125, 295, 296
College students, Indian, 40, 74, 261–64
Collier, John, 11–13, 206, 210, 227
Collier, John, Jr., 56, 62, 63, 203
Colonial period, education policy during, 2–3

Community Action Program (CAP), 66, 85
Community leaders, education as seen by, 182–90
Compulsory school attendance, established (1890s), 8
Concho Demonstration School (Okla.), 238
Control, see Local control; School boards
Coombs, L. Madison, 124
Coyote Stories (reader), 211
Creek Indians, 7, 30, 279
Creek students, 256–57
Crossover phenomenon, 126–28
Crow Indians, 30
Cultural differences, 246–52
  effects of, 247–50
  failure to reconcile, 246–47
  new approaches to handle, 251–52
  scholastic achievement and, 129–31
Culture, see Cultural differences; Indian culture; Two-culture education
Curriculum, 205–21
  in Bethel public school, 61
  in boarding schools, 237–45
  in Cheyenne-Eagle Butte School, 89
  college, 263–64
  in colonial days, 3
  community leaders' attitudes toward, 188–90
  evaluated, 310–12
  Indian culture and language in, 206–15
  Indian dignity and, 205–6
  Indian history and, 215–21
  in Indian school systems, 7
  in Navajo Community College, 269–70
  parental attitudes toward, 172–74
  Project Necessities, 91, 214

in Ramah High School, 258
in Shonto Boarding School, 48–49
teachers' views on, 199–200
in Theodore Roosevelt School, 79–80
See also Vocational curriculum
Curriculum Committee of Navajo Community College, 267–68

Dawes Severalty Act (General Allotment Act; 1887), 7
Day schools
of Bethel, 61–64
boarding schools converted into (1930s), 227
evaluated, 304
Declaration of Indian Purpose (1961), 20
Delaware Indians, 4
Demonstration in Navajo Education (DINE, Inc.), 252
Dick, John, 246, 253
DINE, Inc. (Demonstration in Navajo Education), 252
Direct Job Placement (BIA program), 275
Discipline in boarding schools, 50, 235, 241–42
Diseases
on Cheyenne River Reservation, 86
among Eskimos, 56
Dizmang, Larry H., 152, 153
Dodge, Chee, 39
Dormitories
of Cheyenne-Eagle Butte School, 86
in elementary boarding schools, 233–34
in Rock Point Boarding School, 232, 233
at Rough Rock Demonstration School, 253

in Shonto Boarding School, 49–50
in Theodore Roosevelt School, 77–79, 234
Dormitory programs, BIA sponsored, 228–29
Dropout rates
at Cheyenne-Eagle Butte School, 89
high school, 39–40
among Oglala Sioux students, 248
scholastic achievement and, 134
of urban Indian students, 116–17
Dumont, Robert V., Jr., 176, 247, 250, 251, 305

Eagle Butte (S.D.)
as administrative center, 82–83
industry in, 85
Economic Development Administration (EDA), 85
Economic Opportunity Act (1964), 85
Economic Opportunity, Office of (OEO), 66, 69, 72, 105, 254, 257, 259, 264, 318
Economic policy
1890s–1930s, 7
1960s, 16–17
EDA (Economic Development Administration), 85
Education, 1–22
adult, 45, 49, 90–91, 283
assimilation through, 9, 11, 19–20, 246–47
BIA role in, 33; *see also* Indian Affairs, Bureau of
"civilizing the natives" as, 5–6
Collier-Beatty philosophy of (1930s), 12–13
of colonial period, 2–3
community leaders' view of, 182–90

criticized, 294–301
1890s–1934, 7–9
global evaluation of, 302–13
Meriam Report on, 10–11,
    227–28, 273, 315
1960s–1970s, 15–18, 21–22
termination policy in (1953–
    58), 13–14, 314
urban, need to reorganize,
    292–93: see also Urban In-
    dian students
See also Bilingual education;
    Curriculum; Head Start
    programs; Mission educa-
    tion; Post-high school edu-
    cation; Remedial educa-
    cation; Two-culture educa-
    tion
Education, Office of, 307, 308,
    312
Eells, Walter Crosby, 120
Eisenhower, Dwight D., 277
Elementary and Secondary Edu-
    cation Act (1965), 36, 215,
    298, 308
Elementary boarding schools,
    229–34; see also specific el-
    ementary boarding schools
Employment
    on Cheyenne River Reserva-
        tion, 85
    of Lumbees, 100
    provided by BIA, 12
    provided by Theodore Roose-
        velt School, 81
    in Sells, 67–68
    Shonto Boarding School as
        source of, 42–43
Employment Assistance Service
    (BIA program), 84, 261
Enemy Way (Navajo religious rit-
    ual), 44
English as Second Language
    (ESL), 208–9
English for American Indians

(BIA newsletter), 208
English language instruction,
    206–8
Enrollment
    in BIA operated schools (1968),
        344
    in boarding schools
        1926, 227
        1959–67, 228, 229
        present-day, 222
    college, 74
    in Los Angeles city schools,
        281
    in Ponca City schools, 94
    in Ramah High School, 258
    in Rough Rock School, 252
    in Shonto Boarding School, 46–
        47
Equality of Educational Oppor-
    tunity (Coleman), 285, 296
Erickson, Donald A., 254
Erikson, Erik, 144
Eskimo students
    attendance by, 35, 59
    IQ of, 120
    mental development of, 121–22
    See also Bethel public school
Eskimos
    areas of residence of, 26
    economy of, 28
    local control by, 320
    migration to cities, 273
    number of (1970), 23
    See also Bethel (Alaska)
ESL (English as Second Lan-
    guage), 208–9
Ethnocentrism, effects of, 246–47
Extermination, policy of, 4–5
Extracurricular activities
    at Shonto Boarding School, 49
    at Theodore Roosevelt School,
        80

Faculty at Navajo Community
    College, 269; see also
    Teachers

Family background, scholastic achievement and, 128–29, 299

First National Indian Workshop on School Affairs (1969), 320

Flandreau Indian School (S.D.), 234–36, 239–40

Flathead Indians, 30

Forbes, Jack D., 251

Fort Apache Indian Reservation (Ariz.), 76, 77

Fort Apache Scout (newspaper), 81

Fox Indians, 30

Franklin, Benjamin, 3

Fuchs, Estelle, 262

Funds
  for experimental schools, 252, 257
  inefficient use of, 307–9
  for Navajo Community College, 270–71
  sources of federal, 35–36

Future, self-concept and views of the, 146–47

GED (Graduate Equivalency Degree Program), 91

General Allotment Act (Dawes Severalty Act; 1887), 7

Goodenough, Florence, 120

Goodenough Draw-A-Man Test, 113, 119

Government services, effects of, on Sells, 70–71

Grace Arthur Performance Test of Intelligence, 120

Graduate Equivalency Degree Program (GED), 91

Grandfather Stories (reader), 211

Grant, Ulysses S., 76, 224

Great Sioux Reservation (S.D.), 82, 90

Harkins, Arthur M., 283

Hatteras Indians, 98

Havasupai Indians, 79; *see also* Theodore Roosevelt School

Head Start programs, 305
  in Bethel day schools, 62
  bilingual, 210
  in Eagle Butte, 85
  in Indian Oasis School, 72
  in Rough Rock Demonstration School, 252
  in Shonto Boarding School, 49

Health, *see* Diseases; Mental health

Hearing defects of Eskimo children, 56, 61

Hernandez, Joyce, 153

Hickel, Walter, 18

High school dropout rates, 39–40

High school graduates, number of (1970), 260–61

High schools
  boarding, 234–37
  of Pembroke, 103
  plans for, 60, 63–64, 91
  See also specific high schools; for example: Chilocco Indian School; Flandreau Indian School

Higher education, *see* Post-high school education

Hilkevitch, Rhea R., 120

Hopi Indians, 28, 306

Hopi students, 35

House Concurrent Resolution 108 (1953), 14

Housing conditions
  in Bethel, 56
  on Cheyenne River Reservation, 85–86
  in Robeson County, 101–2
  in Rough Rock, 253
  in Sells, 68–69, 71
  of teachers, 200

Hualapai Indians, 79; *see also* Theodore Roosevelt School

Ignorance about Indians, 216–18
Impact Aid (Public Law 874), 35, 256, 259
Income
of Navajos, at Rough Rock, 253
of Papagos, in Sells, 68
in Ponca City, 93
in Robeson County, 99
Indian Affairs, Bureau of (BIA)
administration of, 297
reorganized, 18–19
created (1836), 5
curriculum and, 91, 206–10, 214, 218, 219
education policy and, 6, 14–16
employment provided by, 12
experimental schools and, 35, 252, 257–59
funds for education and, 307–9
local control and, 312–13, 318–22
post-high school education and, 261, 264, 271, 272
role of, in Sells, 66–67, 71
schools operated by, 8–10, 33, 97
attendance, 34
enrollment (1968), 344
evaluated, 303, 304
termination policy and, 14–15
See also specific schools; for example: Shonto Boarding School; Theodore Roosevelt School
urbanization of Indians and, 275, 277, 279, 285
Indian Arts, Institute of, 234
Indian Bill of Rights (Wheeler-Howard Act; Indian Re-

organization Act of June 18, 1934), 12, 90
Indian centers, 288–93
of Chicago, 109, 114, 288
Indian Claims Commission Act (1946), 13
Indian culture
attitudes toward, 168–69
in curriculum, 206–15
history, 215–21
urban Indian population and, 131
Indian Development Loan Authority, 17
Indian dignity, curriculum and, 205–6
Indian Education: A National Tragedy—A National Challenge (Report), 215, 297, 318
Indian history, 215–21
Indian identity
Indian education and, 306
of Lumbees, 30
at Shonto Boarding School, 52–53
urban Indian students and, 113–15
Indian Oasis School District No. 40 (Sells, Ariz.), 66, 69–76
attendance at, 72–73
issues dealt with by, 73–74
Parent Teacher Council of, 75–76
social life around, 69–70
teachers of, 73–75
Indian population
growth of
1890–1970, 23, 24, 32
Navajos, 42, 43
present-day
characteristics of, 23–24
economic situation, 28–31
school-age
1967, 32–34

by state (1968), 340
by state, 26–27, 340
See also Reservations; Urban Indian population; *and specific tribes*
Indian Reorganization Act of June 18, 1934 (Wheeler-Howard Act; Indian Bill of Rights), 12, 90
Indian Resources Development Act (1967), 17
Indian students
adjustment problems of, 283
attitudes toward schools among, 157–81
differences in, 157–58
lack of hostility, 176–77
rating scales used, 159
self-esteem and, 178–81
attitudes toward teachers among, 162–67
characteristics of, 249–50
college, 40, 261–64
in federally supported public schools (1967–68), 341
mental ability of, 118–22, 126
See also Mental health; Urban Indian students; *and specific Indian students under their tribal origins; for example:* Navajo students
Indian studies programs, 263–64, 269–70
Infant mortality rate, 32
Eskimo, 56
Iowa Indians, 30
IQ (intelligence quotient) of Indian students, 118–22, 126
Isolation
effects of, on teachers, 201–2
scholastic achievement and, 251

Jackson, Jack, 268
Jackson bill (S. 1401), 325

Johnson, Lyndon B., 17, 18, 313, 317, 318
Johnson-O'Malley Act (1934), 12, 36, 227, 259, 293, 304, 312

Kennedy, Edward, 17, 297
Kennedy, Robert F., 17, 153, 297, 300
Kennedy-Mondale bill (S. 2482), 325
Klamath Indians, 14, 30
Kleinfeld, Judith, 121–22
Kuhlmann-Anderson test, 120–21
Kwakiutl students, 250

Land taken from Indians
during allotment period, 7–8
by 1870s, 4
Language instruction, English, 206–8; *see also* Bilingual education
Latin-American students
attitude toward teachers of, 164–65
self-concept of, 139–40
Leighton, Alexander, 155
Leon, Robert, 222, 231–32
Leupp, Francis, 225
Life in boarding schools, 237–45
Life expectancy, Indian (1967 data), 32
Literacy of Cherokee Indians (19th century), 6
Local control, 252–59, 314–26
by Indian school boards, 318–21
National Commission on Indian Education and, 323–26
proponents of, 315–317, 322
Los Angeles (Calif.), 275–79
Los Angeles city schools, 281–83
Lumbee Indians, 29–30
characteristics of, 97
Indian identity of, 30

migration of, 105
social status of, 100–2
tribal origins of, 29–30, 98
Lumbee students, 103–6

McDermott, Walsh, 16
MacDonald, Peter, 270
McGovern, George, 16, 317
MacGregor, Gordon, 176
McNickle, D'Arcy, 155
Magnolia School (Lumberton, N.C.), 104–5
Maladjusted boys, self-concept of, 140
Manuelito (Navajo leader), 39, 246
May 25, 1918, Act of, 9
Medicine, Beatrice, 263
Menominee Indians, 14, 30, 107
Mental ability of Indian students, 118–22
Mental alertness, 113
Mental health, 136–56
  misconceptions about, 136
  self-concept and
    comparative studies, 139–56
    defined, 138–39
"Mental Health of the American Indians, The" (Symposium), 155
Meriam, Lewis, 10, 13, 226, 276
Meriam Report ("The Problem of Indian Administration"), 10–12, 227–28, 273, 315
Mexican American students
  achievement of, 305–6
  in Los Angeles city schools, 281–82
  test scores, 125
Miccosukee Indians, 97
Migrations to cities
  of Canadian Indians, 273–75
  of Lumbees, 105

1930s and 1940s, 277
1960s, 273
Minnesota Multiphasic Personality Inventory (MMPI), 149–50
Mission Educaton, 214, 223–24
  in Bethel, 59, 61, 62
  in colonial period, 2–3
  decreasing, 35
  nature of, 51
  in Sells, 67, 72, 74
MMPI (Minnesota Multiphasic Personality Inventory), 149–50
Mohawk Indians, 30
Monroe, James, 5
Montana Sioux Indians, see Sioux Indians
Montoya, Domingo, 243
Montoya bill (S. 2416), 325
Mortality rate, Indian (1967 data), 32

Nash, Philleo, 16, 255, 259
National Commission on Indian Education, 323–26
National Council on Indian Opportunity, 17, 284, 285, 323–24
National Education Association, 192
National Indian Educaton Advisory Committee to the Commissioner on Indian Affairs, 323
National Indian Education Association, 285
National Indian Education Commission, 309
National Tribal Chairman's Association, 19
Navajo Adult Basic Education programs (Navajo Community College), 270

Navajo college students, 262–63, 268

Navajo Community College (NCC; Ariz.)
administration and control of, 266–67
attendance at, 268
curriculum at, 269–70
funds for, 270–71
importance of, 265

Navajo Community College Bill (1971), 271

Navajo Curriculum Center, 211

Navajo Education Committee, 230

Navajo Indians
in adult education programs, 45
areas of residence of, 28, 30
education policy and, 8–9
Indian Bill of Rights and, 12
Indian identity and, 306
local control and, 316
population growth of, 42, 43
of Rough Rock community, 253
social structure of, 41–43
suicides among, 152–53
urbanization of, 277, 279

Navajo Reservation (Shonto, Ariz.), 39

Navajo Special Education Program, 227–28, 242

Navajo students
college, 262–63, 268
in elementary boarding schools, 230
at Ramah High School, 257–59
school attendance by, 35, 39–40, 45, 268
See also Rough Rock Demonstration School; Shonto Boarding School

Navajo Studies Program (Navajo Community College), 269–70

Navajo Times (newspaper), 214

Navajo Tribal Agency, 277

Navajo Tribal Council, 222, 242, 266, 271

NCC, see Navajo Community College

Necessities, Project (BIA developed curriculum), 91, 214

Neighborhood Youth Corps (NYC), 66

New Mexico, Indian population in, 26, 28

Nez Perce Indians, 30

Nimnicht, Glen, 240

Night Way (Navajo religious ritual), 45

Nixon, Richard M., 1, 17–18, 258, 313

Non-Indian community leaders, education as seen by, 182–90

Non-reservation Indians, 97; see also Lumbee Indians

North Carolina, Indian population in, 26, 29–30

North Dakota, Indian population in, 29

NYC (Neighborhood Youth Corps), 66

Occupations of urban Indians, 279–80

OEO (Office of Economic Opportunity), 66, 69, 72, 105, 254, 257, 259, 264, 318

Oglala Community Boarding School (S.D.), 235, 240

Oglala Sioux Indians, see Sioux Indians

Oklahoma, Indian population in, 26–28

Omaha Indians, 30

Oneida Indians, 19, 30

Onondago Indians, 30

Oriental American students, test scores of, 125
Osage Indians, 28
Ottawa Indians, 30

Paiute Indians, 30
Papago Indians, areas of residence of, 28; see also Sells (Ariz.)
Papago students, college, 74; see also Indian Oasis School District No. 40
Papago Reservation (Ariz.), 65
Papago Tribal Center, 66
Papago Tribal Council, 71
Parent Teacher Council (PTC) of Indian Oasis School, 75–76
Parental attitudes toward schools, 169–81
    basis for, 181
    at Bethel, 61
    at Cheyenne-Eagle Butte School, 89–90
    curriculum, 172–74
    interviews on, 349–53
    school administration, 174–75
    teachers, 170–72, 198–200
    teachers' attitudes and, 195–96
Passamaquody Indians, 31
Patterson, Harold, 154
Peer groups, 248
Pembroke (N.C.)
    Lumbees living in, 101–2
    schools of, 102–3
Penobscot Indians, 31
Personality deviation, mental health and, 149
Petit, Patrick, 290
Phoenix Indian School (Ariz.), 234–35, 238
Piaget, Jean, 121
Pierre School (S.D.), 240
Pima Indians, 28
Pima students, 79; see also

Theodore Roosevelt School
Pine Ridge Sioux Reservation (S.D.), 120, 126, 127, 133, 149, 179, 242–43, 248, 315
Platero, Dillon, 213, 256
Plummer, Abe, 214
Ponca City (Okla.)
    population of, 91–92
    socioeconomic characteristics of, 93–95
Ponca City public schools, enrollment in, 94
Ponca Indians, 91–92
Poorbear, Enos, 242
Population growth
    1890–1970, 23, 24, 32
    of Navajos, 42, 43
Post-high school education, 260–72
    characteristics of college students, 261–64
    increase in, 260–61
    at Navajo Community College, 264–71
Potawatomi Indians, 30
Poverty, scholastic achievement and, 128–29
Pratt, Gen. Richard Henry, 224, 225
Preschool education, see Head Start programs
"Problem of Indian Administration, The" (Meriam Report), 10–12, 227–28, 273, 315
Protestants, see Mission education
Public Law 815, 36
Public Law 874 (Impact Aid), 35, 36, 256, 259
Public schools
    federally supported, number of Indian students in (1967–68), 341

See also City schools; *and specific public schools; for example:* Cheyenne-Eagle Butte School
Pueblo Indians, 28, 277, 279
Pueblo students, 85
Puerto Rican students
achievement of, 305–6
self-concept of, 140
test scores of, 125

Quinault Indians, 30, 154

Ramah High School (N.M.), 35, 257–59, 265
curriculum of, 258
bilingual instruction, 210
Recreational activities in boarding schools, 240–41
Red power movement, 94–95
Rees, Martha, 140
Relocation programs, 4, 275
Remedial education in boarding schools, 239–40
Reservations, 5
Cheyenne River Reservation, 82–86
Fort Apache Indian Reservation, 76, 77
geographical distribution of, 25
Great Sioux Reservation, 82, 90
Navajo Reservation, 39
North and South Dakota, 29
Oklahoma and Arizona, 28
Pine Ridge Sioux Reservation, 120, 126, 127, 133, 149
Rocky Bay Reservation, 256
Yakima Reservation, 30, 214
Road building
in Eagle Butte, 91
in Sells, 71
Robeson County (N.C.)
described, 98–99

economic conditions in, 99–102
Rock Point Boarding School (Ariz.), 209, 229, 232, 233
Rocky Bay Reservation (Mont.), 256
Rocky Bay School (Mont.), 256–57
Roessel, Robert, 316
Roman Catholics, *see* Mission education
Roosevelt, Franklin D., 11–12
Rorschach test, 149
Rough Rock Demonstration School (Ariz.), 35, 209, 232, 252–56, 265
dormitories of, 233–34
evaluated, 254–56
innovations at, 253–54
as precedent, 257, 258
school board of, 320

Sac Indians, 30
Saginaw Indians, 30
St. Francis Mission School (S.D.), 214
Salaries of teachers, 201–2
in Bethel, 60
at Cheyenne-Eagle Butte School, 87–88
Salish Indians, 30
Sando, Joe, 212
Sanitary facilities, absence of
at Cheyenne River Reservation, 86
in Sells, 69
Scholarships, 261–62
Scholastic achievement, 123–35
alienation and, 133
comparative, 305–6
cultural differences and, 249–50
dropout rates and, 134
dual culture problem and, 129–31

factors militating against, 125–26

environmental factors, 128–29, 135, 299

isolation, 251

socioeconomic conditions, 299–300

self-esteem and, 178–81

School administrators, evaluated, 309–10

School boards

of Cheyenne-Eagle Butte School, 89

inclusion of Indian culture in curriculum and, 213–14

Indian, 318–21

of Indian Oasis School District No. 40, 73, 75–76

of Ponca City public schools, 97

of Ramah High School, 258

of Rough Rock Demonstration School, 320

of Shonto Boarding School, 50–51

Schoolmasters' Association (Robeson County, N.C.), 101

Schools

BIA operated, 8–10, 33, 97

attendance, 34

enrollment (1968), 344

evaluated, 303, 304

termination policy and, 14–15

See also specific schools; for example: Shonto Boarding School; Theodore Roosevelt School

developed by Indians, 6–7, 223–24, 257

See also City schools; High schools; Local control; Parental attitudes; Students; Teachers

Self-concept

comparative studies in, 139–56

mental health and, defined, 138–39

Self-determination, stand for, 19, 21–22

Self-esteem

alienation and, 133

dual culture problem and, 131, 132

scholastic achievement and, 178–81

Self-Esteem Inventory, 138, 144

Sells (Ariz.)

effects of expanded government services on, 66–69, 70–71

location of, 65–66

socioeconomic conditions in, 67–69

Semantic Differential Inventory, 138, 139, 141–44, 146, 162–69, 175

Seminole Indians, 7, 31, 97

Seneca Indians, 6, 30

Sex

self-concept and, 144–45

suicide rates by, 151–52

Sex segregation at Theodore Roosevelt School, 80

Shonto Boarding School (Ariz.), 39–53, 229, 232

attendance at, 45

characteristics of Shonto community and, 41–42

dormitory problems at, 49–50

effects of, on traditional religious practices, 44–45

enrollment at, 46–47

Indian identity at, 52–53

local alternatives to, 51–52

location of, 40

school board of, 50–51

as source of employment, 42–44

teachers at, 48–49

Shoshone-Bannock Indians, 30, 152–54

Sioux Indians
  areas of residence of, 29, 30
  local control and, 316
  urbanization of, 279
Sioux students
  achievement of, 126, 127
  adjustment problems of, 247–48
  mental development of, 121
  school attendance by, 35
  urban, 283
  See also Cheyenne-Eagle Butte School
Sitka Conference on Alaskan Native Secondary Education (1968), 64
Social status of Lumbees, 100–2
Social structure of Navajos, 41–43
Social welfare functions of boarding schools, 230–31
Society for the Propagation of the Gospel in Foreign Parts, 223
"Sociocultural Setting of Indian Life, The" (McNickle), 155
Socioeconomic conditions
  in Bethel, 55–56, 60
  in California, 28
  at Cheyenne River Reservation, 84–86
  in North Carolina, 29–30
    Robeson County, 99–102
  North and South Dakota, 29
  scholastic achievement and, 299–300
  in Sells, 67–69
  of urban Indian population, 109, 279–81
  See also Employment; Housing conditions; Income; Occupations; Poverty; Unemployment
South Dakota, Indian population of, 29

Sovereign nations, Indian tribes as, 3–4
Spilka, Bernard, 133, 176
Stanford-Binet test, 120
Stanford Observer (newspaper), 263
Staff at Theodore Roosevelt School, 78–79, 81; see also Teachers
State public schools, see Bethel public school
Steward Indian School, 239–41
Striner, Herbert, 316, 317
Students, college, 40, 261–64; see also Anglo-American students; Black students; Indian students; Latin-American students; Oriental American students; Puerto Rican students
"Suicide Among Yough on the Quinault Indian Reservation" (report), 154
Suicide rates, 137
  comparative, 150–53
  fluctuating, 153–54

Teachers, 191–204
  attitudes of, 193–97, 199
  of Bethel day schools, 62, 63
  of Bethel public school, 60, 201–3
  for bilingual education, 210–11
  characteristics of, 192–93
  of Cheyenne-Eagle Butte School, 87–88
  evaluated, 309–10
  improving work of, 200–4
  Indian, 197–98
  of Indian Oasis School, 73–75
  of Los Angeles city schools, 282, 283
  parental attitudes toward, 170–72, 198–200
  of Ramah High School, 258

of Shonto Boarding School, 48–49
students' attitudes toward, 162–67, 198–200
of Theodore Roosevelt School, 78
Termination policy, 13–15, 314
Test scores, 125
Textbooks
for bilingual education, 210, 211
Indian history in, 216–19
Theodore Roosevelt School (TRS; Fort Apache, Ariz.), 76–80, 229, 232
age range of students at, 79
curriculum at, 79–80
described, 76–78
dormitories of, 77–79, 234
Tonawanda Indians, 30
Topawa Elementary School (Sells, Ariz.), 66
Toyei Boarding School (Ariz.), 209, 229, 234
Transiency of Indian urban population, 109–10
Treaties
number of, concluded 1778–1871), 4
prohibited, 5
Tribal Work Experience Program (Sells, Ariz.), 68
TRIBE, Project, 35, 319, 320
Tribes
differences among, 24
enrollment by, in BIA schools (1968), 344
geographical distribution of, 25–30
as sovereign nations, 3–4
See also Reservations; and specific tribes; for example: Navajo Indians; Sioux Indians
TRS, see Theodore Roosevelt School

Tuscarora Indians, 30
Two-culture education
community leaders favoring, 189–90
teachers and, 196–97
See also Bilingual education

Udall, Stewart, 15
Unemployment
at Cheyenne River Reservation, 84
as major problem, 29
in Shonto, 42, 43
United Scholarship Service, Inc. (Denver, Colo.), 261–62
Urban Indian education, need to reorganize, 292–93; see also Urban Indian students
Urban Indian population, 273–92
of Chicago, 106–9
Indian centers created by, 288–93
Indian culture and, 131
of Los Angeles, 275–79
1928, 1960s and 1970, 273–74
problems faced by, 283–89
socioeconomic characteristics of, 279–81
transiency and anonymity of, 109–10
Urban Indian students
characteristics of, 281–83
dropout rates among, 116–17
Indian identity and, 113–15
interviewed, 112–13
number of, 290
1968 and 1969, 281
problems faced by, 290–92
school attendance, 110–11
Urban schools, see City schools
Ute Indians, 30

Vacuum ideology, defined, 246–47
Values, Indian, 247

Visual defects of Eskimo children, 56, 61
Vital statistics, 1967, 32
Vocational curriculum, 9
  in boarding schools, 237–39
  at Cheyenne-Eagle Butte School, 91
  emphasis on, 219
Voting right, Indians given, 10
Voyat, Gilbert, 121

Warrior, Clyde, 96
Warrior, Della, 94–95
Washington, George, 6
Wax, Murray L., 176, 247, 248, 251, 290, 305, 316, 317
Wax, Rosalie H., 176, 247, 248, 251, 305, 316, 317
WEDA (White Eagle Community Development Association), 95, 96
Werner, Oswald, 211
Wheeler-Howard Act (Indian Reorganization Act of June 18, 1934; Indian Bill of Rights), 12, 90
White community of Ponca City, 93–95
White Eagle School (Ponca City, Okla.), 95–96
White Eagle Community Development Association (WEDA), 95, 96
White House Task Force on Indian Affairs, 15–17, 317–18
Whiteriver Education Conference (1969), 321
Winnebago Indians, 30, 107
Wolcott, H., 250
Wood, Richard G., 367
Woodenlegs, John, 20, 118

Yakima Reservation (Wash.), 30, 214
Yazzie, Allan, 230

O